CHOICE SPECIMENS

OF

AMERICAN LITERATURE,

AND

LITERARY READER,

BEING SELECTIONS FROM THE CHIEF AMERICAN WRITERS,

BY

PROF. BENJ. N. MARTIN, D.D., L.H.D.,

PROFESSOR IN THE UNIVERSITY OF THE CITY OF NEW YORK.

Second Edition, Enlarged and Improved.

NEW YORK:
SHELDON AND COMPANY,
677 BROADWAY.

Entered, according to Act of Congress, in the year 1875,
By SHELDON AND COMPANY,
In the Office of the Librarian of Congress, at Washington.

PREFACE TO THE SECOND EDITION.

THE former edition of this work was prepared simply as a supplement to Shaw's "Choice Specimens of English Literature." Though it extended to a larger size than had been anticipated, and was therefore issued in a separate volume, it still proved so straitened in point of space as to be in some important respects defective and inadequate. The decision of the publishers to reprint it in an enlarged form furnishes to the editor a welcome opportunity to correct its deficiencies, and to make several important emendations.

When the work of collecting suitable extracts from the great body of our literature was fairly entered upon, it soon became apparent that little aid could be had from the earlier manuals. Besides being in great measure obsolete, they were from the beginning disproportionate, and geographically too local in subject and spirit; both of which may be deemed grave defects.

The last twenty years have made great changes in American authorship. Many new names must now be added to the older lists, and many formerly familiar ones must be dropped from them. Hence these extracts have for the most part been derived, with assiduous care, directly from the collected works of our standard authors. This part of my labor has been greatly facilitated by the courtesy of the gentlemen connected with the Society, the Mercantile, and the Astor, Library, whose constant kindness I gratefully acknowledge.

The principal alterations which will be found in this edition are the following.

1. The extracts, formerly, of necessity, brief and fragmentary, have given place to more extended and coherent passages.

2. A much larger space has been allotted to the more eminent authors. Such writers as Franklin, Jefferson, Calhoun, Webster, Wirt, Irving, Cooper, Hawthorne, Channing, Beecher, Prescott, Motley, Shea, Bryant, Poe, Emerson, and Lowell, have been much more adequately exhibited.

3. Many later writers have been added, so that the work more fully represents the rapid development of literary effort among us.

4. A few writers, formerly included, have been dropped from the list, not always as less deserving a place, but sometimes as having less adaptation to the purposes of the book.

Much care has been bestowed upon the dates of the several authors, and in bringing up details of information to the latest period.

The same pains have been taken to furnish a just representation of the writers, too often overlooked in our manuals, of the Southern and Western portions of our country. Though often wanting in mere grace of style, they are apt to be original and vigorous; and often possessing valuable material, they are well worthy of perusal. In all these respects this collection has been carefully elaborated; and the editor hopes that it will be found to give a somewhat proportionate and complete view for its compass, of our best literature.

In adapting the selections to Mr. Tuckerman's interesting "Sketch of American Literature," specimens have generally been taken from several authors in each of his groups. Some names not found in his "Sketch," have been introduced, chiefly for the fuller illustration of the literature of the south and west. In this particular, Coggeshall's "Poets and Poetry of the West" has afforded great assistance. Among the more recent aids of the same kind, I must also mention Davidson's "Living Writers of the South," and Raymond's "Southland Writers." Especial acknowledgment is due to the "Cyclopedia" of the Messrs. Duyckinck; Appleton's "Annual Cyclopedia" has furnished many important dates; and I have occasionally been indebted to the works of Allibone, Cheever, Griswold, Cleveland, Hart, and Underwood. Not only the local literature however, but the several professions, and the great religious denominations, are also represented by prominent writers.

It seemed unnecessary to treat the female writers as a distinct class; they are, therefore, arranged under the departments to which they respectively belong, as Essayists, Novelists, Poets, &c.

I should be claiming a merit which does not belong to me, should I fail to say, that, for much of the labor which this treatise has involved, I am indebted to the co-operation of my brother, Mr. William T. Martin, whose acquaintance with our literature has not often been surpassed, and whose valuable aid and counsel have been freely afforded me.

The hours which have been spent in culling extracts from so many able and entertaining writers, though laborious, have been to the editor full of interest, and often of delight. He trusts that these fruits of his labor will be useful, in imparting, especially to his youthful readers, not only an acquaintance with the best of our national authors, but a taste for literature, and a good ideal of literary excellence, than which few things in intellectual education are more to be esteemed. If successful in these respects, he will be abundantly satisfied; and in this hope, he submits his work to the judgment of the public.

CONTENTS.

CHAPTER I.

1. Religious Writers of the Seventeenth and Eighteenth Centuries.

2. Historical Writers of the Seventeenth and Eighteenth Centuries.

3. Miscellaneous Writers of the Seventeenth and Eighteenth Centuries.

4. Later Religious Writers and Divines.

5. Orators, and Legal and Political Writers, of the Era of the Revolution.

6. Orators, and Legal and Political Writers, of the Era Subsequent to the Revolution.

7. Biographical Writers.

8. History, General and Special.

CHAPTER II.

1. Essayists, Moralists, and Reformers.

2. General and Polite Literature.

3. Later Miscellaneous Writers.

4. Natural History, Scenery, etc.

5. Writers of Travel and Adventure.

6. Novelists and Writers of Fiction.

CHAPTER III.

Poets.

ALPHABETICAL INDEX OF AUTHORS.

(The Figures refer to the Number of the Selection.)

CHOICE SPECIMENS

OF

AMERICAN LITERATURE.

CHAPTER I.

RELIGIOUS WRITERS OF THE SEVENTEENTH AND EIGHTEENTH CENTURIES.

Roger Williams, 1598-1683. (Manual, pp. 480, 512.)

From his "Memoirs."

1. Extent of Religious Freedom.

There goes many a ship to sea, with many hundred souls in one ship, whose weal and woe is common, and is a true picture of a commonwealth, or a human combination or society. It hath fallen out, sometimes, that both Papists and Protestants, Jews and Turks, may be embarked into one ship. Upon which supposal, I affirm that all the liberty of conscience, that ever I pleaded for, turns upon these two hinges ; that none of the Papists, Protestants, Jews, or Turks, be forced to come to the ship's prayers, nor compelled from their own particular prayers or worship, if they practice any. . . . If any of the seamen refuse to perform their service, or passengers to pay their freight ; if any refuse to help, in person or purse, towards the common charges or defence ; if any refuse to obey the common laws or orders of the ship concerning their common peace or preservation ; if any shall mutiny and rise up against their commanders and officers ; if any should preach or write, that there ought to be no commanders nor officers, because all are equal in Christ, therefore no masters nor officers, no laws nor orders, no corrections nor punishments,—I say I never denied but in such cases, whatever is pretended, the commander or commanders may judge, resist, compel, and punish such transgressors, according to their deserts and merits.

Cotton Mather, 1663-1728. (Manual, pp. 479, 512.)

From the "Antiquities," or Book I. of the "Magnalia."

2. PRESERVATION OF NEW ENGLAND PRINCIPLES.

'TIS now time for me to tell my reader, that in *our age*, there has been another essay made, not by French, but by English PROTESTANTS, to fill a certain country in America with *Reformed Churches;* nothing in *doctrine*, little in *discipline*, different from that of Geneva. Mankind will pardon *me*, a native of that country, if smitten with a just fear of encroaching and ill-bodied *degeneracies*, I shall use my modest endeavors to prevent the *loss* of a country so signalized for the *profession* of the purest *Religion*, and for the *protection* of God upon it in that holy profession. I shall count my country *lost*, in the loss of the primitive *principles*, and the primitive *practices*, upon which it was at first established : but certainly one good way to save that *loss*, would be to do something, that the memory of *the great things done for us by our God*, may not be *lost*, and that the story of the circumstances attending the *foundation* and *formation* of this country, and of its *preservation* hitherto, may be impartially handed unto posterity. THIS is the undertaking whereto I now address myself ; and now, *Grant me thy gracious assistances, O my God! that in this my undertaking I may be kept from every false way.*

Jonathan Edwards, 1703-1758. (Manual, p. 479.)

From the "Inquiry, &c., into the Freedom of the Will."

3. MEANING OF THE PHRASE "MORAL INABILITY."

IT must be observed concerning Moral Inability, in each kind of it, that the word *Inability* is used in a sense very diverse from its original import. . . . . In the strictest propriety of speech, a man has a thing in his power, if he has it in his choice, or at his election ; and a man cannot be truly said to be unable to do a thing, when he can do it if he will. It is improperly said, that a person cannot perform those external actions which are dependent on the act of the will, and which would be easily performed, if the act of the will were present. And if it be improperly said, that he cannot perform those external voluntary actions which depend on the will, it is in some respect more improperly said, that he is unable to exert the acts of the will themselves ; because it is more evidently false, with respect to these, that he cannot if he will ; for to say so is a downright contradiction : it is to say he cannot will if he does will. And in this case, not only is it true, that it is easy for a man to do the thing if he will, but the very willing is the doing ; when once he has willed, the thing is performed ; and nothing else remains to be done. Therefore, in these things to ascribe a non-performance to the want of power or ability, is not just ; because the thing wanting is not a being able, but a being willing. There are faculties of mind, and capacity of nature, and everything else sufficient, but a disposition ; nothing is wanting but a will.

Samuel Davies, 1725-1761. (Manual, p. 480.)

From his "Sermons."

4. Life and Immortality Revealed through the Gospel.

So extensive have been the havoc and devastation which death has made in the world for near six thousand years, ever since it was first introduced by the sin of man, that this earth is now become one vast grave-yard or burying-place for her sons. The many generations that have followed upon each other, in so quick a succession, from Adam to this day, are now in the mansions under ground. . . . Some make a short journey from the womb to the grave ; they rise from nothing at the creative fiat of the Almighty, and take an immediate flight into the world of spirits. . . . Like a bird on the wing, they perch on our globe, rest a day, a month, or a year, and then fly off for some other regions. It is evident these were not formed for the purposes of the present state, where they make so short a stay; and yet we are sure they are not made in vain by an all-wise Creator; and therefore we conclude they are young immortals, that immediately ripen in the world of spirits, and there enter upon scenes for which it was worth their while coming into existence. . . . A few creep into their beds of dust under the burden of old age and the gradual decays of nature. In short, the grave is *the place appointed for all living;* the general rendezvous of all the sons of Adam. There the prince and the beggar, the conqueror and the slave, the giant and the infant, the scheming politician and the simple peasant, the wise and the fool, Heathens, Jews, Mahometans, and Christians, all lie equally low, and mingle their dust without distinction. . . . There lie our ancestors, our neighbors, our friends, our relatives, with whom we once conversed, and who were united to our hearts by strong and endearing ties; and there lies our friend, the sprightly, vigorous youth, whose death is the occasion of this funeral solemnity. This earth is overspread with the ruins of the human frame: it is a huge carnage, a vast charnel-house, undermined and hollowed with the graves, the last mansions of mortals.

Nathaniel Emmons,[1] *1745-1840.*

From his "Sermons."

5. THE RIGHT OF PRIVATE JUDGMENT.

THE right of private judgment involves the right of forming our opinions according to the best light we can obtain. After a man knows what others have said or written, and after he has thought and searched the Scriptures, upon any religious sub-

[1] A Congregational clergyman of Massachusetts, original in theology, and eminently lucid in style.

ject, he has a right to form his own judgment exactly according to evidence. He has no right to exercise prejudice or partiality; but he has a right to exercise impartiality, in spite of all the world. After all the evidence is collected from every quarter, then it is the proper business of the understanding or judgment to compare and balance evidence, and to form a decisive opinion or belief, according to apparent truth. We have no more right to judge without evidence than we have to judge contrary to evidence; and we have no more right to doubt without, or contrary to, evidence, than we have to believe without, or contrary to, evidence. We have no right to keep ourselves in a state of doubt or uncertainty, when we have sufficient evidence to come to a decision. The command is, "Prove all things; hold fast that which is good." The meaning is, Examine all things; and after examination, decide what is right.

HISTORICAL WRITERS OF THE SEVENTEENTH AND EIGHTEENTH CENTURIES.

Cadwallader Colden,[1] *1688-1776.*

From "The History of the Five Nations."

6. Conviction of their Superiority.

The *Five Nations* think themselves by nature superior to the rest of mankind. . . . All the nations round them have, for many years, entirely submitted to them, and pay a yearly tribute to them in *wampum;* they dare neither make war nor peace without the consent of the *Mohawks.* Two old men commonly go, about every year or two, to receive this tribute; and I have often had opportunity to observe what anxiety the poor Indians were under while these two old men remained in that part of the country where I was. An old Mohawk

[1] A native of Scotland, but for many years a resident of New York, where he was eminent in politics and science.

Sachem, in a poor blanket and a dirty shirt, may be seen issuing his orders with as arbitrary an authority as a Roman dictator. It is not for the sake of tribute, however, that they make war, but from the notions of glory which they have ever most strongly imprinted on their minds ; and the farther they go to seek an enemy, the greater glory they think they gain ; there cannot, I think, be a greater or stronger instance than this, how much the sentiments impressed on a people's mind conduce to their grandeur. . . . The Five Nations, in their love of liberty and of their country, in their bravery in battle, and their constancy in enduring torments, equal the fortitude of the most renowned Romans.

William Stith, 1755. (Manual, p. 490.)

From "The History of Virginia."

7. THE RULE OF POWHATAN.

ALTHOUGH both himself and people were very barbarous, and void of all letters and civility, yet was there such a government among them, that the magistrates for good command, and the people for due subjection, excelled many places that would be counted very civil. He had under him above thirty inferior Kings or Werowances, who had power of life and death, but were bound to govern according to the customs of their country. However, his will was in all cases, their supreme law, and must be obeyed. They all knew their several lands, habitations, and limits, to fish, fowl, or hunt in. But they held all of their great Werowance, *Powhatan;* to whom they paid tribute of skins, beads, copper, pearl, deer, turkies, wild beasts, and corn. All his subjects reverenced him, not only as a King, but as half a God; and it was curious to behold, with what fear and adoration they obeyed him. For at his feet they presented whatever he commanded; and a frown of his brow would make their greatest Spirits tremble. And indeed it was no wonder; for he was very terrible and tyrannous in punishing such as offended him, with variety of cruelty, and the most exquisite torture.

---

8. Pocahontas in England.

However, Pocahontas was eagerly sought and kindly entertained everywhere. Many courtiers, and others of his acquaintance, daily flocked to Captain Smith to be introduced to her. They generally confessed that the hand of God did visibly appear in her conversion, and that they had seen many English ladies worse favored, of less exact proportion, and genteel carriage than she was. . . . The whole court were charmed and surprised at the decency and grace of her deportment; and the king himself, and queen, were pleased honorably to receive and esteem her. The Lady Delawarr, and those other persons of quality, also waited on her to the masks, balls, plays, and other public entertainments, with which she was wonderfully pleased and delighted. And she would, doubtless, have well deserved, and fully returned, all this respect and kindness, had she lived to arrive in Virginia.

William Smith, 1793. (Manual, p. 490.)

From "The History of the Province of New York."

9. Manners of the Inhabitants.

New York is one of the most social places on the continent. The men collect themselves into weekly evening clubs. The ladies, in winter, are frequently entertained either at concerts of music or assemblies, and make a very good appearance. They are comely, and dress well, and scarce any of them have distorted shapes. Tinctured with a Dutch education, they manage their families with becoming parsimony, good providence, and singular neatness. The practice of extravagant gaming, common to the fashionable part of the fair sex in some places, is a vice with which my countrywomen cannot justly be charged. There is nothing they so generally neglect as reading, and indeed all the arts for the improvement of the mind; in which, I confess, we have set them the example. They are modest, temperate, and charitable; naturally sprightly, sensible, and good-humored; and, by the helps of a more elevated education, would possess all the accomplishments desirable in the sex. Our schools are in the lowest order; the instructors want instruction; and, through a long, shameful neglect of all the arts and sciences, our common speech is extremely corrupt, and the evidences of a bad taste, both as to thought and language, are visible in all our proceedings, public and private.

The history of our diseases belongs to a profession with which I am very little acquainted. Few physicians amongst us are eminent for their skill. Quacks abound like locusts in Egypt, and too many have recommended themselves to a full practice and profitable subsistence. Loud as the call is, to our shame be it remembered, we have no law to protect the lives of the king's subjects from the malpractice of pretenders. Any man, at his pleasure, sets up for physician, apothecary, and chirurgeon. The natural history of this province would of itself furnish a small volume; and, therefore, I leave this also to such as have capacity and leisure to make useful observations in that curious and entertaining branch of natural philosophy.

The clergy of this province are, in general, but indifferently supported, it is true they live easily, but few of them leave any thing to their children. . . . As to the number of our clergymen, it is large enough at present, there being but few settlements unsupplied with a ministry and some superabound. In matters of religion we are not so intelligent in general as the inhabitants of the New England colonies, but both in this respect and good morals we certainly have the advantage of the Southern provinces. One of the king's instructions to our governors recommends the investigation of means for the conversion of negroes and Indians. An attention to both, especially the latter, has been too little regarded. If the missionaries of the English Society for propagating the Gospel instead of being seated in opulent christianized towns had been sent out to preach among the savages, unspeakable political advantages would have flowed from such a salutary measure.

MISCELLANEOUS WRITERS OF THE SEVENTEENTH AND EIGHTEENTH CENTURIES.

John Winthrop, 1587-1649. (Manual, p. 490.)

From his "Life and Letters."

10. True Liberty Defined.

For the other point concerning liberty, I observe a great mistake in the country about that. There is a twofold liberty,—natural (I mean as our nature is now corrupt) and civil, or federal. The first is common to man with beasts and other creatures. By this, man, as he stands in relation to man simply, hath liberty to do what he lists: it is a liberty to evil as well as to good. This liberty is incompatible and inconsistent with authority, and cannot endure the least restraint of the most just authority. The exercise and maintaining of this liberty makes men grow more evil, and, in time, to be worse than brute beasts. This is that great enemy of truth and peace, that wild beast, which all the ordinances of God are bent against, to restrain and subdue it. The other kind of liberty I call civil, or federal; it may also be termed moral, in reference to the covenant between God and man in the moral law, and the politic covenants and constitutions amongst men themselves. This liberty is the proper end and object of authority, and cannot subsist without it; and it is a liberty to that only which is good, just, and honest. This liberty you are to stand for, with the hazard not only of your goods, but of your lives, if need be.

From "The History of New England."

11. Proposed Treatment of the Indians.

We received a letter at the General Court from the magistrates of Connecticut, and New Haven, and of Aquiday,[1] wherein they

[1] The original name of Rhode Island.

declared their dislike of such as would have the Indians rooted out, as being of the cursed race of Ham, and their desire of our mutual accord in seeking to gain them by justice and kindness, and withal to watch over them to prevent any danger by them, &c. We returned answer of our consent with them in all things propounded, only we refused to include those of Aquiday in our answer, or to have any treaty with them.

William Byrd,[1] *1674-1744.*

From "History of the Dividing Line between Virginia and North Carolina."

12. THE GINSENG AND SNAKEROOT PLANTS.

THOUGH practice will soon make a man of tolerable vigor an able footman, yet, as a help to bear fatigue, I used to chew a root of ginseng as I walked along. This kept up my spirits, and made me trip away as nimbly in my half jack-boots as younger men could in their shoes. . . . The Emperor of China sends ten thousand men every year on purpose to gather it. . . . Providence has planted it very thin in every country. Nor, indeed, is mankind worthy of so great a blessing, since health and long life are commonly abused to ill purposes. This noble plant grows likewise at the Cape of Good Hope. It grows also on the northern continent of America, near the mountains, but as sparingly as truth and public spirit.

Its virtues are, that it gives an uncommon warmth and vigor to the blood, and frisks the spirits beyond any other cordial. It cheers the heart even of a man that has a bad wife, and makes him look down with great composure on the crosses of the world. It promotes insensible perspiration, dissolves all phlegmatic and viscous humors that are apt to obstruct the narrow channels of the nerves. It helps the memory, and would quicken even Helvetian dullness. 'Tis friendly to the lungs, much more than scolding itself. It comforts the stomach and strengthens

[1]A native of Virginia;—was sent to England for his education, where he became intimate with the wits of Queen Anne's time. On his return to Virginia, he became a prominent official. He has left very pleasing accounts of his explorations.

the bowels, preventing all colics and fluxes. In one word, it will make a man live a great while, and very well while he does live; and, what is more, it will even make old age amiable, by rendering it lively, cheerful, and good-humored, . . .

I found near our camp some plants of that kind of Rattlesnake root, called star-grass. The leaves shoot out circularly, and grow horizontally and near the ground. The root is in shape not unlike the rattle of that serpent, and is a strong antidote against the bite of it. It is very bitter, and where it meets with any poison, works by violent sweats, but where it meets with none, has no sensible operation but that of putting the spirits into a great hurry, and so of promoting perspiration.

The rattlesnake has an utter antipathy to this plant, insomuch that if you smear your hands with the juice of it, you may handle the viper safely. Thus much I can say on my own experience, that once in July, when these snakes are in their greatest vigor, I besmeared a dog's nose with the powder of this root, and made him trample on a large snake several times, which, however, was so far from biting him, that it perfectly sickened at the dog's approach, and turned his head from him with the utmost aversion.

In our march one of the men killed a small rattlesnake, which had no more than two rattles. Those vipers remain in vigor generally till towards the end of September, or sometimes later, if the weather continues a little warm. On this consideration we had provided three several sorts of rattlesnake root, made up into proper doses, and ready for immediate use, in case any one of the men or their horses had been bitten. . . .

In the low grounds the Carolina gentlemen shewed us another plant, which they said was used in their country to cure the bite of the rattlesnake. It put forth several leaves, in figure like a heart, and was clouded so like the common Assarabacca, that I conceived it to be of that family.

Benjamin Franklin, 1706-1790. (Manual, pp. 478, 486.)

Extract from his Autobiography.

13. GOOD RESOLUTIONS.—THE CROAKER.

I grew convinced, that *truth*, *sincerity*, and *integrity*, in dealings between man and man, were of the utmost importance to the felicity of life, and I formed written resolutions, which still remain in my journal book, to practice them ever while I lived. Revelation had indeed no weight with me, as such; but I entertained an opinion, that, though certain actions might not be bad, *because* they were forbidden by it, or good *because* it commended them; yet probably those actions might be forbidden *because* they were bad for us, or commanded *because* they were beneficial to us, in their own natures, all the circumstances of things considered. And this persuasion, with the kind hand of Providence, or some guardian angel, or accidental favorable circumstances or situations, or all together, preserved me, through this dangerous time of youth, and the hazardous situations I was sometimes in among strangers, remote from the eye and advice of my father, free from any *wilful* gross immorality or injustice, that might have been expected from my want of religion. I say wilful because the instances I have mentioned had something of *necessity* in them, from my youth, inexperience, and the knavery of others. I had therefore a tolerable character to begin the world with; I valued it properly, and determined to preserve it.

We had not been long returned to Philadelphia, before the new types arrived from London. We settled with Keimer and left him by his consent before he heard of it. We found a house to let near the market, and took it. To lessen the rent, which was then but twenty-four pounds a year, though I have since known it to let for seventy, we took in Thomas Godfrey, a glazier, and his family, who were to pay a considerable part of it to us, and we to board with them. We had scarce opened our letters and put our press in order, before George House, an acquaintance of mine, brought a countryman to us, whom he had met in the street, inquiring for a printer. All our cash was now expended in the variety of particulars we had been obliged to procure, and this countryman's five shillings, being our first-fruits, and coming so seasonably, gave me more pleasure than any crown I have since earned; and the gratitude I felt towards House has made me often more ready, than perhaps I otherwise should have been, to assist young beginners.

There are croakers in every country, always boding its ruin. Such a one there lived in Philadelphia; a person of note, an elderly man, with a wise look and a very grave manner of speaking; his name was Samuel Mickle. This gentleman, a stranger to me, stopped me one day at my door, and asked me if I was the young man, who had lately opened a new printing-house? Being answered in the affirmative, he said he was sorry for me, because it was an expensive undertaking, and the expense would be lost; for Philadelphia was a sinking place, the people already half bankrupts, or near being so; all the appearances of the contrary, such as new buildings and the rise of rents, being to his certain knowledge fallacious; for they were in fact among the things that would ruin us. Then he gave me such a detail of misfortunes now existing, or that were soon to exist, that he left me half melancholy. Had I known him before I engaged in this business, probably I never should have done it. This person continued to live in this decaying place, and to declaim in the same strain, refusing for many years to buy a house there, because all was going to destruction; and at last I had the pleasure of seeing him give him five times as much for one, as he might have bought it for when he first began croaking.

From a Letter to Peter Collinson.

14. Franklin's Electrical Kite.

As frequent mention is made in public papers from Europe of the success of the Philadelphia experiment for drawing the electric fire from clouds, by means of pointed rods of iron erected on high buildings, &c., it may be agreeable to the curious to be informed that the same experiment has succeeded in Philadelphia, though made in a different and more easy manner, which is as follows:

Make a small cross of two light strips of cedar, the arms so long as to reach to the four corners of a large thin silk handkerchief, when extended; tie the corners of the handkerchief to the extremities of the cross, so you have the body of a kite; which, being properly accommodated with a tail, loop, and string, will rise in the air, like those made of paper; but this, being of silk, is fitter to bear the wet and wind of a thundergust without tearing. To the top of the upright stick of the cross is to be fixed a very sharp-pointed wire, rising a foot or more above the wood. To the end of the twine, next the hand, is to be tied a silk ribbon, and where the silk and twine join, a key may be fastened. This kite is to be raised when a thundergust appears to be coming on, and the person who holds the string must stand within a door or window, or under some cover, so that the silk ribbon may not be wet; and care must be taken that the twine does not touch the frame of the door or window. As soon as any of the thunder-clouds come over the kite, the pointed wire will draw the electric fire from them, and the kite, with all the twine, will be electrified, and the loose filaments of the twine will stand out every way, and be attracted by an approaching finger. And when the rain has wetted the kite and twine, so that it can conduct the electric fire freely, you will find it stream out plentifully from the key on the approach of your knuckle. At this key the phial may be charged; and all the other electric experiments be performed, which are usually done by the help of a rubbed glass globe or tube, and thereby the sameness of the electric matter with that of lightning be completely demonstrated.

---

15. Motion for Prayers in the Convention.

Mr. President:

The small progress we have made, after four or five weeks close attendance and continual reasonings with each other, our different sentiments on almost every question, several of the last producing as many *Noes* as *Ayes*, is, methinks, a melancholy proof of the imperfection of the human understanding. We indeed seem to *feel* our own want of political wisdom, since we have been running all about in search of it. We have gone back to ancient history for models of government, and examined the different forms of those republics, which, having been originally formed with the seeds of their own dissolution, now no longer exist; and we have viewed modern States all round Europe, but find none of their constitutions suitable to our circumstances.

In this situation of this assembly, groping, as it were, in the dark to find political truth, and scarce able to distinguish it when presented to us, how has it happened, Sir, that we have not hitherto once thought of humbly applying to the Father of Lights to illuminate our understandings? In the beginning of the contest with Britain, when we were sensible of danger, we had daily prayers in this room for the divine protection. Our prayers, Sir, were heard; and they were graciously answered. All of us, who were engaged in the struggle, must have observed frequent instances of a superintending Providence in our favor. To that kind Providence we owe this happy opportunity of consulting in peace on the means of establishing our future national felicity. And have we now forgotten that powerful Friend? or do we imagine we no longer need His assistance? I have lived, Sir, a long time; and the longer I live, the more convincing proofs I see of this truth, *that God governs in the affairs of men*. And if a sparrow cannot fall to the ground without his notice, is it probable that an empire can rise without his aid? We have been assured, Sir, in the Sacred Writings, that "except the Lord build the house, they labor in vain that build it." I firmly believe this; and I also believe, that without his concurring aid, we shall succeed in this political building no better than the builders of Babel; we shall be divided by our little, partial, local interests, our projects will be confounded, and we ourselves shall become a reproach and a by-word down to future ages. And, what is worse, mankind may hereafter, from this unfortunate instance, despair of establishing government by human wisdom, and leave it to chance, war, and conquest.

I therefore beg leave to move,

That henceforth, prayers, imploring the assistance of Heaven and its blessing on our deliberations, be held in this assembly every morning before we proceed to business; and that one or more of the clergy of this city be requested to officiate in that service

---

From his "Essays."

16. THE EPHEMERON. AN EMBLEM.

"IT was," said he, "the opinion of learned philosophers of our race, who lived and flourished long before my time, that this vast world, the Moulin Joly, could not itself subsist more than eighteen hours ; and I think there was some foundation for that opinion, since, by the apparent motion of the great luminary that gives life to all nature, and which in my time has evidently declined considerably towards the ocean at the end of our earth, it must then finish its course, be extinguished in the waters that surround us, and leave the world in cold and darkness, necessarily producing universal death and destruction. I have lived seven of those hours—a great age, being no less than four hundred and twenty minutes of time. How very few of us continue so long ! I have seen generations born, flourish, and expire. . . . And I must soon follow them ; for, by the course of nature, though still in health, I cannot expect to live above seven or eight minutes longer. What now avail all my toil and labor in amassing honey-dew on this leaf, which I cannot live to enjoy !—what the political struggles I have been engaged in for the good of my compatriot inhabitants of this bush, or my philosophical studies for the benefit of our race in general ! for in politics what can laws do without morals ? Our present race of ephemera will, in a course of minutes, become corrupt, like those of other and older bushes, and consequently as wretched. And in philosophy how small our progress ! Alas ! art is long, and life is short. My friends would comfort me with the idea of a name they say I shall leave behind me. . . . But what will fame be to an ephemeron who no longer exists ? and what will become of all history, in the eighteenth hour, when the world itself, even the whole Moulin Joly, shall come to its end, and be buried in universal ruin ?"

LATER RELIGIOUS WRITERS AND DIVINES.

John Woolman,[1] *1720-1772.*

From his "Life and Travels."

17. Remarks on Slavery and Labor.

A people, used to labor moderately for their living, training up their children in frugality and business, have a happier life than those who live on the labor of slaves. Freemen find satisfaction in improving and providing for their families ; but negroes, laboring to support others who claim them as their property, and expecting nothing but slavery during life, have not the like inducement to be industrious. . . . Men having power, too often misapply it : though we make slaves of the negroes, and the Turks make slaves of the Christians, liberty is the natural right of all men equally. . . . The slaves look to me like a burdensome stone to such who burden themselves with them. The burden will grow heavier and heavier, till times change in a way disagreeable to us. . . . I was troubled to perceive the darkness of their imaginations, and, in some pressure of spirits, said the love of ease and gain are the motives, in general, of keeping slaves ; and men are wont to take hold of weak arguments to support a cause which is unreasonable. . . .

I was silent during the meeting for worship, and, when business came on, my mind was exercised concerning the poor slaves, but did not feel my way clear to speak. In this condition I was bowed in spirit before the Lord, and, with tears and

[1] A Quaker preacher, a native of New Jersey, whose Travels and Autobiography have been much admired abroad, notably by Charles Lamb.

inward supplication, besought him so to open my understanding that I might know his will concerning me ; and at length my mind was settled in silence.

At times when I have felt true love open my heart towards my fellow-creatures, and have been engaged in weighty conversation in the cause of righteousness, the instructions I have received under these exercises in regard to the true use of the outward gifts of God, have made deep and lasting impressions on my mind. I have beheld how the desire to provide wealth and to uphold a delicate life has grievously entangled many, and has been like a snare to their offspring, and though some have been affected with a sense of their difficulties, and have appeared desirous at times to be helped out of them, yet for want of abiding under the humbling power of truth, they have continued in these entanglements ; expensive living in parents and children hath called for a large supply, and in answering this call, the faces of the poor have been ground away, and made thin through hard dealing. . .

. . In the uneasiness of body which I have many times felt by too much labor, not as a forced but a voluntary oppression, I have often been excited to think on the original cause of that oppression which is imposed on many in the world. The latter part of the time wherein I labored on our plantation, my heart, through the fresh visitations of heavenly love, being often tender, and my leisure time being frequently spent in reading the life and doctrines of our blessed Redeemer, the account of the sufferings of martyrs, and the history of the first rise of our Society, a belief was gradually settled in my mind, that if such as had great estates, generally lived in that humility and plainness which belong to a Christian life, and laid much easier rents and interests on their lands and moneys, and thus led the way to a right use of things, so great a number of people might be employed in things useful, that labor both for men and other creatures would need to be no more than an agreeable employ, and divers branches of business, which serve chiefly to please the natural inclinations of our minds, and which at present seem necessary to circulate that wealth which some gather, might, in this way of pure wisdom, be discontinued.

John M. Mason,[1] *1770-1829.*

From the Address in behalf of the Bible Society.

18. Grandeur of the Enterprise.

If there be a single measure which can overrule objection, subdue opposition, and command exertion, this is the measure. That all our voices, all our affections, all our hands, should be joined in the grand design of promoting "peace on earth and good will toward man"—that they should resist the advance of misery—should carry the light of instruction into the dominions of ignorance, and the balm of joy to the soul of anguish; and all this by diffusing the oracles of God—addresses to the understanding an argument which cannot be encountered; and to the heart an appeal which its holiest emotions rise up to second. . . .

People of the United States; Have you ever been invited to an enterprise of such grandeur and glory? Do you not value the Holy Scriptures? Value them as containing your sweetest hope; your most thrilling joy? Can you submit to the thought that *you* should be torpid in your endeavors to disperse them, while the rest of Christendom is awake and alert? Shall *you* hang back in heartless indifference, when princes come down from their thrones, to bless the cottage of the poor with the gospel of peace; and imperial sovereigns are gathering their fairest honors from spreading abroad the oracles of the Lord your God. Is it possible that *you* should not see, in this state of human things, a mighty motion of Divine providence? The most heavenly charity treads close upon the march of conflict and blood! The world is at peace! Scarce has the soldier time to unbind his helmet, and to wipe away the sweat from his brow, ere the voice of mercy succeeds to the clarion of battle, and calls the nations from enmity to love!

[1] A Presbyterian clergyman of great distinction, long settled in New York; rarely surpassed in controversial acuteness, and in religious eloquence.

Crowned heads bow to the head which is to wear "many crowns," and, for the first time since the promulgation of Christianity, appear to act in unison for the recognition of its gracious principles, as being fraught alike with happiness to man, and honor to God.

What has created so strange, so beneficent an alteration. This is no doubt the doing of the Lord, and it is marvelous in our eyes. But what instrument has he thought fit chiefly to use. That which contributes in all latitudes and climes to make Christians feel their unity, to rebuke the spirit of strife, and to open upon them the day of brotherly concord—the Bible!—the Bible!—through Bible Societies!

---

19. THE RIGHT OF THE STATE TO EDUCATE.

No sagacity can foretell what characters shall be developed, or what parts performed, by these boys and girls who throng our streets, and sport in our fields. In their tender breasts are concealed the germs, in their little hands are lodged the weapons, of a nation's overthrow or glory. Would it not, then, be madness, would it not be a sort of political suicide, for the commonwealth to be unconcerned what direction their infant powers shall take, or into what habits their budding affections shall ripen? or will it be disputed that the civil authority has a *right* to take care, by a paternal interference on behalf of the children, that the next generation shall not prostrate in an hour, whatever has been consecrated to truth, to virtue, and to happiness by the generations that are past?

Timothy Dwight, 1752-1817. (Manual, pp. 479, 504.)

From "Travels in New England," &c.

20. THE WILDERNESS RECLAIMED.

IN these countries *lands are universally held in fee simple.* Every farmer, with too few exceptions to deserve notice, labors on his own ground, and for the benefit of himself and his family merely. This, also, if I am not deceived, is a novelty; and its influence is seen to be remarkably happy in the industry, sobriety, cheerfulness, personal independence, and universal prosperity of the people at large. . . . A succession of New England villages, composed of neat houses, surrounding neat schoolhouses and churches, adorned with gardens, meadows, and orchards, and exhibiting the universal easy circumstances of the inhabitants, is, at least in my own opinion, one of the most delightful prospects which this world can afford.

The conversion of a wilderness into a desirable residence for man, is an object which no intelligent spectator can behold, without being strongly interested in such a combination of enterprise, patience, and perseverance. Few of those human efforts which have excited the applause of mankind, have demanded equal energy, or merited equal approbation. A forest changed within a short period into fruitful fields covered with houses, schools, and churches, and filled with inhabitants possessing not only the necessaries and comforts, but also the conveniences of life, and devoted to the worship of Jehovah, when seen only in prophetic vision, enraptured the mind even of Isaiah; and when realized, can hardly fail to delight that of a spectator. At least, it may compensate the want of ancient castles, ruined abbeys, and fine pictures.

From the Theology.

21. The Glory of Nature, from God.

There is another and very important view in which this subject demands our consideration. *Theology spreads its influence over the creation and providence of God, and gives to both almost all their beauty and sublimity.* Creation and providence, seen by the eye of theology, and elucidated by the glorious commentary on both furnished in the Scriptures, become new objects to the mind; immeasurably more noble, rich, and delightful, than they can appear to a worldly, sensual mind. The heavens and the earth, and the great as well as numberless events which result from the divine administration, are in themselves vast, wonderful, frequently awful, in many instances solemn, in many exquisitely beautiful, and in a great number eminently sublime. All these attributes, however, they possess, if considered only in the abstract, in degrees very humble and diminutive, compared with the appearance which they make, when beheld as the works of Jehovah. Mountains, the ocean, and the heavens, are majestic and sublime. Hills and valleys, soft landscapes, trees, fruits, and flowers, and many objects in the animal and mineral kingdoms, are beautiful. But what is this beauty, what is this grandeur, compared with that agency of God, to which they owe their being? Think what it is for the Almighty hand to spread the plains, to heave the mountains, and to pour the ocean. Look at the verdure, flowers, and fruits which in the mild season adorn the surface of the earth; the uncreated hand fashions their fine forms, paints their exquisite colors, and exhales their delightful perfumes. In the spring, his life re-animates the world; in the summer and autumn, his bounty is poured out upon the hills and valleys; in the winter, "his way is in the whirlwind and in the storm; and the clouds are the dust of his feet." His hand "hung the earth upon nothing," lighted up the sun in the heavens, and rolls the planets, and the comets through the immeasurable fields of ether. His breath kindled the stars; his voice called into existence worlds innumerable, and filled the expanse with animated being. To all he is present, over all he rules, for all he provides. The mind, attempered to divine contemplation, finds him in every solitude, meets him in every walk, and in all places, and at all times, sees itself surrounded by God.

John Henry Hobart,[1] *1775-1830.*

From a "Sermon."

22. THE DIVINE GLORY IN REDEMPTION.

AT the display of the divine power and glory that created the world, "the morning stars sang together, and all the sons

[1] An eminent divine and bishop of the Episcopal church; a native of Pennsylvania.

of God shouted for joy." Surely not less universal, not less ardent the exultation in those pure and perfect spirits that continually surround the Divine Majesty at the view of the infinite wisdom, love, and power which planned the redemption of a fallen world—which thus devised the mode by which pardon could be extended to the sinner without sanctioning his sin, and favor to the offending rebel against the divine government, without weakening its authority, impeaching its holiness, or subverting its justice. In the nature of the divine Persons thus counselling for man's redemption, it is not for him, blind, and erring, and impotent, it is not for angels, it is not for cherubim or seraphim, for a moment to look. The inner glory of the divine nature burns with a blaze, if I may so with reverence speak, too intense, too radiant, for finite vision. But in its manifestations, in its outer, its more distant rays, shining on the plan of man's redemption, all is mildness, and softness, and peace. Holiness, and justice, and mercy are seen blending their sacred influences, and conveying light and joy in that truth which the counsels of the Godhead alone could render possible. God can be just, and yet justify the sinner.

. . . Let us not, then, neglect this wonderful counsel of God for our salvation; let us not be unaffected by this most stupendous display of divine power, love, and mercy; let us not reject the offers of peace and salvation from the God whom we have offended, and the Sovereign who is finally to judge us. But, on the contrary, let us gratefully adore the mercy and the grace of the Godhead in the plan of redemption, effected in the incarnation, the obedience, the sufferings, the death, and the triumphant resurrection of our Lord and Saviour, Jesus Christ. Let it be our great object to be conformed to the likeness of his death, in mortifying all our corrupt affections, and to experience the power of his resurrection in living a new and holy life, that we may enjoy the new and lively hopes of everlasting glory, which his resurrection assures to all true believers.

Lyman Beecher,[1] *1775-1863.*

From the "Lectures on Political Atheism."

23. THE BEING OF A GOD.

IT is a thing eminently to be desired that there should be a supreme benevolent Intelligence, who is the creator and moral governor of the universe, whose subjects and kingdom shall endure for ever. Such a one the nature of man demands, and his whole soul pants after.

We feel our littleness in presence of the majestic elements of nature, our weakness compared with their power, and our loneliness in the vast universe, unenlightened, unguided, and unblessed, by any intelligence superior to our own. We behold the flight of time, the passing fashion of the world, and the gulf of annihilation curtained with the darkness of an eternal night.

At the side of this vortex, which covers with deep oblivion the past, and impenetrable darkness the future, nature shudders and draws back, and the soul, with sinking heart, looks mournfully around upon this fair creation, and up to these beautiful heavens, and in plaintive accents demands, "Is there, then, no deliverance from this falling back into nothing? Must this conscious being cease—this reasoning, thinking power, and these warm affections, their delightful movements? Must this eye close in an endless night, and this heart fall back upon everlasting insensibility? O, thou cloudless sun, and ye far-distant stars, in all your journeyings in light, have ye discovered no blessed intelligence who called you into being, lit up your fires, marked your orbits, wheels you in your courses, around whom ye roll, and whose praises ye silently celebrate? Are ye empty worlds, and desolate, the sport of chance? or, like our sad earth, are ye peopled with inhabitants, waked up to a brief existence, and hurried reluctantly, from an almost untasted being, back to nothing? O that there were a God, who made you, greater

[1] A Congregational clergyman, prominent, in the early part of this century, for his zeal and piety, and for the eloquence and originality of his sermons; father of a numerous family distinguished in theology and literature.

than ye all, whose being in yours we might see, whose intelligence we might admire, whose will we might obey, and whose goodness we might adore!" Such, except where guilt seeks annihilation as the choice of evils, is the unperverted, universal longing after God and immortality.

William Ellery Channing, 1780-1842. (Manual, p. 480.)

From the Essay on Napoleon Bonaparte.

24. Character of Napoleon.

With powers which might have made him a glorious representative and minister of the beneficent Divinity, and with natural sensibilities which might have been exalted into sublime virtues, he chose to separate himself from his kind, to forego their love, esteem, and gratitude, that he might become their gaze, their fear, their wonder; and for this selfish, solitary good, parted with peace and imperishable renown.

His insolent exaltation of himself above the race to which he belonged, broke out in the beginning of his career. His first success in Italy gave him the tone of a master, and he never laid it aside to his last hour. One can hardly help being struck with the *natural air* with which he arrogates supremacy in his conversation and proclamations. We never feel as if he were putting on a lordly air. In his proudest claims, he speaks from his own mind, and in native language. His style is swollen, but never strained, as if he were conscious of playing a part above his real claims. Even when he was foolish and impious enough to arrogate miraculous powers and a mission from God, his language showed that he thought there was something in his character and exploits to give a color to his blasphemous pretensions. The empire of the world seemed to him to be in a measure his due, for nothing short of it corresponded with his conceptions of himself; and he did not use mere verbiage, but spoke a language to which he gave some credit, when he called his successive conquests "the fulfilment of his destiny."

This spirit of self-exaggeration wrought its own misery, and drew down upon him terrible punishments; and this it did by vitiating and perverting his high powers. First, it diseased his fine intellect, gave imagination the ascendency over judgment, turned the inventiveness and fruitfulness of his mind into rash, impatient, restless energies, and thus precipitated him into projects, which, as the wisdom of his counsellors pronounced, were fraught with ruin. To a man, whose vanity took him out of the rank of human beings, no foundation for reasoning was left. All things seemed possible. His genius and his fortune were not to be bounded by the barriers which experience had assigned to human powers. Ordinary rules did not apply to him. He even found excitement and motives in obstacles before which other men would have wavered; for these would enhance the glory of triumph, and give a new thrill to the admiration of the world. * *

To us there is something radically and increasingly shocking in the thought of one man's will becoming a law to his race; in the thought of multitudes, of vast communities, surrendering conscience, intellect, their affections, their rights, their interests, to the stern mandate of a fellow-creature. When we see one word of a frail man on the throne of France, tearing a hundred thousand sons from their homes, breaking asunder the sacred ties of domestic life, sentencing myriads of the young to make murder their calling, and rapacity their means of support, and extorting from nations their treasures to extend this ruinous sway, we are ready to ask ourselves, Is not this a dream? and, when the sad reality comes home to us, we blush for a race which can stoop to such an abject lot. At length, indeed, we see the tyrant humbled, stripped of power, but stripped by those who, in the main, are not unwilling to play the despot on a narrower scale, and to break down the spirit of nations under the same iron sway.

Manning.

From a Discourse upon Immortality.

25. Grandeur of the Prospect.

To me there is but one objection against immortality, if objection it may be called, and this arises from the very greatness of the truth. My mind sometimes sinks under its weight, is lost in its immensity; I scarcely dare believe that such a good is placed within my reach. When I think of myself, as existing through all future ages, as surviving this earth and that sky, as exempted from every imperfection and error of my present being, as clothed with an angel's glory, as comprehending with my intellect and embracing in my affections, an extent of creation compared with which the earth is a point; when I think of myself as looking on the outward universe with an organ of vision that will reveal to me a beauty and harmony and order not now imagined, and as having an access to the minds of the wise and good, which will make them in a sense my own; when I think of myself as forming friendships with innumerable beings of rich and various intellect and of the noblest virtue, as introduced to the society of heaven, as meeting there the great and excellent, of whom I have read in history, as joined with "the just made perfect" in an ever-enlarging ministry of benevolence, as conversing with Jesus Christ with the familiarity of friendship, and especially as having an immediate intercourse with God, such as the closest intimacies of earth dimly shadow forth;—when this thought of my future being comes to me, whilst I hope, I also fear; the blessedness seems too great; the consciousness of present weakness and unworthiness is almost too strong for hope. But when, in this frame of mind, I look round on the creation, and see there the marks of an omnipotent goodness, to which nothing is impossible, and from which every thing may be hoped; when I see around me the proofs of an Infinite Father, who must desire the perpetual progress of his intellectual offspring; when I look next at the human mind, and see what powers a few years have unfolded, and discern in it the capacity of everlasting improvement; and especially when I look at Jesus, the conqueror of death, the heir of immortality, who has gone as the forerunner of mankind into the mansions of light and purity, I can and do admit the almost overpowering thought of the everlasting life, growth, felicity, of the human soul.

—

From Remarks on the case of the Ship Creole.

26. The Duty of the Free States.

I have now finished my task. I have considered the Duties of the Free States in relation to Slavery, and to other subjects of great and immediate concern. In this discussion I have constantly spoken of Duties as more important than Interests; but these in the end will be found to agree. The energy by which men prosper is fortified by nothing so much as by the lofty spirit which scorns to prosper through abandonment of duty.

I have been called by the subjects here discussed to speak much of the evils of the times, and the dangers of the country; and in treating of these a writer is almost necessarily betrayed into what may seem a tone of despondence. His anxiety to save his country from crime or calamity, leads him to use unconsciously a language of alarm which may excite the apprehension of inevitable misery. But I would not infuse such fears. I do not sympathize with the desponding tone of the day. It may be that there are fearful woes in store for this people; but there are many promises of good to give spring to hope and effort; and it is not wise to open our eyes and ears to ill omens alone. It is to be lamented that men who boast of courage in other trials, should shrink so weakly from public difficulties and dangers, and should spend in unmanly reproaches, or complaints, the strength which they ought to give to their country's safety. But this ought not to surprise us in the present case; for our lot, until of late, has been singularly prosperous, and great prosperity enfeebles men's spirits, and prepares them to despond when it shall have passed away.

The country, we are told, is "ruined." What! the country ruined, when the mass of the population have hardly retrenched a luxury! We are indeed paying, and we ought to pay, the penalty of reckless extravagance, of wild and criminal speculation, of general abandonment to the passion for sudden and enormous gains. But how are we ruined? Is the kind, nourishing earth about to become a cruel step-mother? Or is the teeming soil of this magnificent country sinking beneath our feet? Is the ocean dried up? Are our cities and villages, our schools and churches, in ruins? Are the stout muscles which have conquered sea and land, palsied? Are the earnings of past years dissipated, and the skill which gathered them forgotten? I open my eyes on this ruined country, and I see around me fields fresh with verdure, and behold on all sides the intelligent countenance, the sinewy limb, the kindly look, the free and manly bearing, which indicate any thing but a fallen people. Undoubtedly we have much cause to humble ourselves for the vices which our recent prosperity warmed into being, or rather brought out from the depths of men's souls. But in the reprobation which these vices awaken, have we no proof that the fountain of moral life in the nation's heart is not exhausted. In the progress of temperance, of education, and of religious sensibility, in our land, have we no proof that there is among us an impulse towards improvement, which no temporary crime or calamity can overpower. * * *

After all, there is a growing intelligence in this community; there is much domestic virtue, there is a deep working of Christianity; there is going on a struggle of higher truths with narrow traditions, and of a wider benevolence with social evils; there is a spirit of freedom, a recognition of the equal rights of men; there are profound impulses received from our history, from the virtues of our fathers, and especially from our revolutionary conflict; and there is an indomitable energy, which, after rearing an empire in the wilderness, is fresh for new achievements. * * *

There is one Duty of the Free States of which I have not spoken; it is the duty of Faith in the intellectual and moral energies of the country, in its high destiny, and in the good Providence which has guided it through so many trials and perils to its present greatness. We indeed suffer much, and deserve to suffer more. Many dark pages are to be written in our history. But generous seed is still sown in this nation's mind. Noble impulses are working here. We are called to be witnesses to the world, of a freer, more equal, more humane, more enlightened social existence, than has yet been known. May God raise us to a more thorough comprehension of our work! May he give us faith in the good which we are summoned to achieve! May he strengthen us to build up a prosperity not tainted by slavery, selfishness, or any wrong; but pure, innocent, righteous, and overflowing, through a just and generous intercourse, on all the nations of the earth!

Edward Payson, 1783-1827. (Manual, p. 480.)

From the "Selections."

27. NATURAL RELIGION.

I KNOW that those who hate and despise the religion of Jesus because it condemns their evil deeds, have endeavored to deprive him of the honor of communicating to mankind the glad tidings of life and immortality. I know that they have dragged the mouldering carcass of paganism from the grave, animated her lifeless form with a spark stolen from the sacred altar, arrayed her in the spoils of Christianity, re-lighted her extinguished taper at the torch of revelation, dignified her with the name of natural religion, and exalted her in the temple of reason, as a goddess, able, without divine assistance, to guide mankind to truth and happiness. But we also know, that all her boasted pretensions are vain, the offspring of ignorance, wickedness, and pride. We know that she is indebted to that revelation which she presumes to ridicule, and contemn, for every semblance of truth or energy which she displays. We know that the most she can do, is to find men blind and leave them so; and to lead them still farther astray, in a labyrinth of vice, delusion, and wretchedness. This is incontrovertibly evident, both from past and present experience; and we may defy her most eloquent advocates to produce a single instance in which she has enlightened or reformed mankind. If, as is often asserted, she is able to guide us in the path of truth and happiness, why has she ever suffered her votaries to remain a prey to vice and ignorance. Why did she not teach the learned Egyptians to abstain from worshiping their leeks and onions? Why not instruct the polished Greeks to renounce their sixty thousand gods? Why not persuade the enlightened Romans to abstain from adoring their deified murderers? Why not prevail on the wealthy Phœnicians to refrain from sacrificing their infants to Saturn? Or, if it was a task beyond her power to enlighten the ignorant multitude, reform their barbarous and abominable superstitions, and teach them that they were immortal beings, why did she not, at least, instruct their philosophers in the great doctrine of the immortality of the soul, which they so earnestly labored in vain to discover? They enjoyed the light of reason and natural religion, in its fullest extent, yet so far were they from ascertaining the nature of our future and eternal existence, that they could not determine whether we should exist at all beyond the grave; nor could all their advantages preserve them from the grossest errors, and the most unnatural crimes.

Joseph S. Buckminster, 1784–1812. (Manual, p. 480.)

From the "Sermons."

28. Necessity of Regeneration.

Look back, my hearers, upon your lives, and observe the numerous opinions that you have adopted and discarded, the numerous attachments you have formed and forgotten, and recollect how imperceptible were the revolutions of your sentiments, how quiet the changes of your affections. Perhaps, even now, your minds may be passing through some interesting processes, your pursuits may be taking some new direction, and your character may soon exhibit to the world some unexpected transformation. Compare with this the spiritual regeneration of the heart. So is every one that is born of the Spirit. Perhaps the following may not be an imperfect description of the process that takes place in a mind which is the subject of a radical conversion. The motion of the wind is unseen, its effects are visible ; the trees bend and fields are laid waste ; though the altering sentiments and affections are unnoticed, the altered character obtrudes itself upon our observation. Truths before contemplated without concern, now seize the mind with a grasp too firm to be shaken. The world which is to succeed the present is no longer a subject of accidental thought, of wavering belief, or lifeless speculation ; a region to which no tie binds us, and which no curiosity leads us to explore. To the regenerated mind, the character and condition of man appears in a new, and interesting light. To a being whose existence has but just commenced, death is only a boundary, a line, that marks off the first, the smallest portion of existence. Earth with her retinue of allurements, her band of fascinating syrens, exclaims, "We have lost our hold on this man! He is no longer ours!" Religion welcomes her new adherent ; she beckons him to turn his steps into a new,—a pleasanter path ; and God himself looks down from heaven with complacency and love, illuminating his track by the light of his countenance, marking the first step he takes in religion, and supporting him by the staff of his grace,—the aid of his Holy Spirit. * * * The first objects that engage the dawning mind of the child are objects of sense. That which is born of the flesh is flesh. It is a selfish, sensual creature, ignorant of its Creator, of its destination ; uninclined to the purity, the spirituality, the power of religion ; alienated from the life of God, the life of the soul. Unrenewed by the influence of religious truth, undirected by the guiding hand of an Almighty Father, how shall such a creature reach the regions of immortal bliss ? Is it enthusiasm, is it folly, is it hypocrisy, to say to such a creature, "You must be born again before you can see the kingdom of God?" Is that Redeemer to be disclaimed who offers you his divine aid to form anew your character, to exalt your affections, to enlighten your dreary and desolate understanding?

Nathaniel W. Taylor,[1] *1781–1871.*

From the "Lectures on the Moral Government of God."

29. Proof of Immortality from the Moral Nature of Man.

The argument from *the moral nature* of man is made still more impressive by the superiority of its design and object. If there is no existence for man beyond the present state, what can we suppose to be the design of his Creator in forming him a moral being? What powers, what capacities are involved in his nature! What capacity to enjoy, and what power to impart happiness to others! Who can reflect on the nature of such a creature, his intelligence, his susceptibility, his will, his conscience, the dignity, the excellence of which he is capable, the moral victories and triumphs he may win, his fitness to hold on his way with archangels, strong in advancing all that good which infinite wisdom could devise, and infinite benevolence could love, the graces with which he may be adorned, and the beatitudes with which he may be blessed, and not believe that he is made to be one with the God who has created him—a partaker of his blessedness, a companion of his eternity.

If we consider what an almost total failure there is, even on the part of every good man, to attain in any respect the great end of his creation; how weak in resolution and feeble in heart—how little success in subduing his passions and governing his temper—how much of life is spent before he even begins to live in obedience to the demands of duty and of conscience—how remote he is from the uniform and settled tran-

[1] An eminent Congregational divine, long professor of theology in Yale College, and distinguished by the vigor and originality of his thinking.

quility of perfect virtue—what dissatisfaction he feels with the present, unappeased by all the world can offer—what an impatience and disgust with the littleness of all he finds—what an ever-restless aspiration after nobler and higher things—what anticipations and hopes from futurity never realized here on earth—how does our spirit labor under a sense of the incongruity between his attainments and his powers! and, unless there is a future state, what an insignificance is imparted to all that can be called virtue here on earth, and also to man himself!

Edward Hitchcock, 1793-1864. (Manual, p. 532.)

From "The Religion of Geology."

30. Geological Proof of Divine Benevolence.

My second argument in proof of the divine benevolence is derived from the disturbed, broken, and overturned condition of the earth's crust.

To the casual observer the rocks have the appearance of being lifted up, shattered, and overturned; but it is only the geologist who knows the vast extent of this disturbance. He never finds crystalline, non-fossiliferous rocks which have not been more or less removed from their original position. The older fossiliferous strata exhibit almost equal evidence of the operation of a powerful disturbing force, though sometimes found in their original horizontal position. The newer rocks have experienced less of this agency, though but few of them have not been elevated or dislocated. . . .

If these strata had remained horizontal, as they were originally deposited, it is obvious that all the valuable ores, minerals, and rocks, which man could not have discovered by direct excavation, must have remained forever unknown to him. Now, man has very seldom penetrated the rocks below the depth of half a mile, and rarely so deep as that; whereas, by the elevations, dislocations, and overturnings that have been described, he obtains access to all deposits of useful substances that lie within fifteen or twenty miles of the surface ; and many are thus probably brought to light from a greater depth. He is indebted, then, to this disturbing agency for nearly all the useful metals, coal, rock salt, marble, gypsum, and other useful minerals ; and when we consider how necessary these substances are to civilized society, who will doubt that it was a striking act of benevolence which thus introduced disturbance, dislocation, and apparent ruin into the earth's crust ?

John P. Durbin,[1] *1800.*

From "Observations in the East."

31. First Sight of Mount Sinai.

For two hours we ascended this wild, narrow pass, enclosed between stupendous granite cliffs, whose debris encumbered the defile, often rendering the passage difficult and dangerous. Escaping from the pass, we crossed the head of a basin-like plain, which declined to the south-west, and ascending gradually, gloomy, precipitous, mountain masses rose to view on either hand, with detached snow-beds lying in their clefts. The caravan moved slowly, and apparently with a more solemn, measured tread. The Bedouins became serious and silent, and looked steadily before them, as if to catch the first glimpse of some revered object. The space before us gradually expanded, when suddenly Tualeb, pointing to a black, perpendicular cliff, whose two riven and rugged summits rose some twelve or fifteen hundred feet directly in front of us, exclaimed, "*Gebel Mousa!*" How shall I describe the effect of that announcement? Not a word was spoken by Moslem or Christian, but slowly and silently we advanced into the still expanding plain, our eyes immovably fixed on the frowning precipices of the stern and desolate mountain. We were doubtless on the plain where Israel encamped at the giving of the law, and that grand and gloomy height before us was Sinai, on which God

[1] A native of Kentucky; is deemed one of the most eloquent divines in the Methodist church.

descended in fire, and the whole mountain was enveloped in smoke, and shook under the tread of the Almighty, while his presence was proclaimed by the long, loud peals of repeated thunder, above which the blast of the trumpet was heard waxing louder and louder, and reverberating amid the stern and gloomy mountain heights around; and then God spoke with Moses.

Leonard Bacon, 1802. (Manual, p. 480.)

From a "Missionary Sermon."

32. THE DAY APPROACHING.

THE time is to come when the world will be filled with the knowledge, the fear, and the praise of God Not always will war deluge the earth with fire and blood. Not always will idolatry offend the heavens with its abominations. Not always will despotism, political and spiritual, national and domestic, degrade and corrupt the masses of mankind. Not always will superstition, on the one hand, and infidelity, on the other, reject and despise the blessed revelation of forgiveness for sinners through Jesus, the Lamb of God. Not always will cold philosophy, and erratic enthusiasm, and fanaticism fierce and malignant, conspire to corrupt and pervert the gospel itself, turning even the streams from the fountain of life into waters of bitterness and poison. No, no; the time will come when the sun, in his daily journey round the renovated world, shall waken with his morning beam in every human dwelling the voice of joyful, thankful, spiritual worship. Then shall the boundless soul of Immanuel, who once travailed in the agony of the world's redemption, "be satisfied" with his victories over death and sin. The ransomed of the Lord shall return and come to Zion with songs, and with garlands of everlasting joy; and from the earth, no longer accursed for the sake of man, sorrow and sighing shall flee away.

From the New Englander.

33. The Benefits of Capital.

What wealth can be created without *capital?* Robinson Crusoe, on his lonely island, was a capitalist as well as a laborer and a land-holder. Put him down there without any capital—simply a naked, featherless, two-legged and two-handed, animal, without clothes, without a gun or a fish-hook, without hoe, or hatchet, or knife, or rusty nail, without a particle of food to keep him from fainting, and what will become of him? He gathers perhaps some wild fruits from the bushes; he picks up perhaps some shell-fish from the water's edge; he surprises a fawn or a kid, and throttles it and tears it to pieces with his fingers; he kindles a fire perhaps by rubbing two dry sticks together till they ignite with the friction; and so he keeps himself alive for a few days; but how little progress does he make! * * But let him by any means have a little to begin with in the shape of implements and materials; give him an axe or a spade, a jack-knife, or only a fragment of an iron hoop, give him a gill of seed wheat, or a single potato, or no more than a grain of maize, for planting; and how soon will his condition be changed! He has begun to be, even in this small way, a capitalist; and his labor, drawing something from the past, begins to reach into the future. Instead of spending all his time and strength in a constant scratching for the food of to-day, how soon will he have a blanket of skins, and a hut, and a garden in which he is preparing to-day the food of future months. Give him now a little more capital; let him have the means of stocking his farm with some sort of domestic animals; give him only a steer and a heifer, or even a pair of goats, and how soon will he begin to be rich.

James W. Alexander, 1804-1859. (Manual, p. 480.)

From his "Discourses on Christian Faith and Practice."

34. The Church a Temple.

In surveying the past, we observe a beautiful fitness and an enchanting variety in the materials which have been already built into that part of the edifice which has thus far been reared. How unlike the corps of prophets to the corps of apostles; and how unlike the several individuals of each. We have Scripture authority for placing these among the most honorable and sustaining parts of the fabric, near the corner-stone; for we are "built upon the foundation of the apostles and prophets." Isaiah with his evangelic clarion, Jeremiah with his pastoral reed of sorrows, and David with his many-voiced harp, sometimes loud in notes of triumph, and sometimes subdued to the voice of weeping, stand out with a marked individuality which becomes the more surprising, the more nearly we examine the distinctive features. They may be likened to those immense but goodly stones, carried up in courses, along the precipitous side of the valley, to form the basis for the temple of Solomon. The twelve apostles, including the last, and humanly speaking, the greatest, though brethren, how unlike! Who for an instant, could mistake Paul for Peter, or either of them for John. They occupy salient angles of the great foundation, and lie nearest to the corner-stone, elect and precious. Some of their brethren, though not visible in the front which meets the eye, may have done equal service in the bearing up of the mass. Martyrs and confessors found their place, in succeeding ages, as the wall advanced; some as glorious for ornament as strong for use. When love needed a signal display, amidst the blood of martyrdom, we see it immortalized in an Ignatius and a Polycarp. When stalking heresy needed a front of steel to stand unmoved against all its columns, we find an "Athanasius against the world." When the language of Greece is to be elevated to new dignity by conveying the wonders of Christianity, we hear the golden eloquence of a Basil and a Chrysostom. When Roman philosophy had died out of the world, we behold it revived in an Augustine, the father of the fathers. Later down in ages, we catch glimpses even amidst Romish corruptions of a Bernard and a Kempis. The note of alarm is given to a sleeping carnal church, first by Wicliff, Huss, and Jerome, then by Zwingle, Luther, Calvin, and Knox.

Martin John Spalding,[1] 1810–1872.

From "Sketches of the Early Catholic Missions in Kentucky."

35. Life in the New Settlements.

The early Catholic emigrants to Kentucky, in common with their brethren of other denominations, had to endure many privations and hardships. As we may well conceive, there were few luxuries to be found in the wilderness, in the midst of which they had fixed their new habitations. They often suffered even for the most indispensable necessaries of life. To obtain salt, they had to travel many miles to the licks, through a country infested with savages; and they were often obliged to remain there for several days, until they could procure a supply.

There were then no regular roads in Kentucky. The forests were filled with a luxuriant undergrowth, thickly interspered with the cane, and the whole closely interlaced with the wild pea-vine. These circumstances rendered them nearly impassable; and almost the only chance of effecting a passage through this vegetable wilderness, was by following the paths or *traces* made by the herds of buffalo and other wild beasts. Luckily these traces were numerous, especially in the vicinity of the licks, which the buffalo were in the habit of frequenting, to drink the salt water, or *lick* the earth impregnated with salt.

The new colonists resided in log-cabins, rudely constructed, with no glass in the windows, with floors of dirt, or, in the better sort of dwellings, of puncheons of split timber, roughly hewed with the axe. After they had worn out the clothing brought with them from the old settlements, both men and women were under the necessity of wearing buckskin or home-spun apparel. Such a thing as a store was not known in Kentucky for many years: and the names of broadcloth, ginghams and calicoes, were never even so much as breathed. Moccasins made of buckskin, supplied the place of our modern

[1] Born in Kentucky, and long eminent as a controversial writer and a Prelate of the Roman Catholic church. His "sketches" give much interesting information respecting the early history of that church at the West.

shoes; blankets thrown over the shoulder, answered the purpose of our present fashionable coats and cloaks; and handkerchiefs tied around the head served instead of hats and bonnets. A modern fashionable bonnet would have been a matter of real wonderment in those days of unaffected simplicity.

The furniture of the cabins was of the same primitive character. Stools were used instead of chairs; the table was made of slabs of timber, rudely put together. Wooden vessels and platters supplied the place of our modern plates and china-ware; and a "tin cup was an article of delicate furniture, almost as rare as an iron-fork."[1] The beds were either placed on the floor, or on bedsteads of puncheons, supported by forked pieces of timber, driven into the ground, or resting on pins let into *auger*-holes in the sides of the cabin. Blankets, and bear and buffalo-skins, constituted often the principal bed-covering.

One of the chief resources for food was the chase. All kinds of game were then very abundant; and when the hunter chanced to have a goodly supply of ammunition, his fortune was made for the year. The game was plainly dressed, and served up on wooden platters, with corn-bread, and the Indian dish—the well known *hominy*. The corn was ground with great difficulty, on the laborious hand-mills; for mills of other descriptions were then, and for many years afterwards, unknown in Kentucky.

Such was the simple manner of life led by *our* "pilgrim fathers." They had fewer luxuries, but perhaps were, withal, more happy than their more fastidious descendants. Hospitality was not then an empty name; every log-cabin was freely thrown open to all who chose to share in the best cheer its inmates could afford. The early settlers of Kentucky were bound together by the strong ties of common hardships and dangers—to say nothing of other bonds of union—and they clung together with great tenacity. On the slightest alarm of Indian invasion, they all made common cause, and flew together to the rescue. There was less selfishness, and more generous chivalry;

[1] Marshall,—History of Kentucky.

less bickering, and more cordial charity, then, than at present; notwithstanding all our boasted refinement.

James Henry Thornwell,[1] *1811–1862.*

From the "Discourses on Truth."

36. Evil Tendencies of an Act of Sin.

There is a double tendency in every voluntary determination, one to propagate itself, the other to weaken or support, according to its own moral quality, the general principle of virtue. Every sin, therefore, imparts a proclivity to other acts of the same sort, and disturbs and deranges, at the same time, the whole moral constitution, it tends to the formation of special habits, and to the superinducing of a general debility of principle, which lays a man open to defeat from every species of temptation. The extent to which a single act shall produce this double effect, depends upon its intensity, its intensity depends upon the fullness and energy of will which will enter into it, and the energy of will depends upon the strength of the motives resisted. An act, therefore, which concludes an earnest and protracted conflict, which has not been reached without a stormy debate in the soul, which marks the victory of evil over the love of character, sensibility to shame, the authority of conscience and the fear of God, an act of this sort concentrates in itself the essence of all the single determinations which preceded it, and possesses power to generate a habit and to derange the constitution, equal to that which the whole series of resistances to duty, considered as so many individual instances of transgression, is fitted to impart. By one such act a man is impelled with an amazing momentum in the path of evil. He lives years of sin in a day or an hour. It is always a solemn crisis when the first step is to be taken in a career of guilt, against which nature and education, or any other strong influences protest. The results are unspeakably perilous when a man has to

[1] A Presbyterian divine, and professor of Theology, in South Carolina, his native state: a distinguished theological writer of the South.

fight his way into crime. The victory creates an epoch in his life. He is from that hour, without a miracle of grace, a lost man. The earth is strewed with wrecks of character which were occasioned by one fatal determination at a critical point in life, when the will stood face to face with duty, and had to make its decision deliberately and intensely for evil.

Charles P. McIlvaine,[1] *1799–1873.*

From a Sermon on the Resurrection of Christ.

37. Attestations of the Resurrection.

Here we remark, in general, that his resurrection was the great sign and crowning miracle to which our Lord, all the way of his ministry, to the day of his crucifixion, referred both friends and opposers, for the final confirmation of all his claims and doctrines. He staked all on the promise that he would rise from death. The Jews asked of him a sign, that they might believe. He answered, "There shall no sign be given, but the sign of the prophet Jonas. For as Jonas was three days and nights in the whale's belly, so shall the Son of Man be three days and three nights in the heart of the earth." * * Thus on that single event, the resurrection of Christ, the whole of Christianity, as it all centres in, and depends on him, was made to hinge. Redemption waited the evidence of resurrection. Nothing was to be accounted as sealed and finally certified, till Jesus should deliver himself from the power of death. All of the gospel, all the hopes it brings to us, all the promises with which it comforts us, were taken for their final verdict, as true or false, sufficient or worthless, to the door of that jealously-guarded and stone-sealed sepulchre, waiting the settlement of the question, *will he rise?* * *

But an event so momentous was not left to but one class of

[1] A native of New Jersey; in early life Chaplain and Professor of Moral Philosophy in the Military Academy at West Point, and long the Bishop of Ohio in the Protestant Episcopal Church. His Treatise on the Evidences of Christianity has great merit, and his theological and controversial writings are in high esteem: greatly venerated for his truly evangelical character.

evidences. There was a way by which thousands at once were made to receive as powerful assurance that Christ was risen, as if they had seen him in his risen body. Jesus, before his death, had made a great promise to his disciples, to be fulfilled by him only after his death and resurrection ; a promise impossible to be fulfilled if his resurrection failed ; because then, not only would he be under the power of death, but all his claim to divine power would be brought to nought. It was the promise of the Holy Ghost. "When the Comforter is come whom I will send unto you from the Father, even the Spirit of Truth, which proceedeth from the Father, he shall testify of me, he shall glorify me."

It was after he had "shown himself alive after his passion, by many infallible proofs, being seen of his disciples forty days, and speaking to them of the things pertaining to the Kingdom of God," that the day for the accomplishment of that promise came. The day was that which commemorated the giving of the law on Mount Sinai. It was now to witness the going forth of the gospel from Jerusalem. I need not relate to you the wonderful events of that day of Pentecost, the coming of the Holy Ghost with the "sound as of a rushing mighty wind" that "filled all the house ;" the cloven tongues like as of fire," which sat on each of the disciples; the evidence that it was the Spirit of God which had then come, given in the sudden and astonishing change which immediately came over the apostles, transforming them from weak and timid men to the boldest and strongest; in the change which suddenly came upon the power of their ministry, converting it from the weak agent it had previously been in contact with all the unbelief and wickedness of men into an instrument so mighty that out of a congregation of Jews of all nations, many of whom had probably partaken in the crucifixion of Christ, three thousand that day were bowed down to repentance and subdued to his obedience. * *

Thus was the day of Pentecost, a great day of testimony to the life and divine power, and consequently the resurrection of

Christ. Each of those who heard the divers tongues of the ministry of that day, each of the three thousand, was a witness of the same.

George W. Bethune, 1805–1862. (Manual, p. 487.)

From the "Expository Lectures on the Heidelberg Catechism."

38. Aspirations towards Heaven.

* * Our Christian life is a course through this world, which we are to run looking unto Jesus, at the right hand of the throne of God. The mark of the prize of the high calling is in heaven. Nay, it is the hope of heaven which keeps our souls surely and steadfastly. No matter what other proofs of his being a Christian, a man may think that he has—what moral virtue, what present zeal, what reverence for God and sacred things, what kindness and faithfulness to his fellow-men,—if he have not this longing thirst for heaven, he should doubt his Christianity. The regenerate soul can be satisfied with nothing short of awaking with the divine likeness. We cannot pray aright without hoping for heaven, for there only will the askings of a pious heart be fully granted. We cannot give thanks aright without hoping for heaven, for there are the consummate blessings of the Redeemer's purchase. We cannot serve God aright without hoping for heaven, for there only is our faithfulness to be acknowledged, and our wages paid. Our hopes should be submissive, and our longing patient; we should be willing to remain so long as God has work for us here, but ever with a yearning sense that to depart and be with Christ is far better. Grace in the heart is an ascensive power, ever lifting its desires upward and upward, and so above the temptations of time and earth. We can never drive this world out of our hearts, but by bringing heaven into them. And heaven meets our affections when they ascend, as it met Jesus; and he who so walks, climbing the arduous way from the Valley of Baca to the temple on the mount (for we must walk until we get our wings of angelic strength), will so

approach the heavenly threshold, as, like holy Enoch, he can cross it at a step.

Oh, dear friends, what an advantage have they whose Jesus is in heaven, over those first disciples when they had him with them personally on earth. They were for building tabernacles on Tabor, looking for a temporal kingdom, walking by sight and not by faith ; but our Lord now above, draws up to a better, higher, holier home, our aims, our desires, and our love.

From "A Lecture:" Philadelphia, 1840.

39. The Prospects of Art in the United States.

It is well for those who have sufficient wealth, to bring among us good works of foreign or ancient masters, especially if they allow free access to them for students and copyists. The true gems are, however, rare, and very costly. A single masterpiece would swallow up the whole sum which even the richest of our countrymen would be willing to devote in the way of paintings. I hope, however, soon to see the day when there shall be a fondness for making collections of works by *American artists*, or those resident among us. Such collections, judiciously made, would supply the best history of the rise and progress of the arts in the United States. They would, more than any other means, stimulate artists to a generous emulation. They would reflect high honor upon their possessors, as men who love Art for its own sake, and are willing to serve and encourage it. They would highly gratify the foreigner of taste who comes curious to observe the working of our institutions and our habits of life. He does not cross the sea to find Vandykes and Murillos. He can enjoy them at home ; but he wishes to discover what the children of the West can do in following or excelling European example. The expense of such a collection could not be very great. A few thousands of dollars, less than is often lavished upon the French plate glass and lustres, damask hangings, and Turkey carpets of a pair of parlors (more than which few of our houses can boast), would cover their walls with good specimens of American art, and do far more credit to the taste and heart of the owner.

William R. Williams,[1] ***1804.*** (Manual, p. 480.)

From "The Lectures on the Lord's Prayer."

40. LEAD US NOT INTO TEMPTATION.

WE are warranted in praying to be brought through temptation, when it is not of our own seeking, but of *God's sending.* If we walk without care and without vigilance, if we acknowledge not God in our ways, and take counsel at Ekron, and not at Zion,—leaving the Bible unread, and the closet unvisited,—if the sanctuary and the Sabbath lose their ancient hold upon us, and we then go on frowardly in the way of our own eyes, and after the counsel of our own heart, we have reason to tremble. A conscience quick and sensitive, under the presence of the indwelling Spirit, is like the safety-lamp of the miner, a ready witness and a mysterious guardian against the deathful damps, that unseen, but fatal, cluster around our darkling way. To neglect prayer and watching, is to lay aside that lamp, and then, though the eye see no danger and the ear hear no warning, spiritual death may be gathering around us her invisible vapors, stored with ruin, and rife for a sudden explosion. We are *tempting God,* and shall *we* be delivered ?

And if this be so with the negligent professor of religion, is it not applicable also to the openly careless, who never acknowledged Christ's claims to the heart and the life ?

With an evil nature, and a mortal body, and a brittle and brief tenure of earth, you are traversing perilous paths. Had you God for your friend, your case would be far other than it is. Peril and snare might still beset you ; but you would confront and traverse them, as the Hebrews of old did the weedy bed of the Red Sea, its watery walls guarding their dread way, the pillar of light the vanguard, and the pillar of cloud the

[1] A Baptist divine, born in New York city, where he has long been settled over a church ; eminent for general scholarship and literary ability.

rearguard of their mysterious progress, the ark and the God of the ark piloting and defending them. . . . You are like a presumptuous and unskilful traveller, passing under the arch of the waters of Niagara. The falling cataract thundering above you; a slippery, slimy rock beneath your gliding feet; the smoking, roaring abyss yawning beside you; the imprisoned winds beating back your breath; the struggling daylight coming but mistily to the bewildered eyes,—what is the terror of your condition if your guide, in whose grasp your fingers tremble, be malignant, and treacherous, and suicidal, determined on destroying your life at the sacrifice of his own? He assures you that he will bring you safely through upon the other side of the fall. And SUCH IS SATAN. Lost himself, and desperate, he is set on swelling the number of his compeers in shame, and woe, and ruin.

George B. Cheever, 1807- (Manual, pp. 480, 490.)

From "The Wanderings of a Pilgrim."

41. MONT BLANC.

IT is like those heights of ambition so much coveted in the world, and so glittering in the distance, where, if men live to reach them, they cannot live upon them. They may have all the appliances and means of life, as these French *savants* carried their tents to pitch upon the summit of Mont Blanc; but the peak that looked so warm and glittering in the sunshine, and of such a rosy hue in the evening rays, was too deadly cold, and swept by blasts too fierce and cutting; they were glad to relinquish the attempt, and come down. The view of the party a few hours below the summit, was a sight of deep interest. So was the spectacle of the immeasurable ridges and fields, gulfs and avalanches, heights and depths, unfathomable chasms and impassable precipices, of ice and snow, of such dazzling whiteness, of such endless extent, in such gigantic masses.

From "Lectures on the Pilgrim's Progress."

42. Sin Distorts the Judgment.

On the other hand, those who do not love God, cannot expect to find in his Word a system of truth that will please their own hearts. A sinful heart can have no right views of God, and of course will have defective views of his Word; for sin distorts the judgment, and overturns the balance of the mind on all moral subjects, far more than even the best of men are aware of. There is, there can be, no true reflection of God or of his Word, from the bosom darkened with guilt, from the heart at enmity with him. That man will always look at God through the medium of his own selfishness, and at God's Word through the coloring of his own wishes, prejudices, and fears.

A heart that loves the Saviour, and rejoices in God as its Sovereign, reflects back in calmness the perfect view of his character, which it finds in his Word. Behold on the borders of a mountain lake, the reflection of the scene above, received into the bosom of the lake below! See that crag projecting, the wild flowers that hang out from it, and bend as if to gaze at their own forms in the water beneath. Observe that plot of green grass above, that tree springing from the cleft, and over all, the quiet sky reflected in all its softness and depth from the lake's steady surface. Does it not seem as if there were two heavens. How perfect the reflection! And just as perfect and clear, and free from confusion and perplexity, is the reflection of God's character, and of the truths of his Word, from the quietness of the heart that loves the Saviour, and rejoices in his supreme and sovereign glory.

Now look again. The wind is on the lake, and drives forward its waters in crested and impetuous waves, angry and turbulent. Where is that sweet image? There is no change above: the sky is as clear, the crag projects as boldly, the flowers look just as sweet in their unconscious simplicity; but below, banks, trees, and skies are all mingled in confusion. There is just as much confusion in every unholy mind's idea of God and his blessed Word. God and his truth are always clear, always the same, but the passions of men fill their own hearts with obscurity and turbulence; their depravity is itself obscurity; and through all this perplexity and wilful ignorance, they contend that God is just such a being as they behold him, and that they are very good beings in his sight. We have heard of a defect in the bodily vision, that represents all objects upside down; that man would certainly be called insane, who, under the influence of this misfortune, should so blind his understanding, as to believe and assert that men walked on their heads, and that the trees grew downwards. Now, is it not a much greater insanity for men who in their hearts do not love God, and in their lives perhaps insult and disobey him, to give credit to their own perverted misrepresentations of him and of his Word? As long as men will continue to look at God's truth through the medium of their own pride and prejudice, so long will they have mistaken views of God and eternity, so long will their own self righteousness look better to them for a resting place, than the glorious righteousness of Him, who of God is made unto us our Wisdom, Righteousness, Sanctification, and Redemption.

Horace Bushnell, 1804– (Manual, p. 480.)

From the "Sermons for the New Life."

43. Unconscious Influence.

The Bible calls the good man's life a light, and it is the nature of light to flow out spontaneously in all directions, and fill the world unconsciously with its beams. So the Christian shines, it would say, not so much because he will, as because he is a luminous object. Not that the active influence of Christians is made of no account in the figure, but only that this symbol of light has its propriety in the fact that their unconscious influence is the chief influence, and has the precedence in its power over the world. And yet there are many who will be ready to think that light is a very tame and feeble instrument, because it is noiseless. An earthquake, for example, is to them a much more vigorous, and effective agency. Hear how it comes thundering through the solid foundations of nature. It rocks a whole continent. The noblest works of man—cities, monuments, and temples—are in a moment levelled to the ground or swallowed down the opening gulfs of fire. . . . But let the light of the morning cease, and return no more; let the hour of morning come, and bring with it no dawn; the outcries of a horror-stricken world fill the air, and make, as it were, the darkness audible. The beasts go wild and frantic at the loss of the sun. The vegetable growths turn pale and die. A chill creeps on, and frosty winds begin to howl across the freezing earth. Colder and yet colder is the night. The vital blood, at length, of all creatures stops, congealed. Down goes the frost toward the earth's centre. The heart of the sea is frozen; nay, the earthquakes are themselves frozen in, under their fiery caverns. The very globe itself, too, and all the fellow-planets that have lost their sun, are become mere balls of ice, swinging silent in the darkness. Such is the light which revisits us in the silence of the morning. It make no shock or scar. It would not wake an infant in his cradle. And yet it perpetually new creates the world, rescuing it each morning as a prey from night and chaos. So the Christian is a light, even "the light of the world;" and we must not think that, because he shines insensibly or silently, as a mere luminous object, he is therefore powerless. The greatest powers are ever those which lie back of the little stirs and commotions of nature; and I verily believe that the insensible influences of good men are as much more potent than what I have called their voluntary or active, as the great silent powers of nature are of greater consequence than her little disturbances and tumults. The law of human influence is deeper than many suspect, and they lose sight of it altogether. The outward endeavors made by good men or bad, to sway others, they call their influence; whereas it is, in fact, but a fraction, and in most cases, but a very small fraction, of the good or evil that flows out of their lives.

From "Christ and His Salvation."

44. The True Rest of the Christian.

Once more the analogies of the sleep of Jesus suggest the Christian right, and even duty, of those relaxations, which are necessary, at times, to loosen the strain of life and restore the freshness of its powers. Christ, as we have seen, actually tore himself away from multitudes waiting to be healed, that he might refit himself by sleep. He had a way, too, of retiring often to mountain solitudes and by-places on the sea, partly for the resting of his exhausted energies. Sometimes also he called his disciples off in this manner, saying, "come ye yourselves apart into a desert place and rest awhile." Not that every disciple is, of course, to retire into solitudes and desert places, when he wants recreation. Jesus was obliged to seek such places to escape the continual press of the crowd. In our day, a waking rest of travel, change of scene, new society, is permitted, and when it is a privilege assumed by faithful men, to recruit them for their works of duty they have it by God's sanction, and even as a part of the sound economy of life. Going after a turn of gaiety, or dissipation, not after Christian rest, or going after rest only because you are wearied and worried by selfish overdoings, troubled and spent by toils that serve an idol, is a very different matter. The true blessing of rest is on you, only when you carry a good mind with you, able to look back on works of industry and faithfulness, suspended for a time, that you may do them more effectually. Going in such a frame, you shall rest awhile, as none but such can rest. Nature will dress herself in beauty to your eye, calm thoughts will fan you with their cooling breath, and the joy of the Lord will be strength to your wasted brain and body. Ah, there is no luxury of indulgence to be compared with this true Christian rest! Money will not buy it, shows and pleasures can not woo its approach, no conjuration of art, or contrived gaiety, will compass it even for an hour: but it settles, like dew, unsought, upon the faithful servant of duty, bathing his weariness and recruiting his powers for a new engagement in his calling. Go ye thus apart and rest awhile if God permits.

Albert Taylor Bledsoe,[1] *about 1809–*

From "The Theodicy."

45. Moral Evil Consistent with the Holiness of God.

The argument of the atheist assumes, as we have seen, that a Being of infinite power could easily prevent sin, and cause holiness to exist. It assumes that it is possible, that it implies no contradiction, to create an intelligent moral agent, and place it beyond all liability to sin. But this is a mistake. Almighty power itself, we may say with the most profound reverence, cannot create such a being, and place it beyond the possibility of sinning. If it could not sin, there would be no merit, no virtue, in its obedience. That is to say, it would not be a moral agent at all, but a machine merely. The power to do wrong, as well as to do right, is included in the very idea of a moral and accountable agent, and no such agent can possibly exist without being invested with such a power. To suppose such an agent to be created, and placed beyond all liability to sin, is to suppose it to be what it is, and not what it is, at one and the same time; it is to suppose a creature to be endowed with a power to do wrong, and yet destitute of such a power, which is a plain contradiction. Hence Omnipotence cannot create such a being, and deny to it a power to do evil, or secure it against the possibility of sinning.

Richard Fuller,[2] *1808–*

From a Sermon.

46. The Desire of all Nations shall come. *Haggai* ii. 7.

Follow the adorable Jesus from scene to scene of ever deepening insult and sorrow, tracked everywhere by spies

[1] The most prominent among the living philosophical writers of the South; at present editor of the Southern Review.

[2] A Baptist divine of much distinction; a native of South Carolina, but long settled in Baltimore.

hunting for the precious blood. Behold his sacred face swollen with tears and stripes; and, last of all, ascend Mount Calvary, and view there the amazing spectacle: earth and hell gloating on the gashed form of the Lord of Glory; men and devils glutting their malice in the agony of the Prince of Life; and all the scattered rays of vengeance whieh would have consumed our guilty race, converging and beating in focal intensity upon Him of whom the Eternal twice exclaimed, in a voice from heaven, "This is my beloved Son, in whom I am well pleased." After this, what are our emotions? Can we ever be cold or faithless? No, my brethren, it is impossible, unless we forget this Saviour, and lose sight of that cross on which he poured out his soul for us.

That is an affecting passage in Roman history which records the death of Manlius. At night, and on the Capitol, fighting hand to hand, had he repelled the Gauls, and saved the city, when all seemed lost. Afterwards he was accused; but the Capitol towered in sight of the forum where he was tried, and, as he was about to be condemned, he stretched out his hands, and pointed, weeping, to that arena of his triumph. At this the people burst into tears, and the judges could not pronounce sentence. Again the trial proceeded, but was again defeated; nor could he be convicted until they had removed him to a low spot, from which the Capitol was invisible. And behold my brethren, what I am saying. While the cross is in view, vainly will earth and sin seek to shake the Christian's loyalty and devotion; one look at that purple monument of a love which alone, and when all was dark and lost, interposed for our rescue, and their efforts will be baffled. Low must we sink, and blotted from our hearts must be the memory of that deed, before we can become faithless to the Redeemer's cause, and perfidious to his glory.

Henry Ward Beecher, 1813- (Manual, p. 480.)

From the "Star Papers."

47. A PICTURE IN A COLLEGE AT OXFORD.

I WAS much affected by a head of Christ. Not that it met my ideal of that sacred front, but because it took me in a mood that clothed it with life and reality. For one blessed moment I was with the Lord. I knew him. I loved him. My eyes I could not close for tears. My poor tongue kept silence; but my heart spoke, and I loved and adored. The amazing circuit of one's thoughts in so short a period is wonderful. They circle round through all the past, and up through the whole future; and both the past and future are the present, and are one. For one moment there arose a keen anguish, like a shooting pang, for that which I was; and I thought my heart would break that I could bring but only such a nature to my Lord; but in a moment, as quick as the flash of sunlight which follows the shadow of summer clouds across the fields, there seemed to spring out upon me from my Master a certainty of love so great and noble as utterly to consume my unworth, and leave me shining bright, as if it were impossible for Christ to love a heart without making it pure and beautiful by the resting on it of that illuming affection, just as the sun bathes into beauty the homeliest object when he looks full upon it.

—

48. FROST ON THE WINDOW.

BUT the indefatigable night repairs the desolation. New pictures supply the waste ones. New cathedrals there are, new forests, fringed and blossoming, new sceneries, and new races of extinct animals. We are rich every morning, and poor every noon. One day with us measures the space of two hundred years in kingdoms — a hundred years to build up, and a hundred years to decay and destroy; twelve hours to overspread the evanescent pane with glorious beauty, and twelve to extract and dissipate the pictures. . . . Shall we not reverently and rejoicingly behold in these morning pictures, wrought without color, and kissed upon the window by the cold lips of Winter, another instance of that Divine Beneficence of beauty which suffuses the heavens?

From "Lectures to Young Men."

49. Nature, Designed for our Enjoyment.

The *necessity* of amusement is admitted on all hands. There is an appetite of the eye, of the ear, and of every sense, for which God has provided the material. Gaiety of every degree, this side of puerile levity, is wholesome to the body, to the mind, and to the morals. Nature is a vast repository of manly enjoyments. The magnitude of God's works is not less admirable than its exhilarating beauty. The rudest forms have something of beauty; the ruggedest strength is graced with some charm; the very pins, and rivets, and clasps of nature, are attractive by qualities of beauty, more than is necessary for mere utility. The sun could go down without gorgeous clouds; evening could advance without its evanescent brilliance; trees might have flourished without symmetry; flowers have existed without odor, and fruit without flavor. When I have journeyed through forests, where ten thousand shrubs and vines exist without apparent use; through prairies, whose undulations exhibit sheets of flowers innumerable, and absolutely dazzling the eye with their prodigality of beauty — beauty, not a tithe of which is ever seen by man — I have said, it is plain that God is himself passionately fond of beauty, and the *earth* is his garden, as an *acre* is man's. God has made us like Himself, to be pleased by the universal beauty of the world. He has made provision in nature, in society, and in the family, for amusement and exhilaration enough to fill the heart with the perpetual sunshine of delight.

Upon this broad earth, purfled with flowers, scented with odors, brilliant in colors, vocal with echoing and re-echoing melody, I take my stand against all demoralizing pleasure. Is it not enough that our Father's house is so full of dear delights, that we must wander prodigal to the swine-herd for husks, and to the slough for drink? — when the trees of God's heritage bend over our head and solicit our hand to pluck the golden fruitage, must we still go in search of the apples of Sodom, outside fair and inside ashes.

Men shall crowd to the circus to hear clowns, and see rare feats of horsemanship; but a bird may poise beneath the very sun, or flying downward, swoop from the high heaven; then flit with graceful ease hither and thither, pouring liquid song as if it were a perennial fountain of sound — no man cares for that.

Upon the stage of life, the vastest tragedies are performing in every act; nations pitching headlong to their final catastrophe; others, raising their youthful forms to begin the drama of existence. The world of society is as full of exciting interest, as nature is full of beauty. The great dramatic throng of life is bustling along — the wise, the fool, the clown, the miser, the bereaved, the broken-hearted. Life mingles before us smiles and tears, sighs and laughter, joy and gloom, as the spring mingles the winter-storm and summer-sunshine. To this vast Theatre which God hath builded, where stranger plays are seen than ever author writ, man seldom cares to come. When God dramatizes, when nations act, or all the human kind conspire to educe the vast catastrophe, men sleep and snore, and let the busy scene go on, unlooked, unthought upon. . . . It is my object then, not to withdraw the young from pleasure, but from unworthy pleasures; not to lessen their enjoyments, but to increase them, by rejecting the counterfeit and the vile.

From "Norwood."

50. LIFE IN THE COUNTRY.

IT was this union of seclusion and publicity that made Norwood a place of favorite resort, through the summer, of artists, of languid scholars, and of persons of quiet tastes. There was company for all that shunned solitude, and solitude for all that were weary of company. Each house was secluded from its neighbor. Yards and gardens full of trees and shrubbery, the streets lined with venerable trees, gave the town at a little distance the appearance of having been built in an orchard or a forest-park. A few steps and you could be alone—a few steps too would bring you among crowds. Where else could one watch the gentle conflict between sounds and silence with such dreamy joy ?—or make idleness seem so nearly like meditation ?—or more nimbly chase the dreams of night with even brighter day-dreams, wondering every day what has become of the day before, and each week where the week has gone, and in autumn what has become of the summer, that trod so noiselessly that none knew how swift were its footsteps ! The town filled by July, and was not empty again till late October.

There are but two perfect months in our year—June and October. People from the city usually arrange to miss both. June is the month of gorgeous greens ; October, the month of all colors. June has the full beauty of youth ; October has the splendor of ripeness. Both of them are out-of-door months. If the year has anything to tell you, listen now ! If these months teach the heart nothing, one may well shut up the book of the year.

From "The Life of Jesus the Christ."

51. The Conception of Angels, Superhuman.

The angels of the oldest records are like the angels of the latest. The Hebrew thought had moved through a vast arc of the infinite cycle of truth, between the days when Abraham came from Ur of Chaldea, and the times of our Lord's stay on earth. But there is no development in angels of later over those of an earlier date. They were as beautiful, as spiritual, as pure and noble, at the beginning as at the close of the old dispensation. Can such creatures, transcending earthly experience, and far out-running any thing in the life of man, be creations of the rude ages of the human understanding ?

We could not imagine the Advent stripped of its angelic lore. The dawn without a twilight, the sun without clouds of silver and gold, the morning on the fields without dew-diamonds,—but not the Saviour without his angels? They shine within the Temple, they bear to the matchless mother a message which would have been a disgrace from mortal lips, but which from theirs fell upon her as pure as dew-drops upon the lilies of the plain of Esdraelon. They communed with the Saviour in his glory of transfiguration, sustained him in the anguish of the garden, watched at the tomb; and as they had thronged the earth at his coming, so they seem to have hovered in the air in multitudes at the hour of his ascension. Beautiful as they seem, they are never mere poetic adornments. The occasions of their appearing are grand. The reasons are weighty. Their demeanor suggests and befits the highest conception of superior beings. These are the very elements that a rude age could not fashion. Could a sensuous age invent an order of beings, which, touching the earth from a heavenly height on its most momentous occasions, could still, after ages of culture had refined the human taste and moral appreciation, remain ineffably superior in delicacy, in pure spirituality, to the demands of criticism? Their very coming and going is not with earthly movement. They suddenly are seen in the air as one sees white clouds round out from the blue sky, in a summer's day, that melt back even while one looks upon them. They vibrate between the visible and the invisible. They come without motion. They go without flight. They dawn and disappear. Their words are few, but the Advent Chorus yet is sounding its music through the world.

John McClintock,[1] *1814-1870.*

From a Sermon on "The Ground of Man's Love to God."

52. The Christian the only true Lover of Nature.

It is not too much to say that the only *true* lover of nature, is he that loves God in Christ. It is as with one standing in

[1] Distinguished among the Methodist clergy for eloquence and learning; a native of Pennsylvania.

one of those caves of unknown beauty of which travellers tell us. While it is dark, nothing can be seen but the abyss, or at most, a faint glimmer of ill-defined forms. But flash into it the light of a single torch, and myriad splendors crowd upon the gaze of the beholder. He sees long-drawn colonnades, sparkling with gems ; chambers of beauty and glory open on every hand, flashing back the light a thousand fold increased, and in countless varied hues. So the sense of God's love in the heart gives an eye for nature, and supplies the torch to illuminate its recesses of beauty. For the ear that can hear them, ten thousand voices speak, and all in harmony, the name of God! The sun, rolling in his majesty,—

"And with his tread, of thunder force,
Fulfilling his appointed course,"—

is but a faint and feeble image of the great central Light of the universe. The spheres of heaven, in the perpetual harmony of their unsleeping motion, swell the praise of God ; the earth, radiant with beauty, and smiling in joy, proclaims its Maker's love ; and the ocean,—that

"Glorious mirror, where the Almighty's form
Glasses itself in tempests,"—

as it murmurs on the shore, or foams with its broad billows over the deep, declares its God ; and even the tempests, that, in their "rising wrath, sweep sea and sky," still utter the name of Him who rides upon the whirlwind and directs the storm. In a word, the whole universe is but a temple, with God for its deity, and the redeemed *man* for its worshipper.

Noah Porter,[1] *1811-*

From "The Science of Nature versus the Science of Man.'

53. Science magnifies God.

* * We contend at present only for the position that we cannot have a science of nature which does not regard the spirit of man as a part of nature.

[1] A Congregational divine, born in Connecticut, long Professor of Metaphysics in Yale College, and writer of many critical Essays and Reviews. His treatise on "The Human Intellect," is the most elaborate American work upon Psychology.

But is this all? Do man and nature exhaust the possibilities of being? We cannot answer this question here. But we find suggestions from the spectrum and the spectroscope which may be worth our heeding. The materials with which we have to do in their most brilliant scientific theories seem at first to overwhelm us with their vastness and complexity. The bulks are so enormous, the forces are so mighty, the laws are so wide-sweeping, and at times so pitiless, the distances are so over-mastering, even the uses and beauties are so bewildering, that we bow in mute and almost abject submission to the incomprehensible all; of which we hesitate to affirm aught, except what has been manifest to our observant senses and connected by our inseparable associations. We forget what our overmastering thought has done in subjecting this universe to its interpretations. Its vast distances have been annihilated, for we have connected the distant with the near by the one pervading force which Newton divined We have analyzed the flame that burns in our lamp, and the flame that burns in the sun, by the same instrument,—connecting by a common affinity, at the same instant and under the same eye, two agents, the farthest removed in place and the most subtle in essence. As we have overcome distances, so we have conquered time, reading the story of antecedent cycles with a confidence equal to that with which we forecast the future ages. The philosopher who penetrates the distant portions of the universe by the *omnipresence* of his scientific generalizations, who reads the secret of the sun by the glance of his penetrating eye, has little occasion to deny that all its forces may be mastered by a single all-knowing and *omnipresent* Spirit, and that its secrets can be read by one all-seeing eye. The scientist who evolves the past in his confident thought, under a few grand titles of generalized forces and relations, and who develops and almost gives law to the future by his faith in the persistence of force, has little reason to question the existence of an intellect capable of deeper insight and larger foresight than his own, which can grasp all the past and the future by an all-comprehending intelligence, and can control its wants by a personal energy that is softened to personal tenderness and love.

William Henry Milburn,[1] *1823-*

From "Lectures."

54. The Pioneer Preachers of the Mississippi Valley.

The spoken eloquence of New England is for the most part from manuscript. Her first settlers brought old-world forms, and fashions from the old world, with them. Their preachers were set an appalling distance from their congregations. Between the pulpit, perched far up toward the ceiling, and the seats, was an awful abysmal depth. Above the lofty desk was dimly seen the white cravat, and above that the head of the preacher. His eye was averted and fastened downward upon his manuscript, and his discourse, or exercitation, or whatever it might be, was delivered in a monotonous, regular cadence, probably relieved from time to time by some quaint blunder, the result of indistinct penmanship, or dim religious light. It was not this preacher's business to arouse his audience. The theory of worship of the period was opposed to that. This people did not wish excitement, or stimulus, or astonishment, or agitation. They simply desired informatioe ; they wished to be instructed ; to have their judgment informed, or their reason enlightened. Thus the preacher might safely re main perched up in his far distant unimpassioned eyrie.

But how would such a style of eloquence—if, indeed, truth will permit the name of eloquence to be applied to the reading of matter from a preconcerted manuscript—how would such a style of delivery be received out in the wild West? Place your textual speaker out in the backwoods, on the stump, where a surging tide of humanity streams strongly around him, where the people press up toward him on every side, their

[1] Born in Philadelphia; a Methodist divine, long afflicted with blindness; but widely popular as a preacher and lecturer.

keen eyes intently perusing his to see if he be in real earnest,—"dead in earnest"—and where, as with a thousand darts, their contemptuous scorn would pierce him through if he were found playing a false game, trying to pump up tears by mere acting, or arousing an excitement without feeling it. Would such a style of oratory succeed there? By no means. The place is different; the hearers are different; the time, the thing required, all the circumstances, are totally different. Here, in the vast unwalled church of nature, with the leafy tree-tops for a ceiling, their massy stems for columns; with the endless mysterious cadences of the forest for a choir; with the distant or nearer music and murmur of streams, and the ever-returning voice of birds, sounding in their ears for the made-up music of a picked band of exclusive singers: here stand men whose ears are trained to catch the faintest foot-fall of the distant deer, or the rustle of their antlers against branch or bough of the forest track—whose eyes are skilled to discern the trail of savages who leave scarce a track behind them; and who will follow upon that trail—utterly invisible to the untrained eye—as surely as a blood-hound follows the scent, ten or twenty, or a hundred miles, whose eye and hand are so well practised that they can drive a nail, or snuff a candle, with the long, heavy western rifle. Such men, educated for years, or even generations, in that hard school of necessity, where every one's hand and wood-man's skill must keep his head; where incessant pressing necessities required ever a prompt and sufficient answer in deeds; and where words needed to be but few, and those the plainest and directest, required no delay nor preparation, nor oratorical coquetting, nor elaborate preliminary scribble; no hesitation nor doubts in deeds; no circumlocution in words. To restrain, influence, direct, govern, such a surging sea of life as this, required something very different from a written address.

ORATORS, AND LEGAL AND POLITICAL WRITERS, OF THE ERA OF THE REVOLUTION.

John Dickinson, 1732–1808. (Manual, p. 486.)

From "The Address of Congress to the States." May 26, 1779.

55. The Aspect of the War.

To our constituents we submit the propriety and purity of our intentions, well knowing they will not forget that we lay no burdens upon them but those in which we participate with them—a happy sympathy, that pervades societies formed on the basis of equal liberty. Many cares, many labors, and may we not add, reproaches, are peculiar to us. These are the emoluments of our unsolicited stations; and with these we are content, if YOU approve our conduct. If you do not, we shall return to our private condition, with no other regret than that which will arise from our not having served you as acceptably and essentially as we wished and strove to do, though as cheerfully and faithfully as we could.

Think not we despair of the commonwealth, or endeavor to shrink from opposing difficulties. No! Your cause is too good, your objects too sacred, to be relinquished. We tell you truths because you are freemen, who can bear to hear them, and may profit by them; and when they reach your enemies, we fear not the consequences, because we are not ignorant of their resources or our own. Let your good sense decide upon the comparison. . . .

We well remember what you said at the commencement of this war. You saw the immense difference between your circumstances and those of your enemies, and you knew the quarrel must decide on no less than your lives, liberties, and estates. All these you greatly put to every hazard, resolving rather to die freemen than to live slaves; and justice will oblige the impartial world to confess you have uniformly acted on the same generous principle. Persevere, and you insure peace, freedom, safety, glory, sovereignty, and felicity to yourselves, your children, and your children's children.

Encouraged by favors already received from Infinite Goodness, gratefully acknowledging them, earnestly imploring their continuance, constantly endeavoring to draw them down on your heads by an amendment of your lives, and a conformity to the Divine will, humbly confiding in the protection so often and wonderfully experienced, vigorously employ the means placed by Providence in your hands for completing your labors.

Fill up your battalions—be prepared in every part to repel the incursions of your enemies—place your several quotas in the continental treasury—lend money for public uses—sink the emissions of your respective States—provide effectually for expediting the conveyance of supplies for your armies and fleets, and for your allies—prevent the produce of the country from being monopolized—effectually superintend the behavior of public officers—diligently promote piety, virtue, brotherly love, learning, frugality, and moderation—and may you be approved before Almighty God, worthy of those blessings we devoutly wish you to enjoy.

John Adams, 1735–1826. (Manual, p. 486.)

From his "Life and Works."

56. CHARACTER OF JAMES OTIS.

JAMES OTIS, of Boston, sprang from families among the earliest of the planters of the Colonies, and the most respectable in rank, while the word *rank*, and the idea annexed to it, were tolerated in America. He was a gentleman of general science and extensive literature. He had been an indefatigable student during the whole course of his education in college and at the bar. He was well versed in Greek and Roman history, philosophy, oratory, poetry, and mythology. His classical studies had been unusually ardent, and his acquisitions uncommonly great. . . . It was a maxim which he inculcated on his pupils, as his patron in the profession, Mr. Gridley, had done before him, "*that a lawyer ought never to be without a volume of natural or public law, or moral philosophy, on his table or in his pocket.* In the history, the common law, and statute laws, of England, he had no superior, at least in Boston.

Thus qualified to resist the system of usurpation and despotism, meditated by the British ministry, under the auspices of the Earl of Bute, Mr. Otis resigned his commission from the crown, as Advocate-General,—an office very lucrative at that time, and a sure road to the highest favors of government in America,—and engaged in the cause of his country without fee or reward. His argument, speech, discourse, oration, harangue, —call it by which name you will, was the most impressive upon his crowded audience of any that I ever heard before or since, excepting only many speeches by himself in Faneuil Hall, and in the House of Representatives, which he made from time to time for ten years afterwards. There were no stenographers in those days. Speeches were not printed; and all that was not remembered, like the harangues of Indian orators, was lost in air. Who, at the distance of fifty-seven years, would attempt, upon memory, to give even a sketch of it? Some of the heads are remembered, out of which Livy or Sallust would not scruple to compose an oration for history. I shall not essay an analysis or a sketch of it at present. I shall only say, and I do say in the most solemn manner, that Mr. Otis's oration against "*writs of assistance*" breathed into this nation the breath of life.

From the "Thoughts on Government."

57. Requisites of a Good Government.

The dignity and stability of government in all its branches, the morals of the people, and every blessing of society, depend so much upon an upright and skilful administration of justice, that the judicial power ought to be distinct from both the legislative and executive, and independent upon both, that so it may be a check upon both, as both should be checks upon that.

. . . Laws for the liberal education of youth, especially of the lower class of people, are so extremely wise and useful, that, to a humane and generous mind, no expense for this purpose would be thought extravagant. . . . You and I, my dear friend, have been sent into life at a time when the greatest lawgivers of antiquity would have wished to live. How few of the human race have ever enjoyed an opportunity of making an election of government, more than of air, soil, or climate, for themselves or their children! When, before the present epocha, had three millions of people full power and a fair opportunity, to form and establish the wisest and happiest government that human wisdom can contrive?

Patrick Henry, 1736–1799. (Manual, p. 484.)

From "Speech in the Convention of Virginia." 1775.

58. The Necessity of the War.

I have but one lamp by which my feet are guided, and that is the lamp of experience. I know of no way of judging of the future but by the past. And judging by the past, I wish to know what has been the conduct of the British ministry for the last ten years to justify those hopes with which gentlemen have been pleased to solace themselves and the house. Is it that insidious smile with which our petition has been lately received. Trust it not, Sir, it will prove a snare to your feet. Suffer not yourselves to be betrayed with a kiss. Ask yourselves how this gracious reception of our petition comports with those warlike preparations which cover our waters and darken our land. Are fleets and armies necessary to a work of love and reconciliation? Have we shown ourselves so unwilling to be reconciled that force must be called in to win back our love? Let us not deceive ourselves, sir. These are the implements of war, and subjugation—the last arguments to which kings resort. There is no longer any room for hope. If we wish to be free, if we mean to preserve inviolate those inestimable privileges for which we have been so long contending, if we mean not basely to abandon the noble struggle in which we have been so long engaged, and which we have pledged ourselves never to abandon until the glorious object of our contest is obtained, we must fight, I repeat it, sir, we must fight. An appeal to arms and to the God of Hosts is all that is left us.

They tell us, sir, that we are weak; unable to cope with so formidable an adversary. But when shall we be stronger? Will it be the next week, or the next year? Will it be when we are totally disarmed, and when a British guard shall be stationed in every house? Shall we gather strength by irresolution and inaction? Shall we acquire the means of effectual resistance, by lying supinely on our backs, and hugging the delusive phantom of hope, until our enemies shall have bound us hand and foot?

Sir, we are not weak, if we make a proper use of those means which the God of nature hath placed in our power. Three millions of people, armed in the holy cause of liberty, and in such a country as that which we possess, are invincible by any force which our enemy can send against us. Besides, sir, we shall not fight our battles alone. There is a just God, who presides over the destinies of nations, and who will raise up friends to fight our battles for us. The battle, sir, is not to the strong alone; it is to the vigilant, the active, the brave. Besides, sir, we have no election. If we were base enough to desire it, it is now too late to retire from the contest. There is no retreat but in submission and slavery. Our chains are forged. Their clanking may be heard on the plains of Boston. The war is inevitable—and let it come! I repeat it, sir, let it come!

It is vain, sir, to extenuate the matter. Gentlemen may cry, Peace, peace; but there is no peace. The war is actually begun. The next gale that sweeps from the north will bring to our ears the clash of resounding arms. Our brethren are already in the field. Why stand we here idle? What is it that gentlemen wish? What would they have? Is life so dear, or peace so sweet, as to be purchased at the price of chains and slavery? Forbid it, Almighty God! I know not what course others may take; but as for me, give me liberty, or give me death!

—

From a Speech on the Ratification of the Federal Constitution.

59. NECESSITY OF AMENDMENT BEFORE ADOPTION.

I EXHORT gentlemen to think seriously, before they ratify this constitution, and to indulge a salutary doubt of their being able to succeed in any effort they may make to get amendments after adoption. With respect to that part of the proposal, which says that every power not specially granted to Congress remains with the people; it must be previous to adoption, or it will involve this country in inevitable destruction. To talk of it, as a thing to be subsequently obtained, and not as one of your unalienable rights, is leaving it to the casual opinion of the Congress who shall take up the consideration of that most important right. They will not reason with you about the effect of this constitution. They will not take the opinion of this committee concerning its operation. They will construe it even as they please. If you place it subsequently, let me ask the consequences? Among ten thousand implied powers which they may assume, they may, if we be engaged in war, liberate every one of your slaves if they please. And this must and will be done by men, a majority of whom have not a common interest with you. They will, therefore, have no feeling for *your* interests. . . . . Is it not worth while to turn your eyes for a moment from subsequent amendments, to the real situation of your country? You may have a union, but can you have a lasting union in these circumstances? It will be in vain to expect it. But if you agree to previous amendments, you will have union, firm, solid, permanent. I cannot conclude without saying, that I shall have nothing to do with it, if subsequent amendments be determined upon. Oppressions will be carried on as radically by the majority when adjustments and accommodations will be held up. I say, I conceive it my duty, if this government be adopted before it is amended, to go home. I shall act as I think my duty requires.

Every other gentleman will do the same. Previous amendments, in my opinion, are necessary to procure peace and tranquility. I fear, if they be not agreed to, every movement and operation of government will cease, and how long that baneful thing, *civil discord*, will stay from this country, God only knows. When men are free from restraint, how long will you suspend their fury? The interval between this and bloodshed is but a moment. The licentious and wicked of the community will seize with avidity every thing you hold. In this unhappy situation, what is to be done? It surpasses my stock of wisdom to determine. If you will, in the language of freemen, stipulate that there are rights which no man under heaven can take from you, you shall have me going along with you; but not otherwise.

John Rutledge, 1739–1800. (Manual, p. 484.)

From "Speech on the Judiciary Establishment."

60. An Independent Judiciary the Safeguard of Liberty.

While this shield remains to the states, it will be difficult to dissolve the ties which knit and bind them together. As long as this buckler remains to the people, they cannot be liable to much, or permanent oppression. The government may be administered with violence, offices may be bestowed exclusively upon those who have no other merit than that of carrying votes at elections,—the commerce of our country may be depressed by nonsensical theories, and public credit may suffer from bad intentions; but so long as we have an independent judiciary, the great interests of the people will be safe. Neither the president, nor the legislature, can violate their constitutional rights. Any such attempt would be checked by the judges, who are designed by the constitution to keep the different branches of the government within the spheres of their respective orbits, and say thus far shall you legislate, and no further. Leave to the people an independent judiciary, and they will prove that man is capable of governing himself,—they will be saved from what has been the fate of all other republics, and they will disprove the position that governments of a republican form cannot endure. . .

We are asked by the gentleman from Virginia, if the people want judges to protect them? Yes, sir, in popular governments constitutional checks are necessary for their preservation; the people want to be protected against themselves: no man is so absurd as to propose the people collectedly will consent to the prostration of their liberties; but if they be not shielded by some constitutional checks, they will suffer them to be destroyed—to be destroyed by demagogues, who at the time they are soothing and cajoling the people, with bland and captivating speeches, are forging chains for them; demagogues who carry daggers in their hearts, and seductive smiles in their hypocritical faces, who are dooming the people to despotism, when they profess to be exclusively the friends of the people; against such designs and such artifices, were our constitutional checks made, to preserve the people of this country.

Thomas Jefferson, 1743-1826. (Manual, pp. 486, 490.)

From his "Inaugural Address, March 4th, 1801.

61. ESSENTIAL PRINCIPLES OF AMERICAN GOVERNMENT.

KINDLY separated by nature and a wide ocean from the exterminating havoc of one quarter of the globe, too high-minded to endure the degradations of the others, possessing a chosen country with room enough for our descendants to the hundredth and thousandth generation, entertaining a due sense of our equal right to the use of our own faculties, to the acquisitions of our industry, to honor and confidence from our fellow citizens, resulting not from birth but from our actions and their sense of them, enlightened by a benign religion, professed, indeed, and practised, in various forms, yet all of them including honesty, truth, temperance, gratitude, and the love of man; acknowledging and adoring an overruling Providence, which by all its dispensations proves that it delights in the happiness of man here and his greater happiness hereafter ; with all these blessings, what more is necessary to make us a happy and prosperous people? Still one thing more, fellow-citizens, a wise and frugal government, which shall restrain men from injuring one another, which shall leave them otherwise free to regulate their own pursuits of industry and improvement, and shall not take from the mouth of labor the bread it has earned. This is the sum of good government, and this is necessary to close the circle of our felicities.

About to enter, fellow-citizens, on the exercise of duties which comprehend everything dear and valuable to you, it is proper that you should understand what I deem the essential principles of our government, and consequently those which ought to shape its administration. I will compress them within the narrowest compass they will bear, stating the general principle, but not all its limitations. Equal and exact justice to all men, of whatever state or persuasion, religious, or political ; peace, commerce, and honest friendship, with all nations, entangling alliances with none ; the support of the state governments in all their rights, as the most competent administrations for our domestic concerns and the surest bulwarks against anti-republican tendencies ; the preservation of the general government in its whole constitutional vigor, as the sheet anchor of our peace at home and safety abroad ; a jealous care of the right of election by the people, a mild and safe corrective of abuses which are lopped by the sword of revolution where peaceable remedies are unprovided ; absolute acquiesence in the decisions of the majority, the vital principle of republics, from which there is no appeal but to force, the vital principle and immediate parent of despotism ; a well disciplined militia, our best reliance in peace and for the first moments of war, till regulars may relieve them ; the supremacy of the civil over the military authority ; economy in the public expense, that labor may be lightly burdened ; the honest payment of our debts and sacred preservation of the public faith ; encouragement of agriculture, and of commerce as its handmaid ; the diffusion of information and the arraignment of all abuses at the bar of public reason; freedom of religion; freedom of the press; freedom of person under the protection of the *habeas corpus*; and trial by juries impartially selected; these principles form the bright constellation which has gone before us, and guided our steps through an age of revolution and reformation. The wisdom of our sages and the blood of our heroes have been devoted to their attainment. They should be the creed of our political faith, the text of civil instruction, the touchstone by which to try the services of those we trust; and should we wander from them in moments of error or alarm, let us hasten to retrace our steps and to regain the road which alone leads to peace, liberty, and safety.

---

62. Character of Washington.

His mind was great and powerful, without being of the very first order; his penetration strong, though not so acute as a Newton, Bacon, or Locke; and as far as he saw no judgment was ever sounder. It was slow in operation, being little aided by invention or imagination, but sure in conclusion. Hence the common remark of his officers, of the advantage he derived from councils of war, where hearing all suggestions, he selected whatever was best; and certainly no General ever planned his battles more judiciously. But if deranged during the course of the action, if any member of his plan was dislocated by sudden circumstances, he was slow in re-adjustment. The consequence was that he often failed in the field, and rarely against an enemy in station, as at Boston and York. He was incapable of fear, meeting personal dangers with the calmest unconcern. Perhaps the strongest feature in his character was prudence; never acting until every circumstance, every consideration was maturely weighed; refraining if he saw a doubt, but when once decided, going through with his purpose, whatever obstacles opposed. His integrity was most pure, his justice the most inflexible I have ever known; no motives of interest or consanguinity, of friendship or hatred, being able to bias his decision. He was indeed in every sense of the words, a wise, a good, and a great man. His temper was naturally irritable, and high toned ; but reflection and resolution had obtained a firm and habitual ascendancy over it. If ever however it broke its bonds, he was most tremendous in his wrath. In his expenses he was honorable, but exact ; liberal in contributions to whatever promised utility, but frowning and unyielding on all visionary projects, and all unworthy calls on his charity. His heart was not warm in its affections ; but he exactly calculated every man's value, and gave him a solid esteem proportioned to it. His person, you know, was fine, his stature exactly what one would wish, his deportment easy, erect, and noble ; the best horseman of his age, and the most graceful figure that could be seen on horseback. Although in the circle of his friends, where he might be unreserved with safety, he took a free share in conversation, his colloquial talents were not above mediocrity, possessing neither copiousness of ideas, nor fluency of words. In public, when called on for a sudden opinion, he was unready, short, and embarrassed. Yet he wrote readily, rather diffusely, in an easy and correct style. This he had acquired by conversation with the world, for his education was merely reading, writing, and common arithmetic, to which he added surveying at a later day. His time was employed in action chiefly, reading little, and that only in agriculture and English history. His correspondence became necessarily extensive, and with journalizing his agricultural proceedings, occupied most of his leisure hours within doors. On the whole, his character was in its mass, perfect ; in nothing, bad ; in few points indifferent ; and it may truly be said that never did nature and fortune combine more perfectly to make a man great.

—

From the "Notes on Virginia."

63. Geographical Limits of the Elephant and the Mammoth. 1781.

From the thirtieth degree of south latitude to the thirtieth of north are nearly the limits which nature has fixed for the existence and multiplication of the elephant known to us. Proceeding thence northwardly to thirty-six and a half degrees, we enter those assigned to the mammoth. The farther we advance north, the more their vestiges multiply, as far as the earth has been explored in that direction ; and it is as probable as otherwise, that this progression continues to the pole itself, if land extends so far. The centre of the frozen zone, then, may be the acme of their vigor, as that of the torrid is of the elephant. Thus nature seems to have drawn a belt of separation between these two tremendous animals, whose breadth indeed is not precisely known, though at present we may suppose it to be about six and a half degrees of latitude ; to have assigned to the elephant the regions south of these confines, and those north to the mammoth, founding the constitution of the one in her extreme of heat, and that of the other in the extreme of cold. When the Creator has therefore separated their nature as far as the extent of the scale of animal life allowed to this planet would permit, it seems perverse to declare it the same, from a partial resemblance of their tusks and bones. But to whatever animal we ascribe these remains, it is certain such a one has existed in America, and that it has been the largest of all terrestrial beings.

---

64. The Unhappy Effects of Slavery.

There must doubtless be an unhappy influence on the manners of our people produced by the existence of slavery among us. . . . With the morals of the people, their industry also is destroyed. For in a warm climate no man will labor for himself who can make another labor for him. This is so true, that of the proprietors of slaves a very small proportion indeed are ever seen to labor. And can the liberties of a nation be thought secure when we have removed their only firm basis—a conviction in the minds of the people that they are the gift of God ? that they are not to be violated but with his wrath ? Indeed, I tremble for my country when I reflect that God is just ; that his justice cannot sleep forever ; that considering numbers, nature, and natural means only, a revolution of the wheel of fortune, an exchange of situation, is among possible events ; that it may become propable by supernatural interference. The Almighty has no attribute which can take sides with us in such a contest. But it is impossible to be temperate, and to pursue this subject through the various considerations of policy, of morals, of history, natural and civil. We must be contented to hope they will force their way into every one's mind. I think a change already perceptible since the origin of the present revolution. The spirit of the master is abating, that of the slave is rising from the dust, his condition mollifying, the way I hope preparing, under the auspices of Heaven, for a total emancipation.

John Jay, 1745-1829. (Manual, pp. 484, 486.)

From the "Address from the Convention." December 23, 1776.

65. An Appeal to Arms.

Rouse, brave citizens ! Do your duty like men ; and be persuaded that Divine Providence will not permit this western world to be involved in the horrors of slavery. Consider that, from the earliest ages of the world, religion, liberty, and reason have been bending their course towards the setting sun. The holy Gospels are yet to be preached to these western regions ; and we have the highest reason to believe that the Almighty will not suffer slavery and the gospel to go hand in hand. It cannot, it will not be.

But if there be any among us dead to all sense of honor and love of their country ; if deaf to all the calls of liberty, virtue, and religion ; if forgetful of the magnanimity of their ancestors, and the happiness of their children ; if neither the examples nor the success of other nations, the dictates of reason and of nature, or the great duties they owe to their God, themselves, and their posterity, have any effect upon them ; if neither the injuries they have received, the prize they are contending for, the future blessings or curses of their children, the applause or the reproach of all mankind, the approbation or displeasure of the great Judge, or the happiness or misery consequent upon their conduct, in this and a future state can move them,—then let them be assured that they deserve to be slaves, and are entitled to nothing but anguish and tribulation. . . . Let them forget every duty, human and divine, remember not that they have children, and beware how they call to mind the justice of the Supreme Being.

Alexander Hamilton, 1757–1804. (Manual, pp. 484, 486.)

From "Vindication of the Funding System."

66. CHARACTER OF THE DEBT.

A PERSON who, unacquainted with the fact, should learn the history of our debt from the declamations with which certain newspapers are perpetually charged, would be led to suppose that it is the mere creature of the *present* government, for the purpose of burthening the people with taxes, and producing an artificial and corrupt influence over them ; he would, at least, take it for granted that it had been contracted in the pursuit of some wanton or vain project of ambition or glory ; he would scarcely be able to conceive that every part of it was the relict of a war which had given independence, and preserved liberty to the country ; that the present government found it as it is, in point of magnitude (except as to the diminutions made by itself), and has done nothing more than to bring under a regular regimen and provision, what was before a scattered and heterogeneous mass.

And yet this is the simple and exact state of the business. The whole of the debt embraced by the provisions of the funding system, consisted of the unextinguished principal and arrears of interest, of the debt which had been contracted by the United States in the course of the late war with Great Britain, and which remained uncancelled, and the principal and arrears of interest of the separate debts of the respective States contracted during the same period, which remained, *outstanding, and unsatisfied, relating to services and supplies for carrying on the war.* Nothing more was done by that system, than to incorporate these two species of debt into the mass, and to make for the whole, one general, comprehensive provision. There is therefore, no arithmetic, no logic, by which it can be shown that the funding system has augmented the aggregate debt of the country. The sum total is manifestly the same; though the parts which were before divided are now united. There is, consequently, no color for an assertion, that the system in question either created any *new* debt, or made any addition to the *old.*

And it follows, that the collective burthen upon the people of the United States must have been as great *without* as *with* the union of the different portions and descriptions of the debt. The only difference can be, that without it that burthen would have been otherwise distributed, and would have fallen with unequal weight, instead of being equally borne as it now is.

These conclusions which have been drawn respecting the non-increase of the debt, proceed upon the presumption that every part of the public debt, as well that of the States individually, as that of the United States, was to have been honestly paid. If there is any fallacy in this supposition, the inferences may be erroneous; but the error would imply the disgrace of the United States, or parts of them,—a disgrace from which every man of true honor and genuine patriotism will be happy to see them rescued.

When we hear the epithets, "vile matter," "corrupt mass," bestowed upon the public debt, and the owners of it indiscriminately maligned as the harpies and vultures of the community, there is ground to suspect that those who hold the language, though they may not dare to avow it, contemplate a more summary process for getting rid of debts than that of paying them. Charity itself cannot avoid concluding from the language and conduct of some men, (and some of them of no inconsiderable importance,) that in their vocabularies *creditor* and *enemy* are synonymous terms, and that they have a laudable antipathy against every man to whom they owe money, either as individuals or as members of the society.

From a "Letter to Lafayette." October 6, 1789.

67. The French Revolution.

I have seen, with a mixture of pleasure and apprehension, the progress of events which have lately taken place in your country. As a friend to mankind and to liberty, I rejoice in the efforts which you are making to establish it, while I fear much for the final success of the attempts, for the fate of those I esteem who are engaged in them, and for the danger in case of success, of innovations greater than will consist with the real felicity of your nation. If your affairs still go well when this reaches you, you will ask why this foreboding of ill, when all the appearances have been so much in your favor. I will tell you: I dread disagreements among those who are now united (which will be likely to be improved by the adverse party) about the nature of your constitution; I dread the vehement character of your people, whom I fear you may find it more easy to bring on, than to keep within proper bounds after you have put them in motion. I dread the interested refractoriness of your nobles, who cannot all be gratified, and who may be unwilling to submit to the requisite sacrifices. And I dread the reveries of your philosophic politicians, who appear in the moment to have great influence, and who, being mere speculatists, may aim at more refinement than suits either with human nature, or the composition of your nation.

Fisher Ames, 1758-1808. (Manual, p. 487.)

From the "Speech on the British Treaty." April 15, 1795.

68. Obligation of National Good Faith.

The consequences of refusing to make provision for the treaty are not all to be foreseen. By rejecting, vast interests are committed to the sport of the winds: chance becomes the arbiter of events, and it is forbidden to human foresight to count their number, or measure their extent. Before we resolve to leap into this abyss, so dark and so profound, it becomes us to pause, and reflect upon such of the dangers as are obvious and inevitable. If this assembly should be wrought into a temper to defy these consequences, it is vain, it is deceptive, to pretend that we can escape them. It is worse than weakness to say, that as to public faith, our vote has already settled the question. Another tribunal than our own is already erected; the public opinion, not merely of our own country, but of the enlightened world, will pronounce a judgment that we cannot resist, that we dare not even affect to despise.

. . . This, sir, is a cause that would be dishonored and betrayed if I contented myself with appealing only to the understanding. It is too cold, and its processes are too slow, for the occasion. I desire to thank God that since he has given me an intellect so fallible, he has impressed upon me an instinct that is sure. On a question of shame and honor, reasoning is sometimes useless, and worse. I feel the decision in my pulse; if it throws no light upon the brain, it kindles a fire at the heart.

What is patriotism? Is it a narrow affection for the spot where a man was born? Are the very clods where we tread entitled to this ardent preference, because they are greener? No, sir, this is not the character of the virtue, and it soars higher for its object. It is an extended self-love, mingling with all the enjoyments of life, and twisting itself with the minutest filaments of the heart. It is thus we obey the laws of society, because they are the laws of virtue. In their authority we see not the array of force and terror, but the venerable image of our country's honor. Every good citizen makes that honor his own, and cherishes it not only as precious, but as sacred. He is willing to risk his life in its defence; and is conscious that he gains protection, while he gives it. For what rights of a citizen will be deemed inviolable, when a state renounces the principles that constitute their security? Or, if his life should not be invaded, what would its enjoyments be in a country odious in the eyes of strangers, and dishonored in his own? Could he look with affection and veneration to such a country as his parent? The sense of having one would die within him; he would blush for his patriotism, if he retained any, and justly, for it would be a vice; he would be a banished man in his native land.

I see no exception to the respect that is paid among nations to the law of good faith. If there are cases in this enlightened period when it is violated, then are none when it is decried. It is the philosophy of politics, the religion of governments. It is observed by barbarians; a whiff of tobacco smoke, or a string of beads, gives not merely binding force, but sanctity, to treaties. Even in Algiers, a truce may be bought for money; but when ratified, even Algiers is too wise or too just, to disown and annul its obligation. Thus we see, neither the ignorance of savages, nor the principles of an association for piracy and rapine, permit a nation to despise its engagements. If, sir, there could be a resurrection from the foot of the gallows, if the victims of justice could live again, collect together, and form a society, they would, however loath, soon find themselves obliged to make justice, that justice under which they fell, the fundamental law of their state. They would perceive it was their interest to make others respect, and they would, therefore, soon pay some respect themselves, to the obligations of good faith.

Gouverneur Morris, 1752–1816. (Manual, p. 484.)

From a "Report to Congress in 1780."

69. Qualifications of a Minister of Foreign Affairs.

A minister of foreign affairs should have a genius quick, lively, penetrating; should write on all occasions with clearness and perspicuity; be capable of expressing his sentiments with dignity, and conveying strong sense and argument in easy and agreeable diction; his temper mild, cool, and placid; festive, insinuating, and pliant, yet obstinate; communicative, and yet reserved. He should know the human face and heart, and the connections between them; should be versed in the laws of nature and nations, and not ignorant of the civil and municipal law; should be acquainted with the history of Europe, and with the interests, views, commerce, and productions of the commercial and maritime powers; should know the interests and commerce of America, understand the French and Spanish languages, at least the former, and be skilled in the modes and forms of public business; a man educated more in the world than in the closet, that by use, as well as by nature, he may give proper attention to great objects, and have proper contempt for small ones. He should be attached to the independence of America, and the alliance with France, as the great pillars of our politics; and this attachment should not be slight and accidental, but regular, consistent, and founded in strong conviction. His manners, gentle and polite; above all things, honest, and least of all things, avaricious. His circumstances and connections should be such as to give solid pledges for his fidelity; and he should by no means be disagreeable to the prince with whom we are in alliance, his ministers, or subjects.

William Pinkney,[1] *1764–1820.*

From "Speech in the Maryland Legislature." 1798.

70. Responsibility for Slavery.

For my own part, I would willingly draw the veil of oblivion over this disgusting scene of iniquity, but that the present abject state of those who are descended from these kidnapped sufferers, perpetually brings it forward to the memory.

But wherefore should we confine the edge of censure to our ancestors, or those from whom they purchased? Are not we equally guilty? *They* strewed around the seeds of slavery; *we* cherish and sustain the growth. *They* introduce the system; *we*

[1] Highly distinguished as a lawyer, orator, and diplomatist; a native of Maryland.

enlarge, invigorate, and confirm it. Yes, let it be handed down to posterity, that the people of Maryland, who could fly to arms with the promptitude of Roman citizens, when the hand of oppression was lifted up against themselves; who could behold their country desolated and their citizens slaughtered; who could brave with unshaken firmness every calamity of war before they would submit to the smallest infringement of their rights—that this very people could yet see thousands of their fellow-creatures, within the limits of their territory, bending beneath an unnatural yoke, and, instead of being assiduous to destroy their shackles, be anxious to immortalize their duration, so that a nation of slaves might forever exist in a country whose freedom is its boast.

—

From "Speech in the Nereide Case."

71. War, and American Belligerent Rights.

* * I THROW into the opposite scale the ponderous claim of War; a claim of high concernment, not to us only, but to the world; a claim connected with the maritime strength of this maritime state, with public honor and individual enterprise, with all those passions and motives which can be made subservient to national success and glory, in the hour of national trial and danger. I throw into the same scale the venerable code of universal law, before which it is the duty of this Court, high as it is in dignity, and great as are its titles to reverence, to bow down with submission. I throw into the same scale a solemn treaty, binding upon the claimant and upon you. In a word, I throw into that scale the rights of belligerent America, and, as embodied with them, the rights of these captors, by whose efforts and at whose cost the naval exertions of the government have been seconded, until our once despised and drooping flag has been made to wave in triumph, where neither France nor Spain could venture to show a prow. You may call these rights by what name you please. You may call them *iron* rights:—I care not. It is more than enough for me that they

are RIGHTS. It is more than enough for me that they come before you encircled and adorned by the laurels which we have torn from the brow of the naval genius of England: that they come before you recommended, and endeared, and consecrated by a thousand recollections, which it would be baseness and folly not to cherish, and that they are mingled in fancy and in fact with all the elements of our future greatness. . . . .

We are now, thank God, once more at peace. Our belligerent rights may therefore sleep for a season. May their repose be long and profound! But the time must arrive when the interests and honor of this great nation will command them to awake; and when it does arrive, I feel undoubting confidence that they will rise from their slumber in the fullness of their strength and majesty, unenfeebled and unimpaired by the judgment of this high court.

The skill and valor of our infant navy, which has illuminated every sea, and dazzled the master states of Europe by the splendor of its triumphs, have given us a pledge which I trust will continue to be dear to every American heart, and to influence the future course of our policy, that the ocean is destined to acknowledge the youthful dominion of the West.

James Madison, 1751-1836. (Manual, p. 486.)

From his "Report of Debates in the Federal Convention."

72. VALUE OF A RECORD OF THE DEBATES.

THE close of the war, however, brought no cure for the public embarrassments. The states relieved from the pressure of foreign danger, and flushed with the enjoyment of independent and sovereign power, instead of a diminished disposition to part with it, persevered in omissions, and in measures, incompatible with their relations to the federal government, and with those among themselves.

. . . It was known that there were individuals who had betrayed a bias towards monarchy, and there had always been some not unfavorable to a partition of the Union into several confederacies; either from a better chance of figuring on a sectional theatre, or that the sections would require stronger governments, or by their hostile conflicts lead to a monarchical consolidation. The idea of dismemberment had recently made its appearance in the newspapers.

Such were the defects, the deformities, the diseases, and the ominous prospects, for which the convention were to provide a remedy, and which ought never to be overlooked in expounding and appreciating the constitutional charter—the remedy that was provided.

The curiosity I had felt during my researches into the history of the most distinguished confederacies, particularly those of antiquity, and the deficiency I found in the means of satisfying it, more especially in what related to the process, the principles, the reasons, and the anticipations, which prevailed in the formation of them, determined me to preserve, as far as I could, an exact account of what might pass in the convention whilst executing its trust—with the magnitude of which I was fully impressed, as I was by the gratification promised to future curiosity by an authentic exhibition of the objects, the opinions, and the reasonings, from which the new system of government was to receive its peculiar structure and organization. Nor was I unaware of the value of such a contribution to the fund of materials for the history of a constitution, on which would be staked the happiness of a people great even in its infancy, and possibly the cause of liberty throughout the world.

Of the ability and intelligence of those who composed the Convention the debates and proceedings may be a test, as the character of the work which was the offspring of their deliberations must be tested by the experience of the future added to that of nearly half a century that has passed.

But whatever may be the judgment pronounced on the competency of the architects of the Constitution, or whatever may be the destiny of the edifice prepared by them, I feel it a duty to express my profound and solemn conviction, derived from my intimate opportunity of observing and appreciating the views of the Convention, collectively and individually, that there never was an assembly of men, charged with a great, and arduous trust, who were more pure in their motives, or more exclusively or anxiously devoted to the object committed to them, than were the members of the Federal Convention of 1787, to the object of devising and proposing a constitutional system which should best supply the defects of that which it was to replace, and best secure the permanent liberty and happiness of their country.

—

73. Inscription for a Statue of Washington.

The General Assembly of Virginia have caused this statue to be erected as a monument of affection and gratitude to George Washington, who, uniting to the endowments of the hero the virtues of the patriot, and exerting both in establishing the liberties of his country, has rendered his name dear to his fellow-citizens, and given to the world an immortal example of true glory.

John Randolph, 1773-1832. (Manual, p. 487.)

From a Speech in the Virginia Convention.

74. "Change is not Reform."

Sir, I see no wisdom in making this provision for future changes. You must give Governments time to operate on the People, and give the People time to become gradually assimilated to their institutions. Almost any thing is better than this state of perpetual uncertainty. A People may have the best form of Government that the wit of man ever devised, and yet, from its uncertainty alone, may, in effect, live under the worst Government in the world. Sir, how often must I repeat, that *change* is not *reform?* I am willing that this new Constitution shall stand as long as it is possible for it to stand; and that, believe me, is a very short time. Sir, it is vain to deny it. They may say what they please about the old Constitution,—the defect is not there. It is not in the form of the old edifice,—neither in the design nor in the elevation; it is in the *material*, it is in the People of Virginia. To my knowledge that People are changed from what they have been. The four hundred men who went out with David were *in debt*. The fellow-laborers of Catiline were *in debt*. The partizans of Cæsar were *in debt*. And I defy you to show me a desperately indebted People, anywhere, who can bear a regular, sober Government. I throw the challenge to all who hear me. I say that the character of the good old Virginia planter,—the man who owned from five to twenty slaves, or less, who lived by hard work, and who paid his debts,—is passed away. A new order of things is come. The period has arrived of living by one's wits; of living by contracting debts that one cannot pay; and above all, of living by office-hunting.

Sir, what do we see? Bankrupts,—branded-bankrupts,—giving great dinners, sending their children to the most expensive schools, giving grand parties, and just as well received as anybody in society! I say that, in such a state of things, the old Constitution was too good for them,—they could not bear it. No, Sir; they could not bear a freehold suffrage, and a property representation. I have always endeavored to do the People justice; but I will not flatter them,—I will not pander to their appetite for change. I will do nothing to provide for change. I will not agree to any rule of future apportionment, or to any provision for future changes, called amendments to the Constitution. Those who love change,—who delight in public confusion, who wish to feed the cauldron, and make it bubble,—may vote if they please for future changes. But by what spell, by what formula, are you going to bind the People to all future time? The days of Lycurgus are gone by, when we could swear the People not to alter the Constitution until he should return. You may make what entries on parchment you please; give me a Constitution that will last for half a century; that is all I wish for. No Constitution that you can make will last the one-half of half a century. Sir, I will stake anything, short of my salvation, that those who are malcontent now, will be more malcontent, three years hence, than they are at this day. I have no favor for this Constitution. I shall vote against its adoption, and I shall advise all the people of my district to set their faces, aye, and their shoulders, too, against it.

—

From "Letters to a young Relative."

75. The Error of Decayed Families.

One of the best and wisest men I ever knew has often said to me that a decayed family could never recover its loss of rank in the world, until the members of it left off talking and dwelling upon its former opulence. This remark, founded in a long and clear observation of mankind, I have seen verified in numerous instances in my own connections, who, to use the words of my oracle, will never thrive until they can become poor folks. He added, they may make some struggles, and with apparent success, to recover lost ground; they may, and sometimes do, get half way up again; but they are sure to fall back, unless, reconciling themselves to circumstances, they become in form, as well as in fact, poor folks.

John Kent, 1763-1847. (Manual, pp. 488, 504.)

From "Commentaries on American Law."

76. Law of the States.

The judicial power of the United States is necessarily limited to national objects. The vast field of the law of property, the very extensive head of equity jurisdiction, and the principal rights and duties which flow from our civil and domestic relations, fall within the control, and we might almost say the exclusive cognizance, of the state governments. We look essentially to the state courts for protection to all these momentous interests. They touch, in their operation, every chord of human sympathy, and control our best destinies. It is their province to reward and to punish. Their blessings and their terrors will accompany us to the fireside, and "be in constant activity before the public eye." The elementary principles of the common law are the same in every state, and equally enlighten and invigorate every part of our country. Our municipal codes can be made to advance with equal steps with that of the nation, in discipline, in wisdom, and in lustre, if the state governments (as they ought in all honest policy) will only render equal patronage and security to the administration of justice. The true interests and the permanent freedom of this country require that the jurisprudence of the individual states should be cultivated, cherished, and exalted, and the dignity and reputation of the state authorities sustained, with becoming pride. In their subordinate relation to the United States, they should endeavor to discharge the duty which they owe to the latter, without forgetting the respect which they owe to themselves. In the appropriate language of Sir William Blackstone, and which he applies to the people of his own country, they should be "loyal, yet free ; obedient, vet independent."

Edward Livingston,[1] *1764-1836.*

From the "Report on the Penal Code for Louisiana."

77. THE PROPER OFFICE OF THE JUDGE.

JUDGES are generally men who have grown old in the practice at the bar. With the knowledge which this experience gives, they acquire a habit, very difficult to be shaken off, of taking a side in every question that they hear debated, and when the mind is once enlisted, their passions, prejudices, and professional ingenuity are always arrayed on the same side, and furnish arms for the contest. Neutrality cannot, under these circumstances, be expected ; but the law should limit as much

[1] Was born in New York; eminent as a statesman, and as the author of a code of laws for Louisiana, his adopted state.

as possible, the evil that this almost inevitable state of things must produce. In the theory of our law, judges are the counsel for the accused, in practice they are, with a few honorable exceptions, his most virulent prosecutors. The true principles of criminal jurisprudence require that they should be neither. Perfect impartiality is incompatible with these duties. A good judge should have no wish that the guilty should escape, or that the innocent should suffer; no false pity, no undue severity, should bias the unshaken rectitude of his judgment; calm in deliberation, firm in resolve, patient in investigating the truth, tenacious of it when discovered, he should join urbanity of manners, to dignity of demeanor, and an integrity above suspicion, to learning and talent; such a judge is what, according to the true structure of our courts, he ought to be,—the protector, not the advocate of the accused; his judge, not his accuser; and while executing these functions, he is the organ by which the sacred will of the law is pronounced. Uttered by such a voice, it will be heard, respected, felt, obeyed; but impose on him the task of argument, of debate; degrade him from the bench to the bar; suffer him to overpower the accused with his influence, or to enter the lists with his advocate, to carry on the contest of sophisms, of angry arguments, of tart replies, and all the wordy war of forensic debate; suffer him to do this, and his dignity is lost; his decrees are no longer considered as the oracles of the law; they are submitted to, but not respected; and even the triumph of his eloquence or ingenuity, in the conviction of the accused, must be lessened by the suspicion that it has owed its success to official influence, and the privilege of arguing without reply. For these reasons, the judge is forbidden to express any opinion on the facts which are alleged in evidence, much less to address any argument to the jury; but his functions are confined to expounding the law, and stating the points of evidence on which the recollection of the jury may differ.

John Quincy Adams, 1767-1848. (Manual, pp. 487, 504.)

From the "Speech on the Right of Petition."

78. The Right of Petition Universal.

Sir, it is well known, that, from the time I entered this House, down to the present day, I have felt it a sacred duty to present any petition, couched in respectful language, from any citizen of the United States, be its object what it may; be the prayer of it that in which I could concur, or that to which I was utterly opposed. It is for the sacred right of petition that I have adopted this course. . . . Where is your law which says that the mean, and the low, and the degraded, shall be deprived of the right of petition, if their moral character is not good? Where, in the land of freemen, was the right of petition ever placed on the exclusive basis of morality and virtue? Petition is *supplication*—it is *entreaty*—it is *prayer!* And where is the degree of vice or immorality which shall deprive the citizen of the right to *supplicate* for a boon, or to *pray for mercy!* Where is such a law to be found? . . . And what does your law say? Does it say that, before presenting a petition, you shall look into it, and see whether it comes from the virtuous, and the great, and the mighty. No, sir; it says no such thing. The right of petition belongs to *all.* And so far from refusing to present a petition because it might come from those low in the estimation of the world, it would be an additional incentive, if such incentive were wanting.

—

From a "Discourse on the Jubilee of the Constitution."

79. The Administration of Washington.

When Solon, by the appointment of the people of Athens, had formed, and prevailed upon them to adopt a code of fundamental laws, the best that they would bear, he went into voluntary banishment for ten years, to save his system from the batteries of rival statesmen working upon popular passions and prejudices excited against his person. In eight years of a turbulent and tempestuous administration, Washington had settled upon firm foundations the practical execution of the Constitution of the United States. In the midst of the most appalling obstacles, through the bitterest internal dissensions, and the most formidable combinations of foreign antipathies and cavils, he had subdued all opposition to the Constitution itself; had averted all dangers of European war; had redeemed the captive children of his country from Algiers; had reduced by chastisement, and conciliated by kindness, the most hostile of the Indian tribes; had restored the credit of the nation, and redeemed their reputation of fidelity to the performance of their obligations; had provided for the total extinguishment of the public debt; had settled the union upon the immovable foundation of principle; and had drawn around his head, for the admiration and emulation of after times, a brighter blaze of glory than had ever encircled the brows of hero or statesman, patriot or sage.

The administration of Washington fixed the character of the Constitution of the United States, as a practical system of government, which it retains to this day. Upon his retirement, its great antagonist, Mr. Jefferson, came into the government again, as Vice-President of the United States, and four years after succeeded to the Presidency itself. But the funding system and the bank were established. The peace with both the great belligerent powers of Europe was secured. The disuniting doctrines of unlimited separate State sovereignty were laid aside. Louisiana, by a stretch of power in Congress, far beyond the highest tone of Hamilton, was annexed to the Union—and although dry-docks, and gun-boats, and embargoes, and commercial restrictions, still refused the protection of the national arm to commerce, and although an overweening love of peace, and a reliance upon reason as a weapon of defence against foreign aggression, eventuated in a disastrous though glorious war with the gigantic power of Britain,—the Constitution as construed by Washington, still proved an effective government for the country.

Henry Clay, 1777-1852. (Manual, p. 486.)

From a "Speech in the United States Senate," March 24, 1818.

80. Emancipation of the South American States.

Our Revolution was mainly directed against the mere theory of tyranny. We had suffered comparatively but little; we had, in some respects, been kindly treated; but our intrepid and intelligent forefathers saw, in the usurpation of the power to levy an inconsiderable tax, the long train of oppressive acts that were to follow. They rose; they breasted the storm; they achieved our freedom. Spanish America for centuries has been doomed to the practical effects of an odious tyranny. If we were justified, she is more than justified.

I am no propagandist. I would not seek to force upon other nations our principles and our liberty if they did not want them. I would not disturb the repose even of a detestable despotism. But if an abused and oppressed people will their freedom; if they seek to establish it; if, in truth, they have established it,—we have a right, as a sovereign power, to notice the fact, and to act as circumstances and our interest require. I will say, in the language of the venerated father of my country, "born in a land of liberty, my anxious recollections, my sympathetic feelings, and my best wishes, are irresistibly excited, whensoever, in any country, I see an oppressed nation unfurl the banners of freedom."

From the "Speech in the Senate on the Compromise Bill."

81. Dangers of Disunion.

South Carolina must perceive the embarrassments of her situation. She must be desirous,—it is unnatural to suppose that she is not,—to remain in the Union. What! a State whose heroes in its gallant ancestry fought so many glorious battles along with the other States of this Union,—a State with which this confederacy is linked by bonds of such a powerful character! I have sometimes fancied what would be her condition if she goes out of this Union; if her five hundred thousand people should at once be thrown upon their own resources. She is out of the Union. What is the consequence? She is an independent power. What then does she do? She must have armies and fleets, and an expensive government; have foreign missions; she must raise taxes; enact this very tariff, which has driven her out of the Union, in order to enable her to raise money, and to sustain the attitude of an independent power. If she should have no force, no navy to protect her, she would be exposed to piratical incursions. Their neighbor, St. Domingo, might pour down a horde of pirates on her borders, and desolate her plantations. She must have her embassies; therefore she must have a revenue. And, let me tell you, there is another consequence, an inevitable one. She has a certain description of persons recognized as property South of the Potomac, and West of the Mississippi, which would be no longer recognized as such, except within their own limits. This species of property would sink to one half of its present value, for it is Louisiana and the southwestern States which are her great market.

* * * * * * * * * *

If there be any who want civil war, who want to see the blood of any portion of our countrymen spilt, I am not one of them. I wish to see war of no kind; but, above all, I do not desire to see a civil war. When war begins, whether civil or foreign, no human sight is competent to foresee when, or how, or where it is to terminate. But when a civil war shall be lighted up in the bosom of our own happy land, and armies are marching, and commanders are winning their victories, and fleets are in motion on our coast, tell me if you can tell me, if any human being can tell its duration? God alone knows where such a war would end. In what a state will our institutions be left? In what state our liberties? I want no war; above all, no war at home

John C. Calhoun, 1782-1850. (Manual, p. 486.)

From his "Speech on the Bill to regulate the Power of Removal."

82. DANGERS OF AN UNLIMITED POWER OF REMOVAL FROM OFFICE.

LET us not be deceived by names. The power in question is too great for the chief magistrate of a free state. It is in its nature an imperial power; and if he be permitted to exercise it, his authority must become as absolute as that of the autocrat of all the Russias. To give him the power to dismiss at his will and pleasure, without limitation or control, is to give him an absolute and unlimited control over the subsistence of almost all who hold office under government. Let him have the power, and the sixty thousand who now hold employments under government would become dependent upon him for the means of existence. . . . I know that there are many virtuous and high-minded citizens who hold public office; but it is not, therefore, the less true that the tendency of the power of dismissal is such as I have attributed to it; and that, if the power be left unqualified, and the practice be continued as it has of late, the result must be the complete corruption and debasement of those in public employment. . . .

I have seen the spirit of independent men, holding public office, sink under the dread of this fearful power, too honest and too firm to become the instruments of the flatterers of power, yet too prudent, with all the consequences before them, to whisper disapprobation of what, in their hearts, they condemned. Let the present state of things continue, let it be understood that none are to acquire the public honors or to retain them, but by flattery and base compliance, and in a few generations the American character will become utterly corrupt and debased.

From the "Address on the relation of the States to the General Government."

83. PECULIAR MERIT OF OUR POLITICAL SYSTEM.

HAPPILY for us, we have no artificial and separate classes of society. We have wisely exploded all such distinctions; but we are not, on that account, exempt from all contrariety of interests, as the present distracted and dangerous condition of our country, unfortunately, but too clearly proves. With us they are almost exclusively geographical, resulting mainly from difference of climate, soil, situation, industry, and production; but are not, therefore, less necessary to be protected by an adequate constitutional provision, than where the distinct interests exist in separate classes. The necessity is, in truth, greater, as such separate and dissimilar geographical interests are more liable to come into conflict, and more dangerous, when in that state, than those of any other description: so much so, that *ours is the first instance on record where they have not formed, in an extensive territory, separate and independent communities, or subjected the whole to despotic sway.* That such may not be our unhappy fate also, must be the sincere prayer of every lover of his country.

So numerous and diversified are the interests of our country, that they could not be fairly represented in a single government, organized so as to give to each great and leading interest a separate and distinct voice, as in governments to which I have referred. A plan was adopted better suited to our situation, but perfectly novel in its character. The powers of government were divided, not, as heretofore, in reference to classes, but geographically. One General Government was formed for the whole, to which were delegated all the powers supposed to be necessary to regulate the interests common to all the States, leaving others subject to the separate control of the States, being, from their local and peculiar character, such that they could not be subject to the will of a majority of the whole Union, without the certain hazard of injustice and oppression. It was thus that the interests of the whole were subjected, as they ought to be, to the will of the whole, while the peculiar and local interests were left under the control of the States separately, to whose custody only they could be safely confided. This distribution of power, settled solemnly by a constitutional compact, to which all the States are parties, constitutes the peculiar character and excellence of our political system. It is truly and emphatically *American, without example or parallel.*

To realize its perfection, we must view the General Government and those of the States as a whole, each in its proper sphere independent; each perfectly adapted to its respective objects; the States acting separately, representing and protecting the local and peculiar interests; and acting jointly through one General Government, with the weight respectively assigned to each by the Constitution, representing and protecting the interest of the whole, and thus perfecting, by an admirable but simple arrangement, the great principle of representation and responsibility, without which no government can be free or just. To preserve this sacred distribution as originally settled, by coercing each to move in its prescribed orbit, is the great and difficult problem, on the solution of which the duration of our Constitution, of our union, and, in all probability, our liberty depends. How is this to be effected?

From his "Works."

84. Concurrent Majorities Supersede Force.

It has been already shown, that the same constitution of man which leads those who govern to oppress the governed,—if not prevented,—will, with equal force and certainty, lead the latter to resist oppression, when possessed of the means of doing so peaceably and successfully. But absolute governments, of all forms, exclude all other means of resistance to their authority, than that of force; and, of course, leave no other alternative to the governed, but to acquiesce in oppression, however great it may be, or to resort to force to put down the government. But the dread of such a resort must necessarily lead the government to prepare to meet force in order to protect itself; and hence, of necessity, force becomes the conservative principle of all such governments.

On the contrary, the government of the concurrent majority, where the organism is perfect, excludes the possibility of oppression, by giving to each interest, or portion, or order,—where there are established classes,—the means of protecting itself, by its negative, against all measures calculated to advance the peculiar interests of others at its expense. Its effect, then, is to cause the different interests, portions, or orders,—as the case may be, to desist from attempting to adopt any measure calculated to promote the prosperity of one, or more, by sacrificing that of others; and thus to force them to unite in such measures only as would promote the prosperity of all, as the only means to prevent the suspension of the action of the government;—and, thereby, to avoid anarchy, the greatest of all evils. It is by means of such authorized and effectual resistance, that oppression is prevented, and the necessity of resorting to force superseded, in governments of the concurrent majority;—and, hence, compromise, instead of force, becomes their conservative principle.

It would, perhaps, be more strictly correct to trace the conservative principle of constitutional governments to the necessity which compels the different interests, or portions, or orders, to compromise,—as the only way to promote their respective prosperity, and to avoid anarchy,—rather than to the compromise itself. No necessity can be more urgent and imperious, than that of avoiding anarchy. It is the same as that which makes government indispensable to preserve society; and is not less imperative than that which compels obedience to superior force. Traced to this source, the voice of a people,—uttered under the necessity of avoiding the greatest of calamities, through the organs of a government so constructed as to suppress the expression of all partial and selfish interests, and to give a full and faithful utterance to the sense of the whole community, in reference to its common welfare,—may without impiety, be called *the voice of God.* To call any other so, would be impious.

Daniel Webster, 1782–1852. (Manual, pp. 478, 486.)

From the "Reply to Hayne, in the United States Senate."

85. INESTIMABLE VALUE OF THE FEDERAL UNION.

I CANNOT, even now, persuade myself to relinquish it, without expressing once more my deep conviction, that, since it respects nothing less than the union of the states, it is of most vital and essential importance to the public happiness. I profess, sir, in my career hitherto, to have kept steadily in view the prosperity and honor of the whole country, and the preservation of our Federal Union. It is to that Union we owe our safety at home, and our consideration and dignity abroad. It is to that Union we are chiefly indebted for whatever makes us most proud of our country. That Union we reached only by the discipline of our virtues in the severe school of adversity. It had its origin in the necessities of disordered finance, prostrate commerce, and ruined credit. Under its benign influences, these great interests immediately awoke, as from the dead, and sprang forth with newness of life. Every year of its duration has teemed with fresh proofs of its utility and its blessings; and although our territory has stretched out wider and wider, and our population spread farther and farther, they have not outrun its protection or its benefits. It has been to us all a copious fountain of national, social, personal happiness. I have not allowed myself, sir, to look beyond the Union, to see what might lie hidden in the dark recess behind. I have not coolly weighed the chances of preserving liberty, when the bonds that unite us together shall be broken asunder. I have not accustomed myself to hang over the precipice of disunion, to see whether, with my short sight, I can fathom the depth of the abyss below; nor could I regard him as a safe counsellor in the affairs of this government, whose thoughts should be mainly bent on considering, not how the Union should be best preserved, but how tolerable might be the condition of the people when it shall be broken up and destroyed. While the Union lasts, we have high, exciting, gratifying prospects spread out before us, for us and our children. Beyond that I do not seek to penetrate the veil. God grant that, in my day at least, that curtain may not rise. God grant that, on my vision never may be opened what lies behind. When my eyes shall be turned to behold, for the last time, the sun in heaven, may I not see him shining on the broken and dishonored fragments of a once glorious Union; on states dissevered, discordant, belligerent; on a land rent with civil feuds, or drenched, it may be, in fraternal blood! Let their last feeble and lingering glance rather behold the gorgeous ensign of the republic, now known and honored throughout the earth, still full high advanced, its arms and trophies streaming in their original lustre, not a stripe erased or polluted, nor a single star obscured,—bearing for its motto no such miserable interrogatory as, *What is all this worth?* nor those other words of delusion and folly, *Liberty first, and Union afterwards;* but everywhere, spread all over in characters of living light, blazing on all its ample folds, as they float over the sea and over the land, and in every wind under the whole heavens, that other sentiment, dear to every American heart—Liberty *and* Union, now and forever, one and inseparable!

From the "Speech at the Laying of the Corner Stone of the Bunker Hill Monument."

86. Object of the Monument.

Let it not be supposed that our object is to perpetuate national hostility, or even to cherish a mere military spirit. It is higher, purer, nobler. We consecrate our work to the spirit of national independence, and we wish that the light of peace may rest upon it forever. We rear a memorial of our conviction of that unmeasured benefit which has been conferred on our own land, and of the happy influences which have been produced, by the same events, on the general interests of mankind. We come, as Americans, to mark a spot which must forever be dear to us and our posterity. We wish that whoever, in all coming time, shall turn his eye hither, may behold that the place is not undistinguished where the first great battle of the Revolution was fought. We wish that this structure may proclaim the magnitude and importance of that event to every class and every age. We wish that infancy may learn the purpose of its erection, from maternal lips, and that weary and withered age may behold it, and be solaced by the recollections which it suggests. We wish that labor may look up here, and be proud in the midst of its toil. We wish that in those days of disaster, which, as they come upon all nations, must be expected to come upon us also, desponding patriotism may turn its eyes hitherward, and be assured that the foundations of our national power are still strong. We wish that this column, rising towards heaven among the pointed spires of so many temples dedicated to God, may contribute also to produce, in all minds, a pious feeling of dependence and gratitude. We wish, finally, that the last object to the sight of him who leaves his native shore, and the first to gladden his who revisits it, may be something which shall remind him of the liberty and the glory of his country. Let it rise! let it rise, till it meet the sun in his coming; let the earliest light of the morning gild it, and parting day linger and play on its summit.

From his "Works."

87. BENEFITS OF THE CONSTITUTION.

ITS benefits are not exclusive. What has it left undone, which any government could do, for the whole country? In what condition has it placed us? Where do we now stand? Are we elevated, or degraded, by its operation? What is our condition, under its influence, at the very moment when some talk of arresting its power and breaking its unity? Do we not feel ourselves on an eminence? Do we not challenge the respect of the whole world? What has placed us thus high? What has given us this just pride? What else is it, but the unrestrained and free operation of that same Federal Constitution, which it has been proposed now to hamper, and manacle, and nullify? Who is there among us, that, should he find himself on any spot of the earth where human beings exist, and where the existence of other nations is known, would not be proud to say, I am an American? I am a countryman of Washington? I am a citizen of that Republic, which although it has suddenly sprung up, yet there are none on the globe who have ears to hear, and have not heard of it,—who have eyes to see and have not read of it,—who know any thing,—and yet do not know of its existence and its glory? And, gentlemen, let me now reverse the picture. Let me ask, who is there among us, if he were to be found to-morrow in one of the civilized countries of Europe, and were there to learn that this goodly form of Government had been overthrown—that the United States were no longer united—that a death-blow had been struck upon their bond of Union—that they themselves had destroyed their chief good and their chief honor,—who is there, whose heart would not sink within him? Who is there, who would not cover his face for very shame?

At this very moment, gentlemen, our country is a general refuge for the distressed and the persecuted of other nations. Whoever is in affliction from political occurrences in his own country, looks here for shelter. Whether he be republican, flying from the oppression of thrones—or whether he be monarch or monarchist, flying from thrones that crumble and fall under or around him,—he feels equal assurance, that if he get foothold on our soil, his person is safe, and his rights will be respected.

And who will venture to say, that in any government now existing in the world, there is greater security for persons or property than in that of the United States? We have tried these popular institutions in times of great excitement and commotion; and they have stood substantially firm and steady, while the fountains of the great deep have been elsewhere broken up; while thrones, resting on ages of prescription, have tottered and fallen; and while in other countries, the earthquake of unrestrained popular commotion has swallowed up all law, and all liberty, and all right, together. Our Government has been tried in peace, and it has been tried in war, and has proved itself fit for both. It has been assailed from without, and it has successfully resisted the shock; it has been disturbed within, and it has effectually quieted the disturbance. It can stand trial—it can stand assault—it can stand adversity, —it can stand every thing, but the marring of its own beauty, and the weakening of its own strength. It can stand every thing, but the effects of our own rashness, and our own folly. It can stand everything, but disorganization, disunion, and nullification.

—

From his Correspondence with Lord Ashburton.

88. THE RIGHT OF CHANGING ALLEGIANCE.

ENGLAND acknowledges herself overburdened with population of the poorer classes. Every instance of the emigration of persons of those classes is regarded by her as a benefit. England, therefore, encourages emigration; means are notoriously supplied to emigrants, to assist their conveyance, from public funds; and the New World, and most especially these United States, receive the many thousands of her subjects thus ejected from the bosom of their native land by the necessities of their condition. They come away from poverty and distress in over-crowded cities, to seek employment, comfort, and new homes, in a country of free institutions, possessed by a kindred race, speaking their own language, and having laws and usages in many respects like those to which they have been accustomed; and a country which, upon the whole, is found to possess more attractions for persons of their character and condition, than any other on the face of the globe. It is stated that, in the quarter of the year ending with June last, more than twenty-six thousand emigrants left the single port of Liverpool for the United States, being four or five times as many as left the same port within the same period, for the British Colonies and all other parts of the world. Of these crowds of emigrants, many arrive in our cities in circumstances of great destitution, and the charities of the country, both public and private, are severely taxed to relieve their immediate wants. In time they mingle with the new community in which they find themselves, and seek means of living. Some find employment in the cities, others go to the frontiers, to cultivate lands reclaimed from the forest; and a greater or less number of the residue, becoming in time naturalized citizens, enter into the merchant service under the flag of their adopted country.

Now, my Lord, if war should break out between England and a European power, can any thing be more unjust, any thing more irreconcilable to the general sentiments of mankind, than that England should seek out these persons, thus encouraged by her, and compelled by their own condition, to leave their native homes, tear them away from their new employments, their new political relations, and their domestic connections, and force them to undergo the dangers and hardships of military service for a country which has thus ceased to be their own country? Certainly, certainly, my Lord, there can be but one answer to this question. Is it not far more reasonable that England should either prevent such emigration of her subjects, or that, if she encourage and promote it, she should leave them, not to the embroilment of a double and contradictory allegiance, but to their own voluntary choice, to form such relations, political or social, as they see fit, in the country where they are to find their bread, and to the laws and institutions of which they are to look for defence and protection.

Joseph Story, 1779-1845. (Manual, pp. 487, 531.)

From his "Miscellaneous Writings."

89. Chief Justice Marshall.

When can we expect to be permitted to behold again so much moderation united with so much firmness, so much sagacity with so much modesty, so much learning with so much experience, so much solid wisdom with so much purity, so much of every thing to love and admire, with nothing—absolutely nothing, to regret? What, indeed, strikes us as the most remarkable in his whole character, even more than his splendid talents, is the entire consistency of his public life and principles. There is nothing in either which calls for apology or concealment. Ambition has never seduced him from his principles, nor popular clamor deterred him from the strict performance of duty. Amid the extravagances of party spirit he has stood with a calm and steady inflexibility, neither bending to the pressure of adversity, nor bounding with the elasticity of success. He has lived as such a man should live, (and yet, how few deserve the commendation!) by and with his principles. Whatever changes of opinion have occurred in the course of his long life, have been gradual and slow; the results of genius acting upon larger materials, and of judgment matured by the lessons of experience.

If we were tempted to say, in one word, what it was in which he chiefly excelled other men, we should say, in wisdom—in the union of that virtue, which has ripened under the hardy discipline of principles, with that knowledge which has constantly sifted and refined its old treasures, and as constantly gathered new. The constitution, since its adoption, owes more to him than to any other single mind, for its true interpretation and vindication. Whether it lives or perishes, his exposition of its principles will be an enduring monument to his fame, as long as solid reasoning, profound analysis, and sober views of government, shall invite the leisure, or command the attention, of statesmen and jurists. . . . Yet it may be affirmed by those who have had the privilege of intimacy with Mr. Chief Justice Marshall, that he rises, rather than falls, with the nearest survey; and that in the domestic circle he is exactly what a wife, a child, a brother, and a friend would most desire. In that magical circle, admiration of his talents is forgotten in the indulgence of those affections and sensibilities which are awakened only to be gratified.

From his "Miscellanies."

90. Dignity of American Jurisprudence.

The most delicate, and at the same time the proudest attribute of American jurisprudence, is the right of its judicial tribunals to decide questions of constitutional law. In other governments these questions cannot be entertained or decided by courts of justice; and, therefore, whatever may be the theory of the constitution, the legislative authority is practically omnipotent, and there is no means of contesting the legality or justice of a law, but by an appeal to arms. This can be done only when oppression weighs heavily and grievously on the whole people, and is then resisted by all because it is felt by all. But the oppression that strikes at a humble individual, though it robs him of character, or fortune, or life, is remediless; and, if it becomes the subject of judicial enquiry, judges may lament, but cannot resist, the mandates of the legislature. Far different is the case in our country; and the privilege of bringing every law to the test of the constitution belongs to the humblest citizen, who owes no obedience to any legislative act which transcends the constitutional limits. * *

The discussion of constitutional questions throws a lustre round the bar, and gives a dignity to its functions, which can rarely belong to the profession in any other country. Lawyers are here emphatically placed as sentinels upon the outposts of the constitution, and no nobler end can be proposed for their ambition or patriotism than to stand as faithful guardians of the constitution, ready to defend its legitimate powers, and to stay the arm of legislative, executive, or popular oppression. If their eloquence can charm, when it vindicates the innocent, and the suffering under private wrongs; if their learning and genius can, with almost superhuman witchery, unfold the mazes and intricacies by which the minute links of title are chained to the adamantine pillars of the law;—how much more glory belongs to them when this eloquence, this learning, and this genius, are employed in defence of their country; when they breathe forth the purest spirit of morality and virtue in support of the rights of mankind; when they expound the lofty doctrines which sustain and connect, and guide the destinies of nations; when they combat popular delusions at the expense of fame, and friendship, and political honors; when they triumph by arresting the progress of error and the march of power, and drive back the torrent that threatens destruction equally to public liberty and to private property, to all that delights us in private life, and all that gives grace and authority in public office.

Lewis Cass,[1] *1782-1866.*

From his "Report of the Secretary of War." December 1831.

91. POLICY OF REMOVING THE INDIANS.

THE associations which bind the Indians to the land of their forefathers are strong and enduring; and these must be broken by their emigration. But they are also broken by our citizens, who every day encounter all the difficulties of similar changes in pursuit of the means of support. And the experiments that have been made satisfactorily show that, by proper precautions and liberal appropriations, the removal and establishment of the Indians can be effected with little comparative trouble to them, or us. . . . If they remain, they must decline, and eventually disappear. Such is the result of all experience. If they remove, they may be comfortably established, and their moral and physical condition ameliorated. . . .

The great moral debt we owe to this unhappy race is universally felt and acknowledged. Diversities of opinion exist respecting the proper mode of discharging this obligation, but its validity is not denied.

Indolent in his habits, the Indian is opposed to labor; improvident in his mode of life, he has little foresight in providing, or care in preserving. Taught from infancy to reverence his own

[1] A native of New Hampshire, but for many years a citizen of Michigan: conspicuous in public life, and a writer of high authority on Indian and military affairs, and the settlement of the north-west.

traditions and institutions, he is satisfied of their value, and dreads the anger of the Great Spirit, if he should depart from the customs of his fathers. Devoted to the use of ardent spirits, he abandons himself to its indulgence without restraint. War and hunting are his only occupations. . . . Shall they be advised to remain, or remove? If the former, their fate is written in the annals of their race; if the latter, we may yet hope to see them renovated in character and condition, by our example and instruction, and their exertions.

Rufus Choate, 1799-1859. (Manual, p. 487.)

From his "Lectures and Addresses."

92. Conservative Force of the American Bar.

Is it not so that in its nature, in its functions, in the intellectual and practical habits which it forms, in the opinions to which it conducts, in all its tendencies and influences of speculation and action, it is, and ought to be, professionally and peculiarly such an element and such an agent, that it contributes, or ought to be held to contribute, more than all things else, or as much as anything else, to preserve our organic forms, our civil and social order, our public and private justice, our constitutions of government, even the Union itself? In these crises through which our liberty is to pass, may not, must not, this function of conservatism become more and more developed, and more and more operative? May it not one day be written, for the praise of the American Bar, that it helped to keep the true idea of the state alive and germinant in the American mind; that it helped to keep alive the sacred sentiments of obedience, and reverence, and justice, of the supremacy of the calm and grand reason of the law over the fitful will of the individual and the crowd; that it helped to withstand the pernicious sophism that the successive generations, as they come to life, are but as so many successive flights of summer flies, without relations to the past or duties to the future, and taught instead that all—all the dead, the living, the unborn—were one moral person—one for action, one for suffering, one for responsibility; that the engagements of one age may bind the conscience of another; the glory or the shame of a day may brighten or stain the current of a thousand years of continuous national being?

From the "Address before the New England Society of New York."

93. The Age of the Pilgrims, our Heroic Period.

I have said that I deemed it a great thing for a nation, in all the periods of its fortunes, to be able to look back to a race of founders, and a principle of institution, in which it might seem to see the realized idea of true heroism. That felicity, that pride, that help, is ours. Our past—both its great eras, that of settlement, and that of independence—should announce, should compel, should spontaneously evolve as from a germ, a wise, moral, and glorious future. These heroic men and women should not look down on a dwindled posterity. It should seem to be almost of course, too easy to be glorious, that they who keep the graves, bear the name, and boast the blood, of men in whom the loftiest sense of duty blended itself with the fiercest spirit of liberty, should add to their freedom, justice; justice to all men, to all nations; justice, that venerable virtue, without which freedom, valor, and power, are but vulgar things.

And yet is the past nothing, even our past, but as you, quickened by its examples, instructed by its experiences, warned by its voices, assisted by its accumulated instrumentality, shall reproduce it in the life of to-day. Its once busy existence, various sensations, fiery trials, dear-bought triumphs; its dynasty of heroes, all its pulses of joy and anguish, and hope and fear, and love and praise, are with the years beyond the flood. "The sleeping and the dead are but as pictures." Yet, gazing on these, long and intently, and often, we may pass into the likeness of the departed,—may emulate their labors, and partake of their immortality.

William H. Seward,[1] *1801-1872.*

"Oration on Lafayette," July 16th, 1834.

94. His Military Services in America.

There were indeed other and heroic volunteers from European countries, but they were either exiles who had no homes, or they were soldiers by profession, who followed the sword wherever a harvest was to be reaped with it. . . . Lafayette's first act in America gave new evidence of disinterestedness and magnanimity. He found the small patriot army rent asunder by jealous feuds growing out of ambition for preferment. What revolution, however holy, has not suffered by such evils! How many a revolution has been lost by them! Schuyler, the brave, the high-spirited, and wise, now the victim of an intrigue, was hesitating whether to submit to a privation of rank justly due him, or to resign. Putnam's recent promotion produced bitter complaints; and Gates was laboring night and day, aided by a powerful faction, to displace Washington from the chief command. The correspondence of the Father of his country, now first published, reveals the fact that the compensation attached to military rank was by no means an unimportant object of the universal rage for preferment, which then threatened to break up the army. Lafayette set a noble example to the republican chiefs. He declined the tender of a commission as major-general, with the emoluments, and stipulated, on the contrary, for leave to serve without reward, and even without a command, until he should have made a title to it by actual achievements. He won his commission by the blood he gave to his adopted country in the battle of Brandywine, by rallying the troops in the retreat at Chester Bridge, and by his brave resistance and capture, with the aid of militia-men, of a superior force of British and Hessian regulars; and thus, without exciting murmurs among his compatriots, and with the thanks of Congress, he

[1] A prominent statesman, formerly Governor of New York, of which state he is a native. He is known in literature by many addresses, speeches, and diplomatic papers, often of high merit.

rose to the command of a division in the army of the United States. Lavish of gold, as he had already shown that he was lavish of blood, he clothed and equipped these troops, numbering two thousand, at his own expense; and they soon became, under his exact but affectionate discipline, the favorite corps of the whole army. . . .

Lafayette stood second to Washington in the affections of the American people, and in the applauses of the friends of liberty throughout the world. Certainly whatever honors that people could have conferred upon any one would have been sure to wait on him. Let those who think that preferment, power, and applause are always the chief objects of human ambition, look now at this illustrious and yet youthful personage, cheerfully resigning his command, and without one murmur of regret for the honors laid down, or one glance towards the honors gathering before him, taking affectionate leave of his companions in arms, and their great chief, and returning to his native land, to resume there the duties he owed as a subject and member of the state, in France.

Abraham Lincoln,[1] *1809–1865.*

"Speech at the Dedication of the National Cemetery at Gettysburg," November 19, 1863.

95. OBLIGATION TO THE PATRIOT DEAD.

FOURSCORE and seven years ago our fathers brought forth upon this continent a new nation, conceived in liberty, and dedicated to the proposition that all men are created equal. Now we are engaged in a great civil war, testing whether that nation, or any nation so conceived and so dedicated, can long endure. We are met on a great battle-field of that war. We have come to dedicate a portion of that field as a final resting-place for those who here gave their lives that that nation might live. It

[1] Born in Kentucky; a prominent lawyer and statesman of Illinois; was elected President of the United States in 1860; was eminent for his profound appreciation of the subsequent struggle, and for his patriotic appeals in behalf of the nation. Assassinated April 13, 1865.

is altogether fitting and proper that we should do this. But in a larger sense we cannot dedicate, we cannot consecrate, we cannot hallow this ground. The brave men, living and dead, who struggled here, have consecrated it far above our power to add or detract. The world will little note, nor long remember, what we say here; but it can never forget what they did here. It is for us, the living, rather to be dedicated here to the unfinished work which they who fought here, have thus far so nobly advanced. It is rather for us to be here dedicated to the great task remaining before us, that from these honored dead we take increased devotion to that cause for which they gave the last full measure of devotion; that we here highly resolve that these dead shall not have died in vain; that this nation, under God, shall have a new birth of freedom, and that governments of the people, by the people, and for the people, shall not perish from the earth.

Charles Sumner, 1811–1874. (Manual, p. 487.)

From the "Speech in the Senate on the Nebraska and Kansas Bill," May 25, 1854.

96. Prospective Results of the Bill.

Sir, the bill which you are now about to pass is at once the worst and the best bill on which Congress ever acted. Yes, sir, worst and best at the same time.

It is the worst bill, inasmuch as it is a present victory of slavery. In a Christian land, and in an age of civilization, a time-honored statute of freedom is struck down, opening the way to all the countless woes and wrongs of human bondage. Among the crimes of history, another is about to be recorded, which no tears can blot out, and which, in better days, will be read with universal shame.

But there is another side, to which I gladly turn. Sir, it is the best bill on which Congress ever acted; for it annuls all past compromises with slavery, and makes all future compromises impossible. Thus it puts freedom and slavery face to face, and bids them grapple. Who can doubt the result? It opens wide the door of the future, when, at last, there will really be a North, and the slave power will be broken; when this wretched despotism will cease to dominate over our government, no longer impressing itself upon everything at home and abroad; when the national government shall be divorced in every way from slavery, and according to the true intention of our fathers, freedom shall be established by Congress everywhere, at least beyond the local limits of the states.

Thus, sir, now standing at the very grave of freedom in Kansas and Nebraska, I lift myself to the vision of that happy resurrection, by which freedom will be secured, not only in these territories, but everywhere under the national government. More clearly than ever before, I now penetrate that "All-Hail-Hereafter" when slavery must disappear. Proudly I discern the flag of my country, as it ripples in every breeze, at last become in reality, as in name, the Flag of Freedom, undoubted, pure, and irresistible. Am I not right, then, in calling this bill the best on which Congress ever acted?

Sorrowfully I bend before the wrong you are about to commit. Joyfully I welcome all the promises of the future.

From the "Speech for Union against the Slave Power," June 8, 1848.

97. HEROIC EFFORTS CANNOT FAIL.

THERE are occasions of political difference, I admit, when it may become expedient to vote for a person who does not completely represent our sentiments. There are some matters that come legitimately within the range of expediency and compromise. The Tariff and the Currency are unquestionably of this character. If a candidate differs from me, more or less, on these, I may yet be disposed to vote for him. But the question now before the country is of another character. This will not admit of compromise. It is not within the domain of expediency. *To be wrong on this is to be wholly wrong.* It is not merely expedient for us to defend Freedom, when assailed, but our duty so to do, unreservedly, and careless of consequences. Who is there in this assembly that would help to fasten a fetter upon Oregon or Mexico? Who is there that would not oppose every effort for this purpose? Nobody. Who is there, then, that can vote for Taylor or Cass?

But it is said that we shall throw away our votes, and that our opposition will fail. Sir! no honest, earnest effort in a good cause ever fails. It may not be crowned with the applause of men; it may not seem to touch the goal of immediate worldly success, which is the end and aim of so much of life. But still it is not lost. It helps to strengthen the weak with new virtue; to arm the irresolute with proper energy; to animate all with devotion to duty, which in the end conquers all. Fail! Did the martyrs fail, when with their precious blood they sowed the seed of the Church? Did the discomfited champions of Freedom fail, who have left those names in history which can never die? Did the three hundred Spartans fail, when, in the narrow pass, they did not fear to brave the innumerable Persian hosts, whose very arrows darkened the sun? No! Overborne by numbers, crushed to earth, they have left an example which is greater far than any victory. And this is the least we can do. Our example shall be the source of triumph hereafter. It will not be the first time in history that the hosts of Slavery have outnumbered the champions of Freedom. But where is it written that Slavery finally prevailed.

* * * * *

Returning to our forefathers for our principles, let us borrow, also, something of their courage and union. Let us summon to our sides the majestic forms of those civil heroes, whose firmness in council was equalled only by the firmness of Washington in war. Let us listen again to the eloquence of the elder Adams, animating his associates in Congress to independence: let us hang anew upon the sententious wisdom of Franklin; let us be enkindled, as were the men of other days, by the fervid devotion to Freedom, which flamed from the heart of Jefferson.

Deriving instruction from our enemies, let us also be taught by the Slave Power. The two hundred thousand slaveholders are always united in purpose. Hence their strength. Like arrows in a quiver, they cannot be broken. The friends of Freedom have thus far been divided. *Union*, then, must be our watchword,—union among men of all parties. By such a union we shall consolidate an opposition which must prevail.

From a Speech, September 10, 1863.

98. Our Foreign Relations.

It only remains that the Republic should lift itself to the height of its great duties. War is hard to bear,—with its waste, its pains, its wounds, its funerals. But in this war we have not been choosers. We have been challenged to the defence of our country, and in this sacred cause, to crush Slavery. There is no alternative. Slavery began the combat, staking its life, and determined to rule or die. That we may continue freemen there must be no slaves; so that our own security is linked with the redemption of a race. Blessed lot, amidst the harshness of war, to wield the arms and deal the blows under which the monster will surely fall! * *

But while thus steady in our purpose at home, we must not neglect that proper moderation abroad, which becomes the consciousness of our strength and the nobleness of our cause. The mistaken sympathy which foreign powers now bestow upon slavery,—or it may be the mistaken insensibility,—under the plausible name of "neutrality," which they profess,—will be worse for them than for us. For them it will be a record of shame which their children would gladly wash out with tears. For us it will be only another obstacle vanquished in the battle for civilization, where unhappily false friends are mingled with open enemies. Even if the cause shall seem for a while imperilled from foreign powers, yet our duties are none the less urgent. If the pressure be great, the resistance must be greater; nor can there be any retreat. Come weal or woe, this is the place for us to stand.

I know not if a republic like ours can count even now upon the certain friendship of any European power, unless it be the republic of William Tell. The very name is unwelcome to the full-blown representatives of monarchical Europe, who forget how proudly, even in modern history, Venice bore the title of *Serenissima Respublica.* It will be for us to change all this, and we shall do it. Our successful example will be enough. Thus far we have been known chiefly through that vital force which slavery could only degrade, but not subdue. Now at last, by the death of slavery, will the republic begin to live. For what is life without liberty? Stretching from ocean to ocean,—teeming with population, bountiful in resources of all kinds, and thrice-happy in universal enfranchisement, it will be more than conqueror. Nothing too vast for its power; nothing too minute for its care. Triumphant over the foulest wrong ever inflicted, after the bloodiest war ever waged, it will know the majesty of right and the beauty of peace, prepared always to uphold the one, and to cultivate the other. Strong in its own mighty stature, filled with all the fulness of a new life, and covered with a panoply of renown, it will confess that no dominion is of value which does not contribute to human happiness. Born in this latter day, and the child of its own struggles, without ancestral claims, but heir of all the ages,—it will stand forth to assert the dignity of man, and wherever any member of the human family is to be succored, there its voice will reach,—as the voice of Cromwell reached across France even to the persecuted mountaineers of the Alps. Such will be this republic;—upstart among the nations. Aye! as the steam-engine, the telegraph, and chloroform are upstart. Comforter and helper like these, it can know no bounds to its empire over a willing world. But the first stage is the death of slavery.

From "Prophetic Voices about America."

99. National Greatness Attainable through Peace.

Such are some of the prophetic voices about America, differing in character and importance, but all having one augury, and opening one vista, illimitable in extent and vastness. Farewell to the idea of Montesquieu, that a republic can exist only in a small territory. . . . . . .

Such grandeur may justly excite anxiety rather than pride, for duties are in corresponding proportion. There is occasion for humility also, as the individual considers his own insignificance in the transcendent mass. The tiny polyp, in its unconscious life, builds the everlasting coral; each citizen is little more than the industrious insect. The result is accomplished by continuous and combined exertion. Millions of citizens, working in obedience to nature, can accomplish anything. Of course, war is an instrumentality which a true civilization disowns. Here some of our prophets have erred. Sir Thomas Browne was so much overshadowed by his own age, that his vision was darkened by "great armies," and even "hostile and piratical attacks" on Europe. It was natural that D'Aranda, schooled in worldly affairs, should imagine the new-born power ready to seize the Spanish possessions. Among our own countrymen, Jefferson looked to war for the extension of dominion. The Floridas, he says on one occasion, "are ours on the first moment of war, and until a war they are of no particular necessity to us." Happily they were acquired in another way. Then again, while declaring that no constitution was ever before so calculated as ours for extensive empire and self-government, and insisting upon Canada as a component part, he calmly says that "this would be, of course, in the first war." Afterwards, while confessing a longing for Cuba, "as the most interesting addition that could ever be made to our system of States," he says that "he is sensible that this can never be obtained, even with her own consent, without war." Thus at each stage is the baptism of blood. In much better mood the good Bishop recognized empire as moving gently in the pathway of light. All this is much clearer now than when he prophesied. It is easy to see that empire obtained by force is unrepublican and offensive to that first principle of our Union according to which all just government stands only on the consent of the governed. Our country needs no such ally as war. Its destiny is mightier than war. Through peace it will have every thing. This is our talisman. Give us peace, and population will increase beyond all experience ; resources of all kinds will multiply infinitely ; arts will embellish the land with immortal beauty, the name of Republic will be exalted, until every neighbor, yielding to irresistible attraction, will seek a new life in becoming a part of the great whole ; and the national example will be more puissant than army or navy for the conquest of the world.

Alexander H. Stephens,[1] *1812–.*

From Appendix to "The Constitutional View."

100. Origin of the American Flag.

The stars, as a matter of course, represent states. The origin of the stripes, I think, if searched out, would be found to be a little curious. All I know upon that point is, that on the 4th day of July, 1776, after the Declaration of Independence was carried, a committee was appointed by Congress, consisting of Mr. Jefferson, Dr. Franklin, and John Adams, to prepare a *device* for a *seal* of the United States. . . . This seal, as reported, or the *device* in full, as reported, was never adopted. But in it we see the emblems, in part, which are still preserved in the flag.

The stripes, or lines, which, on Mr. Jefferson's original plan, were to designate the six quarterings of the shield, as signs of the six countries from which our ancestors came, are now, I believe, considered as representations of the old thirteen states,

[1] One of the most eminent public men of the south ; a native of Georgia.

and with most persons the idea of a shield is lost sight of. You perceive that, by drawing six lines or stripes on a shield figure, it will leave seven spaces of the original color, and of course give thirteen apparent stripes; hence the idea of their being all intended to represent the old thirteen states. My opinion is, that this was the origin of the stripes. Mr. Jefferson's quartered shield for a seal device was seized upon as a national emblem, that was put upon the flag. We have now the stars as well as the stripes. When each of these was adopted I cannot say; but the flag, as it now is, was designed by Captain Reid, as I tell you, and adopted by Congress.

BIOGRAPHICAL WRITERS.

Benjamin Rush,[1] *1745–1813.*

From "Essays, Literary, Moral," etc.

101. THE LIFE OF EDWARD DRINKER, A CENTENARIAN.

HE saw and heard more of those events which are measured by time, than have ever been seen or heard since the age of the patriarchs; he saw the same spot of earth which at one period of his life was covered with wood and bushes, and the receptacle of beasts and birds of prey, afterwards become the seat of a city not only the first in wealth and arts in the new, but rivalling, in both, many of the first cities in the old world. He saw regular streets where he once pursued a hare; he saw churches rising upon morasses where he had often heard the croaking of frogs; he saw wharves and warehouses where he had often seen Indian savages draw fish from the river for their daily subsistence; and he saw ships of every size and use in those streams where he had often seen nothing but Indian canoes. . . . He saw the first treaty ratified between the newly confederated powers of America and the ancient mon-

[1] A native of Pennsylvania, eminent as a writer, and especially as a teacher and practitioner of medicine.

archy of France, with all the formalities of parchment and seals, on the same spot, probably, where he once saw William Penn ratify his first and last treaty with the Indians, without the formality of pen, ink, or paper. . . . He saw the beginning and end of the empire of Great Britain in Pennsylvania. He had been the subject of seven successive crowned heads, and afterwards became a willing citizen of a republic; for he embraced the liberties and independence of America in his withered arms, and triumphed in the last years of his life in the salvation of his country

---

John Marshall, 1755-1835. (Manual, p. 490.)

From the "History of the American Colonies."

102. THE CONQUEST OF CANADA.

DURING these transactions, General Amherst was taking measures for the annihilation of the remnant of French power in Canada. He determined to employ the immense force under his command for the accomplishment of this object, and made arrangements during the winter to bring the armies from Quebec, Lake Champlain, and Lake Ontario, to act against Montreal. * *

The junction of these armies presenting before Montreal a force not to be resisted, the Governor offered to capitulate. In the month of September, Montreal, and all other places within the government of Canada, then remaining in the possession of France, were surrendered to his Britannic majesty. The troops were to be transported to France, and the Canadians to be protected in their property, and the full enjoyment of their religion.

That colossal power which France had been long erecting in America, with vast labor and expense; which had been the motive for one of the most extensive and desolating wars of modern times, was thus entirely overthrown. The causes of this interesting event are to be found in the superior wealth and population of the colonies of England, and in her immense naval strength; an advantage, in distant war, not to be counterbalanced by the numbers, the discipline, the courage, and the military talents, which may be combined in the armies of an inferior maritime power.

The joy diffused throughout the British dominions by this splendid conquest, was mingled with a proud sense of superiority, which did not estimate with exact justice the relative means employed by the belligerents. In no part of those dominions was this joy felt in a higher degree, or with more reason, than in America. In that region, the wars between France and England had assumed a form, happily unknown to other parts of the civilized world. Not confined as in Europe, to men in arms,—women and children were its common victims. It had been carried by the savage to the fire-side of the peaceful peasant, where the tomahawk and the scalping-knife were applied indiscriminately to every age, and to either sex. The hope was now fondly indulged that these scenes, at least in the northern and middle colonies, were closed forever.

John Armstrong,[1] *1759-1843.*

From the Life of General Wayne.

103. STORMING OF STONY POINT

WAYNE, believing that few things were impracticable to discipline and valor, after a careful reconnoissance, adopted the project, and hastened to give it execution. Beginning his march on the 15th from Sandy Beach, he at eight o'clock in the evening took a position within a mile and a half of his object. By the organization given to the attack, the regiments of Febiger and Meigs, with Hull's detachment, formed the column of the right; and the regiment of Butler and Murfey's detachment, that of the left. A party of twenty men, furnished with axes for pioneer duty, and followed by a sustaining corps of one hundred and fifty men with unloaded arms, pre-

[1] An officer of the revolutionary army, and a conspicuous actor in the war of 1812; has written chiefly on military affairs.

ceded each column, while a small detachment was assigned to purposes merely of demonstration.

At half after eleven o'clock, the hour fixed on for the assault, the columns were in motion ; but from delays made inevitable by the nature of the ground, it was twenty minutes after twelve before this commenced, when neither the morass, now overflowed by the tide, nor the formidable and double row of *abattis*, nor the high and strong works on the summit of the hill, could for a moment damp the ardor or stop the career of the assailants, who, in the face of an incessant fire of musketry and a shower of shells and grape-shot, forced their way through every obstacle, and with so much concert of movement, that both columns entered the fort and reached its centre, nearly at the same moment. Nor was the conduct of the victors less conspicuous for humanity than for valor. Not a man of the garrison was injured after the surrender ; and during the conflict of battle, all were spared who ceased to make resistance.

The entire American loss in this enterprise, so formidable in prospect, did not exceed one hundred men. The pioneer parties, necessarily the most exposed, suffered most. Of the twenty men led by Lieutenant Gibbons of the Sixth Pennsylvania Regiment, seventeen were killed or wounded. Wayne's own escape on this occasion was of the hair-breadth kind. Struck on the head by a musket-ball, he fell ; but immediately rising on one knee, he exclaimed, " March on, carry me into the fort ; for should the wound be mortal, I will die at the head of the column." The enemy's loss in killed and captured amounted to six hundred and seven men. This affair, the most brilliant of the war, covered the commanding general with laurels.

Charles Caldwell,[1] *1772-1853.*

From his "Autobiography."

104. A Lecture of Dr. Rush.

At length, however, though the class of the winter, all told, amounted to less than a hundred, a sufficient number had ar-

[1] A native of North Carolina; prominent as a physician and controversialist.

rived to induce the professors to commence their lectures; and the introductory of Dr. Rush was a performance of deep and touching interest, and never, I think, to be forgotten (while his memory endures), by any one who listened to it, and was susceptible of the impression it was calculated to make. It consisted in a well-written and graphical description of the terrible sweep of the late pestilence; the wild dismay and temporary desolation it had produced; the scenes of family and individual suffering and woe he had witnessed during its ravages; the mental dejection, approaching despair, which he himself had experienced, on account of the entire failure of his original mode of practice in it, and the loss of his earliest patients (some of them personal friends); the joy he felt on the discovery of a successful mode of treating it; the benefactions which he had afterwards the happiness to confer; and the gratulations with which, after the success of his practice had become known, he was often received in sick and afflicted families. The discourse, though highly colored, and marked by not a few figures of fancy and bursts of feeling, was, notwithstanding, sufficiently fraught with substantial matter to render it no less instructive than it was fascinating.

Thomas H. Benton, 1783–1858. (Manual, p. 487.)

From the "Thirty Years' View of the United States Senate."

105. THE CHARACTER OF MACON.[1]

HE was above the pursuit of wealth, but also above dependence and idleness, and, like an old Roman of the elder Cato's time, worked in the fields at the head of his slaves in the intervals of public duty, and did not cease this labor until advancing age rendered him unable to stand the hot sun of summer. . . . I think it was the summer of 1817,—that was the last time (he told me) he tried it, and found the sun too hot for him,—then sixty years of age, a senator, and the refuser of all office. How often I think of him, when I see at Washington

[1] Nathaniel Macon, United States Senator from North Carolina.

robustious men going through a scene of supplication, tribulation, and degradation, to obtain office, which the salvation of the soul does not impose upon the vilest sinner! His fields, his flocks, and his herds, yielded an ample supply of domestic productions. A small crop of tobacco—three hogsheads when the season was good, two when bad—purchased the exotics which comfort and necessity required, and which the farm did not produce. He was not rich, but rich enough to dispense hospitality and charity, to receive all guests in his house, from the president to the day laborer—no other title being necessary to enter his house but that of an honest man; . . . and above all, he was rich enough to pay as he went, and never to owe a dollar to any man.

. . . He always wore the same dress,—that is to say, a suit of the same material, cut, and color, superfine navy-blue,—the whole suit from the same piece, and in the fashion of the time of the Revolution, and always replaced by a new one before it showed age. He was neat in his person, always wore fine linen, a fine cambric stock, a fine fur hat with a brim to it, fair top-boots—the boot outside of the pantaloons, on the principle that leather was stronger than cloth.

. . . He was an habitual reader and student of the Bible, a pious and religious man, and of the "*Baptist persuasion*," as he was accustomed to express it.

Alexander Slidell Mackenzie, 1803-1845.

(Manual, pp. 490, 505.)

From the Life of Commodore Decatur.

106. Recapture, and Burning of the Frigate "Philadelphia," at Tripoli.

When all were safely assembled on the deck of the Intrepid, (for so admirably had the service been executed that not a man was missing, and only one slightly wounded,) Decatur gave the order to cut the fasts and shove off. The necessity for prompt obedience and exertion was urgent. The flames had now gained the lower rigging, and ascended to the tops; they darted furiously from the ports, flashing from the quarter gallery round the mizzen of the Intrepid, as her stern dropped clear of the ship. To estimate the perils of their position, it should be borne in mind, that the fire had been communicated by these fearless men to the near neighborhood of both magazines of the Philadelphia. The Intrepid herself was a fire ship, having been supplied with combustibles, a mass of which, ready to be converted into the means of destroying other vessels of the enemy, if the opportunity should offer, lay in barrels on her quarter deck, covered only with a tarpaulin.

With destruction thus encompassing them within and without, Decatur and his brave followers were unmoved. Calmly they put forth the necessary exertion, breasted the Intrepid off with spars, and pressing on their sweeps, caused her slowly to withdraw from the vicinity of the burning mass. A gentle breeze from the land came auspiciously at the same moment, and wafted the Intrepid beyond the reach of the flames, bearing with it, however, a shower of burning embers, fraught with danger to a vessel laden with combustibles, had not discipline, order, and calm self-possession, been at hand for her protection. Soon this peril was also left behind, and Decatur and his followers were at a sufficient distance to contemplate securely the spectacle which the Philadelphia presented. Hull, spars, and rigging, were now enveloped in flames. As the metal of her guns became heated, they were discharged in succession from both sides, serving as a brilliant salvo in honor of the victory, and not harmless for the Tripolitans, as her starboard battery was fired directly into the town.

The town itself, the castles, the minarets of the mosques, and the shipping in the harbor, were all brought into distinct view by the splendor of the conflagration. It served also to reveal to the enemy the cause of their disaster, in the little Intrepid, as she slowly withdrew from the harbor. The shot of the shipping and castles fell thickly around her, throwing up columns of spray, which the brilliant light converted into a new ornament of the scene. Only one shot took effect, and that passed through her top-gallant sail. Three hearty American cheers were now given in mingled triumph and derision. Soon after, the boats of the Siren joined company, and assisted in towing the Intrepid out of the harbor. The cables of the Philadelphia having burned off, she drifted on the rocks near the westward entrance of the harbor; and then the whole spectacle, so full of moral sublimity, considering the means by which it had been effected, and of material grandeur, had its appropriate termination in the final catastrophe of her explosion.

Nor were the little band of heroes on board the Intrepid the only exulting spectators of the scene. Lieutenant Stewart and his companions on board the Siren, watching with intense interest, beheld in the conflagration a pledge of Decatur's success; and Captain Bainbridge, with his fellow-captives in the dungeons of Tripoli, saw in it a motive of national exultation, and an earnest that a spirit was at work to hasten the day of their liberation.

I. F. H. Claiborne,[1] *About 1804–.*

From "Life and Times of General Samuel Dale."

107. Tecumseh's Speech to the Creek Indians.

I saw the Shawnees issue from their lodge; they were painted black, and entirely naked except the flap about their loins. Every weapon but the war-club,—then first introduced among the Creeks,—had been laid aside. An angry scowl sat on all their visages; they looked like a procession of devils. Tecumseh led, the warriors followed, one in the footsteps of the other. The Creeks, in dense masses, stood on each side of the path, but the Shawnees noticed no one; they marched to the pole in the centre of the square, and then turned to the left.

[1] Was born in Mississippi; by profession a lawyer, and for some years a member of Congress; author of several biographical works of interest, chiefly relating to the Southwest.

. . They then marched in the same order to the Council, or King's house,—as it was termed in ancient times, and drew up before it. The Big Warrior and the leading men were sitting there. The Shawnee chief sounded his war-whoop,—a most diabolical yell, and each of his followers responded. Tecumseh then presented to the Big Warrior a wampum belt of five different-colored stands, which the Creek chief handed to his warriors, and it was passed down the line. The Shawnee pipe was then produced ; it was large, long, and profusely decorated with shells, beads, and painted eagle and porcupine quills. It was lighted from the fire in the centre, and slowly passed from the Big Warrior along the line. All this time not a word had been uttered ; every thing was still as death ; even the winds slept, and there was only the gentle rustle of the falling leaves. At length Tecumseh spoke, at first slowly, and in sonorous tones, but soon he grew impassioned, and the words fell in avalanches from his lips. His eyes burned with supernatural lustre, and his whole frame trembled with emotion ; his voice resounded over the multitude,—now sinking in low and musical whispers, now rising to its highest key, hurling out his words like a succession of thunderbolts. His countenance varied with his speech ; its prevalent expression was a sneer of hatred and defiance ; sometimes a murderous smile ; for a brief interval a sentiment of profound sorrow pervaded it ; and at the close, a look of concentrated vengeance, such, I suppose, as distinguishes the arch-enemy of mankind. I have heard many great orators, but I never saw one with the vocal powers of Tecumseh, or the same command of the muscles of his face.

. . . Had I been deaf, the play of his countenance would have told me what he said. Its effect on that wild, superstitious, untutored, and warlike assemblage may be conceived : not a word was said, but stern warriors, the "stoics of the woods," shook with emotion, and a thousand tomahawks were brandished in the air. Even the Big Warrior, who had been true to the whites, and remained faithful during the war, was for the moment visibly affected, and more than once I saw his huge hand clutch, spasmodically, the handle of his knife. . .

When he resumed his seat, the northern pipe was again passed round in solemn silence. The Shawnees then simultaneously leaped up with one appalling yell, and danced their tribal war-dance, going through the evolutions of battle, the scout, the ambush, the final struggle, brandishing their war-clubs, and screaming, in terrific concert, an infernal harmony fit only for the regions of the damned

---

George Washington Greene,[1] *1811–.*

From The Life of General Greene.

108. Foreign Officers in the Revolutionay Army.

. . Mrs. Greene had joined her husband early in January, bringing with her her summer's acquisition, a stock of French that quickly made her little parlor the favorite resort of foreign officers. There was often to be seen Lafayette, not yet turned of twenty-one, though a husband, a father, and a major-general; graver somewhat in his manners than strictly belonged either to his years or his country ; and loved and trusted by all, by Washington and Greene especially. Steuben, too, was often there, wearing his republican uniform, as, fifteen years before, he had worn the uniform of the despotic Frederick ; as deeply skilled in the ceremonial of a court as in the manœuvring of an army ; with a glittering star on his left breast, that bore witness to the faithful service he had rendered in his native Germany ; and revolving in his accurate mind designs which were to transform this mass of physical strength, which Americans had dignified with the name of army, into a real army which Frederick himself might have accepted. He had but little English at his command as yet, but at his side there was a mercurial young Frenchman, Peter Duponceau, who knew how to interpret both his graver thoughts and the lighter gallantries with which the genial old soldier loved to season his intercourse with the wives and daughters of his new fellow-citizens. As the years passed away, Duponceau himself became a celebrated man, and loved

[1] Born in Rhode Island ; a grandson of the distinguished General Greene of the Revolution, whose life he has written, with many interesting details of that struggle.

to tell the story of these checkered days. Another German, too, De Kalb, was sometimes seen there, taller, statelier, graver than Steuben, with the cold, observant eye of the diplomatist, rather than the quick glance of the soldier, though a soldier too, and a brave and skillful one; caring very little about the cause he had forsaken his noble chateau and lovely wife to fight for, but a great deal about the promotion and decorations which his good service here was to win him in France; for he had made himself a Frenchman, and served the King of France, and bought him French lands, and married a French wife. Already before this war began, he had come hither in the service of France to study the progress of the growing discontent; and now he was here again an American major-general, led partly by the ambition of rank, partly by the thirst of distinction, but much, too, by a certain restlessness of nature, and longing for excitement and action, not to be wondered at in one who had fought his way up from a butlership to a barony. He and Steuben had served on opposite sides during the Seven Years War, though born both of them on the same bank of the Rhine; and though when Steuben first came, De Kalb was in Albany, yet in May they must have met more than once. How did they feel towards each other, the soldier of Frederick, and the soldier of Louis? If we had known more about this, we should have known better, perhaps, why Lafayette, a fast friend of De Kalb, speaks of the "methodic mediocrity" of Steuben, and Steuben of the "vanity and presumption" of the young major-general.

In the same circle, too, was the young Fleury whom we have seen bearing himself so gallantly at Fort Mifflin, and who, a year after, was to render still more brilliant service at Stony Point; and the Marquis de la Rouerie, concealing his rank under the name of Armand, and combatting an unsuccessful love by throwing himself headlong into the tumult of war; and Mauduit Duplessis, whose skill as an engineer had been proved at Red Bank, and who about this time was breveted Lieutenant-Colonel, at Washington's recommendation, for "gallant conduct at Brandywine and Germantown," and "distinguished services at Fort Mercer," and a "degree of modesty not always found in men who have performed brilliant actions," but whom neither modesty nor gallantry could save from a fearful death at San Domingo; and Gimat, aide to Lafayette now, but who afterwards led Lafayette's van as colonel in the successful assault of the British redoubts at Yorktown; and La Colombe, who was to serve Lafayette faithfully in France as he served him here; and Ternant, distinguished in America, France, and Holland, but who this year rendered invaluable service to American discipline by his aid in carrying out the reforms of Steuben. Kosciusko was in the north, but Poland had still another representative, the gallant Pulaski, who had done good service during the last campaign, and who the very next year was to lay down his life for us at the siege of Savannah.

James Parton, 1822-. (Manual, pp. 490, 532.)

From "Life and Times of Aaron Burr."

109. Career and Character of Burr.

To judge this man, to decide how far he was unfortunate, and how far guilty; how much we ought to pity, and how much to blame him,—is a task beyond my powers. And what occasion is there for judging him, or for judging any one? We all know that his life was an unhappy failure. He failed to gain the small honors at which he aimed; he failed to live a life worthy of his opportunities; he failed to achieve a character worthy of his powers. It was a great, great pity. And any one is to be pitied, who, in thinking of it, has any other feelings than those of compassion—compassion for the man whose life was so much less a blessing to him than it might have been, and compassion for the country, which after producing so rare and excellent a kind of man, lost a great part of the good he might have done her.

The great error of his career, as before remarked, was his

turning politician. He was too good for a politician, and not great enough for a statesman. . .

If his expedition had succeeded, it was in him, I think, to have run a career in Spanish America similar to that of Napoleon in Europe. Like Napoleon, he would have been one of the most amiable despots, and one of the most destructive. Like Napoleon, he would have been sure, at last, to have been overwhelmed in a prodigious ruin. Like Napoleon, he would have been idolized and execrated. Like Napoleon, he would have had his half dozen friends to go with him to St. Helena. Like Napoleon, he would have justified to the last, with the utmost sincerity, nearly every action of his life.

We live in a better day than he did. Nearly every thing is better now in the United States than it was fifty years ago, and a much larger proportion of the people possess the means of enjoying and improving life. If some evils are more obvious and rampant than they were, they are also better known, and the remedy is nearer. . .

Politics, apart from the pursuit of office, have again become real and interesting. The issue is distinct and important enough to justify the intense concern of a nation. To a young man coming upon the stage of life with the opportunities of Aaron Burr, a glorious and genuine political career is possible. The dainty keeping aloof from the discussion of public affairs, which has been the fashion until lately, will not again find favor with any but the very stupid, for a long time to come. The intellect of the United States once roused to the consideration of political questions, will doubtless be found competent to the work demanded of it.

The career of Aaron Burr can never be repeated in the United States. That of itself is a proof of progress. The game of politics which he played is left, in these better days, to far inferior men, and the moral license which he and Hamilton permitted themselves, is not known in the circles they frequented. But the graver errors, the radical vices, of both men belong to human nature, and will always exist to be shunned and battled.

From "Famous Americans."

110. Henry Clay's Career at the Western Bar.

It is surprising how addicted to litigation were the earlier settlers of the Western States. The imperfect surveys of land, the universal habit of getting goods on credit at the store, and "difficulties" between individuals ending in bloodshed, filled the court calendars, with land disputes, suits for debt, and exciting murder cases, which gave to lawyers more importance and better chances of advancement than they possessed in the older States. Mr. Clay had two strings to his bow. Besides being a man of red-tape and pigeon-holes, exact, methodical, and strictly attentive to business, he had a power over a Kentucky jury such as no other man has ever wielded. To this day nothing pleases aged Kentuckians better than to tell stories which they heard their fathers tell of Clay's happy repartees to opposing counsel, his ingenious cross-questioning of witnesses, his sweeping torrents of invective, his captivating courtesy, his melting pathos. Single gestures, attitudes, tones, have come down to us through two or three memories, and still please the curious guest at Kentucky firesides. But when we turn to the cold records of this part of his life, we find little to justify his traditional celebrity. It appears that the principal use to which his talents were applied during the first years of his practice at the bar, was in defending murderers. He seems to have shared the feeling which then prevailed in the Western country, that to defend a prisoner at the bar is a nobler thing than to assist in defending the public against his further depredations; and he threw all his force into the defence of some men who would have been "none the worse for a hanging." One day, in the streets of Lexington, a drunken fellow whom he had rescued from the murderer's doom, cried out, "Here comes Mr. Clay, who saved my life." "Ah! my poor fellow," replied the advocate, "I fear I have saved too many like you, who ought to be hanged." The anecdotes printed of his exploits in cheating the gallows of its due, are of a quality which shows that the power of this man over a jury lay much in his manner. His delivery, which "bears absolute sway in oratory," was bewitching and irresistible, and gave to quite common-place wit and very questionable sentiment, an amazing power to please and subdue.

From an Article in the Atlantic Monthly.

111. Western Theatres.

At the West, along with much reckless and defiant unbelief in every thing high and good, there is also a great deal of that terror-stricken pietism which refuses to attend the theatre unless it is very bad indeed, and is called "Museum." This limits the business of the theatre; and as a good theatre is necessarily a very expensive institution, it improves very slowly, although the Western people are in precisely that state of development and culture to which the drama is best adapted and is most beneficial. We should naturally expect to find the human mind, in the broad, magnificent West, rising superior to the prejudices originating in the little sects of little lands. So it will rise in due time. So it has risen, in some degree. But mere grandeur of nature has no educating effect upon the soul of man ; else Switzerland would not have supplied Paris with footmen, and the hackmen of Niagara would spare the tourist. It is only a human mind that can instruct a human mind.

* * * * * *

To witness the performance, and to observe the rapture expressed upon the shaggy and good-humored countenances of the boatmen, was interesting, as showing what kind of banquet will delight a human soul, starved from its birth. It likes a comic song very much, if the song refers to fashionable articles of ladies costume, or holds up to ridicule members of Congress, policemen, or dandies. It is not averse to a sentimental song, in which "Mother, dear," is frequently apostrophized. It delights in a farce from which most of the dialogue has been cut away, while all the action is retained,—in which people are continually knocked down, or run against one another with great violence. It takes much pleasure in seeing Horace Greeley play a part in a negro farce, and become the victim of designing colored brethren. But what joy, when the beauteous Terpsichorean nymph bounds upon the scene, rosy with paint, glistening with spangles, robust with cotton and cork, and bewildering with a cloud of gauzy skirts! What a vision of beauty to a man who has seen nothing for days and nights but the hold of a steamboat and the dull shores of the Mississippi!

HISTORY, GENERAL AND SPECIAL.

John Heckewelder,[1] *1743–1823.*

From the "Narrative" of the Moravian Missions among the Indians.

112. Settlements of the Christian Indians.

Both these congregations, being supplied with missionaries and schoolmasters, were so prosperous that they became the admiration of visitors, some of whom thought it next to a miracle that, by the light of the gospel, a savage race should be brought to live together in peace and harmony, and above all devote themselves to religion. The people residing in the neighborhood of those places were also intimate with these Indians, and both were serviceable to each other; one instance of which is here inserted. In February of the year 1761, a white man, who had lost a child, came to Nain weeping, and begging that the Indian Brethren would assist him and his wife to search for his child, which had been missing since the day before. Several of the Indian Brethren immediately went to the house of the parents, and discovered the footsteps of the child, and tracing the same for the distance of two miles, found the child in the woods, wrapped up in its petticoat, and shiver-

[1] Prominent among the Moravian clergy for his experience of missionary life among the American Indians, for his knowledge of the Indian languages, and for his lifelong devotion to the missionary work.

ing with cold. The joy of the parents was so great that they reported the circumstance wherever they went. To some of the white people, who had been in dread of the near settlement of these Indians, this incident was the means of making them easy, and causing them to rejoice in having such good neighbors.

. . . The war being over, the Indians who had been engaged in it freely confessed to their friends and relations, and to some white people they had heretofore been acquainted with, that "the Brethren's settlements had been as a stumbling-block to them; that had it not been for these, they would most assuredly have laid waste the whole country from the mountains to Philadelphia; and that many plans had been formed for destroying these settlements."

Jeremy Belknap, 1744-1798. (Manual, p. 490.)

From "The History of New Hampshire."

113. THE MAST PINE.

ANOTHER thing worthy of observation is the aged and majestic appearance of the trees, of which the most noble is the mast pine. This tree often grows to the height of one hundred and fifty, and sometimes two hundred feet. It is straight as an arrow, and has no branches but very near the top. It is from twenty to forty inches in diameter at its base, and appears like a stately pillar, adorned with a verdant capital, in form of a cone. Interspersed among these are the common forest trees of various kinds.

When a mast tree is to be felled, much preparation is necessary. So tall a stick, without any limbs nearer the ground than eighty or a hundred feet, is in great danger of breaking in the fall. To prevent this the workmen have a contrivance which they call *bedding* the tree, which is thus executed. They know in what direction the tree will fall; and they cut down a number of smaller trees which grow in that direction; or if there be none, they draw others to the spot, and place them so that the falling tree may lodge on their branches; which breaking or yielding under its pressure, render its fall easy and safe. A time of deep snow is the most favorable season, as the rocks are then covered, and a natural bed is formed to receive the tree. When fallen, it is examined, and if to appearance it be sound, it is cut in the proportion of three feet in length to every inch of its diameter, for a mast; but if intended for a bow-sprit or a yard, it is cut shorter. If it be not sound throughout, or if it break in falling, it is cut into logs for the saw-mill. . . .

When a mast is to be drawn on the snow, one end is placed on a sled, shorter, but higher than the common sort, and rests on a strong block, which is laid across the middle of the sled. . In descending a long and steep hill they have a contrivance to prevent the load from making too rapid a descent. Some of the cattle are placed behind it; a chain which is attached to their yokes is brought forward and fastened to the hinder end of the load, and the resistance which is made by these cattle checks the descent. This operation is called *tailing*. The most dangerous circumstance is the passing over the top of a sharp hill, by which means the oxen which are nearest to the tongues are sometimes suspended, till the foremost cattle can draw the mast so far over the hill as to give them opportunity to recover the ground. In this case the drivers are obliged to use much judgment and care to keep the cattle from being killed. There is no other way to prevent this inconvenience than to level the roads.

David Ramsay, 1749-1815. (Manual, p. 491.)

From "The History of the Revolution in South Carolina."

114. Feeling of the Province toward Great Britain.

In South Carolina, an enemy to the Hanoverian succession, or to the British constitution, was scarcely known. The inhabitants were fond of British manners even to excess. They for the most part, sent their children to Great Britain for education, and spoke of that country under the endearing appellation of Home. They were enthusiasts for that sacred plan of civil and religious happiness under which they had grown up and flourished. . . . Wealth poured in upon them from a thousand channels. The fertility of the soil generously repaid the labor of the husbandman, making the poor to sing, and industry to smile, through every corner of the land. None were indigent but the idle and unfortunate. Personal independence was fully within the reach of every man who was healthy and industrious. The inhabitants, at peace with all the world, enjoyed domestic tranquility, and were secure in their persons and property. They were also completely satisfied with their government, and wished not for the smallest change in their political constitution.

In the midst of these enjoyments, and the most sincere attachment to the mother country, to their king and his government, the people of South Carolina, without any original design on their part, were step by step drawn into an extensive war, which involved them in every species of difficulty, and finally dissevered them from the parent state.

. . Every thing in the colonies contributed to nourish a spirit of liberty and independence. They were planted under the auspices of the English constitution in its purity and vigor. Many of their inhabitants had imbibed a large portion of that spirit which brought one tyrant to the block, and expelled another from his dominions. They were communities of separate, independent individuals, for the most part employed in cultivating a fruitful soil, and under no general influence but of their own feelings and opinions; they were not led by powerful families, or by great officers in church or state. . . Every inhabitant was, or easily might be, a freeholder. Settled on lands of his own, he was both farmer and landlord. Having no superior to whom he was obliged to look up, and producing all the necessaries of life from his own grounds, he soon became independent. His mind was equally free from all the restraints of superstition. No ecclesiastical establishment invaded the rights of conscience, or fettered the free-born mind. At liberty to act and think as his inclination prompted, he disdained the ideas of dependence and subjection.

Henry Lee,[1] *1756-1818.*

From "Memoirs" of the War in the South.

115. Clarke's Services against the Indians.

John Rodgers Clarke, colonel in the service of Virginia against our neighbors the Indians in the revolutionary war, was among our best soldiers, and better acquainted with the Indian warfare than any officer in our army. This gentleman, after one of his campaigns, met in Richmond several of our cavalry officers, and devoted all his leisure in ascertaining from them the various uses to which horse were applied, as well as the manner of such application. The information he acquired determined him to introduce this species of force against the Indians, as that of all others the most effectual.

By himself, by Pickens, and lately by Wayne, was the accuracy of Clarke's opinion justified. . . .

The Indians, when fighting with infantry, are very daring. This temper of mind results from his consciousness of his superior fleetness; which, together with his better knowledge of woods, assures to him extrication out of difficulties, though desperate. This is extinguished when he finds that he is to save himself from the pursuit of horse, and with its extinction falls that habitual boldness.

---

116. The Career of Captain Kirkwood.

The State of Delaware furnished one regiment only; and certainly no regiment in the army surpassed it in soldiership.

[1] In the revolutionary war he was distinguished as a cavalry officer, and subsequently, in political life, as a writer and speaker.

The remnant of that corps, less than two companies, from the battle of Camden, was commanded by Captain Kirkwood, who passed through the war with high reputation; and yet, as the line of Delaware consisted of but one regiment, and that regiment was reduced to a captain's command, Kirkwood never could be promoted in regular routine—a very glaring defect in the organization of the army, as it gave advantages to parts of the same army denied to other portions of it. The sequel is singularly hard. Kirkwood retired, upon peace, as a captain; and when the army under St. Clair was raised to defend the west from the Indian enemy, this veteran resumed his sword as the eldest captain in the oldest regiment.

In the decisive defeat of the 4th of November,[1] the gallant Kirkwood fell, bravely sustaining his point of the action. It was the thirty-third time he had risked his life for his country; and he died as he had lived, the brave, meritorious, unrewarded Kirkwood.

Peter S. Duponceau,[2] *1760-1844.*

From "An Address."

117. CHARACTER OF PENN.

WILLIAM PENN stands the first among the lawgivers whose names and deeds are recorded in history. Shall we compare him with Lycurgus, Solon, Romulus, those founders of military commonwealths, who organized their citizens in deadly array against the rest of their species, taught them to consider their fellow-men as barbarians, and themselves as alone worthy to rule over the earth? . . . But see William Penn, with weaponless hand, sitting down peaceably with his followers, in the midst of savage nations whose only occupation was shedding the blood of their fellow-men, disarming them by his justice, and teaching them, for the first time, to view a stranger without distrust. See them bury their tomahawks in his pres-

[1] St. Clair's defeat.

[2] An eminent jurist and philologist, of French origin, but for many years a citizen of Philadelphia.

ence, so deep that man shall never be able to find them again. See them, under the shade of the thick groves of Coaquannock, extend the bright chain of friendship, and solemnly promise to preserve it as long as the sun and moon shall endure. See him then, with his companions, establishing his commonwealth on the sole basis of religion, morality, and universal love, and adopting, as the fundamental maxim of his government, the rule handed down to us from Heaven, "Glory to God on high, and on earth peace and good will towards men."

Charles J. Ingersoll,[1] *1782-1862.*

From the "Historical Sketch" of the War of 1812.

118. Calhoun Characterized

John Caldwell Calhoun was the same slender, erect, and ardent logician, politician, and sectarian, in the House of Representatives in 1814 that he is in the Senate of 1847. Speaking with aggressive aspect, flashing eye, rapid action and enunciation, unadorned argument, eccentricity of judgment, unbounded love of rule, impatient, precipitate, kind temper, excellent in colloquial attractions, caressing the young, not courting rulers; conception, perception, and demonstration quick and clear, with logical precision arguing paradoxes, and carrying home conviction beyond rhetorical illustration; his own impressions so intense as to discredit, scarcely listen to, any other suggestions; well educated and informed.

---

119. Battle of Chippewa.

In a fair national trial of the military faculties, courage, activity, and fortitude, discipline, gunnery, and tactics, for the first time the palm was awarded by Englishmen to Americans over Englishmen. Without fortuitous advantage the Americans proved too much for the redoubtable English, though

[1] A native of Pennsylvania; long conspicuous in the law, literature, and political life.

superior in number, therefore universally arrogating to themselves even with inferior numbers, a mastery but faintly questioned by most Americans; no accident to depreciate the triumph of the younger over the older nation; no more fortune than what favors the bravest.

Physical and even corporeal national characteristics, did not escape comparison in this normal contest. The American rather more active and more demonstrative than his ancestors, many of the officers of imposing figure, Scott and McNeill particularly, towering with gigantic stature above the rest, stood opposed in striking contrast to the short, thick, brawny, burly Briton, hard to overcome. . . . The Marquis of Tweedale, with his sturdy, short person, and stubborn courage, represented the British. . . . Even the names betokened at once consanguinity and hostility. Scott, McNeill, and McRee, in arms against Gordon, Hay, and Maconochie. And the harsh Scotch nomenclature, compared with the more euphonious savage Canada, Chippewa, Niagara, which latter modern English prosody has corrupted from the measure of Goldsmith's Traveller:—

> "Where wild Oswego spreads her swamps around,
> And Niagara stuns with thundering sound."

. . Mankind impressed by numbers and bloodshed, regard the second more extensive battle near the falls of Niagara, on the 25th of the same month, between the same parties with British reinforcements, known as the battle of Bridgewater, as more important than its precursor. . . . The victory of Chippewa was the resurrection or birth of American arms, after their prostration by so long disuse, and when at length taken up again, by such continual and deplorable failures, that the martial and moral influence of the first decided victory opened and characterized an epoch in the annals and intercourse of the two kindred and rival nations, whose language is to be spoken, as their institutions are rapidly spreading, throughout most of mankind. Fought between only some three or four thousand men in both armies, at a place remote from either of their countries, the battle of Chippewa may not bear vulgar comparison with the great military engagements of modern Europe. . . . The charm of British military invincibility was as effectually broken, by a single brigade, as that of naval supremacy was by a single frigate, as much as if a large army or fleet had been the agent.

Henry M. Brackenridge,[1] *1786–.* (Manual, p. 505.)

From "Recollections of the West."

120. OLD ST. GENEVIEVE, IN MISSOURI.

THE house of M. Beauvais was a long, low building, with a porch or shed in front, and another in the rear; the chimney occupied the center, dividing the house into two parts, with each a fireplace. One of these served for dining-room, parlor, and principal bed-chamber; the other was the kitchen; and each had a small room taken off at the end for private chambers or cabinets. There was no loft or garret, a pair of stairs being a rare thing in the village. The furniture, excepting the beds and the looking-glass, was of the most common kind. . . . The yard was enclosed with cedar pickets, eight or ten inches in diameter, and six feet high, placed upright, sharpened at the top, in the manner of a stockade fort. In front the yard was narrow, but in the rear quite spacious, and containing the barn and stables, the negro quarters, and all the necessary offices of a farm-yard. Beyond this, there was a spacious garden enclosed with pickets. . . .

The pursuits of the inhabitants were chiefly agricultural, although all were more or less engaged in traffic for peltries with the Indians, or in working the lead mines in the interior. Peltry and lead constituted almost the only circulating medium. All politics, or discussions of the affairs of government were entirely unknown; the commandant took care of all that sort of thing. But instead of them, the processions and ceremonies of the church, and the public balls, furnished ample

[1] Distinguished in literature and as a political writer; a native of Pennsylvania.

matter for occupation and amusement. Their agriculture was carried on in a field of several thousand acres, enclosed at the common expense, and divided into lots. . . . Whatever they may have gained in some respects, I question very much whether the change of government has contributed to increase their happiness. About a quarter of a mile off, there was a village of Kickapoo Indians, who lived on the most friendly terms with the white people. The boys often intermingled with those of the white village, and practised shooting with the bow and arrow—an accomplishment which I acquired with the rest, together with a little smattering of the Indian language, which I forgot on leaving the place.

Gulian C. Verplanck, 1786–1870. (Manual, p. 487.)

From the "Literary and Historical Discourses."

121. THE SCHOOLMASTER.

The schoolmaster's occupation is laborious and ungrateful; its rewards are scanty and precarious. He may indeed be, and he ought to be animated by the consciousness of doing good, that best of all consolations, that noblest of all motives. But that too must be often clouded by doubt and uncertainty. Obscure and inglorious as his daily occupation may appear to learned pride or worldly ambition, yet to be truly successful and happy he must be animated by the spirit of the same great principles which inspired the most illustrious benefactors of mankind. If he bring to his task high talent and rich acquirement, he must be content to look into distant years for the proof that his labors have not been wasted, that the good seed which he daily scatters abroad does not fall on stony ground and wither away, or among thorns to be choked by the cares, the delusions, or the vices of the world. He must solace his toils with the same prophetic faith that enabled the greatest of modern philosophers,[1] amidst the neglect or contempt of his own times, to regard himself as sowing the seeds of truth for posterity and the care of

[1] Bacon.

Heaven. He must arm himself against disappointment and mortification with a portion of that same noble confidence which soothed the greatest of modern poets when weighed down by care and danger, by poverty, old age, and blindness, still

> "——In prophetic dreams he saw
> The youth unborn with pious awe
> Imbibe each virtue from his sacred page."

He must know and he must love to teach his pupils not the meager elements of knowledge, but the secret and the use of their own intellectual strength, exciting and enabling them hereafter to raise for themselves the veil which covers the majestic form of Truth. He must feel deeply the reverence due to the youthful mind fraught with mighty though undeveloped energies and affections, and mysterious and eternal destinies. Thence he must have learned to reverence himself and his profession, and to look upon its otherwise ill-requited toils as their own exceeding great reward.

If such are the difficulties and the discouragements, such the duties, the motives, and the consolations of teachers who are worthy of that name and trust, how imperious then the obligation upon every enlightened citizen who knows and feels the value of such men to aid them, to cheer them, and to honor them.

But let us not be content with barren honor to buried merit. Let us prove our gratitude to the dead by faithfully endeavoring to elevate the station, to enlarge the usefulness, and to raise the character of the schoolmaster amongst us. Thus shall we best testify our gratitude to the teachers and guides of our own youth, thus best serve our country, and thus most effectually diffuse over our land light, and truth, and virtue.

John W. Francis, 1789-1861. (Manual, pp. 487, 532.)

From his "Reminiscences."

122. Public Changes during a Single Lifetime.

He who has passed a period of some three score years and upward, some faithful Knickerbocker for instance, native born, and ever a resident among us, whose tenacious memory enables him to meditate upon the thirty thousand inhabitants at the time of his birth, with the almost oppressive population of some seven hundred thousand which the city at present contains; who contrasts the cheap and humble dwellings of that earlier date, with the costly and magnificent edifices which now beautify the metropolis; who studies the sluggish state of the mechanic arts at the dawn of the Republic, and the mighty demonstrations of skill which our Fulton, and our Stevens, our Douglas, our Hoe, and our Morse, have produced; who remembers the few and humble water-craft conveyances of days past, and now beholds the majestic leviathans of the ocean which crowd our harbors; who contemplates the partial and trifling commercial transactions of the Confederacy, with the countless millions of commercial business which engross the people of the present day, in our Union; who estimates the offspring of the press, and the achievements of the telegraph, he who has been the spectator of all this, may be justly said to have lived the period of many generations, and to have stored within his reminiscences the progress of an era the most remarkable in the history of his species.

If he awakens his attention to a consideration of the progress of intellectual and ethical pursuits, if he advert to the prolific demonstrations which surround him for the advancement of knowledge, literary and scientific, moral and religious, the indomitable spirit of the times strikes him with more than logical conviction. The beneficence and humanity of his countrymen may be pointed out by contemplating her noble free schools, her vast hospitals and asylums for the alleviation of physical distress and mental infirmities; with the reflection that all these are the triumphs of a self-governed people, accomplished within the limited memory of an ordinary life. Should reading enlarge the scope of his knowledge, let him study the times of the old Dutch Governors, when the Ogdens erected the first church in the fort of New Amsterdam, in 1642, and then survey the vast panoramic view around him of the two hundred and fifty and more edifices, now consecrated to the solemnities of religious devotion. It imparts gratification to know that the old Bible which was used in that primary church of Van Twiller is still preserved by a descendant of the builder, a precious relic of the property of the older period, and of the devotional impulse of those early progenitors. To crown the whole, time in its course has recognized the supremacy of political and religious toleration, and established constitutional freedom on the basis of equal rights and even and exact justice to all men. That New York has given her full measure of toil, expenditure, and talent in furtherance of these vast results, by her patriots and statesmen, is proclaimed in grateful accents by the myriad voice of the nation at large.

William Meade, 1789-1862.

From the "Old Churches &c. of Virginia."

123. Character of the Early Virginia Clergy.

It has been made a matter of great complaint against the Legislature of Virginia, that it should not only have withdrawn the stipend of sixteen thousand weight of tobacco from the clergy, but also have seized upon the glebes. I do not mean to enter on the discussion of the legality of that act, or of the motives of those who petitioned for it. Doubtless there were many who sincerely thought that it was both legal and right, and that they were doing God and religion a service by it. I hesitate not, however, to express the opinion, in which I have been and am sustained by many of the best friends of the Church then and ever since, that nothing could have been more injurious to the cause of true religion in the Episcopal Church, or to its growth in any way, than the continuance of either stipend or glebes. Many clergymen of the most unworthy character would have been continued among us, and such a revival as we have seen have never taken place. . . . Not merely have the pious members of the Church taken this view of the subject, since the revival of it under other auspices, but many of those who preferred the Church at that day, for other reasons than her evangelical doctrine and worship, saw that it was best that she should be thrown upon her own resources. I had a conversation with Mr. Madison, soon after he ceased to be President of the United States, in which I became assured of this. He himself took an active part in promoting the act for the putting down the establishment of the Episcopal Church, while his relative was Bishop of it, and all his family connection attached to it. . . .

It may be well here to state, what will more fully appear when we come to speak of the old glebes and churches in a subsequent number, that the character of the laymen of Virginia for morals and religion was in general greatly in advance of that of the clergy. The latter, for the most part, were the refuse or more indifferent of the English, Irish, and Scotch Episcopal churches, who could not find promotion and employment at home. The former were natives of the soil, and descendants of respectable ancestors, who migrated at an early period. . . . Some of the vestries, as their records painfully show, did what they could to displace unworthy ministers, though they often failed through defect of law. In order to avoid the danger of having evil ministers fastened upon them, as well as from the scarcity of ministers, they made much use of lay-readers as substitutes. . . . The reading of the service and sermons in private families, which contributed so much to the preservation of an attachment to the Church in the same, was doubtless promoted by this practice of lay-reading. Those whom Providence raised up to resuscitate the fallen Church of Virginia can testify to the fact that the families who descended from the above mentioned, have been their most effective supports. . . . And when, in the providence of God, they are called on to leave their ancient homes, and form new settlements in the distant South and West, none are more active and reliable in transplanting the Church of their Fathers.

Jared Sparks, 1794-1866. (Manual, p. 490.)

From "The Life of General Stark."

124. The Battle of Bennington.

The German troops with their battery were advantageously posted upon a rising ground, at a bend in the Wollamsac (a tributary of the Hoosac), on its north bank. The ground fell off to the north and west, a circumstance of which Stark skilfully took advantage. Peters' corps of Tories were entrenched on the other side of the stream, in lower ground, and nearly in front of the German Battery. The little river, that meanders through the scene of the action, is fordable in all places. Stark was encamped upon the same side of it as the Germans, but, owing to its serpentine course, it crossed his line of march twice on his way to their position. Their post was carefully reconnoitered at a mile's distance, and the plan of attack was arranged in the following manner. Colonel Nichols, with two hundred men, was detached to attack the rear of the enemy's left, and Colonel Herrick, with three hundred men, to fall upon the rear of their right, with orders to form a junction before they made the assault. Colonels Hubbard and Stickney were also ordered to advance with two hundred men on their right, and one hundred in front, to divert their attention from the real point of attack. The action commenced at three o'clock in the afternoon, on the rear of the enemy's left, when Colonel Nichols, with great precision, carried into effect the dispositions of the commander. His example was followed by every other portion of the little army. General Stark himself moved forward slowly in front, till he heard the sound of the guns from Colonel Nichols' party, when he rushed upon the Tories, and in a few moments the action became general. "It lasted," says Stark, in his official report, "two hours, and was the hottest I ever saw. It was like one continued clap of thunder." The Indians, alarmed at the prospect of being enclosed between the parties of Nichols and Herrick, fled at the commencement of the action, their main principle of battle array being to contrive or to escape, an ambush or an attack in the rear. The Tories were soon driven over the river, and were thus thrown in confusion on the Germans, who were forced from their breast-work. Baum made a brave and resolute defence. The German dragoons, with the discipline of veterans, preserved their ranks unbroken, and, after their ammunition was expended, were led to the charge by their Colonel with the sword; but they were overpowered and obliged to give way, leaving their artillery and baggage on the field.

They were well enclosed in two breast-works, which, owing to the rain on the 15th, they had constructed at leisure. But notwithstanding this protection, with the advantage of two pieces of cannon, arms and ammunition in perfect order, and an auxiliary force of Indians, they were driven from their entrenchments by a band of militia just brought to the field, poorly armed, with few bayonets, without field-pieces, and with little discipline. The superiority of numbers on the part of the Americans, will, when these things are considered, hardly be thought to abate anything from the praise due to the conduct of the commander, or the spirit and courage of his men.

—

From the "Life of Count Pulaski."

125. HIS SERVICES, DEATH, AND CHARACTER.

(The Battle of Brandywine.)—On that occasion, Count Pulaski, as well as Lafayette, was destined to strike his first blow in defence of American liberty. Being a volunteer, and without command, he was stationed near General Washington till towards the close of the action, when he asked the command of the General's body guard,—about thirty horse, and advanced rapidly within pistol-shot of the enemy, and after reconnoitering their movements, returned and reported that they were endeavoring to cut off the line of retreat, and particularly the train of baggage. He was then authorized to collect as many of the scattered troops as came in his way, and employ them according to his discretion, which he did in a manner so prompt and bold, as to effect an important service in the retreat of the army; fully sustaining, by his conduct and courage, the reputation for which the world had given him credit. Four days after this event, he was appointed by Congress to the command of the cavalry, with the rank of brigadier general.

(Before Charleston in 1779.)—Scarcely waiting till the enemy had crossed the ferry, Pulaski sallied out with his legion and a few mounted volunteers, and made an assault upon the advanced parties. With the design of drawing the British into an ambuscade, he stationed his infantry on low ground behind a breast-work, and then rode forward a mile, with his cavalry in the face of a party of light-horse, with whom he came to close quarters, and kept up a sharp skirmish till he was compelled to retreat by the increasing numbers of the enemy. His coolness, courage, and disregard of personal danger, were conspicuous throughout the rencounter, and the example of this prompt and bold attack had great influence in raising the spirits of the people, and inspiring the confidence of the inexperienced troops then assembled in the city. The infantry, impatient to take part in the conflict, advanced to higher ground in front of the breast-work and thus the scheme of an ambuscade was defeated.

(His death at Savannah.)—The cavalry were stationed in the rear of the advanced columns, and in the confusion which appeared in front, and in the obscurity caused by the smoke, Pulaski was uncertain where he ought to act. To gain information on this point, he determined to ride forward in the heat of the conflict, and called to Captain Bentalou to accompany him. They had proceeded but a short distance, when they heard of the havoc that had been produced in the swamp among the French troops. Hoping to animate these troops by his presence, he rushed onward, and while riding swiftly to the place where they were stationed, he received a wound in the groin from a swivel-shot, and fell from his horse near the abattis. Captain Bentalou was likewise wounded by a musket-ball. Count Pulaski was left on the field till nearly all the troops had retreated, when some of his men returned, in the face of the enemy's guns, and took him to the camp.

(His character.)—He possessed in a remarkable degree, the power of winning and controlling men, a power so rare that it may be considered not less the fruit of consummate art than the gift of nature. Energetic, vigilant, untiring in the pursuit of an object, fearless, fertile in resources, calm in danger, resolute and persevering under discouragements, he was always prepared for events, and capable of effecting his purposes with the best chance of success. . . . He embraced our cause as his own, harmonizing as it did with his principles and all the noble impulses of his nature, the cause of liberty and of human rights; he lost his life in defending it; thus acquiring the highest of all claims to a nation's remembrance and gratitude.

William H. Prescott, 1796-1859. (Manual, p. 494.)

From the "History of Ferdinand and Isabella."

126. MORAL CONSEQUENCES OF THE DISCOVERY OF AMERICA.

WHATEVER be the amount of physical good or evil immediately resulting to Spain from her new discoveries, their moral consequences were inestimable. The ancient limits of human thought and action were overleaped; the veil which had covered the secrets of the deep for so many centuries was removed; another hemisphere was thrown open; and a boundless expansion promised to science, from the infinite varieties in which nature was exhibited in these unexplored regions. The success of the Spaniards kindled a generous emulation in their Portuguese rivals, who soon after accomplished their long-sought passage into the Indian seas, and thus completed the great circle of maritime discovery. It would seem as if Providence had postponed this grand event, until the possession of America, with its stores of precious metals, might supply such materials for a commerce with the east, as should bind together the most distant quarters of the globe. The impression made on the enlightened minds of that day is evinced by the tone of gratitude and exultation, in which they indulge, at being permitted to witness the consummation of these glorious events, which their fathers had so long, but in vain, desired to see.

The discoveries of Columbus occurred most opportunely for the Spanish nation, at the moment when it was released from its tumultuous struggle in which it had been engaged for so many years with the Moslems. The severe schooling of these wars had prepared it for entering on a bolder theater of action, whose stirring and romantic perils raised still higher the chivalrous spirit of the people. The operation of this spirit was shown in the alacrity with which private adventurers embarked in expeditions to the New World, under cover of the general license, during the last two years of this century. Their efforts, combined with those of Columbus, extended the range of discovery from its original limits, twenty-four degrees of north latitude, to probably more than fifteen south, comprehending some of the most important territories in the western hemisphere. Before the end of 1500, the principal groups of the West India islands had been visited, and the whole extent of the southern continent coasted from the Bay of Honduras to Cape St. Augustine. One adventurous mariner, indeed, named Lepe, penetrated several degrees south of this, to a point not reached by any other voyager for ten or twelve years after. A great part of the kingdom of Brazil was embraced in this extent, and two successive Castilian navigators landed and took formal possession of it for the crown of Castile, previous to its reputed discovery by the Portuguese Cabral; although the claims to it were relinquished by the Spanish Government, conformably to the famous line of demarkation established by the treaty of Tordesillas.

While the colonial empire of Spain was thus every day enlarging, the man to whom it was all due was never permitted to know the extent, or the value of it. He died in the conviction in which he lived, that the land he had reached was the long-sought Indies. But it was a country far richer than the Indies; and had he on quitting Cuba struck into a westerly, instead of southerly direction, it would have carried him into the very depths of the golden regions, whose existence he had so long and vainly predicted. As it was, he "only opened the gates," to use his own language, for others more fortunate than himself; and, before he quitted Hispaniola for the last time, the young adventurer arrived there, who was destined by the conquest of Mexico to realize all the magnificent visions, which had been derided only as visions, in the lifetime of Columbus.

—

From "The History of the Conquest of Mexico."

127. PICTURE-WRITING OF THE MEXICANS.

WHILE these things were passing, Cortés observed one of Teuhtlile's attendants busy with a pencil, apparently delineating some object. On looking at his work, he found that it was a sketch, on canvas, of the Spaniards, their costumes, arms, and, in short, different objects of interest, giving to each its appropriate form and color. This was the celebrated picture-writing of the Aztecs, and as Teuhtlile informed him, this man was employed in portraying the various objects for the eye of Montezuma, who would thus gather a more vivid notion of their appearance than from any description by words. Cortés was pleased with the idea; and as he knew how much the effect would be heightened by converting still life into action, he ordered out the cavalry on the beach, the wet sands of which afforded a firm footing for the horses. The bold and rapid movements of the troops, as they went through their military exercises, the apparent ease with which they managed the fiery animals on which they were mounted, the glancing of their weapons, and the shrill cry of the trumpet, all filled the spectators with astonishment; but when they heard the thunders of the cannon, and witnessed the volumes of smoke and flame issuing from these terrible engines, and the rushing sound of the balls, as they dashed through the trees of the neighboring forest, shivering their branches into fragments, they were filled with consternation, from which the Aztec chief himself was not wholly free.

Nothing of all this was lost on the painters, who faithfully recorded, after their fashion, every particular, not omitting the ships—"the water-houses," as they called them—of the strangers, which, with their dark hulls and snow-white sails reflected from the water, were swinging lazily at anchor on the calm bosom of the bay. All was depicted with a fidelity that excited in their turn the admiration of the Spaniards, who, doubtless unprepared for this exhibition of skill, greatly overestimated the merits of the execution.

From "The History of the Conquest of Peru."

128. Ransom and Doom of the Inca.

THESE articles consisted of goblets, ewers, salvers, vases of every shape and size, ornaments and utensils for the temples and the royal palaces, tiles and plates for the decoration of the public edifices, curious imitations of different plants and animals. Among the plants, the most beautiful was the Indian corn, in which the golden ear was sheathed in its broad leaves of silver, from which hung a rich tassel of threads of the same precious metal. A fountain was also much admired, which sent up a sparkling jet of gold, while birds and animals of the same material played in the waters at its base. The delicacy of the workmanship of some of these, and the beauty and ingenuity of the design, attracted the admiration of better judges than the rude Conquerors of Peru.

Before breaking up these specimens of Indian art, it was determined to send a quantity, which should be deducted from the royal fifth, to the Emperor. It would serve as a sample of the ingenuity of the natives, and would show him the value of his conquests. A number of the most beautiful articles was selected, to the amount of a hundred thousand ducats, and Hernando Pizarro was appointed to be the bearer of them to Spain.

The doom of the Inca was proclaimed by sound of trumpet in the great square of Caxamalca; and, two hours after sunset, the Spanish soldiery assembled by torch-light in the *plaza* to witness the execution of the sentence. It was on the twenty-ninth of August, 1533. Atahuallpa was led out chained hand and foot,—for he had been kept in irons ever since the great excitement had prevailed in the army respecting an assault. Father Vicente de Valverde was at his side, striving to administer consolation, and, if possible, to persuade him at this last hour to abjure his superstition and embrace the religion of his Conquerors. He was willing to save the soul of his victim from the terrible expiation in the next world, to which he had so cheerfully consigned his mortal part in this.

During Atahuallpa's confinement the friar had repeatedly expounded to him the Christian doctrines, and the Indian monarch discovered much acuteness in apprehending the discourse of his teacher. But it had not carried conviction to his mind, and though he listened with patience, he had shown no disposition to renounce the faith of his fathers. The Dominican made a last appeal to him in this solemn hour; and, when Atahuallpa was bound to the stake, with the fagots that were to kindle his funeral pile lying around him, Valverde, holding up the cross, besought him to embrace it, and be baptized, promising that by so doing the painful death to which he had been sentenced should be commuted for the milder form of the *garrote,*—a mode of punishment by strangulation, used for criminals in Spain.

The unhappy monarch asked if this were really so, and, on its being confirmed by Pizarro, he consented to abjure his own religion, and receive baptism. The ceremony was performed by Father Valverde, and the new convert received the name of Juan de Atahuallpa,—the name of Juan being conferred in honor of John the Baptist, on whose day the event took place.

Atahuallpa expressed a desire that his remains might be transported to Quito, the place of his birth, to be preserved with those of his maternal ancestors. Then turning to Pizarro, as a last request, he implored him to take compassion on his young children, and receive them under his protection. Was there no other one in that dark company who stood grimly around him, to whom he could look for the protection of his offspring? Perhaps he thought there was no other so competent to afford it, and that the wishes so solemnly expressed in that hour might meet with respect even from his Conqueror. Then, recovering his stoical bearing, which for a moment had been shaken, he submitted himself calmly to his fate,—while the Spaniards, gathering around, muttered their *credos* for the salvation his soul. Thus by the death of a vile malefactor perished the last of the Incas.

George Bancroft, 1800–. (Manual, pp. 487, 491, 531.)

From the "History of the United States."

129. Virginia and its Inhabitants in Early Times.

The genial climate and transparent atmosphere delighted those who had come from the denser air of England. Every object in nature was new and wonderful. The loud and frequent thunder-storms were phenomena that had been rarely witnessed in the colder summers of the north; the forests, majestic in their growth, and free from underwood, deserved admiration for their unrivalled magnificence; the purling streams and the frequent rivers, flowing between alluvial banks, quickened the ever-pregnant soil into an unwearied fertility; the strangest and the most delicate flowers grew familiarly in the fields; the woods were replenished with sweet barks and odors; the gardens matured the fruits of Europe, of which the growth was invigorated and the flavor improved by the activity of the virgin mould. Especially the birds, with their gay plumage and varied melodies, inspired delight; every traveller expressed his pleasure in listening to the mocking-bird, which carolled a thousand several tunes, imitating and excelling the notes of all its rivals. The humming-bird, so brilliant in its plumage, and so delicate in its form, quick in motion, yet not fearing the presence of man, hunting about the flowers like the bee gathering honey, rebounding from the blossoms into which it dips its bili, and as soon returning "to renew its addresses to its delightful objects," was ever admired as the smallest and the most beautiful of the feathered race. The rattlesnake, with the terrors of its alarms and the power of its venom; the opossum, soon to become as celebrated for the care of its offspring as the fabled pelican; the noisy frog, booming from the shallows like the English bittern; the flying squirrel; the myriads of pigeons, darkening the air with the immensity of their flocks, and, as men believed, breaking with their weight the boughs of trees on which they alighted,—were all honored with frequent commemoration, and became the subjects of the strangest tales. The concurrent relation of all the Indians justified the belief that, within ten days journey towards the setting of the sun, there was a country where gold might be washed from the sand, and where the natives themselves had learned the use of the crucible; but definite and accurate as were the accounts, inquiry was always baffled; and the regions of gold remained for two centuries an undiscovered land.

Various were the employments by which the calmness of life was relieved. George Sandys, an idle man, who had been a great traveller, and who did not remain in America, a poet, whose verse was tolerated by Dryden and praised by Isaac Walton, beguiled the ennui of his seclusion by translating the whole of Ovid's Metamorphoses. To the man of leisure the chase furnished a perpetual resource. It was not long before the horse was multiplied in Virginia; and to improve that noble animal was early an object of pride, soon to be favored by legislation. Speed was especially valued, and "the planters pace" became a proverb. . .

---

130. CONTRAST OF ENGLISH AND FRENCH COLONIZATION IN AMERICA.

IN Asia, the victories of Clive at Plassy, of Coote at the Wandewash, and of Watson and Pococke on the Indian seas, had given England the undoubted ascendency in the East Indies, opening to her suddenly the promise of untold treasures and territorial acquisitions without end.

In America, the Teutonic race, with its strong tendency to individuality and freedom, was become the master from the Gulf of Mexico to the Poles; and the English tongue, which but a century and a half before had for its entire world a part only of two narrow islands on the outer verge of Europe, was now to spread more widely than any that had ever given expression to human thought.

Go forth, then, language of Milton and Hampden, language of my country, take possession of the North American continent! Gladden the waste places with every tone that has been rightly struck on the English lyre, with every English word that has been spoken well for liberty and for man! Give an echo to the now silent and solitary mountains; gush out with the fountains that as yet sing their anthems all day long without response; fill the valleys with the voices of love in its purity, the pledges of friendship in its faithfulness; and as the morning sun drinks the dewdrops from the flowers all the way from the dreary Atlantic to the Peaceful Ocean, meet him with the joyous hum of the early industry of freemen! Utter boldly and spread widely through the world the thoughts of the coming apostles of the people's liberty, till the sound that cheers the desert shall thrill through the heart of humanity, and the lips of the messenger of the people's power, as he stands in beauty upon the mountains, shall proclaim the renovating tidings of equal freedom for the race! . . . .

France, of all the states on the continent of Europe the most powerful by territorial unity, wealth, numbers, industry, and culture, seemed also by its place marked out for maritime ascendency. Set between many seas, it rested upon the Mediterranean, possessed harbors on the German Ocean, and embraced within its wide shores and jutting headlands, the bays and open waters of the Atlantic; its people, infolding at one extreme the offspring of colonists from Greece, and at the other, the hardy children of the Northmen, were called, as it were, to the inheritance of life upon the sea. The nation, too, readily conceived or appropriated great ideas, and delighted in bold resolves. Its travellers had penetrated farthest into the fearful interior of unknown lands; its missionaries won most familiarly the confidence of the aboriginal hordes; its writers described with keener and wiser observation the forms of nature in her wildness, and the habits and languages of savage man; its soldiers,—and every lay Frenchman in America owed military service,—uniting beyond all others celerity with courage, knew best how to endure the hardships of forest life and to triumph in forest warfare. Its ocean chivalry had given a name and a colony to Carolina, and its merchants a people to Acadia. The French discovered the basin of the St. Lawrence; were the first to explore and possess the banks of the Mississippi, and planned an American empire that should unite the widest valleys and most copious inland waters of the world.

But new France was governed exclusively by the monarchy of its metropolis; and was shut against the intellectual daring of its philosophy, the liberality of its political economists, the movements of its industrial genius, its legal skill, and its infusion of Protestant freedom. Nothing representing the new activity of thought in modern France, went to America. Nothing had leave to go there but what was old and worn out.

The colonists from England brought over the forms of the government of the mother country, and the purpose of giving them a better development and a fairer career in the western world. The French emigrants took with them only what belonged to the past, and nothing that represented modern freedom. The English emigrants retained what they called English privileges, but left behind in the parent country English inequalities, the monarch, and nobility, and prelacy. French America was closed against even a gleam of intellectual independence; nor did it contain so much as one dissenter from the Roman Church; English America had English liberties in greater purity and with far more of the power of the people than England. Its inhabitants were self-organized bodies of freeholders, pressing upon the receding forests, winning their way farther and farther forward every year, and never going back. They had schools, so that in several of the colonies there was no one to be found beyond childhood, who could not read and write; they had the printing press scattering among them books, and pamphlets, and many newspapers; they had a ministry chiefly composed of men of their own election. In private life they were accustomed to take care of themselves; in public affairs they had local legislatures, and municipal self-direction. And now this continent from the Gulf of Mexico to where civilized life is stayed by barriers of frost, was become their dwelling-place and their heritage.

From "The History of the United States."

131. Death of Montcalm.

But already the hope of New France was gone. Born and educated in camps, Montcalm had been carefully instructed, and was skilled in the language of Homer as well as in the art of war. Greatly laborious, just, disinterested, hopeful even to rashness, sagacious in council, swift in action, his mind was a well-spring of bold designs; his career in Canada a wonderful struggle against inexorable destiny. Sustaining hunger and cold, vigils and incessant toil, anxious for his soldiers, unmindful of himself, he set, even to the forest-trained red men, an example of self-denial and endurance, and in the midst of corruption made the public good his aim. Struck by a musket ball, as he fought opposite Monckton, he continued in the engagement, till, in attempting to rally a body of fugitive Canadians in a copse near St. John's gate, he was mortally wounded.

On hearing from the surgeon that death was certain, "I am glad of it," he cried; "how long shall I survive?" "Ten or twelve hours, perhaps less." "So much the better; I shall not live to see the surrender of Quebec." To the council of war he showed that in twelve hours all the troops near at hand might be concentrated and renew the attack before the English were intrenched. When De Ramsay, who commanded the garrison, asked his advice about defending the city, "To your keeping," he replied, "I commend the honor of France. As for me, I shall pass the night with God, and prepare myself for death." Having written a letter recommending the French prisoners to the generosity of the English, his last hours were given to the hope of endless life, and at five the next morning he expired.

From "The History of the United States."

132. CHARACTER OF THE DECLARATION OF INDEPENDENCE.

FROM the fullness of his own mind, without consulting one single book, Jefferson drafted the declaration, he submitted it separately to Franklin and to John Adams, accepted from each of them one or two unimportant verbal corrections, and on the twenty-eighth of June reported it to Congress, which now on the second of July immediately after the resolution of independence entered upon its consideration. During the remainder of that day and the next two, the language, the statements, and the principles of the paper were closely scanned.

. . . .

This immortal state paper, which for its composer was the aurora of enduring fame, was "the genuine effusion of the soul of the country at that time," the revelation of its mind, when, in its youth, its enthusiasm, its sublime confronting of danger, it rose to the highest creative powers of which man is capable. The bill of rights which it promulgates, is of rights that are older than human institutions, and spring from the eternal justice that is anterior to the state. Two political theories divided the world: one founded the commonwealth on the reason of state, the policy of expediency, the other on the immutable principles of morals; the new republic, as it took its place among the powers of the world, proclaimed its faith in the truth and reality and unchangeableness of freedom, virtue, and right. The heart of Jefferson in writing the declaration, and of Congress in adopting it, beat for all humanity; the assertion of right was made for the entire world of mankind, and all coming generations, without any exception whatever; for the proposition which admits of exceptions can never be self-evident. As it was put forth in the name of the ascendant people of that time, it was sure to make the circuit of the world, passing everywhere through the despotic countries of Europe; and the astonished nations as they read that all men are created equal, started out of their lethargy, like those who have been exiles from childhood, when they suddenly hear the dimly remembered accents of their mother tongue.

—

133. Earlier Policy of Spain in the American Revolution.

The King of France, whilst he declared his wish to make no conquest whatever in the war, held out to the King of Spain, with the consent of the United States, the acquisition of Florida; but Florida had not power to allure Charles the Third, or his ministry, which was a truly Spanish ministry, and wished to pursue a truly Spanish policy. There was indeed one word which, if pronounced, would be a spell potent enough to alter their decision; a word that calls the blood into the cheek of a Spaniard as an insult to his pride, a brand of inferiority on his nation. That word was Gibraltar. Meantime, the King of Spain declared that he would not then, nor in the future, enter into the quarrel of France and England; that he wished to close his life in tranquility, and valued peace too highly to sacrifice it to the interests or opinions of another.

So the flags of France and the United States went together into the field against Great Britain, unsupported by any other government, yet with the good wishes of all the peoples of Europe. The benefit then conferred on the United States was priceless. In return, the revolution in America came opportunely for France. . . . For the blessing of that same France, America brought new life and hope; she superseded scepticism by a wise and prudent enthusiasm in action, and bade the nation that became her ally lift up its heart from the barrenness of doubt to the highest affirmation of God and liberty, to freedom and union with the good, the beautiful, and the true.

J. G. M. Ramsey,[1] *about 1800–.*

From "The Annals of Tennessee."

134. SKETCH OF GENERAL JOHN SEVIER.

THE Etowah campaign was the last military service rendered by Sevier, and the only one for which he ever received compensation from the government. For nearly twenty years he had been constantly engaged in incessant and unremitted service. He was in thirty-five battles, some of them hardly contested, and decisive. He was never wounded, and in all his campaigns and battles was successful and the victor. He was careful of the lives of his soldiery; and, although he always led them to the victory, he lost, in all his engagements with the enemy, but fifty-six men. The secret of his invariable success was the impetuosity and vigor of his charge. Himself an accomplished horseman, a graceful rider, passionately fond of a spirited charger, always well mounted, at the head of his dragoons, he was at once in the midst of the fight. His rapid movement, always unexpected and sudden, disconcerted the enemy, and, at the first onset, decided the victory. He was the first to introduce the Indian war-whoop in his battles with the savages, the Tories, and the British. More harmless than the leaden missile, it was not less efficient, and was always the precursor and attendant of victory. The prisoners at King's Mountain said, "We could stand your fighting; but your cursed hallooing confused us. We thought the mountains had regiments, instead of companies." Sevier's enthusiasm was contagious; he imparted it to his men. He was the idol of the soldiery; and his orders were obeyed cheerfully, and executed with precision. In a military service of twenty years, one instance is not known of insubor-

[1]A native of Tennessee. His Annals contain much valuable material.

dination on the part of the soldier, or of discipline by the commander.

Sevier's troops were generally his neighbors, and the members of his own family. Often no public provision was made for their pay, equipments, or subsistence. These were furnished by himself, being at once commander, commissary, and paymaster. The soldiery rendezvoused at his house, which often became a cantonment; his fields, ripe or unripe, were given up to his horsemen; powder and lead, provisions, clothing, even all he had, belonged to his men.

The Etowah campaign terminated the military services of General Sevier. Hereafter, we will have to record his not less important agency in the civil affairs of Tennessee.

Charles Gayarré, 1805–. (Manual, p. 490.)

From the "History of Louisiana."

135. General Jackson at New Orleans.

His very physiognomy prognosticated what soul was encased within the spare but well-ribbed form which had that "lean and hungry look" described by England's greatest bard as bespeaking little sleep of nights, but much of ambition, self-reliance, and impatience of control. His lip and eye denoted the man of unyielding temper, and his very hair, slightly silvered, stood erect like quills round his wrinkled brow, as if they scorned to bend. Some sneered, it is true, at what they called a military tyro, at the impromptu general who had sprung out of the uncouth lawyer and the unlearned judge, who in arms had only the experience of a few months, acquired in a desultory war against wild Indians, and who was, not only without any previous training to his new profession, but also without the first rudiments of a liberal education, for he did not even know the orthography of his own native language. Such was the man who, with a handful of raw militia, was to stand in the way of the veteran troops of England, whose boast it was to have triumphed over one of the greatest captains known in history.

But those who entertained such distrust had hardly come in contact with General Jackson, when they felt that they had to deal with a master-spirit. True, he was rough hewn from the rock, but rock he was, and of that kind of rock which Providence chooses to select as a fit material to use in its structures of human greatness. True, he had not the education of a lieutenant in a European army; but what lieutenant, educated or not, who had the will and the remarkable military adaptation so evident in General Jackson's intellectual and physical organization, ever remained a subaltern? Much less could General Jackson fail to rise to his proper place in a country where there was so much more elbow-room, and fewer artificial obstacles than in less favored lands. But, whatever those obstacles might have been, General Jackson would have overcome them all. His will was of such an extraordinary nature that, like Christian faith, it could almost have accomplished prodigies and removed mountains. It is impossible to study the life of General Jackson without being convinced that this is the most remarkable feature of his character. His will had, as it were, the force and the fixity of fate; that will carried him triumphantly through his military and civil career, and through the difficulties of private life. So intense and incessantly active this peculiar faculty was in him, that one would suppose that his mind was nothing but will—a will so lofty that it towered into sublimity. In him it supplied the place of genius—or, rather, it was almost genius. On many occasions, in the course of his long, eventful life, when his shattered constitution made his physicians despair of preserving him, he seemed to continue to live merely because it was his will; and when his unconquerable spirit departed from his enfeebled and worn-out body, those who knew him well might almost have been tempted to suppose that he had not been vanquished by death, but had at last consented to repose. This man, when he took the command at New Orleans, had made up his mind to beat the English; and, as that mind was so constituted that it was not susceptible of entertaining much doubt as to the results of any of its resolves, he went to work with an innate confidence which transfused itself into the population he had been sent to protect.

Brantz Mayer, 1809–. (Manual, p. 490.)

From "Mexico, Aztec," &c.

136. REKINDLING THE SACRED FIRE.

AT the end of the Aztec or Toltec cycle of fifty-two years,—for it is not accurately ascertained to which of the tribes the astronomical science of Tenochtitlan is to be attributed,—these primitive children of the New World believed that the world was in danger of instant destruction. Accordingly, its termination became one of their most serious and awful epochs, and they anxiously awaited the moment when the sun would be blotted out from the heavens, and the globe itself resolved once more into chaos. As the cycle ended in the winter, the season of the year, with its drearier sky and colder air, in the lofty regions of the valley, added to the gloom that fell upon the hearts of the people. On the last day of the fifty-two years, all the fires in temples and dwellings were extinguished, and the natives devoted themselves to fasting and prayer. They destroyed alike their valuable and worthless wares; rent their garments, put out their lights, and hid themselves for awhile in solitude. . . .

At dark on the last dread evening,—as soon as the sun had set, as they imagined, forever,—a sad and solemn procession of priests and people marched forth from the city to a neighboring hill, to rekindle the "New Fire." This mournful march was called "the procession of the gods," and was supposed to be their final departure from their temples and altars.

As soon as the melancholy array reached the summit of the hill, it reposed in fearful anxiety until the Pleiades reached the zenith in the sky, whereupon the priests immediately began the sacrifice of a human victim, whose breast was covered with a wooden shield, which the chief *flamen* kindled by friction. When the sufferer received the fatal stab from the sacrificial knife of *obsidian*, the machine was set in motion on his bosom until the blaze had kindled. The anxious crowd stood round with fear and trembling. Silence reigned over nature and man. Not a word was uttered among the countless multitude that thronged the hill-sides and plains, whilst the priest performed his direful duty to the gods. At length, as the first sparks gleamed faintly from the whirling instrument, low sobs and ejaculations were whispered among the eager masses. As the sparks kindled into a blaze, and the blaze into a flame, and the flaming shield and victim were cast together on a pile of combustibles which burst at once into the brightness of a conflagration, the air was rent with the joyous shouts of the relieved and panic-stricken Indians. Far and wide over the dusky crowds beamed the blaze like a star of promise. Myriads of upturned faces greeted it from hills, mountains, temples, terraces, teocallis, house-tops, and city walls; and the prostrate multitudes hailed the emblem of light, life, and fruition, as a blessed omen of the restored favor of their gods, and the preservation of their race for another cycle. At regular intervals, Indian couriers held aloft brands of resinous wood, by which they transmitted the "New Fire" from hand to hand, from village to village, and town to town, throughout the Aztec empire. Light was radiated from the imperial or ecclesiastical center of the realm. In every temple and dwelling it was rekindled from the sacred source; and when the sun rose again on the following morning, the solemn procession of priests, princes, and subjects, which had taken up its march from the capital on the preceding night with solemn steps, returned once more to the abandoned capital, and, restoring the gods to their altars, abandoned themselves to joy and festivity, in token of gratitude and relief from impending doom.

Albert James Pickett,[1] ***1858–.*** (Manual, p. 490.)

From "The History of Alabama."

137. THE INDIANS AND THE EARLY SETTLERS OF ALABAMA.

DURING my youthful days, I was accustomed to be much with the Creek Indians, hundreds of whom came almost daily

[1] A native of North Carolina, who removed in early life to Alabama. His "History" abounds in interesting matter.

to the trading-house. For twenty years I frequently visited the Creek nation. Their green-corn dances, ball plays, war ceremonies, and manners and customs, are all fresh in my recollection. In my intercourse with them I was thrown into the company of many old white men called "Indian country men," who had for years conducted a commerce with them. Some of these men had come to the Creek nation before the Revolutionary War, and others, being tories, had fled to it during the war, and after it to escape from whig persecution. They were unquestionably the shrewdest and most interesting men with whom I ever conversed. Generally of Scotch descent, many of them were men of some education. All of them were married to Indian wives, and some of them had intelligent and handsome children. . . . . I often conversed with the chiefs while they were seated in the shades of the spreading mulberry and walnut, upon the banks of the beautiful Tallapoosa. As they leisurely smoked their pipes, some of them related to me the traditions of their country. I occasionally saw Choctaw and Cherokee traders, and learned much from them. I had no particular object in view, at that time, except the gratification of a curiosity which led me, for my own satisfaction alone, to learn something of the early history of Alabama.

Charles Wentworth Upham, 1802 (Manual, pp. 490, 532.)

From the "History of Witchcraft and Salem Village."

138. Defeat of the Indian King Philip.

The Indians were carrying all before them. Philip was spreading conflagration, devastation, and slaughter around the borders, and striking sudden and deadly blows into the heart of the country. It was evident that he was consolidating the Indian power into irresistible strength. . . . From other scouting parties it became evident that this opinion was correct, and that the Indians were collecting stores and assembling their warriors somewhere, to fall upon the colonies at the first opening of spring. Further information made it certain that their place of gathering was in the Narragansett country, in the south-westerly part of the colony of Rhode Island. There was no alternative but, as a last effort, to strike the enemy at that point with the utmost available force. . . . It was between one and two o'clock in the afternoon, and the short winter day was wearing away. Winslow saw the position at a glance, and, by the promptness of his decision, proved himself a great captain. He ordered an instant assault. The Massachusetts troops were in the van, the Plymouth, with the commander-in-chief, in the center, the Connecticut in the rear. The Indians had erected a block-house near the entrance, filled with sharpshooters, who also lined the palisades. The men rushed on, although it was into the jaws of death, under an unerring fire. The block-house told them where the entrance was. The companies of Moseley and Davenport led the way. Moseley succeeded in passing through. Davenport fell beneath three fatal shots, just within the entrance. Isaac Johnson, captain of the Roxbury company, was killed while on the log. But death had no terrors to that army. The center and rear divisions pressed up to support the front, and fill the gaps, and all equally shared the glory of the hour. Enough survived the terrible passage to bring the Indians to a hand-to-hand fight within the fort. After a desperate struggle of nearly three hours, the savages were driven from their stronghold, and with the setting of that sun their power was broken. Philip's fortunes had received a decided overthrow, and the colonies were saved. In all military history there is not a more daring exploit. Never, on any field, has more heroic prowess been displayed.

John Lothrop Motley, 1814–. (Manual, p. 532.)

From "The History of the United Netherlands."

139. CHARACTER OF ALVA.

FERDINANDO ALVAREZ DE TOLEDO, Duke of Alva, was now in in his sixtieth year. He was the most successful and experienced general of Spain, or of Europe. No man had studied more deeply, or practiced more constantly, the military science. In the most important of all arts at that epoch he was the most consummate artist. In the only honorable profession of the age he was the most thorough and the most pedantic professor. Having proved in his boyhood at Fontarabia, and in his maturity at Mühlberg, that he could exhibit heroism and headlong courage when necessary, he could afford to look with contempt upon the witless gibes which his enemies had occasionally perpetrated at his expense. . . . "Recollect," said he to Don John of Austria, "that the first foes with whom one has to contend are one's own troops—with their clamors for an engagement at this moment, and their murmurs about results at another; with their 'I thought that the battle should be fought,' or, 'It was my opinion that the occasion ought not to be lost.' "

On the whole, the Duke of Alva was inferior to no general of his age. As a disciplinarian, he was foremost in Spain, perhaps in Europe. A spendthrift of time, he was an economist of blood; and this was, perhaps, in the eye of humanity, his principal virtue. . . . Such were his qualities as a military commander. As a statesman, he had neither experience nor talent. As a man, his character was simple. He did not combine a great variety of vices; but those which he had were colossal, and he possessed no virtues. He was neither lustful nor intemperate; but his professed eulogists admitted his enormous avarice, while the world has agreed that such an amount of stealth and ferocity, of patient vindictiveness and universal blood-thirstiness, were never found in a savage beast of the forest, and but rarely in a human bosom.

—

From "The History of the United Netherlands."

140. Siege and Abandonment of Ostend.

The Archduke Albert and the Infanta Isabella entered the place in triumph, if triumph it could be called. It would be difficult to imagine a more desolate scene. The artillery of the first years of the seventeenth century was not the terrible enginery of destruction that it has become in the last third of the nineteenth, but a cannonade, continued so steadily and so long, had done its work. There were no churches, no houses, no redoubts, no bastions, no walls, nothing but a vague and confused mass of ruin. Spinola conducted his imperial guests along the edge of extinct volcanoes, amid upturned cemeteries, through quagmires, which once were moats, over huge mounds of sand, and vast shapeless masses of bricks and masonry, which had been forts. He endeavored to point out places where mines had been exploded, where ravelins had been stormed, where the assailants had been successful, and where they had been bloodily repulsed. But it was all loathsome, hideous rubbish. There were no human habitations, no hovels, no casemates. The inhabitants had burrowed at last in the earth, like the dumb creatures of the swamps and forests. In every direction the dykes had burst, and the sullen wash of the liberated waves, bearing hither and thither the floating wreck of fascines and machinery, of planks and building materials, sounded far and wide over what should have been dry land. The great ship channel, with the unconquered Half-moon upon one side and the incomplete batteries and platforms of Bucquoy on the other, still defiantly opened its passage to the sea, and the retiring fleets of the garrison were white in the offing. All around was the grey expanse of stormy ocean, without a cape or a headland to break its monotony, as the surges rolled mournfully in upon a desolation more dreary than their own. The atmosphere was murky and surcharged with rain, for the wild, equinoctial storm which had held Maurice spell-bound, had been raging over land and sea for many days. At every step the unburied skulls of brave soldiers who had died in the cause of freedom, grinned their welcome to the conquerors. Isabella wept at the sight. She had cause to weep. Upon that miserable sandbank more than a hundred thousand men had laid down their lives by her decree, in order that she and her husband might at last take possession of a most barren prize. This insignificant fragment of a sovereignty which her wicked old father had presented to her on his deathbed—a sovereignty which he had no more moral right or actual power to confer than if it had been in the planet Saturn—had at last been appropriated at the cost of all this misery. It was of no great value, although its acquisition had caused the expenditure of at least eight millions of florins, divided in nearly equal proportions between the two belligerents. It was in vain that great immunities were offered to those who would remain, or who would consent to settle in the foul Golgotha. The original population left the place in mass. No human creatures were left save the wife of a freebooter and her paramour, a journeyman blacksmith. This unsavory couple, to whom entrance into the purer atmosphere of Zeeland was denied, thenceforth shared with the carrion crows the amenities of Ostend.

From the Preface to the "Rise of the Dutch Republic."

141. The Rise of the Dutch Republic.

The rise of the Dutch Republic must ever be regarded as one of the leading events of modern times. Without the birth of this great commonwealth, the various historical phenomena of the sixteenth and following centuries must have either not existed, or have presented themselves under essential modifications. . . . From the handbreadth of territory called the province of Holland, rises a power which wages eighty years' warfare with the most potent empire upon earth, and which, during the progress of the struggle, becoming itself a mighty state, and binding about its own slender form a zone of the richest possessions of earth, from pole to tropic, finally dictates its decrees to the empire of Charles.

. . To the Dutch Republic, even more than to Florence at an earlier day is the world indebted for practical instruction in that great science of political equilibrium which must always become more and more important as the various states of the civilized world are pressed more closely together, and as the struggle for pre-eminence becomes more feverish and fatal. Courage and skill in political and military combinations enabled

William the Silent to overcome the most powerful and unscrupulous monarch of his age. The same hereditary audacity and fertility of genius placed the destiny of Europe in the hands of William's great-grandson, and enabled him to mould into an impregnable barrier the various elements of opposition to the overshadowing monarchy of Louis XIV. As the schemes of the Inquisition and the unparalled tyranny of Philip, in one century led to the establishment of the Republic of the United Provinces, so, in the next, the revocation of the Nantes Edict and the invasion of Holland are avenged by the elevation of the Dutch Stadholder upon the throne of the stipendiary Stuarts.

To all who speak the English language, the history of the great agony through which the republic of Holland was ushered into life must have peculiar interest, for it is a portion of the records of the Anglo-Saxon race—essentially the same whether in Friesland, England, or Massachusetts.

. . The great Western Republic, therefore—in whose . . . veins flows much of that ancient and kindred blood received from the nation once ruling a noble portion of its territory, and tracking its own political existence to the same parent spring of temperate human liberty—must look with affectionate interest upon the trials of the elder commonwealth. . . The lessons of history and the fate of free states can never be sufficiently pondered by those upon whom so large and heavy a responsibility for the maintenance of rational human freedom rests.

Alexander B. Meek,[1] *1814-1865.* (Manual, p. 523.)

From "Romantic Passages in Southwestern History."

142. EXILED FRENCH OFFICERS IN ALABAMA.

UPON the colony they bestowed the name of Marengo, which is still preserved in the county. Other relics of their nomen-

[1] One of the few writers of Alabama. The "Romantic passages" is a book of great interest.

clature, drawn similarly from battles in which some of them had been distinguished, are to be found in the villages of Linden and Arcola. . . .

Who that would have looked upon Marshal Grouchy or General Lefebvre, as, dressed in their plain, rustic habiliments,—the straw hat, the homespun coat, the brogan shoes,—they drove the plough in the open field, or wielded the axe in the new-ground clearing, would, if unacquainted with their history, have dreamed that those farmer-looking men had sat in the councils of monarchs, and had headed mighty armies in the fields of the sternest strife the world has ever seen? "Do you know, sir," said a citizen to a traveller, who, in 1819, was passing the road from Arcola to Eaglesville,—"do you know, sir, who is that fine-looking man who has just ferried you across the creek?" "No. Who is he?" was the reply. "That," said the citizen, "is the officer who commanded Napoleon's advanced guard when he returned from Elba." This was Colonel Raoul, now a general in France.

---

143. The Youth of the Indian Chief Weatherford.

But the mind of the young Indian, though grasping with singular readiness the knowledge thus imparted, was subject to stronger tastes and propensities; and he indulged in all the wild pursuits and amusements of the youth of his nation with an alacrity and spirit which won their approval and admiration. He became one of the most active, athletic, and swift-footed participants in their various games and dances, and was particularly expert and successful, as a hunter, in the use of the rifle and the bow. He was also noted, even in his youth, for his reckless daring as a rider, and his graceful feats of horsemanship, which the fine stables of his father enabled him to indulge. To use the words of an old Indian woman who knew him at this period, "The squaws would quit hoeing corn, and smile and gaze upon him as he rode by the corn-patch."

Abel Stevens,[1] *1815–.*

From "The History of Methodism."

144. THE EARLY METHODIST CLERGY IN AMERICA.

THEY composed a class which, perhaps, will never be seen again. They were distinguished by native mental vigor, shrewdness, extraordinary knowledge of human nature, many of them by overwhelming natural eloquence, the effects of which on popular assemblies are scarcely paralleled in the history of ancient or modern oratory, and not a few by powers of satire and wit which made the gainsayer cower before them. To these intellectual attributes they added great excellences of the heart, a zeal which only burned more fervently where that of ordinary men would have grown faint, a courage that exulted in perils, a generosity which knew no bounds, and left most of them in want in their latter days, a forbearance and co-operation with each other which are seldom found in large bodies, an entire devotion to one work, and, withal, a simplicity of character which extended even to their manners and their apparel. They were likewise characterized by rare physical abilities. They were mostly robust. The feats of labor and endurance which they performed, in incessantly preaching in villages and cities, among slave huts and Indian wigwams, in journeyings seldom interrupted by stress of weather, in fording creeks, swimming rivers, sleeping in forests,—these, with the novel circumstances with which such a career frequently brought them into contact, afford examples of life and character which, in the hands of genius, might be the materials for a new department of romantic literature. They were men who labored as if the judgment fires were about to break out on the world, and time to end with their day. They were precisely the men whom the moral wants of the new world at the time demanded.

[1] A prominent clergyman of the Methodist church. His History of Methodism is a work of great research and value. A native of Pennsylvania.

Francis Parkman, 1823–. (Manual, pp. 496, 505.)

From "The Conspiracy of Pontiac."

145. Hunters and Trappers.

These rude and hardy men, hunters and traders, scouts and guides, who ranged the woods beyond the English borders, and formed a connecting link between barbarism and civilization, have been touched upon already. They were a distinct, peculiar class, marked with striking contrasts of good and evil. Many, though by no means all, were coarse, audacious, and unscrupulous; yet, even in the worst, one might often have found a vigorous growth of warlike virtues, an iron endurance, an undespairing courage, a wondrous sagacity, and singular fertility of resource. In them was renewed, with all its ancient energy, that wild and daring spirit, that force and hardihood of mind, which marked our barbarous ancestors of Germany and Norway. These sons of the wilderness still survive. We may find them to this day, not in the valley of the Ohio, nor on the shores of the lakes, but far westward on the desert range of the buffalo, and among the solitudes of Oregon. Even now, while I write, some lonely trapper is climbing the perilous defiles of the Rocky Mountains, his strong frame cased in time-worn buck-skin, his rifle griped in his sinewy hand. Keenly he peers from side to side, lest Blackfoot or Arapahoe should ambuscade his path. The rough earth is his bed, a morsel of dried meat and a draught of water are his food and drink, and death and danger his companions. No anchorite could fare worse, no hero could dare more; yet his wild, hard life has resistless charms; and while he can wield a rifle, he will never leave it. Go with him to the rendezvous, and he is a stoic no more. Here, rioting among his comrades, his native appetites break loose in mad excess, in deep carouse, and desperate gaming. Then follow close the quarrel, the challenge, the fight,—two rusty rifles and fifty yards of prairie.

From "The Discovery of the Great West."

146. EXPLORATION OF THE MISSISSIPPI RIVER.

THE river twisted among the lakes and marshes choked with wild rice; and, but for their guides, they could scarcely have followed the perplexed and narrow channel. It brought them at last to the portage; where, after carrying their canoes a mile and a half over the prairie and through the marsh, they launched them on the Wisconsin, bade farewell to the waters that flowed to the St. Lawrence, and committed themselves to the current that was to bear them they knew not whither,—perhaps to the Gulf of Mexico, perhaps to the South Sea or the Gulf of California. They glided calmly down the tranquil stream, by islands choked with trees and matted with entangling grape-vines; by forests, groves, and prairies,—the parks and pleasure-grounds of a prodigal nature; by thickets and marshes and broad bare sand-bars; under the shadowing trees, between whose tops looked down from afar the bold brow of some woody bluff. At night, the bivouac,—the canoes inverted on the bank, the flickering fire, the meal of bison-flesh or venison, the evening pipes and slumber beneath the stars; and when in the morning they embarked again, the mist hung on the river like a bridal veil; then melted before the sun, till the glassy water and the languid woods basked breathless in the sultry glare.

On the 17th of June, they saw on their right the broad meadows, bounded in the distance by rugged hills, where now stand the town and fort of Prairie du Chien. Before them, a wide and rapid current coursed athwart their way, by the foot of lofty heights wrapped thick in forests. They had found what they sought, and "with a joy," writes Marquette, "which I cannot express," they steered forth their canoes on the eddies of the Mississippi.

Turning southward, they paddled down the stream, through a solitude unrelieved by the faintest trace of man. A large fish, apparently one of the huge cat-fish of the Mississippi, blundered against Marquette's canoe with a force which seems to have startled him; and once, as they drew in their net, they caught a "spade-fish," whose eccentric appearance greatly astonished them. At length, the buffalo began to appear, grazing in herds on the great prairies which then bordered the river; and Marquette describes the fierce and stupid look of the old bulls, as they stared at the intruders through the tangled mane which nearly blinded them.

John Gilmary Shea,[1] *1824–*.

From "The History of Catholic Missions among the Indians."

147. Difficulties of the Enterprise.

The discovery of America, like every other event in the history of the world, had, in the designs of God, the great object of the salvation of mankind. In that event, more clearly, perhaps, than it is often given to us here below, we can see and adore that Providence which thus gave to millions, long sundered from the rest of man by pathless oceans, the light of the gospel, and the proffered boon of redemption. . . .

The field was one as yet unmatched for extent and difficulty. That region now studded with cities and towns, traversed in every direction by the panting steam-car or lightning telegraph, was then an almost unbroken forest, save where the wide prairie rolled its billows of grass towards the western mountains, or was lost in the sterile, salt, and sandy plains of the southwest. No city raised to heaven spire, dome, or minaret; no plough turned up the rich, alluvial soil; no metal dug from the bowels of the earth had been fashioned into instruments to aid man in the arts of peace and war. . . .

The simplest arts of civilized life were unknown. In one little section of the Gila and Rio Grande, the people spun and wove a native cotton, manufactured a rude pottery, and lived in

[1] This writer is much distinguished for his numerous works, most of which relate to the early missions of the Roman Catholic church in America. He is a native of New York.

houses or castle-towns of unburnt bricks. Elsewhere the canoe or cabin of bark or hides, and the arabesque mat, denoted the highest point of social progress.

Elsewhere the whole country was inhabited by tribes of a nomadic character, rarely collected in villages except at particular seasons, or for specific objects, though here and there were found more sedentary tribes in villages of bark, encircled by walls of earth, or palisades of wood, whose institutions, commercial spirit, and agriculture, superior to that of the wild rovers, seemed to show the remnant of some more civilized tribe in a state of decadence. Around each isolated tribe lay an unbroken wilderness extending for miles on every side, where the braves roamed, hunters alike of beasts and men. So little intercourse or knowledge of each other existed, so desolate was the wilderness that a vagabond tribe might wander from one extreme of the continent to another, and language alone could tell the nation to which they belonged.

The whole country was thus occupied by comparatively small, but hostile tribes, so numerous, that almost every river and every lake has handed down the name of a distinct nation. In form, in manners, and in habits, these tribes presented an almost uniform appearance: language formed the great distinctive mark to the European, though the absence of a feather or a line of paint disclosed to the native the tribe of the wanderer whom he met.

The country itself presented a thousand obstacles: there was danger from flood, danger from wild beasts, danger from the roving savage, danger from false friends, danger from the furious rapids on rivers, danger of loss of sight, of health, of use of motion and of limbs, in the new, strange life of an Indian wigwam. . . .

Once established in a tribe, the difficulties were increased. After months, nay, years, of teaching, the missionaries found that the fickle savage was easily led astray; never could they form pupils to our life and manners. The nineteenth century failed, as the seventeenth failed, in raising up priests from among the Iroquois or the Algonquins; and at this day a pupil of the Propaganda, who disputed in Latin on theses of Peter Lombard, roams at the head of a half-naked band in the billowy plains of Nebraska.

From "Introduction to Early Voyages," etc.

148. Exploration of the Mississippi River.

Many a river lives embalmed in history and in historic verse. The Euphrates, the Nile, the Jordan, the Tiber, and the Rhine typify the course of empires and dynasties. Countries have been described *per flumina*, but these streams possess renown rather from some city that frowned on their currents, or some battle fought and won on their banks. The great River of our West, from its immense length and the still increasing importance of its valley, possesses a history of its own. Its discovery by the Spanish adventurers, a Cabeza de Vaca, a De Soto, a Tristan, who reached, crossed, or followed it, is its period of early romance, brilliant, brief, and tragic. Its exploration by Marquette and La Salle follows,—work of patient endurance and investigation, still tinged with that light of heroism that hovers around all who struggle with difficulty and adversity to attain a great and useful end. Then come the early voyages depicting the successive stages of its banks from a wilderness to civilization.

The death of La Salle in Texas in his attempt to reach Illinois closes the chapter of exploration. Iberville opens a new period by his voyage to the mouth of the Mississippi, which crowning the previous efforts, gave the valley of the great river to civilization, Christianity, and progress. The river had become an object of rivalry. English, French, and Spanish at the same moment sought to secure its mouth, but fortune favored the bold Canadian, and the white flag reared by La Salle was planted anew.

. . . At the moment when these narratives take us to the valley of the Mississippi, that immense territory presented a strange contrast to its present condition. From its head waters amid the lakes of Minnesota to its mouth; from its western springs in the heart of the Rocky mountains to its eastern cradle in the Alleghanies, all was yet in its primeval state. The Europeans had but one spot, Tonty's little fort; no white men roamed it but the trader or the missionary. With a sparse and scattered Indian population, the country teeming with buffalo, deer, and game, was a scene of plenty. The Indian has vanished from its banks with the game that he pursued. The valley numbers as many states now as it did white men then; a busy, enterprising, adventurous, population, numbering its millions, has swept away the unprogressive and unassimilating red man. The languages of the Illinois, the Quapaw, the Tonica, the Natchez, the Ouma, are heard no more by the banks of the great water; no calumet now throws round the traveller its charmed power; the white banner of France floated long to the breeze, but with the flag of England and the standard of Spain all disappeared we may say within a century. For fifty years one single flag met the eye, and appealed to the heart of the inhabitants of the shores of the Mississippi.[1] Two now divide it: let us hope that the altered flag may soon resume its original form, and meet the heart's warm response at the mouth as at the source of the Mississippi.

John Gorham Palfrey, 1796–. (Manual, pp. 504, 532.)

From the "History of New England."

149. HAPPINESS OF WINTHROP'S CLOSING YEARS.

HE was greatly privileged in living so long. Just before he died, that ecclesiastical arrangement had been made, which he might naturally hope would preserve the churches of New England in purity, peace, and strength, to remote times. Religious and political dissensions, which had disturbed and threatened the infant Church and the forming State, appeared to be effectually composed. The tribunals, carefully constituted

[1] In allusion to the Rebellion.

for the administration of impartial and speedy justice, understood and did their duty, and commanded respect. The education of the generations which were to succeed had been provided for with an enlightened care. The College had bountifully contributed its ripe first-fruits to the public service; and the novel system of a universal provision of the elements of knowledge at the public cost, had been inaugurated with all circumstances of encouragement.

A generation was coming forward which remembered nothing of what Englishmen had suffered in New England for want of the necessaries and comforts of life. The occupations of industry were various and remunerative. Land was cheap, and the culture of it yielded no penurious reward to the husbandman; while he who chose to sell his labor was at least at liberty to place his own estimate upon it, and found it always in demand. The woods and waters were lavish of gifts which were to be had simply for the taking. The white wings of commerce, in their long flight to and from the settler's home, wafted the commodities which afford enjoyment and wealth to both sender and receiver. The numerous handicrafts, which in its constantly increasing division of labor, a thriving society employs, found liberal recompense; and manufactures on a larger scale were beginning to invite accumulations of capital and associated labor.

The Confederacy of the Four Colonies was an humble, but a substantial, power in the world. It was known to be such by its French, Dutch, and savage neighbors; by the alienated communities on Narragansett Bay; and by the rulers of the mother country.

During Winthrop's last ten years, nowhere else in the world had Englishmen been so happy as under the generous government which his mind inspired and regulated. What one mind could do for a community's well-being, his had done. The prosecution of the issues he had wrought for was now to be committed to the wisdom and courage of a younger generation, and to the course of events, under the continued guidance of a propitious Providence.

CHAPTER II.

ESSAYISTS, MORALISTS, AND REFORMERS.

Joseph Dennie, 1768-1812. (Manual, p. 497.)

From "The Lay Preacher."

150. REFLECTIONS ON THE SEASONS.

"Truly the light is sweet, and a pleasant thing it is for the eyes to behold the sun."

THE sensitive Gray, in a frank letter to his friend West, assures him that, when the sun grows warm enough to tempt him from the fireside, he will, like all other things, be the better for his influence; for the sun is an old friend, and an excellent nurse, &c. This is an opinion which will be easily entertained by every one who has been cramped by the icy hand of Winter, and who feels the gay and renovating influence of Spring. In those mournful months when vegetables and animals are alike coerced by cold, man is tributary to the howling storm and the sullen sky, and is, in the phrase of Johnson, a "slave to gloom;" but when the earth is disencumbered of her load of snows, and warmth is felt, and twittering swallows are heard, he is again jocund and free. Nature renews her charter to her sons. . . . Hence is enjoyed, in the highest luxury,—

"Day, and the sweet approach of even and morn,
And sight of vernal bloom and summer's rose,
And flocks, and herds, and human face divine."

It is nearly impossible for me to convey to my readers an idea of the "vernal delight" felt at this period by the Lay Preacher, far declined in the vale of years. My spectral figure, pinched by the rude gripe of January, becomes as thin as that "dagger of lath" employed by the vaunting Falstaff, and my mind, affected by the universal desolation of winter, is nearly as vacant of joy and bright ideas as the forest is of leaves and the grove is of song. Fortunately for my happiness, this is only periodical spleen. Though in the bitter months, surveying my attenuated body, I exclaim with the melancholy prophet, "My leanness, my leanness! woe is me!" and though, adverting to the state of my mind, I behold it "all in a robe of darkest grain," yet when April and May reign in sweet vicissitude, I give, like Horace, care to the winds, and perceive the whole system excited by the potent stimulus of sunshine. . . . I have myself in winter felt hostile to those whom I could smile upon in May, and clasp to my bosom in June.

William Gaston,[1] *1778-1844.*

From "Essays and Addresses."

151. The Importance of Integrity.

The first great maxim of human conduct—that which it is all-important to impress on the understandings of young men, and recommend to their hearty adoption—is, above all things, in all circumstances, and under every emergency, to preserve a clean heart and an honest purpose. . . . Without it, neither genius nor learning, neither the gifts of God, nor human exertions, can avail aught for the accomplishment of the great objects of human existence. Integrity is the crowning virtue,—integrity is the pervading principle which ought to regulate, guide, control, and vivify every impulse, device, and action. Honesty is sometimes spoken of as a vulgar virtue; and perhaps, that honesty which barely refrains from outraging the positive rules ordained by society for the protection of property, and which ordinarily pays its debts and performs its engagements, however useful and commendable a quality, is not to be numbered among the highest efforts of human virtue. But that integrity which, however tempting the opportunity, or however secure against detection, no selfishness nor resentment, no lust of power, place, favor, profit, or pleasure, can cause to swerve from the strict rule of right, is the perfection of man's moral nature. In this sense, the poet was right when he pronounced "an honest man's the noblest work of God." It is almost inconceivable what an erect and independent spirit this high endowment communicates to the man, and what a moral intrepidity and vivifying energy it imparts to his character. . . . Erected on such a basis, and built up of such materials, fame is enduring. Such is the fame of our Washington—of the man "inflexible to ill, and obstinately just." While, therefore, other monuments, intended to perpetuate human greatness, are daily mouldering into dust, and belie the proud inscriptions which they bear, the solid, granite pyramid of his glory lasts from age to age, imperishable, seen afar off, looming high over the vast desert, a mark, a sign, and a wonder, for the wayfarers though this pilgrimage of life.

Jesse Buel,[1] *1778-1839.* (Manual, p. 504.)

From "The Farmer's Instructor."

152. Extent and Defects of American Agriculture.

We have associated, gentlemen, to increase the pleasures and profits of rural labor, to enlarge the sphere of useful knowledge, and, by concentrating our energies, to give them greater effect in advancing the public good. In no country does the agricultural class bear so great a proportion to the whole population as in this. In England one-third of the inhabitants only are employed in husbandry; in France, two-thirds; in Italy, a little more than three-fourths; while in the United States the agricultural portion probably exceeds five-sixths. And in no country does the agricultural population exercise such a controlling political power, contribute so much to the wealth, or tend so strongly to give an impress to the character of a nation as in the United States. Hence it may be truly said of us that our agriculture is our nursing mother,

[1] A prominent lawyer and statesman of North Carolina.

which nurtures, and gives growth, and wealth, and character to our country. . . . Knowing no party, and confined to no sect, its benefits and its blessings, like dews from heaven, fall upon all.

. . . Our agriculture is greatly defective. It is susceptible of much improvement. How shall we effect this improvement? The old are *too old to learn*, or, rather, to unlearn what have been the habits of their lives. The young cannot learn as they ought to learn, and as the public interests require, because they have no suitable school for their instruction. We have no place where they can learn the *principles* upon which the *practice* of agriculture is based, none where they can be instructed in all the modern improvements of the art.

Much injury has been done to the cause of agriculture by sanguine speculations, which have only led to expense and disappointments; but all works on agriculture are not of that character; nor should it be forgotten that theory is the parent of practical knowledge, and that the very systems which farmers themselves adopt, were originally founded upon those theories which they so much affect to despise. Neither can it be denied that systems grounded upon theory alone, unsupported by experiment, are properly viewed with distrust; for the most plausible reasoning upon the operations of nature, without accompanying proof deduced from facts, may lead to a wrong conclusion, and it is often difficult to separate that which is really useful, from that which is merely visionary. . . . Prudence, therefore, dictates the necessity of caution; but ignorance is opposed to every change, from the mere want of judgment to discriminate between that which is purely speculative, and that which rests upon a more solid foundation.

Robert Walsh, 1784-1859. (Manual, p. 504.)

From "Didactics, Social, Literary, &c."

153. False Sympathy with Criminals.

Whatever the impulse to guilt, some suppression or aberration of the reason may ever be alleged and admitted. In this mode, however, sentimentalists might argue or whine away the whole body of crimes and punishments. It is the duty of every true friend of humanity and order, to protest against perverted sensibilities or sophistical refinements, which find warrant or apology for depraved appetites,—for the worst distemperature of the mind, and the most fatal catastrophes,—in natural propension, and unrestrained feeling. Spurious sympathy is a more prolific evil than sanguinary rigor, useless and pernicious as the latter is, in our humble opinion. Public executions do more harm than good,—but are not worse than morbid public commiseration and entreaty for criminals, to whom the real justice of the law has been applied, after fair and merciful trial. . . .

Many of the worst criminals, who, in different ages and countries, have justly suffered ignominious death on the wheel, the block, or the gallows, were men of "extraordinary character," of singular acuteness, of the most decided spirit. To acknowledge this fact is not to applaud their conduct, or admire their general ultimate character. . . .

We have constantly remembered what we early read in the works of Mr. Burke, that it is the propensity of degenerate minds to admire or worship *splendid wickedness;* that, with too many persons, the ideas of justice and morality are fairly conquered and overpowered by guilt when it is grown gigantic, and happens to be associated with the lustre of genius, the glare of fashion, or the robes of power. Against this species of degeneracy or illusion it has been our uniform endeavor to guard ourselves, and our conscientious practice to warn and exhort others. The integrity and delicacy of the moral sense, whether in individuals or communities, form a most important subject of the care of all public writers and speakers, in all transactions by which, or the history or treatment of which, the public judgment and feelings may be affected. Hence, when mail robbers or murderers are to be tried or executed, we should be disposed to avoid all extraordinary bustle, or concern, or voluminous details about their fate; we should deem it the true policy of practical ethics to abstain from everything calculated to produce adventitious interest or consequence for the culprits. It is not with pleasure that we hear of the crowds that besiege the door of the court-room, or see in the newspapers the many columns of evidence, with an endless repetition of trifling circumstances, any more than we can rejoice for the cause of moral and social order when convicted highwaymen or murderers are carried to the gallows as *saints*, and hung amidst vast assemblages, either merely indulging a callous curiosity, or losing all the horror of their offences in emotions of compassion or admiration, awakened by the dramatic nature of the whole scene.

Thomas S. Grimke,[1] *1786–1834.*

From "Addresses, Scientific and Literary."

154. Literary Excellence of the English Bible.

The translation of the Bible, in the reign of James I., is the most remarkable and interesting event in the history of translations. . . . The great excellence of the translation is due to six considerations. *First*, it was made under a very solemn sense of the important duty devolved on those who were thus selected. Hence arose that prevailing air of dignity, gravity, simplicity, which is so conspicuous. *Secondly*, the translators came to the task looking to the *thoughts*, not to the *style*. Their object was not that of all other translators, to imitate and rival the beauty of *style*. Their sole object was to render faithfully, and in a plain, appropriate style, the *thoughts* of the sacred

[1] A native of South Carolina, distinguished in the law and in literature.

writers. Hence they became *thoroughly imbued with the spirit* of the original, and gave an incomparably better version of the Hebrew and Greek Testaments than any or all of them together could have done of any classic. Had each of them left us translations of some classic, I hesitate not to say they would not now have been found in any library but as mere curiosities. *Thirdly*, the number of persons employed contributed very much to prevent any *personal* style from prevailing, and gave to the whole an air of plain, simple uniformity. *Fourthly*, the era was providential in one important view. As the translation was made before all the bitterness of sectarian spirit distracted the English Protestant church, it was executed far less with a view to party differences than could have been the case at any time afterwards. *Fifthly*, fortunately the only great religious difference that could have affected it was the dispute with the Catholic church, and, as to that, all Protestants were agreed in England on every important point. *Sixthly*, the English language was then at the happiest stage of its progress, with all the strength, simplicity, and clearness of the elder literature, whilst, at the same time, it was free from the cant of the age of Charles I. and Cromwell, from the vulgarity and levity of that of Charles II., and from the artificial character of that of Anne.

Such a translation is an illustrious monument of the age, the nation, the language. It is, properly speaking, less a translation than an original, having most of the merit of the *former* as to *style*, and all the merit of the *latter* as to *thought*. It is the noblest, best, most finished classic of the English tongue.

Henry C. Carey, 1793–. (Manual, p. 504.)

From "Principles of Social Science."

155. AGRICULTURE AS A SCIENCE.

THAT agriculture may become a science, it is indispensable that man always repay to the great bank from which he has drawn his food, the debt he thereby has contracted. The earth, as has been already said, gives nothing, but is ready to lend everything; and when the debts are punctually repaid, each successive loan is made on a larger scale; but when the debtor fails in punctuality, his credit declines, and the loans are gradually diminished, until at length he is turned out from house and home. No truth in the whole range of science is more readily susceptible of proof than that the community which limits itself to the exportation of raw produce must end by the exportation of men, and those men the slaves of nature, even when not actually bought and sold by their fellow men.

. . . With the growth of commerce, the necessity for moving commodities back and forth steadily declines, with constant improvement in the machinery of transportation, and diminution in the risk of losses of the kind that are covered by insurance against dangers of the sea, or those of fire. The treasures of the earth then become developed, and stone and iron take the place of wood in all constructions, while the exchanges between the miner of coal and of iron—of the man who quarries the granite, and him who raises the food—rapidly increase in quantity, and diminish the necessity for resorting to the distant market.

Edmund Ruffin, 1793-1865.

From "An Essay on Calcareous Manures."

156. Improvement of Acid Soils.

Nearly all the woodland now remaining in lower Virginia, and also much of the land which has long been arable, is rendered unproductive by acidity; and successive generations have toiled on such land, almost without remuneration, and without suspecting that their worst virgin land was then richer than their manured lots appeared to be. The cultivator of such soil, who knows not its peculiar disease, has no other prospect than a gradual decrease of his always scanty crops. But if the evil is once understood, and the means of its removal are within his reach, he has reason to rejoice that his soil was so constituted as to be preserved from the effects of the improvidence of his forefathers, who would have worn out any land not almost indestructible. The presence of acid, by restraining the productive powers of the soil, has, in a great measure, saved it from exhaustion; and after a course of cropping, which would have utterly ruined soils much better constituted, the powers of our acid land remain not greatly impaired, though dormant, and ready to be called into action by merely being relieved of its acid quality. A few crops will reduce a new acid field to so low a rate of product, that it scarcely will pay for its cultivation; but no great change is afterwards caused by continuing scourging tillage and grazing, for fifty years longer. Thus our acid soils have two remarkable and opposite qualities,—both proceeding from the same cause; they can neither be enriched by manure, nor impoverished by cultivation, to any great extent. Qualities so remarkable deserve all our powers of investigation; yet their very frequency seems to have caused them to be overlooked; and our writers on agriculture have continued to urge those who seek improvement, to apply precepts drawn from English authors, to soils which are totally different from all those for which their instructions were intended.

Francis Wayland, 1796–1865. (Manual, pp. 487, 502, 504.)

From "The Limitations of Human Responsibility."

157. Superiority of the Moral Sentiments.

It is a common remark, that, whenever it has been thought necessary to arouse the mind of man to enterprises of great pith and moment, the appeal has always been made to his moral sentiments. Hence, among the most ancient nations, it was the invariable custom to accompany the declaration of war with religious ceremonies; and if, in later times, this custom has become somewhat less usual, the change itself, in a more remarkable manner, illustrates the tendency of our nature. . . . But let victory declare for the assailed, let the invader become the invaded, let it become necessary to stimulate men to put forth the highest effort of human daring, and the sacred names of conscience, of duty to family, to country, and to God, are universally invoked, and the Supreme Being is urgently appealed to, to succor the cause of a sinking commonwealth. It is, perhaps, worth while to remark, in passing, that this consciousness of right is a source of power which belongs specially to the oppressed, and which, other things being equal, will always insure to them the victory; and, when other things are not equal, it is frequently sufficient, of itself, to outweigh a vast preponderance of physical force. It is, morever, efficient in proportion to the purity of the moral principle of a people. We hence perceive the elements of superiority which, by the constitution of our nature, have been bestowed upon virtue.

Another illustration of the power of the moral principle, is seen in the sentiments with which we contemplate the character of confessors, martyrs, and men of every age, who have sacrificed every thing else for the sake of adherence to righteousness. The highest glory of human nature is to love right better than life, and to obey the dictates of conscience at every conceivable hazard. Even falsehood, when sealed with blood, acquires not unfrequently, for a time, an irrepressible power. Truth, when uttered from the stake, or on the scaffold, becomes absolutely irresistible. We admire Plato, surrounded by listening princes, and vieing with them in oriental magnificence; but we venerate Socrates in his dungeon, patiently suffering death for holding forth the truth; and the dictates of our own bosoms spontaneously assign to him the highest place among the uninspired teachers of wisdom. Or, to turn to more awful examples, the foundations of the Christian religion were laid in blood. The Captain of our salvation "was obedient unto death, the death of the cross." The martyrdoms of the early age of the church gave to the world examples of the love of right, of which it had never before conceived even the possibility, and thus set on foot a moral reformation, which is destined to work in the character of man a universal transformation.

Horace Mann, 1796–1859. (Manual, p. 532.)

From "Lectures on various Subjects."

158. Thoughts for a Young Man.

In this country most young men are poor. Time is the rock from which they are to hew out their fortunes; and health, enterprise, and integrity, the instruments with which to do it. For this, diligence in business, abstinence from pleasures, privation even, of everything that does not endanger health, are to be joyfully welcomed and borne. When we look around us, and see how much of the wickedness of the world springs from poverty, it seems to sanctify all honest efforts for the acquisition of an independence; but when an independence is acquired, then comes the moral crisis, then comes an Ithuriel test, which shows whether a man is higher than a common man, or lower than a common reptile. In the duty of accumulation—and I call it a *duty*, in the most strict and literal signification of that word—all below a competence is most valuable, and its acquisition most laudable; but all above a fortune is a misfortune. It is a misfortune to him who amasses it; for it is a voluntary continuance in the harness of a beast of burden, when the soul should enfranchise and lift itself up into a higher region of pursuits and pleasures. It is a persistence in the work of providing goods for the body after the body has already been provided for; and it is a denial of the higher demands of the soul, after the time has arrived, and the means are possessed, of fulfilling those demands. . . Because the lower service was once necessary, and has, therefore, been performed, it is a mighty wrong, when, without being longer necessary, it usurps the sacred rights of the higher.

Orestes A. Brownson, 1800–. (Manual, p. 480.)

From "New Views."

159. The Duty of Progress.

Progress is the end for which man was made. To this end it is his duty to direct all his enquiries, all his systems of religion and philosophy, all his institutions of politics and society, all the productions of his genius and taste, in one word, all the modes of his activity. This is his duty. Hitherto, he has performed it but blindly, without knowing, and without admitting it. Humanity has but to-day, as it were, risen to self-consciousness, to a perception of its own capacity, to a glimpse of its inconceivably grand and holy destiny. Heretofore it has failed to recognize clearly its duty. It has advanced, but not designedly. not with foresight; it has done it instinctively, by the aid of the invisible but safe-guiding hand of its Father. Without knowing what it did, it has condemned progress while it was progressing. It has stoned the prophets and reformers, even while it was itself reforming and uttering glorious prophecies of its future condition. But the time has now come for humanity to understand itself, to accept the law imposed upon it for its own good, to foresee its end, and march with intention steadily towards it. Its future religion is the religion of progress. The true priests are those who can quicken in mankind a desire for progress, and urge them forward in the direction of the true, the good, the perfect.

From "The Convert."

160. Politics of Catholic Europe in the Seventeenth Century despotic.

In France, Spain, Portugal, and a large part of Italy, all through the seventeenth century, the youth were trained in the maxim, The prince is the State, and his pleasure is law. Bossuet, in his politics, did only faithfully express the political sentiments and convictions of his age, shared by the great body of Catholics as well as of non-Catholics. Rational liberty had few defenders, and they were exiled, like Fénelon, from the court. The politics of Philip II. of Spain, of Richelieu, Mazarin, and Louis XIV. in France, which were the politics of Catholic Europe, hardly opposed, except by the popes, through the greater part of the sixteenth and the whole of the seventeenth centuries, tended directly to enslave the people, and to restrict the freedom and efficiency of the church. Had either Philip, or, after him, Louis, succeeded, by linking the Catholic cause to his personal ambition, in realizing his dream of universal monarchy, Europe would most likely have been plunged into a political and social condition as unenviable as that into which old Asia has been plunged for these four hundred years; and it may well be believed that it was Providence that raised and directed the tempest that scattered the Grand Armada, and that gave victory to the arms of Eugene and Marlborough.

Theodore Dwight Woolsey, 1801–.

From his "Introduction to the Study of International Law."

161. IMPORTANCE OF THE STUDY.

FROM all that has been said it has become apparent that the study of international law is important, as an index of civilization, and not to the student of law only, but to the student of history. In our land, especially, it is important, on more than one account, that this science should do its share in enlightening educated minds. One reason for this lies in the new inducements which we, as a people, have to swerve from national rectitude. Formerly our interests threw us on the side of unrestricted commerce, which is the side towards which justice inclines, and we lived far within our borders with scarcely the power to injure or be injured, except on the ocean. Now we are running into the crimes to which strong nations are liable. Our diplomatists unblushingly moot the question of taking foreign territory by force if it cannot be purchased; our executive prevents piratical expeditions against the lands of neighboring States as feebly and slowly as if it connived at them; we pick quarrels to gain conquests; and at length, after more than half a century of public condemnation of the slave-trade, after being the first to brand it as piracy, we hear the revival of the trade advocated as a right, as a necessity. Is it not desirable that the sense of justice, which seems fading out of the national mind before views of political expediency or destiny, should be deepened and made fast by that study which frowns on national crimes?

And, again, every educated person ought to become acquainted with national law, because he is a responsible member of the body politic; because there is danger that party views will make our doctrine in this science fluctuating, unless it is upheld by large numbers of intelligent persons; and because the executive, if not controlled, will be tempted to assume the province of interpreting international law for us. As it regards the latter point it may be said, that while Congress has power to define offences against the laws of nations, and thus, if any public power, to pronounce authoritatively what the law of nations is, the executive through the Secretary of State, in practice, gives the lead in all international questions. In this way the Monroe doctrine appeared; in this way most other positions have been advanced; and perhaps this could not be otherwise. But we ought to remember that the supreme executives in Europe have amassed power by having diplomatic relations in their hands, that thus the nation may become involved in war against its will, and that the prevention of evils must lie, if there be any, with the men who have been educated in the principles of international justice.

I close this treatise here, hoping that it may be of some use to my native land, and to young men who may need a guide in the science of which it treats.

Taylor Lewis, 1802–.[1]

From "The Six Days of Creation."

162. UNITY OF THE MOSAIC ACCOUNT.

ANOTHER striking trait of the Mosaic cosmogony is its unbroken wholeness or unity. . . . Be it invention or inspiration, it is the invention or the inspiration of one mind. Other cosmogonies, though bearing unmistakable evidence of their descent from the Mosaic, have had successive deposits, in successive series, of mythological strata. This stands towering out in lonely sublimity, like the everlasting granite of the Alps or the Himalaya, as compared with the changing alluvium of the Nile or the Ganges. As the serene air that ever surrounds the head of Mont Blanc excels in purity the mists of the fen, so does the lofty theism of the Mosaic account rise high above the nature-worship of the Egyytian and Hesiodean theogonies. "In the beginning God made the heavens and the earth. And the earth was waste and void, and darkness was upon the face of the deep. And the Spirit of God brooded over the waters. And God said, Let there be light, and it was light. And God saw the light that it was fair, and God divided the light from the darkness. And thus there was an evening and a morning—one day!" What is there like it, or to be at all compared with it, in any mythology on earth? There it stands, high above them all, and remote from them all, in its air of great antiquity, in its unaccountableness, in its serene truthfulness, in its unapproachable sublimity, in that impress of divine majesty and ineffable holiness which even the unbelieving neologist has been compelled to acknowledge, and by which every devout reader feels that the first page in Genesis is forever distinguished from any mere human production.

[1] Born in New York; a prolific writer, eminent for his profound scholarship, his wide acquaintance with Oriental and Biblical literature, and his originality and freedom of mind: long Professor of Greek in Union College.

From "State Rights."

163. Cruel Intestine Wars caused by National Division.

If it were Death alone! But "Hell follows hard after." What a heaving Tartarus was Greece, when all hope of a true nationality was given up! From Corcyra to Rhodes, from Byzantium to Cyrene, one bloody scene of faction, "sedition, privy conspiracy, and rebellion." In the cities, in the isles, in the colonies, banishments, confiscations, ostracisms, and cruel deaths. The most ferocious parties everywhere, fomented in the smaller States by the influence of the larger, and kept alive in the leading cities by the continual presence of foreign emissaries. With us it would be far more like Satan's kingdom, inasmuch as our states are more numerous, relatively more petty, and, from the increased powers of modern knowledge and modern invention, capable of the greater mutual mischief.

We are not prophesying at random. Here is our old guide-book. The road is all mapped out, the way surveyed, by which we march to ruin. All the dire calamities of Greece may be traced to this word autonomia.[1]

. . . Greece presented the first great proof of a fact of which we are now in danger of furnishing another and more terrible example to the world. It is the utter impossibility of peace, in a territory made by nature a geographical unity, inhabited by a people, or peoples, of one lineage, one language, bound together in historical reminiscences, yet divided into petty sovereign States too small for any respectable nationalities themselves, and yet preventing any beneficent nationality as a whole. No animosities have been so fierce as those existing among people thus geographically and politically related. No wars with each other have been so cruel; no home factions have been so incessant, so treacherous, and so debasing. The very ties that draw them near only awaken occasions of strife, which would not have existed between tribes wholly alien to each other in language and religion.

[1] State sovereignty.

Horace Greeley,[1] *1811-1873.*

From a "Lecture on the Emancipation of Labor."

164. THE PROBLEM OF LABOR.

The worker of the nineteenth century stands a sad and care-worn man. Once in a while a particular flowery Fourth of July oration, political harangue, or Thanksgiving sermon, catching him well filled with creature comforts, and a little inclined to soar starward, will take him off his feet, and for an hour or two he will wonder if ever human lot was so blessed as that of the free-born American laborer. He hurrahs, and is ready to knock any man down who will not readily and heartily agree that this is a great country, and our industrious classes the happiest people on earth. . . . The hallucination passes off, however, with the silvery tones of the orator, and the exhilarating fumes of the liquor which inspired it. The inhaler of the bewildering gas bends his slow steps at length to his sorry domicile, or wakes therein on the morrow, in a sober and practical mood. His very exaltation, now past, has rendered him more keenly susceptible to the deficiencies and impediments which hem him in: his house seems narrow, his food coarse, his furniture scanty, his prospects gloomy, and those of his children more sombre, if possible; and as he hurries off to the day's task which he has too long neglected, and for which he has little heart, he too falls into that train of thought which is beginning to encircle the globe, and of which the burden may be freely rendered thus: "Why should those by whose toil all comforts and luxuries are produced, or made available, enjoy so scanty a share of them? Why should a man able and eager to work, ever stand idle for want of employment in a world where so much needful work impatiently awaits the doing? Why should a man be required to surrender something of his independence, in accepting the employment which will enable him to earn by honest effort the bread of his family? Why should the man

[1] The well-known journalist of New York; conspicuous for his many writings on social and political reform, his reminiscences, &c.; a native of New Hampshire.

who faithfully labors for another, and receives therefor less than the product of his labor, be currently held the obliged party, rather than he who buys the work and makes a good bargain of it? In short, why should Speculation and Scheming ride so jauntily in their carriages, splashing honest Work as it trudges humbly and wearily by on foot?" Such, as I interpret it, is the problem which occupies and puzzles the knotted brain of Toil in our day.

—

From an Address on Success in Business.

165. The Beneficence of Labor-Saving Inventions.

There is, if not an ever-increasing need, an ever-increasing consciousness of need, of labor-saving inventions and machinery. And, if those inventions should render labor twenty times as productive as it is to-day, should make this a general rule, that all human labor shall produce twenty times as much as it does to-day—there would be no glut of products, as so many mistakenly apprehend. There would only be a very much fuller and broader satisfaction of human needs. Our wants are infinite. They expand and dilate on every side, according to our means—often very much in advance of our means,—of satisfying them. If labor shall become—as I doubt not it will become at an early day, far more productive, far more effective, than it is now, we shall hear nothing like a complaint that there are no more wants to be satisfied, but the contrary. And yet, we know the fact is deplorably true, that the time is scarcely yet remote when the laboring class, distinctively so called, set its face resolutely against new inventions—set to work deliberately to destroy labor-saving machinery, and so to act as more and more to throw labor back into the barbaric period when probably every yard of cloth cost a day's labor, as did every bushel of grain. England herself, it is computed now does the work, by means of steam and machinery, of eight hundred millions of men. And yet English wants are no more satisfied to-day than they were a thousand years ago. I do not say they are altogether unsatisfied ; but I say that the consciousness of want, the demand for products, is just as keen to-day; and I have not a doubt that if inventions could be introduced into China whereby the labor of her people should be rendered fifty times as effective as it is to-day, you would find not a dearth of employment as a consequence, but rather an increase of activity and an increased demand for labor. To-day British capital and British talent are fairly grid-ironing the ancient plains and slopes of Hindostan with British canals, irrigating, and railroads. It is their *gold* they say; but it is not British capital, so much as British genius and British confidence, that are required. There is wealth enough in India, more gold and silver and gems, probably to-day than in Europe, for the precious metals always flow thither, and they very seldom flow thence.

—

From "Recollections of a Busy Life."

166. LITERATURE AS A VOCATION; THE EDITOR.

No other public teacher lives so wholly in the present, as the Editor; and the noblest affirmations of unpopular truth,—the most self-sacrificing defiance of a base and selfish Public Sentiment that regards only the most sordid ends, and values every utterance solely as it tends to preserve quiet and contentment, while the dollars fall jingling into the merchant's drawer, the land-jobber's vault, and the miser's bag,—can but be noted in their day, and with their day forgotten. It is his cue to utter silken and smooth sayings,—to condemn Vice so as not to interfere with the pleasures, or alarm the consciences of the vicious,—to praise and champion Liberty so as not to give annoyance or offence to Slavery, and to commend and glorify Labor without attempting to expose or repress any of the gainful contrivances by which Labor is plundered and degraded. Thus sidling dexterously between somewhere and nowhere, the Able Editor of the Nineteenth Century may glide through life respectable and in good case, and lie down to his long rest with the non-achievements of his life emblazoned on the very whitest marble, surmounting and glorifying his dust.

There is a different and sterner path,—I know not whether there be any now qualified to tread it,—I am not sure that even one has ever followed it implicitly, in view of the certain meagerness of its temporal rewards, and the haste wherewith any fame acquired in a sphere so thoroughly ephemeral as the Editor's, must be shrouded by the dark waters of oblivion. This path demands an ear ever open to the plaints of the wronged and the suffering, though they can never repay advocacy, and those who mainly support newspapers will be annoyed and often exposed by it; a heart as sensitive to oppression and degradation in the next street as if they were practised in Brazil or Japan; a pen as ready to expose and reprove the crimes whereby wealth is amassed and luxury enjoyed in our own country at this hour, as if they had only been committed by Turks or Pagans in Asia, some centuries ago. Such an Editor, could one be found or trained, need not expect to lead an easy, indolent, or wholly joyous life,—to be blessed by Archbishops, or followed by the approving shouts of ascendant majorities; but he might find some recompense for their loss, in the calm verdict of an approving conscience; and the tears of the despised and the friendless, preserved from utter despair by his efforts and remonstrances, might freshen for a season the daisies that bloomed above his grave.

—

From "The Crystal Palace and its Lessons."

167. Tranquility of Rural Life.

As for me, long tossed on the stormiest waves of doubtful conflict and arduous endeavor, I have begun to feel, since the shades of forty years fell upon me, the weary tempest-driven voyager's longing for land, the wanderer's yearning for the hamlet where in childhood he nestled by his mother's knee, and was soothed to sleep on her breast. The sober down-hill of life dispels many illusions, while it developes or strengthens within us the attachment, perhaps long smothered or overlaid, for "that dear hut, our home." And so I, in the sober afternoon of life, when its sun, if not high, is still warm, have bought me a few acres of land in the broad, still country, and bearing thither my household treasures, have resolved to steal from the city's labors and anxieties at least one day in each week, wherein to revive as a farmer, the memories of my childhood's humble home. And already I realize that the experiment cannot cost so much as it is worth. Already I find in that day's quiet, an antidote and a solace for the feverish, festering cares of the weeks which environ it. Already, my brook murmurs a soothing even-song to my burning, throbbing brain; and my trees, gently stirred by the fresh breezes, whisper to my spirit something of their own quiet strength and patient trust in God. And thus do I faintly realize, though but for a brief and flitting day, the serene joy which shall irradiate the Farmer's vocation, when a fuller and truer education shall have refined and chastened his animal cravings, and when Science shall have endowed him with her treasures, redeeming Labor from drudgery, while quadrupling its efficiency, and crowning with beauty and plenty our bounteous, beneficent Earth.

Theodore Parker, about *1812-1860.*

(Manual, p. 531.)

From "Lessons from the World of Nature," &c.

168. WINTER AND SPRING.

IN the hard, cold winter of our northern lands, how do we feel a longing for the presence of life! Then we love to look on a pine or fir tree, which seems the only living thing in the woods, surrounded by dead oaks, birches, maples, looking like the gravestones of buried vegetation: that seems warm and living then; and at Christmas, men bring it into meeting-houses and parlors, and set it up, full of life, and laden with kindly gifts for the little folk. Then even the unattractive crow seems half sacred, through the winter bearing messages of promise from the perished autumn to the advancing spring—this dark forerunner of the tuneful tribes which are to come. We feel a longing for fresh, green nature, and so in the shelter of our houses keep some little Aaron's rod, budding alike with promise and memory; or in some hyacinth or Dutchman's tulip we keep a prophecy of flowers, and start off some little John to run before, and with his half-gospel tell of some great Emmanuel, and signify to men that the kingdom of heavenly beauty is near at hand. Now that forerunner disappears, for the desire of all nations has truly come; the green grass is creeping everywhere, and it is spangled with many flowers that came unasked. . . .

What if there was a spring time of blossoming but once in a hundred years! How would men look forward to it, and old men, who had beheld its wonders, tell the story to their children, how once all the homely trees became beautiful, and earth was covered with freshness and new growth! How would young men hope to become old, that they might see so glad a sight! And when beheld, the aged man would say, "Lord, now lettest thou thy servant depart in peace, for mine eyes have seen thy salvation."

—

From an "Installation Sermon," January 4th, 1846.

169. The True Idea of a Christian Church.

The saints of olden time perished at the stake; they hung on gibbets; they agonized upon the rack; they died under the steel of the tormentor. It was the heroism of our fathers' day that swam the unknown seas; froze in the woods; starved with want and cold; fought battles with the red right hand. It is the sainthood and heroism of our day that toils for the ignorant, the poor, the weak, the oppressed, the wicked. Yes, it is our saints and heroes who fight fighting; who contend for the slave, and his master too, for the drunkard, the criminal; yes, for the wicked or the weak in all their forms. . . . But the saints and the heroes of this day, who draw no sword, whose right hand is never bloody, who burn in no fires of wood or sulphur, nor languish briefly on the hasty cross; the saints and heroes who, in a worldly world, dare to be men; in an age of conformity and selfishness, speak for Truth and Man, living for noble aims, men who will swear to no lies howsoever popular; who will honor no sins, though never so profitable, respectable, and ancient; men who count Christ not their master, but teacher, friend, brother, and strive like him to practice all they pray; to incarnate and make real the Word of God, these men I honor far more than the saints of old. . . . Racks and fagots soon waft the soul to God, stern messengers, but swift. A boy could bear that passage,—the martyrdom of death. But the temptation of a long life of neglect, and scorn, and obloquy, and shame, and want, and desertion by false friends; to live blameless though blamed, cut off from human sympathy, that is the martyrdom of to-day. I shed no tears for such martyrs. I shout when I see one; I take courage and thank God for the real saints, prophets and heroes of to-day. . . . Yea, though now men would steal the rusty sword from underneath the bones of a saint or hero long deceased, to smite off therewith the head of a new prophet, that ancient hero's son; though they would gladly crush the heart out of him with the tombstones they piled up for great men, dead and honored now; yet in some future day, that mob penitent, baptized with a new spirit, like drunken men returned to sanity once more, shall search through all this land for marble white enough to build a monument to that prophet whom their fathers slew; they shall seek through all the world for gold of fineness fit to chronicle such names. I cannot wait; but I will honor such men now, not adjourn the warning of their voice, and the glory of their example, till another age! The church may cast out such men; burn them with the torments of an age too refined in its cruelty to use coarse fagots and the vulgar axe! It is no loss to these men; but the ruin of the church. I say the Christian church of the nineteenth century must honor such men, if it would do a church's work; must take pains to make such men as these, or it is a dead church, with no claim on us, except that we bury it. A true church will always be the church of martyrs. The ancients commenced every great work with a victim! We do not call it so; but the sacrifice is demanded, got ready, and offered by unconscious priests long ere the enterprise succeeds. Did not Christianity begin with a martyrdom?

—

From "Historic Americans."

170. Character of Franklin.

His was the morality of a strong, experienced person, who had seen the folly of wise men, the meanness of proud men, the baseness of honorable men, and the littleness of great men, and made liberal allowances for the failures of all men. If the final end to be reached were just, he did not always inquire about the provisional means which led thither. He knew that the right line is the shortest distance between two points, in morals as in mathematics, but yet did not quarrel with such as attained the point by a crooked line. Such is the habit of politicians, diplomatists, statesmen, who look on all men as a commander looks on his soldiers, and does not ask them to join the church or keep their hands clean, but to stand to their guns and win the battle.

Thus, in the legislature of Pennsylvania, Franklin found great difficulty in carrying on the necessary measures for military defence, because a majority of the Assembly were Quakers, who, though friendly to the success of the revolution founded contrary to their principles, refused to vote the supplies of war. So he caused them to vote appropriations to purchase bread, flour, wheat, *or other grain.* The Government said, "I shall take the money, for I understand very well their meaning,—other grain is gunpowder." He afterwards moved the purchase of a fire-engine, saying to his friend, "Nominate me on the committee, and I will nominate you; we will buy a great gun, which is certainly a fire engine; the Quakers can have no objection to that."

Such was the course of policy that Franklin took, as I think, to excess; but yet I believe that no statesman of that whole century did so much to embody the eternal rules of right in the customs of the people, and to make the constitution of the universe the common law of all mankind; and I cannot bestow higher praise than that, on any man whose name I can recall. He mitigated the ferocities of war. He built new hospitals, and improved old ones. He first introduced this humane principle into the Law of Nations, that in time of war, private property on land shall be unmolested, and peaceful commerce continued, and captive soldiers treated as well as the soldiers of the captors. Generous during his life-time, his dead hand still gathers and distributes blessings to the mechanics of Boston, and their children. True is it that

"Him only pleasure leads and peace attends,
Whose means are pure and spotless as his ends."

But it is a great thing in this stage of the world to find a man whose *ends* are pure and spotless. Let us thank him for that.

From "Historic Americans."

171. CHARACTER OF THOMAS JEFFERSON.

OF all those who controlled the helm of affairs during the time of the Revolution, and while the Constitution and the forms of our National and State Institutions were carefully organized, there is none who has been more generally popular, more commonly beloved, more usually believed to be necessary to the Legislation and Administration of his country, than Thomas Jefferson. It may not be said of him that of all those famous men he could least have been spared; for in the rare and great qualities for patiently and wisely conducting the vast affairs of State and Nation in pressing emergencies, he seems to have been wanting. But his grand merit was this—that while his powerful opponents favored a strong government, and believed it necessary thereby to repress what they called the lower classes, he, Jefferson, believed in Humanity; believed in a true Democracy. He respected labor and education, and upheld the right to education of all men. These were the Ideas in which he was far in advance of all the considerable men, whether of his State or of his Nation—ideas which he illustrated through long years of his life and conduct. The great debt that the Nation owes to him is this—that he so ably and consistently advocated these needful opinions, that he made himself the head and the hand of the great party that carried these ideas into power, that put an end to all possibility of class-government, made naturalization easy, extended the suffrage and applied it to judicial office, opened a still wider and better education to all, and quietly inaugurated reforms, yet incomplete, of which we have the benefit to this day, and which, but for him, we might not have won against the party of Strong Government, except by a difficult and painful Revolution.

Wendell Phillips,[1] *1811-.*

From "A Lecture delivered in December, 1861."

172. The War for the Union.

I would have government announce to the world that we understand the evil which has troubled our peace for seventy years, thwarting the natural tendency of our institutions, sending ruin along our wharves and through our workshops every ten years, poisoning the national conscience. We know well its character. But democracy, unlike other governments, is strong enough to let evils work out their own death — strong enough to face them when they reveal their proportions. It

[1] A native of Massachusetts: a vigorous thinker and speaker on the great moral and political topics of the day, and the most eloquent of the Anti-Slavery leaders.

was in this sublime consciousness of strength, not of weakness, that our fathers submitted to the well-known evil of slavery, and tolerated it until the viper we thought we could safely tread on, at the touch of disappointment, starts up a fiend whose stature reaches the sky. But our cheeks do not blanch. Democracy accepts the struggle. After this forbearance of three generations, confident that she has yet power to execute her will, she sends her proclamation down to the Gulf — freedom to every man beneath the stars, and death to every institution that disturbs our peace, or threatens the future of the republic.

From His "Speeches, Lectures," &c.

173. CHARACTER OF TOUSSAINT L'OUVERTURE.

ABOVE the lust of gold, pure in private life, generous in the use of his power, it was against such a man that Napoleon sent his army, giving to General Leclerc,— the husband of his beautiful sister Pauline,— thirty thousand of his best troops, with orders to re-introduce slavery. Among these soldiers came all of Toussaint's old mulatto rivals and foes.

* * * * * * *

Mounting his horse, and riding to the eastern end of the island, Samana, he looked out on a sight such as no native had ever seen before. Sixty ships of the line, crowded by the best soldiers of Europe, rounded the point. They were soldiers who had never yet met an equal, whose tread, like Cæsar's, had shaken Europe,— soldiers who had scaled the Pyramids, and planted the French banners on the walls of Rome. He looked a moment, counted the flotilla, let the reins fall on the neck of his horse, and, turning to Christophe, exclaimed: "All France is come to Hayti; they can only come to make us slaves; and we are lost." He then recognized the only mistake of his life,— his confidence in Bonaparte, which had led him to disband his army.

Returning to the hills, he issued the only proclamation which bears his name and breathes vengeance: "My children, France comes to make us slaves. God gave us liberty; France has no right to take it away. Burn the cities, destroy the harvests, tear up the roads with cannon, poison the wells, show the white man the hell he comes to make"; and he was obeyed. When the great William of Orange saw Louis XIV. cover Holland with troops, he said, "Break down the dykes, give Holland back to ocean"; and Europe said, "Sublime!" When Alexander saw the armies of France descend upon Russia, he said: "Burn Moscow, starve back the invaders"; and Europe said, "Sublime!" This black saw all Europe marshalled to crush him, and gave to his people the same heroic example of defiance.

Thomas Starr King, 1824-1864.

(Manual, p. 532.)

From "Patriotism and other Papers."

174. GREAT PRINCIPLES AND SMALL DUTIES.

IF we go to Nature for our morals, we shall learn the necessity of perfection in the smallest act. Infinite skill is not exhausted nor concentrated in the structure of a firmament, in drawing the orbit of a planet, in laying the strata of the earth, in rearing the mountain cone. The care for the bursting flower is as wise as the forces displayed in the rolling star; the smallest leaf that falls and dies unnoticed in the forest is wrought with a beauty as exquisite as the skill displayed in the sturdy oak. All the wisdom of Nature is compressed and revealed in the sting of the bee; and the pride of human art is mocked by the subtile mechanism and cunning structure of a fly's foot and wing. However minute the task, it reveals the polish of perfection. Omnipotent skill is stamped on the infinitely small, as on the infinitely great. It is a moral stenography like this which we need in daily life. . . .

The lesson of Christianity, then, urged and enforced by Nature, is the inestimable worth of common duties, as manifesting the greatest principles; it bids us attain perfection, not by striving to do dazzling deeds, but by making our experience divine; it tells us that the Christian hero will ennoble the humblest field of labor; that nothing is mean which can be performed as duty; but that religious virtue, like the touch of Midas, converts the humblest call of conscience into spiritual gold.

The Greek philosopher, Plato, has left an instructive and beautiful poetic picture of the judgment of souls, when they had been collected from the regions of temporary bliss and pain, and suffered once more to return to the duties and pleasures of earthly life. The spirits advanced by lot, to make their choice of the condition and form under which they should re-enter the world. The dazzling and showy fortunes, the lives of kings and warriors and statesmen were soon exhausted; and the spirit of Ulysses, who had been the wisest prince among all the Greeks, came last to choose. He advanced with sorrow, fearing that his favorite condition had been selected by some more fortunate soul who had gone before him. But, to his surprise and pleasure, Ulysses found that the only life which had not been chosen was the lot of an obscure and private man, with its humble cares and quiet joys; the lot which he, the wisest, would have selected, had his turn come first; the life for which he had longed, since he had felt the folly and meanness of station, wealth, and power. . . .

CHAPTER III.

GENERAL AND POLITE LITERATURE.

William Wirt, 1772-1834. (Manual, pp. 487, 490.)

From the "Life of Patrick Henry."

175. HENRY'S EXAMPLE NO ARGUMENT FOR INDOLENCE.

I CANNOT learn that he gave in his youth any evidence of that precocity which sometimes distinguishes uncommon genius. His companions recollect no instance of premature wit, no striking sentiment, no flash of fancy, no remarkable beauty or strength of expression, and no indication however slight, either of that impassioned love of liberty, or of that adventurous daring and intrepidity, which marked so strongly his future character. So far was he indeed from exhibiting any one prognostic of this greatness, that every omen foretold a life at best, of mediocrity, if not of insignificance. His person is represented as having been coarse, his manners uncommonly awkward, his dress slovenly, his conversation very plain, his aversion to study invincible, and his faculties almost entirely benumbed by indolence. No persuasion could bring him either to read or to work. On the contrary, he ran wild in the forest like one of the *Aborigines* of the country, and divided his life between the dissipation and uproar of the chase, and the languor of inaction.

His propensity to observe and comment upon the human character, was, so far as I can learn, the only circumstance which distinguished him advantageously from his youthful companions. This propensity seems to have been born with him, and to have exerted itself instinctively, the moment that a new subject was presented to his view. Its action was incessant, and it became at length almost the only intellectual exercise in which he seemed to take delight. To this cause, may be traced that consummate knowledge of the human heart which he finally attained, and which enabled him when he came upon the public stage, to touch the springs of passion with a master hand, and to control the resolutions and decisions of his hearers with a power almost more than mortal.

From what has been already stated, it will be seen how little education had to do with the formation of this great man's mind. He was indeed a mere child of nature, and nature seems to have been too proud and too jealous of her work, to permit it to be touched by the hand of art. She gave him Shakespeare's genius, and bade him, like Shakespeare, to depend on that alone. Let not the youthful reader, however, deduce from the example of Mr. Henry, an argument in favor of indolence, and the contempt of study. Let him remember that the powers which surmounted the disadvantage of those early habits, were such as very rarely appear upon this earth. Let him remember, too, how long the genius even of Mr. Henry was kept down, and hidden from the public view, by the sorcery of those pernicious habits; through what years of poverty and wretchedness they doomed him to struggle; and let him remember, that at length, when in the zenith of his glory, Mr. Henry himself, had frequent occasions to deplore the consequences of his early neglect of literature, and to bewail the ghosts of his departed hours.

—

From "Eulogium on Adams and Jefferson."

176. JEFFERSON'S SEAT AT MONTICELLO.

APPROACHING the house on the east, the visitor instinctively paused, to cast around one thrilling glance at this magnificent panorama, and then passed to the vestibule, where, if he had not been previously informed, he would immediately perceive that he was entering the house of no common man. In the spacious and lofty hall which opens before him, he marks no tawdry and unmeaning ornaments, but before, on the right, on the left, all around, the eye is struck and gratified with objects of science and taste, so classed and arranged as to produce their finest effect. On one side, specimens of sculpture set out in such order as to exhibit . . . the historical progress of that art, from the first rude attempts of the aborigines of our country up to that exquisite and finished bust of the great patriot himself, from the master-hand of Ceracchi On the other side, the visitor sees displayed a vast collection of specimens of Indian art—their paintings, weapons, ornaments, and manufactures; on another, an array of the fossil productions of our country, mineral and animal, the polished remains of those colossal monsters that once trod our forests, and are no more; and a variegated display of the branching honors of those "monarchs of the waste," that still people the wilds of the American continent.

From this hall he was ushered into a noble saloon, from which the glorious landscape of the west again bursts upon his view; and which within is hung thick around with the finest productions of the pencil—historical paintings of the most striking subjects from all countries and all ages, the portraits of distinguished men and patriots both of Europe and America, and medallions and engravings in endless profusion.

While the visitor was yet lost in the contemplation of these treasures of the arts and sciences, he was startled by the approach of a strong and sprightly step; and, turning with instinctive reverence to the door of entrance, he was met by the tall, and animated, and stately figure of the patriot himself, his countenance beaming with intelligence and benignity, and his outstretched hand, with its strong and cordial pressure, confirming the courteous welcome of his lips; and then came that charm of manner and conversation that passes all description—so cheerful, so unassuming, so free, and easy, and frank, and kind, and gay, that even the young, and overawed, and embarrassed visitor at once forgot his fears, and felt himself by the side of an old and familiar friend.

Timothy Flint, 1780–1840. (Manual, p. 490.)

From "Recollections of the Mississippi Valley."

177. THE WESTERN BOATMAN.

THERE is no wonder that the way of life which the boatman lead, in turn extremely indolent and extremely laborious, for days together requiring little or no effort, and attended with no danger, and then on a sudden laborious and hazardous beyond the Atlantic navigation, generally plentiful as it regards food, and always so as it regards whiskey, should always have seductions that prove irresistible to the young people that live near the banks of the river. The boats float by their dwellings on beautiful spring mornings, when the verdant forest, the mild and delicious temperature of the air, the delightful azure of the sky of this country, the fine bottom on the one hand, and the romantic bluff on the other, the broad and smooth stream rolling calmly down through the forest, and floating the boat gently forward,—all these circumstances harmonize in the excited youthful imagination. The boatmen are dancing to the violin on the deck of their boat. They scatter their wit among the girls on the shore, who come down to the water's edge to see the pageant pass. The boat glides on until it disappears behind a point of wood; at this moment, perhaps, the bugle, with which all the boats are provided, strikes up its note in the distance, over the water. These scenes, and these notes, echoing from the bluffs of the beautiful Ohio, have a charm for the imagination, which, although I have heard a thousand times repeated, and at all hours, and in all positions, is even to me always new, and always delightful. No wonder that to the young, who are reared in these remote regions, with that restless curiosity which is fostered by solitude and silence, who witness scenes like these so frequently,—no wonder that the severe and unremitting labors of agriculture, performed directly in the view of such scenes, should become tasteless and irksome.

Washington Irving, 1783–1859.

(Manual, pp. 478, 498.)

From "Knickerbocker's History of New York."

178. From "Title and Table of Contents."

A history of New York, from the beginning of the world to the end of the Dutch dynasty, . . . being the only authentic history of the times that ever hath been or ever will be published, by Diedrick Knickerbocker. . . . Book I., chap. i. Description of the World. . . . Book II., chap. i. . . . Also of Master Hendrick Hudson, his discovery of a strange country. . . . Chap. vii. How the people of Pavonia migrated from Communipaw to the Island of Manhattan. . . . Chap. ix. How the city of New Amsterdam waxed great under the protection of St. Nicholas, and the absence of laws and statutes. Book III., chap. iii. How the town of New Amsterdam arose out of mud, and came to be marvellously polished and polite, together with a picture of the manners of our great-great-grandfathers. . . . Book IV., chap. vi. Projects of William the Testy for increasing the currency; he is outwitted by the Yankees. The great Oyster War. . . . Book V., chap. viii. How the Yankee crusade against the New Netherlands was baffled by the sudden outbreak of witchcraft among the people of the East . . . Book VII., chap. ii. How Peter Stuyvesant labored to civilize the community. How he was a great promoter of holydays. How he instituted kissing on New Year's Day. . . . Chap. iii. How troubles thicken on the province. How it is threatened by the Helderbergers,—the Merrylanders, and the Giants of the Susquehanna.

---

179. The Army at New Amsterdam.

First of all came the Van Bummels, who inhabit the pleasant borders of the Bronx. These were short, fat men, wearing exceeding large trunk-breeches, and are renowned for feats of the trencher; they were the first inventors of suppawn, or mush and milk. . . . Lastly came the Knickerbockers, of the great town of Schahticoke, where the folks lay stones upon the houses in windy weather, lest they should be blown away. These derive their name, as some say, from *Knicker*, to shake, and *Beker*, a goblet, indicating thereby that they were sturdy tosspots of yore; but in truth, it was derived from *Knicker*, to nod, and *Bocken*, books, plainly meaning that they were great nodders or dozers over books: from them did descend the writer of this History.

From the "Tales of a Traveller."

180. A MOTHER'S MEMORY.

A PART of the church-yard is shaded by large trees. Under one of them my mother lay buried. You have no doubt thought me a light, heartless being. I thought myself so; but there are moments of adversity which let us into some feelings of our nature to which we might otherwise remain perpetual strangers.

I sought my mother's grave: the weeds were already matted over it, and the tombstone was half hid among nettles. I cleared them away, and they stung my hands; but I was heedless of the pain, for my heart ached too severely. I sat down on the grave, and read, over and over again, the epitaph on the stone.

It was simple,—but it was true. I had written it myself. I had tried to write a poetical epitaph, but in vain; my feelings refused to utter themselves in rhyme. My heart had gradually been filling during my lonely wanderings; it was now charged to the brim, and overflowed. I sunk upon the grave, and buried my face in the tall grass, and wept like a child. Yes, I wept in manhood upon the grave, as I had in infancy upon the bosom, of my mother. Alas! how little do we appreciate a mother's tenderness while living! how heedless are we in youth of all her anxieties and kindness! But when she is dead and gone; when the cares and coldness of the world come withering to our hearts; when we find how hard it is to find true sympathy;—how few love us for ourselves; how few will befriend us in our misfortunes—then it is that we think of the mother we have lost. It is true I had always loved my mother, even in my most heedless days; but I felt how inconsiderate and ineffectual had been my love. My heart melted as I retraced the days of infancy, when I was led by a mother's hand, and rocked to sleep in a mother's arms, and was without care or sorrow. "O my mother!" exclaimed I, burying my face again in the grass of the grave, "O that I were once more by your side; sleeping never to wake again on the cares and troubles of this world."

I am not naturally of a morbid temperament, and the violence of my emotion gradually exhausted itself. It was a hearty, honest, natural discharge of grief which had been slowly accumulating, and gave me wonderful relief. I rose from the grave as if I had been offering up a sacrifice, and I felt as if that sacrifice had been accepted.

I sat down again on the grass, and plucked one by one the weeds from her grave: the tears trickled more slowly down my cheeks, and ceased to be bitter. It was a comfort to think that she had died before sorrow and poverty came upon her child, and all his great expectations were blasted.

I leaned my cheek upon my hand, and looked upon the landscape. Its quiet beauty soothed me. The whistle of a peasant from an adjoining field came cheerily to my ear. I seemed to respire hope and comfort with the free air that whispered through the leaves, and played lightly with my hair, and dried the tears upon my cheek. A lark, rising from the field before me, and leaving as it were a stream of song behind him as he rose, lifted my fancy with him. He hovered in the air just above the place where the towers of Warwick castle marked the horizon, and seemed as if fluttering with delight at his own melody. "Surely," thought I, "if there were such a thing as a transmigration of souls, this might be taken for some poet let loose from earth, but still revelling in song, and carolling about fair fields and lordly towers."

—

From "The Life and Voyages of Columbus."

181. Columbus a Prisoner.

The arrival of Columbus at Cadiz, a prisoner, and in chains, produced almost as great a sensation as his triumphant return from his first voyage. It was one of those striking and obvious facts, which speak to the feelings of the multitude, and preclude the necessity of reflection. No one stopped to inquire into the case. It was sufficient to be told that Columbus was brought home in irons from the world he had discovered. A general burst of indignation arose in Cadiz, and its neighboring city, Seville, which was immediately echoed throughout all Spain. . . . However Ferdinand might have secretly felt disposed towards Columbus, the momentary tide of public feeling was not to be resisted. He joined with his generous queen in her reprobation of the treatment of the admiral, and both sovereigns hastened to give evidence to the world, that his imprisonment had been without their authority, and contrary to their wishes.

—

182. His Arrival at Court.

He appeared at court in Granada, on the 17th of December, not as a man ruined and disgraced, but richly dressed, and attended by an honorable retinue. He was received by their majesties with unqualified favor and distinction. When the queen beheld this venerable man approach, and thought on all that he had deserved, and all that he had suffered, she was moved to tears. Columbus had borne up firmly against the rude conflicts of the world; he had endured with lofty scorn the injuries and insults of ignoble men; but he possessed strong and quick sensibility. When he found himself thus kindly received by his sovereigns, and beheld tears in the benign eyes of Isabella, his long-suppressed feelings burst forth. He threw himself upon his knees, and for some time could not utter a word for the violence of his tears and sobbings.

From Wolfert's Roost.

183. "A Time of Unexampled Prosperity."

. . . Every now and then the world is visited by one of these delusive seasons, when "the credit system," as it is called, expands to full luxuriance; every body trusts every body; a bad debt is a thing unheard of; the broad way to certain and sudden wealth lies plain and open, and men are tempted to dash forward boldly, from the facility of borrowing.

Promissory notes, interchanged between scheming individuals, are liberally discounted at the banks, which become so many mints to coin words into cash; and as the supply of words is inexhaustible, it may readily be supposed what a vast amount of promissory capital is soon in circulation. Every one now talks in thousands; nothing is heard but gigantic operations in trade, great purchases and sales of real property, and immense sums made at every transfer. All, to be sure, as yet exists in promise; but the believer in promises calculates the aggregate as solid capital, and falls back in amazement at the amount of public wealth, "the unexampled state of public prosperity!"

Now is the time for speculative and dreaming or designing men. They relate their dreams and projects to the ignorant and credulous, dazzle them with golden visions, and set them maddening after shadows. The example of one stimulates another; speculation rises on speculation; bubble rises on bubble; every one helps with his breath to swell the windy superstructure, and admires and wonders at the magnitude of the inflation he has contributed to produce.

Speculation is the romance of trade, and casts contempt upon all its sober realities. It renders the stock-jobber a magician, and the exchange a region of enchantment. It elevates the merchant into a kind of Knight-errant, or rather a commercial Quixote. The slow but sure gains of snug percentage become despicable in his eyes: no "operation" is thought worthy of attention, that does not double or treble the investment. No business is worth following, that does not promise an immediate fortune. As he sits musing over his ledger, with pen behind his ear, he is like LaMancha's hero in his study, dreaming over his books of chivalry. His dusty counting-house fades before his eyes, or changes into a Spanish mine; he gropes after diamonds, or dives after pearls. The subterranean garden of Aladdin is nothing to the realms of wealth that break upon his imagination.

When a man of business, therefore, hears on every side rumors of fortunes suddenly acquired; when he finds banks liberal, and brokers busy; when he sees adventurers flush of paper capital, and full of scheme and enterprise; when he perceives a greater disposition to buy than to sell; when trade overflows its accustomed channels, and deluges the country; when he hears of new regions of commercial adventure, of distant marts and distant mines, swallowing merchandise and disgorging gold; when he finds joint stock companies of all kinds forming; railroads, canals, and locomotive engines, springing up on every side; when idlers suddenly become men of business, and dash into the game of commerce as they would into the hazards of the faro table; when he beholds the streets glittering with new equipages, palaces conjured up by the magic of speculation; tradesmen flushed with sudden success, and vying with each other in ostentatious expense; in a word, when he hears the whole community joining in the theme of "unexampled prosperity," let him look upon the whole as a "weather breeder," and prepare for the impending storm.

From The Life of Washington.

184. Death and Burial of Braddock.

The proud spirit of Braddock was broken by his defeat. He remained silent the first evening after the battle, only ejaculating at night, "Who would have thought it!" He was equally silent the following day; yet hope still seemed to linger in his breast, from another ejaculation: "We shall better know how to deal with them another time!"

He was grateful for the attentions paid to him by Captain Stewart and Washington, and more than once, it is said, expressed his admiration of the gallantry displayed by the Virginians in the action. It is said, moreover, that in his last moments, he apologized to Washington for the petulance with which he had rejected his advice, and bequeathed to him his favorite charger and his faithful servant, Bishop, who had helped to convey him from the field.

Some of these facts, it is true, rest on tradition, yet we are willing to believe them, as they impart a gleam of just and generous feeling to his closing scene. He died on the night of the 13th, at the Great Meadows, the place of Washington's discomfiture in the preceding year. His obsequies were performed before break of day. The chaplain having been wounded, Washington read the funeral service. All was done in sadness, and without parade, so as not to attract the attention of lurking savages, who might discover and outrage his grave. It is doubtful even whether a volley was fired over it, that last military honor which he had recently paid to the remains of an Indian warrior. The place of his sepulture, however, is still known, and pointed out.

Reproach spared him not, even when in his grave. The failure of the expedition was attributed both in England and America, to his obstinacy, his technical pedantry, and his military conceit. He had been continually warned to be on his guard against ambush and surprise, but without avail. Had he taken the advice urged on him by Washington and others, to employ scouting parties of Indians and rangers, he would never have been so signally surprised and defeated.

Still his dauntless conduct on the field of battle shows him to have been a man of fearless spirit; and he was universally allowed to be an accomplished disciplinarian. His melancholy end, too, disarms censure of its asperity. Whatever may have been his faults and errors, he in a manner expiated them by the hardest lot that can befall a brave soldier, ambitious of renown—an unhonored grave in a strange land; a memory clouded by misfortune, and a name for ever coupled with defeat.

—

185. Baron Steuben in the Revolutionary Army.

The committee having made their report, the baron's proffered services were accepted with a vote of thanks for his disinterestedness, and he was ordered to join the army of Valley Forge. That army, in its ragged condition and squalid quarters, presented a sorry aspect to a strict disciplinarian from Germany, accustomed to the order and appointments of European camps; and the baron often declared, that under such circumstances no army in Europe could be kept together for a single month. The liberal mind of Steuben, however, made every allowance; and Washington soon found in him a consummate soldier, free from pedantry or pretension.

* * * * * *

For a time, there was nothing but drills throughout the camp, then gradually came evolutions of every kind. The officers were schooled as well as the men. The troops, says a person who was present in the camp, were paraded in a single line with shouldered arms; every officer in his place. The baron passed in front, then took the musket of each soldier in hand, to see whether it was clean and well polished, and examined whether the men's accoutrements were in good order.

He was sadly worried for a time with the militia; especially when any manœuvre was to be performed. The men blundered in their exercise; the baron blundered in his English; his French and German were of no avail; he lost his temper, which was rather warm; swore in all three languages at once, which made the matter worse, and at length called his aide to his assistance, to help him curse the blockheads as it was pretended—but no doubt to explain the manœuvre.

Still the grand marshal of the court of Hohenzollern mingled with the veteran soldier of Frederick, and tempered his occasional bursts of impatience; and he had a kind generous heart, that soon made him a favorite with the men. His discipline extended to their comforts. He inquired into their treatment by the officers. He examined into the doctor's reports; visited the sick; and saw that they were well lodged and attended.

He was an example, too, of the regularity and system he exacted. One of the most alert and indefatigable men in the camp; up at day-break if not before, whenever there were to be any important manœuvres, he took his cup of coffee and smoked his pipe while his servant dressed his hair, and by sunrise he was in the saddle, equipped at all points, with the star of his order of knighthood glittering on his breast, and was off to the parade, alone, if his suite were not ready to attend him.

The strong good sense of the baron was evinced in the manner in which he adapted his tactics to the nature of the army and the situation of the country, instead of adhering with bigotry to the systems of Europe. His instructions were appreciated by all. The officers received them gladly and conformed to them. The men soon became active and adroit. The army gradually acquired a proper organization, and began to operate like a great machine; and Washington found in the baron an intelligent, disinterested, truthful coadjutor, well worthy of the badge he wore of the Order of *Fidelity*.

Richard Henry Wilde, 1789-1847.

(Manual, pp. 501, 521.)

From "Conjectures concerning Torquato Tasso."

186. Interest of Tasso's Life.

There is scarcely any poet whose life excites a more profound and melancholy interest than that of Torquato Tasso.

His short and brilliant career of glory captivates the imagination, while the heart is deeply affected by his subsequent misfortunes. Greater fame and greater misery have seldom been the lot of man, and a few brief years sufficed for each extreme.

An exile even in his boyhood, the proscription and confiscation suffered by his father deprived him of home and patrimony. Honor and love, and the favor of princes, and enthusiastic praise, dazzled his youth. Envy, malice, and treachery, tedious imprisonment and imputed madness, insult, poverty, and persecution, clouded his manhood. The evening of his days was saddened by a troubled spirit, want, sickness, bitter memories, and deluded hopes; and when at length a transient gleam of sunshine fell upon his prospects, death substituted the immortal for the laurel crown.

Mystery adds its fascination to his story. The causes of his imprisonment are hidden in obscurity: it is still disputed whether he was insane or not.

. . . Few points of literary history, therefore, are more interesting, or more obscure, than the love, the madness, and the imprisonment of Tasso.

George Ticknor, 1791–1871. (Manual, p. 502.)

From "The History of Spanish Literature."

187. Design of Cervantes in writing Don Quixote.

His purpose in writing the Don Quixote has sometimes been enlarged by the ingenuity of a refined criticism, until it has been made to embrace the whole of the endless contrast between the poetical and the prosaic in our natures,—between heroism and generosity on one side, as if they were mere illusions, and a cold selfishness on the other, as if it were the truth and reality of life. But this is a metaphysical conclusion drawn from views of the work at once imperfect and exaggerated; a conclusion contrary to the spirit of the age, which was not given to a satire so philosophical and generalizing, and contrary to the character of Cervantes himself, as we follow it from the time when he first became a soldier, through all his trials in Algiers, and down to the moment when his warm and trusting heart dictated the Dedication of "Persiles and Sigismunda" to the Count de Lemos. His whole spirit, indeed, seems rather to have been filled with a cheerful confidence in human virtue. and his whole bearing in life seems to have been a contradiction to that discouraging and saddening scorn for whatever is elevated and generous, which such an interpretation of the Don Quixote necessarily implies.

* * * * * * *

At the very beginning of the work, he announces it to be his sole purpose to break down the vogue and authority of books of chivalry, and at the end of the whole he declares anew in his own person, that "he had no other desire than to render abhorred of men the false and absurd stories contained in books of chivalry;" exulting in his success as an achievement of no small moment. And such, in fact, it was, for we have abundant proof that the fanaticism for these romances was so great in Spain, during the sixteenth century, as to have become matter of alarm to the more judicious. . . .

To destroy a passion that had struck its roots so deeply in the character of all classes of men, to break up the only reading which at that time could be considered widely popular and fashionable, was certainly a bold undertaking, and one that marks anything rather than a scornful or broken spirit, or a want of faith in what is most to be valued in our common nature. The great wonder is, that Cervantes succeeded. But that he did there is no question. No book of chivalry was written after the appearance of Don Quixote, in 1605; and from the same date, even those already enjoying the greatest favor ceased, with one or two unimportant exceptions, to be reprinted; so that, from that time to the present, they have been constantly disappearing, until they are now among the rarest of literary curiosities—a solitary instance of the power of genius to destroy, by a single well-timed blow, an entire department, and that, too, a flourishing and favored one, in the literature of a great and proud nation.

The general plan Cervantes adopted to accomplish this object, without, perhaps, foreseeing its whole course, and still less all its results, was simple as well as original. In 1605 he published the first part of Don Quixote, in which a country gentleman of La Mancha, full of genuine Castilian honor and enthusiasm, gentle and dignified in his character, trusted by his friends, and loved by his dependants—is represented as so completely crazed by long reading the most famous books of chivalry, that he believes them to be true, and feels himself called on to become the impossible knight-errant they describe, —nay, actually goes forth into the world to defend the oppressed and avenge the injured, like the heroes of his romances.

James Hall, 1793–1868. (Manual, p. 510.)

From "Statistics of the West."

188. DESCRIPTION OF A PRAIRIE.

IMAGINE a stream of a mile in width, whose waters are as transparent as those of the mountain spring, flowing over beds of rock or gravel. Fancy the prairie commencing at the water's edge—a natural meadow covered with grass and flowers, rising, with a gentle slope, for miles, so that in the vast panorama thousands of acres are exposed to the eye. The prospect is bounded by a range of low hills, which sometimes approach the river, and again recede, and whose summits, which are seen gently waving along the horizon, form the level of the adjacent country. . . . The timber is scattered in groves and strips, the whole country being one vast illimitable prairie, ornamented by small collections of trees. . . . But more often we see the single tree, without a companion near, or the little clump, composed of a few dozen oaks or elms; and not unfrequently, hundreds of acres embellished with a kind of open woodland, and exhibiting the appearance of a splendid park, decorated with skill and care by the hand of taste. Here we behold the beautiful lawn enriched with flowers, and studded with trees, which are so dispersed about as not to intercept the prospect, standing singly, so as not to shade the ground, and occasionally collected in clusters, while now and then the shade deepens into the gloom of the forest, or opens into long vistas and spacious plains, destitute of tree or shrub.

When the eye roves off from the green plain, to the groves, or points of timber, these also are found . . . robed in the most attractive hues. The rich undergrowth is in full bloom. The red-bud, the dog-wood, the crab-apple, the wild plum, the cherry, the wild rose, are abundant in all the rich lands; and the grape-vine, though its blossom is unseen, fills the air with fragrance. The variety of the wild fruit and flowering shrubs is so great, and such the profusion of the blossoms with which they are bowed down, that the eye is regaled almost to satiety.

The gayety of the prairie, its embellishments, and the absence of the gloom and savage wildness of the forest, all contribute to dispel the feeling of lonesomeness which usually creeps over the mind of the solitary traveler in the wilderness. Though he may not see a house nor a human being, and is conscious that he is far from the habitations of men, he can scarcely divest himself of the idea that he is traveling through scenes embellished by the hand of art. The flowers so fragile, so delicate, and so ornamental, seem to have been tastefully disposed to adorn the scene. The groves and clumps of trees appear to have been scattered over the lawn to beautify the landscape; and it is not easy to avoid that illusion of the fancy which persuades the beholder, that such scenery has been created to gratify the refined taste of civilized man.

Henry R. Schoolcraft, 1793–1864. (Manual, p. 504.)

From "Oneota."

189. THE CHIPPEWA INDIAN.

OF all the existing branches of the Algonquin stock in America, this extensive and populous tribe appears to have the strongest claims to intellectual distinction, on the score of their traditions, so far at least, as the present state of our inquiries extends. They possess in their curious fictitious legends and lodge-tales, a varied and exhaustless fund of tradition, which is repeated from generation to generation. These legends hold, among the wild men of the north, the relative rank of story-books; and are intended both to amuse and instruct. This people possess also the art of picture writing in a degree which denotes that they have been, either more careful, or more fortunate, in the preservation of this very ancient art of the human race. Warriors, and the bravest of warriors, they are yet an intellectual people.

. . . They believe that the great Spirit created material matter, and that He made the earth and heavens, by the power of His will. . . . He made one great and master-spirit of evil, to whom He also gave assimilated and subordinate evil spirits having something of his own nature, to execute his will. Two antagonist powers, they believe, were thus placed in the world, who are continually striving for the mastery, and who have power to affect the lives and fortunes of men. This constitutes the ground-work of their religion, sacrifices, and worship.

They believe that animals were created before men, and that they originally had rule on the earth. By the power of necromancy, some of these animals were transformed to men, who, as soon as they assumed this new form, began to hunt the animals, and make war against them. It is expected that these animals will resume their human shapes, in a future state, and hence their hunters feign some clumsy excuses for their present policy of killing them. They believe that all animals, and birds, and reptiles, and even insects, possess reasoning faculties, and have souls. It is in these opinions, that we detect the ancient doctrine of transmigration.

One of the most curious opinions of this people is their belief in the mysterious and sacred character of fire. They obtain sacred fire, for all national and ecclesiastical purposes, from the flint. Their national pipes are lighted with this fire. It is symbolical of purity. Their notions of the boundary between life and death, which is also symbolically the limit of the material verge between this and a future state, are revealed in connection with the exhibition of flames of fire. They also make sacrifices by fire of some part of the first fruits of the chase. These traits are to be viewed, perhaps, in relation to their ancient worship of the sun, above noticed, of which the traditions and belief are still generally preserved. The existence of the numerous classes of jossakeeds, or mutterers (the word is from the utterance of sounds low on the earth), is a trait that will remind the reader of a simliar class of men in early ages in the eastern hemisphere. These persons constitute, indeed, the Magi of our western forests.

Edward Everett, 1794–1865. (Manual, pp. 487, 531.)

From "Orations and Speeches."

190. Astronomy, for all Time.

There is much by day to engage the attention of the observatory; the sun, his apparent motions, his dimensions, the spots on his disk (to us the faint indications of movements of unimagined grandeur in his luminous atmosphere), a solar eclipse, a transit of the inferior planets, the mysteries of the spectrum—all phenomena of vast importance and interest. But night is the astronomer's accepted time; he goes to his delightful labors when the busy world goes to its rest. A dark pall spreads over the resorts of active life; terrestrial objects, hill and valley, and rock and stream, and the abodes of men, disappear; but the curtain is drawn up which concealed the heavenly hosts. There they shine and there they move, as they moved and shone to the eyes of Newton and Galileo, of Kepler and Copernicus, of Ptolemy and Hipparchus; yea, as they moved and shone when the morning stars sang together, and all the sons of God shouted for joy. All has changed on earth; but the glorious heavens remain unchanged. The plough has passed over the remains of mighty cities, the homes of powerful nations are desolate, the languages they spoke are forgotten; but the stars that shone for them are shining for us; the same eclipses run their steady cycle; the same equinoxes call out the flowers of spring, and send the husbandman to the harvest; the sun pauses at either tropic, as he did when his course began; and sun and moon, and planet and satellite, and star, and constellation, and galaxy, still bear witness to the power, the wisdom, and the love of Him who placed them in the heavens, and upholds them there.

—

191. Description of the Sunrise.

Much, however, as we are indebted to our observatories for elevating our conceptions of the heavenly bodies, they present even to the unaided sight, scenes of glory which words are too feeble to describe. I had occasion, a few weeks since, to take the early train from Providence to Boston; and for this purpose rose at two o'clock in the morning. Everything around was wrapt in darkness and hushed in silence, broken only by what seemed at that hour the unearthly clank and rush of the train. It was a mild, serene, midsummer's night,—the sky was without a cloud,—the winds were whist. The moon, then in the last quarter, had just risen, and the stars shone with a spectral lustre, but little affected by her presence. Jupiter, two hours high, was the herald of the day; the Pleiades, just above the horizon, shed their sweet influence in the east; Lyra sparkled near the zenith; Andromeda veiled her newly-discovered glories from the naked eye, in the south; the steady pointers, far beneath the pole, looked meekly up from the depths of the north, to their sovereign.

Such was the glorious spectacle as I entered the train. As we proceeded, the timid approach of twilight became more perceptible; the intense blue of the sky began to soften; the smaller stars, like little children, went first to rest; the sister beams of the Pleiades soon melted together; but the bright constellations of the west and north remained unchanged. Steadily the wondrous transfiguration went on. Hands of angels, hidden from mortal eyes, shifted the scenery of the heavens; the glories of night dissolved into the glories of the dawn. The blue sky now turned more softly gray; the great watch-stars shut up their holy eyes; the east began to kindle. Faint streaks of purple soon blushed along the sky; the whole celestial concave was filled with the inflowing tides of the morning light, which came pouring down from above in one great ocean of radiance; till at length, as we reached the Blue Hills, a flash of purple fire blazed out from above the horizon, and turned the dewy tear-drops of flower and leaf, into rubies and diamonds. In a few seconds, the everlasting gates of the morning were thrown wide open, and the lord of day, arrayed in glories too severe for the gaze of man, began his state.

I do not wonder at the superstition of the ancient Magians, who in the morning of the world, went up to the hill-tops of Central Asia, and ignorant of the true God, adored the most glorious work of His hand. But I am filled with amazement when I am told that in this enlightened age, and in the heart of the Christian world, there are persons who can witness this daily manifestation of the power and wisdom of the Creator, and yet say in their hearts, "there is no God."

From a Discourse on the Discovery and Colonization of America.

192. THE CELTIC IMMIGRATION.

THIS great Celtic race is one of the most remarkable that has appeared in history. Whether it belongs to that extensive Indo-European family of nations, which, in ages before the dawn of history, took up a line of march in two columns from Lower India, and moving westward by both a northern and a southward route, finally diffused itself over Western Asia, Northern Africa, and the greater part of Europe; or whether, as others suppose, the Celtic race belongs to a still older stock, and was itself driven down upon the south and into the west of Europe by the overwhelming force of the Indo-Europeans, is a question which we have no time at present to discuss. However it may be decided, it would seem that for the first time, as far as we are acquainted with the fortunes of this interesting race, they have found themselves in a really prosperous condition, in this country. Driven from the soil in the west of Europe, to which their forefathers clung for two thousand years, they have at length, and for the first time in their entire history, found a real home in a land of strangers. Having been told, in the frightful language of political economy, that at the daily table which Nature spreads for the human family there is no cover laid for them in Ireland, they have crossed the ocean to find occupation, shelter, and bread, on a foreign but friendly soil.

This "Celtic Exodus," as it has been aptly called, is to all the parties immediately connected with it one of the most important events of the day. To the emigrants themselves it may be regarded as a passing from death to life. It will benefit Ireland by reducing a surplus population, and restoring a sounder and juster relation of capital and labor. It will benefit the laboring classes in England, where wages have been kept down to the starvation-point by the struggle between native population and the inhabitants of the sister island, for that employment and food, of which there is not enough for both. This benefit will extend from England to ourselves, and will lessen the pressure of that competition which our labor is obliged to sustain, with the ill-paid labor of Europe. In addition to all this, the constant influx into America of stout and efficient hands supplies the greatest want in a new country, which is that of labor, gives value to land, and facilitates the execution of every species of private enterprise and public work.

I am not insensible to the temporary inconveniences which are to be set off against these advantages, on both sides of the water. Much suffering attends the emigrant, there, on his passage, and after his arrival. It is possible that the value of our native labor may have been depressed by too sudden and extensive a supply from abroad; and it is certain that our asylums and alms-houses are crowded with foreign inmates, and the resources of public and private benevolence have been heavily drawn upon. These are considerable evils, but they have perhaps been exaggerated.

Hugh S. Legaré, 1797–1843. (Manual, p. 487.)

From his "Collected Writings."

193. The Study of the Ancient Classics.

Not to have the curiosity to study the learned languages is not to have any vocation at all for literature: it is to be destitute of liberal curiosity and of enthusiasm; to mistake a self-sufficient and superficial dogmatism for philosophy, and that complacent indolence which is the bane of all improvement, for a proof of the highest degree of it. . . .

All that we ask, then, is, that a boy should be thoroughly taught the ancient languages from his eighth to his sixteenth year, or thereabouts, in which time he will have his taste formed, his love of letters completely, perhaps enthusiastically, awakened, his knowledge of the principles of universal grammar perfected, his memory stored with the history, the geography, and the chronology of all antiquity, and with a vast fund of miscellaneous literature besides, and his imagination kindled with the most beautiful and glowing passages of Greek and Roman poetry and eloquence; all the rules of criticism familiar to him—the sayings of sages and the achievements of heroes indelibly impressed upon his heart. He will have his curiosity fired for further acquisition, and find himself in possession of the golden keys which open all the recesses where the stores of knowledge have ever been laid up by civilized man. The consciousness of strength will give him confidence, and he will go to the rich treasures themselves, and take what he wants, instead of picking up eleemosynary scraps from those whom, in spite of himself, he will regard as his betters in literature. He will be let into that great communion of scholars throughout all ages and all nations,—like that more awful communion of saints in the holy church universal,—and feel a sympathy with departed genius, and with the enlightened and the gifted minds of other countries, as they appear before him, in the transports of a sort of vision beatific, bowing down at the same shrines, and flowing with the same holy love of whatever is most pure, and fair, and exalted, and divine in human nature.

—

From a Review of Kent's Commentaries.

194. DISADVANTAGES OF COLONIAL LIFE.

IT is our misfortune, in one sense, to have succeeded, at the very outset of our career, to an over-grown inheritance in the literature of the mother country, and to have stood for a century in that political and social relation towards her, which was of all others most unfavorable to any originality in genius and opinions. Our good fathers piously spoke of England as their *home.* The inferiority—the discouraging and degrading inferiority—implied in a state of colonial dependence, chilled the enthusiasm of talent, and repressed the aspirations of ambition. Our youth were trained in English schools to classical learning and good manners; but no scholarship—great as we believe its efficacy to be—can either inspire or supply, the daring originality and noble pride of genius, to which, by some mysterious law of nature, the love of country and a national spirit seem to be absolutely necessary. We imported our opinions ready-made—"by balefuls," if it so pleases the Rev. Sidney Smith. We were taught to read by English school-masters—and to reason by English authors—English clergymen filled our pulpits, English lawyers our courts—and above all things, we deferred to and dreaded the dictatorial authority and withering contempt of English criticism. It is difficult to imagine a state of things more fatal to intellectual dignity and enterprise, and the consequences were such as might have been anticipated. What is still more lamentable, although the cause has in a good measure ceased, the effect continues, nor do we see any remedy for the evil until our youth shall be taught to go up to the same original and ever-living fountains of all literature, at which the Miltons, and the Barrows, and the Drydens drank in so much of their enthusiasm and inspiration, and to cast off entirely that slavish dependence upon the opinions of others which they must feel, who take their knowledge of what it is either their duty, their interest, or their ambition to learn, at second hand.

Francis L. Hawks, 1798–1866. (Manual, p. 480.)

From "Narrative of the United States Expedition to Japan."

195. Japan interesting in many Aspects.

Viewed in any of its aspects, the empire of Japan has long presented to the thoughtful mind an object of uncommon interest. And this interest has been greatly increased by the mystery with which, for the last two centuries, an exclusive policy has sought to surround the institutions of this remarkable country. . . .

The political inquirer, for instance, has wished to study in detail the form of government, the administration of laws, and the domestic institutions, under which a nation systematically prohibiting intercourse with the rest of the world has attained to a state of civilization, refinement, and intelligence, the mere glimpses of which so strongly invite further investigation.

The student of physical geography, aware how much national characteristics are formed or modified by peculiarities of physical structure in every country, would fain know more of the lands and the seas, the mountains and the rivers, the forests and the fields, which fall within the limits of this almost *terra incognita.*

. . . The man of commerce asks to be told of its products and its trade, its skill in manufactures, the commodities it needs, and the returns it can supply.

The scholar asks to be introduced to its literature, that he may contemplate in historians, poets, and dramatists (for Japan has them all), a picture of the national mind.

The Christian desires to know the varied phases of their superstition and idolatry, and longs for the dawn of that day when a purer faith and more enlightened worship shall bring them within the circle of Christendom.

Amid such a diversity of pursuits as we have enumerated, a common interest unites all in a common sympathy; and hence the divine and the philosopher, the navigator and the naturalist, the man of business and the man of letters, have alike joined in a desire for the thorough exploration of a field at once so extensive and so inviting.

George P. Marsh, 1801–. (Manual, p. 532.)

From "Lectures on the English Language."

196. METHOD OF LEARNING ENGLISH.

THE groundwork of English, indeed, can be, and best is, learned at the domestic fireside—a school for which there is no adequate substitute; but the knowledge there acquired is not, as in homogeneous languages, a root, out of which will spontaneously grow the flowers and the fruits which adorn and enrich the speech of man. English has been so much affected by extraneous, alien, and discordant influences, so much mixed with foreign ingredients, so much overloaded with adventitious appendages, that it is to most of those who speak it, in a considerable degree, a conventional and arbitrary symbolism. The Anglo-Saxon tongue has a craving appetite, and is as rapacious of words, and as tolerant of forms, as are its children, of territory and of religions. But in spite of its power of assimilation, there is much of the speech of England which has never become connatural to the Anglican people; and its grammar has passively suffered the introduction of many syntactical combinations, which are not merely irregular, but repugnant. I shall not here inquire whether this condition of English is an evil. There are many cases where a complex and cunningly-devised machine, dexterously guided, can do that which the congenital hand fails to accomplish; but the computing of our losses and gains, the striking of our linguistic balance, belongs elsewhere. Suffice it to say, that English is not a language which teaches itself by mere unreflecting usage. It can only be mastered, in all its wealth, in all its power, by conscious, persistent labor; and therefore, when all the world is awaking to the value of general philological science, it would ill become us to be slow in recognizing the special importance of the study of our own tongue.

—

From "Man and Nature."

197. The Evergreens of Southern Europe.

The multitude of species, intermixed as they are in their spontaneous growth, gives the American forest landscape a variety of aspect not often seen in the woods of Europe; and the gorgeous tints which nature repeats from the dying dolphin to paint the falling leaf of the American maples, oaks, and ash trees, clothe the hill-sides and fringe the watercourses with a rainbow splendor of foliage, unsurpassed by the brightest groupings of the tropical flora. It must be admitted, however, that both the northern and the southern declivities of the Alps exhibit a nearer approximation to this rich and multifarious coloring of autumnal vegetation than most American travellers in Europe are willing to allow; and, besides, the small deciduous shrubs, which often carpet the forest glades of these mountains, are dyed with a ruddy and orange glow, which, in the distant landscape, is no mean substitute for the scarlet and crimson and gold and amber of the trans-atlantic woodland.

No American evergreen known to me resembles the umbrella pine sufficiently to be a fair object of comparison with it. A cedar, very common above the Highlands on the Hudson, is extremely like the cypress, straight, slender, with erect, compressed ramification, and feathered to the ground, but its foliage is neither so dark nor so dense, the tree does not attain the majestic height of the cypress, nor has it the lithe flexibility of that tree. In mere shape, the Lombardy poplar nearly resembles this latter, but it is almost a profanation to compare the two, especially when they are agitated by the wind; for under such circumstances, the one is the most majestic, the other the most ungraceful, or—if I may apply such an expression to any thing but human affectation of movement—the most awkward of trees. The poplar trembles before the blast, flutters, struggles wildly, dishevels its foliage, gropes around with its feeblest branches, and hisses as in impotent passion. The cypress gathers its limbs still more closely to its stem, bows a gracious salute rather than an humble obeisance to the tempest, bends to the winds with an elasticity that assures you of its prompt return to its regal attitude, and sends from its thick leaflets a murmur like the roar of the far-off ocean.

George H. Calvert, 1803–. (Manual pp. 503, 505.)

From "First Years in Europe."

198. Estimate of Coleridge.

That Coleridge with his mental pockets full of gold, and with a mine in fee wherefrom he not only replenished his daily purse but enriched his neighbors, should now and then borrow a guinea, is a fact at which we should rather smile than frown, or, more fitly, pass by without special sensation, seeing what has been the practice of the highest,—a practice which may with full ethical assent be regarded as a privilege inherent in their supremacy, the free use of all knowledge collected and experience acquired, no matter when, where, or by whom, being a natural right of him *who has the genius to turn it to best account.* That in certain cases where acknowledgment was due it was not made, we may ascribe to opinion; or to defects which broke the complete rotundity of such a circle of endowments that without this breach they would have swollen their possessor to almost preterhuman proportions, empowering him to "bestride the narrow world like a Colossus."

Let the truth be spoken of all men. Let no man's greatness be a bar to full utterance; but let temperance and charity—duties peculiarly imperative when uttering derogatory truth—be especially observed towards a resplendent suffering brother like Coleridge, suffering from his own weakness, but on that very account entitled to a tenderer consideration from those who are themselves endowed to feel and claim something more than common human affinity with a nature so large and so susceptive. Could but a tithe of the fresh insights he has given us be allowed as an offset against his short-comings, never, from any scholar of sound sensibilities, would a whisper be heard against his name. Under the coarse, rusty, one-pronged spur of sectarian or political rancor, or from the knawing consciousness of sterile inferiority to a creative mind, plenty of people are ready and eager to try, with their net-work of flimsy phrases, to cramp the play of a giant's limbs, or, with the slow slimy poison of envy and malice, to spot and deform his beauty and his symmetry. To such, to the half-eyed and the half-souled, to the prosaic and the unsympathetic, be left all harsh condemnation of Coleridge.

For the living, not for the dead, are these inadequate words spoken. The writings of Coleridge—in tone high, refined. noble; in expression rich, choice, copious; in spirit as pure as the sun's light; intellectually of rare breadth and mellowness and brilliancy—are a healthful power in literature, their influence solely for good, warming, strengthening, elevating. As for Coleridge himself, his is an immortal name; and as he walks through the ages his robes adjusting themselves with varying grace, in harmony with the mutations of opinion, his inward life will be ever fresh to his fellow-men, while his detractors will be shaken from him as *gryllidæ* from the tunic of the superb Diana.

Ralph Waldo Emerson, 1803- (Manual pp. 478, 503, 531.)

From "Essays," Second Series.

199. Influence of Nature.

THERE are days which occur in this climate, at almost any season of the year, wherein the world reaches its perfection; when the air, the heavenly bodies, and the earth, make a harmony, as if Nature would indulge her offspring; when, in these bleak upper sides of the planet, nothing is to desire that we have heard of the happiest latitudes, and we bask in the shining hours of Florida and Cuba; when everything that has life gives sign of satisfaction, and the cattle that lie on the ground seem to have great and tranquil thoughts. These halcyons may be looked for with a little more assurance in that pure October weather which we distinguish by the name of Indian summer. The day, immeasurably long, sleeps over the broad hills, and warm, wide fields. To have lived through all its sunny hours seems longevity enough. The solitary places do not seem quite lonely. At the gates of the forest, the surprised man of the world is forced to leave his city estimates of great and small, wise and foolish. The knapsack of custom falls off his back with the first step he makes into these precincts. Here is sanctity which shames our religions, and reality which discredits our heroes.

From "Society and Solitude."

200. The Power of Childhood.

The perfection of the providence for childhood is easily acknowledged. The care which covers the seed of the tree under tough husks and stony cases, provides, for the human plant, the mother's breast and the father's house. The size of the nestler is comic, and its tiny beseeching weakness is compensated perfectly by the happy patronizing look of the mother, who is a sort of high reposing Providence toward it. Welcome to the parents the puny struggler, strong in his weakness, his little arms more irresistible than the soldier's, his lips touched with persuasion which Chatham and Pericles in manhood had not. His unaffected lamentations when he lifts up his voice on high, or, more beautiful, the sobbing child,—the face all liquid grief, as he tries to swallow his vexation,—soften all hearts to pity, and to mirthful and clamorous compassion. The small despot asks so little that all reason and all nature are on his side. His ignorance is more charming than all knowledge, and his little sins more bewitching than any virtue. His flesh is angels' flesh, all alive. "Infancy," said Coleridge, "presents body and spirit in unity: the body is all animated." All day, between his three or four sleeps, he coos like a pigeon-house, sputters, and spurs, and puts on his faces of importance; and when he fasts, the little Pharisee fails not to sound his trumpet before him. By lamp-light he delights in shadows on the wall; by daylight, in yellow and scarlet. Carry him out of doors,—he is overpowered by the light and the extent of natural objects, and is silent. Then presently begins his use of his fingers, and he studies power, the lesson of his race. First it appears in no great harm, in architectural tastes. Out of blocks, thread-spools, cards, and checkers, he will build his pyramid with the gravity of Palladio. With an acoustic apparatus of whistle and rattle, he explores the laws of sound. But chiefly, like his senior countrymen, the young American studies new and speedier modes of transportation. Mistrusting the cunning of his small legs, he wishes to ride on the necks and shoulders of all flesh. The small enchanter nothing can withstand, no seniority of age, no gravity of character; uncles, aunts, grandsires, grandams, fall an easy prey: he conforms to nobody, all conform to him; all caper and make mouths, and babble, and chirrup to him. On the strongest shoulders he rides, and pulls the hair of laurelled heads.

---

201. MAN MUST WORK IN HARMONY WITH PRINCIPLES.

CIVILIZATION depends on morality. Everything good in man leans on what is higher. This rule holds in small as in great. Thus, all our strength and success in the work of our hands depend on our borrowing the aid of the elements. You have seen a carpenter on a ladder with a broad-axe, chopping upward chips from a beam. How awkward! At what disadvantage he works! But see him on the ground, dressing his timber under him. Now, not his feeble muscles, but the force of gravity brings down the axe; that is to say, the planet itself splits his stick. The farmer had much ill-temper, laziness, and shirking, to endure from his hand-sawyers until one day he bethought him to put his saw-mill on the edge of a waterfall; and the river never tires of turning his wheel; the river is good-natured, and never hints an objection.

We had letters to send: couriers could not go fast enough, nor far enough; broke their wagons, foundered their horses, bad roads in spring, snow-drifts in winter, heat in summer;

could not get the horses out of a walk. But we found out that the air and earth were full of electricity; and always going our way,—just the way we wanted to send. *Would he take a message?* Just as lief as not; had nothing else to do; would carry it in no time. Only one doubt occurred, one staggering objection,—he had no carpet bag, no visible pockets, no hands, not so much as a mouth, to carry a letter. But, after much thought and many experiments, we managed to meet the conditions, and to fold up the letter in such invisible compact form as he could carry in those invisible pockets of his, never wrought by needle and thread,—and it went like a charm.

I admire still more than the saw-mill the skill which, on the sea-shore, makes the tides drive the wheels and grind corn, and which thus engages the assistance of the moon like a hired hand, to grind, and wind, and pump, and saw, and split stone, and roll iron.

Now that is the wisdom of a man, in every instance of his labor, to hitch his wagon to a star, and see his chore done by the gods themselves. That is the way we are strong, by borrowing the might of the elements. The forces of steam, gravity, galvanism, light, magnets, wind, fire, serve us day by day, and cost us nothing.

Our astronomy is full of examples of calling in the aid of these magnificent helpers. Thus, on a planet so small as ours, the want of an adequate base for astronomical measurements is early felt, as, for example, in detecting the parallax of a star. But the astronomer, having by an observation fixed the place of a star, by so simple an expedient as waiting six months, and then repeating his observation, contrived to put the diameter of the earth's orbit, say two hundred millions of miles, between his first observation and his second, and this line afforded him a respectable base for his triangle.

All our arts aim to win this vantage. We cannot bring the heavenly powers to us, but, if we will only choose our jobs in directions in which they travel, they will undertake them with the greatest pleasure. It is a peremptory rule with them, that *they never go out of their road.* We are dapper little busybodies, and run this way and that way superserviceably; but they swerve never from their foreordained paths,—neither the sun, nor the moon, nor a bubble of air, nor a mote of dust.

And as our handiworks borrow the elements, so all our social and political action leans on principles. To accomplish anything excellent, the will must work for catholic and universal ends. A puny creature walled in on every side, as Daniel wrote,—

> "Unless above himself he can,
> Erect himself, how poor a thing is man!"

but when his will leans on a principle, when he is the vehicle of ideas, he borrows their omnipotence. Gibraltar may be strong, but ideas are impregnable, and bestow on the hero their invincibility. "It was a great instruction," said a saint in Cromwell's war, "that the best courages are but beams of the Almighty." Hitch your wagon to a star. Let us not fag in paltry works which serve our pot and bag alone. Let us not lie and steal. No god will help. We shall find all their teams going the other way. Charles's Wain, Great Bear, Orion, Leo, Hercules: every god will leave us. Work rather for those interests which the divinities honor and promote,—justice, love, freedom, knowledge, utility.

—

202. Rules for Reading.

Be sure, then, to read no mean books. Shun the spawn of the press on the gossip of the hour. Do not read what you shall learn without asking, in the street and the train. Dr. Johnson said, "he always went into stately shops;" and good travelers stop at the best hotels; for, though they cost more, they do not cost much more, and there is the good company and the best information. In like manner, the scholar knows that the famed books contain, first and last, the best thoughts and facts. Now and then, by rarest luck, in some foolish grub street is the gem we want. But in the best circles is the best information. If you should transfer the amount of your reading day by day from the newspaper to the standard authors.—But who dare speak of such a thing.

The three practical rules, then, which I have to offer, are: 1st. Never read any book that is not a year old. 2d. Never read any but famed books. 3d. Never read any but what you like; or, in Shakespeare's phrase,

"No profit goes where is no pleasure ta'en:
In brief, sir, study what you most affect."

Montaigne says, "Books are a languid pleasure;" but I find certain books vital and spermatic, not leaving the reader what he was: he shuts the book a richer man. I would never willingly read any others than such.

John Russell Bartlett, 1805-.

From the "Personal Narrative of Explorations," &c.

203. LYNCH LAW AT EL PASO.

ON the present occasion, circumstances rendered it necessary for safety, as well as for the purpose of warning the desperate gang who were now about to have their deserts, that all should be doubly armed. In the court-room, therefore, where one of the most solemn scenes of human experience was enacting, all were armed save the prisoners. There sat the judge, with a pistol lying on the table before him; the clerks and attorneys wore revolvers at their sides; and the jurors were either armed with similar weapons, or carried with them the unerring rifle. The members of the commission and citizens, who were either guarding the prisoners or protecting the court, carried by their sides a revolver, a rifle, or a fowling-piece, thus presenting a scene more characteristic of feudal times than of the nineteenth century. The fair but sun-burnt complexion of the

American portion of the jury, with their weapons resting against their shoulders, and pipes in their mouths, presented a striking contrast to the swarthy features of the Mexicans, muffled in checkered *serapes*, holding their broad-brimmed glazed hats in their hands, and delicate cigarritos in their lips. The reckless, unconcerned appearance of the prisoners, whose unshaven faces and dishevelled hair gave them the appearance of Italian bandits rather than of Americans or Englishmen, the grave and determined bearing of the bench; the varied costume and expression of the spectators and members of the Commission, clad in serapes, blankets, or overcoats, with their different weapons, and generally with long beards, made altogether one of the most remarkable groups which ever graced a court-room. . . .

The evidence being closed, a few remarks were now made by the prosecuting attorney, followed by the charge of the judge, when the case was given to the jury. In a short time they returned into court with a verdict of guilty, against William Craig, Marcus Butler, and John Wade; upon whom the judge then pronounced sentence of death.

The prisoners were now escorted to the little plaza or open square in front of the village church, where the priest met them, to give such consolation as his holy office would afford. But their conduct, notwithstanding the desire on the part of all to afford them every comfort their position was susceptible of, continued reckless and indifferent, even to the last moment. Butler alone was affected. He wept bitterly, and excited much sympathy by his youthful appearance, being but 21 years of age. His companions begged him "not to cry, as he could die but once."

The sun was setting when they arrived at the place of execution. The assembled spectators formed a guard around a small alamo, or poplar tree, which had been selected for the gallows. It was fast growing dark, and the busy movements of a large number of the associates of the condemned, dividing and collecting again in small bodies at different points around and outside of the party, and then approaching nearer to the centre, proved that an attack was meditated, if the slightest opportunity should be given. But the sentence of the law was carried into effect.

Nathaniel Parker Willis, 1807–1867.

(Manual, pp. 504, 519.)

From "Pencillings by the Way."

204. The American Abroad.

It is a queer feeling to find oneself a *foreigner*. One can not realize long at a time how his face or his manners should have become peculiar; and after looking at a print for five minutes in a shop-window, or dipping into an English book, or in any manner throwing off the mental habit of the instant, the curious gaze of the passer-by, or the accent of a strange language, strikes one very singularly. Paris is full of foreigners of all nations, and of course physiognomies of all characters may be met everywhere; but, differing as the European nations do decidedly from each other, they differ still more from the American. Our countrymen, as a class, are distinguishable wherever they are met; not as Americans however, for of the habits and manners of our country, people know nothing this side the water. But there is something in an American face, of which I never was aware till I met them in Europe, that is altogether peculiar. The French take the Americans to be English; but an Englishman, while he presumes him his countryman, shows a curiosity to know who he is, which is very foreign to his usual indifference. As far as I can analyze it, it is the independent, self-possessed bearing of a man unused to look up to any one as his superior in rank, united to the inquisitive, sensitive, communicative expression which is the index to our national character. The first is seldom possessed in England but by a man of decided rank, and the latter is never possessed by an Englishman at all. The two are united in no other nation. Nothing is easier than to tell the rank of an Englishman, and nothing puzzles an European more than to know how to rate the pretensions of an American. . . .

From "Ephemera."

205. CHARACTER AND WRITINGS OF JAMES HILLHOUSE.

LIKE the public feeling, the condition and powers of criticism toward an author's fame, are essentially changed by his death. His personal character, and the events of his life—the foreground, so to speak, in the picture of his mind, are, till this event, wanting to the critical perspective; and when the hand to correct is cold, and the ear to be caressed and wounded is sealed, some of the uses of censure, and all reserve in comparison and final estimate, are done away.

* * * * * * *

Such men as Hillhouse are not common, even in these days of universal authorship. In accomplishment of mind and person, he was probably second to no man. His poems show the first. They are fully conceived, nicely balanced, exquisitely finished—works for the highest taste to relish, and for the severest student in dramatic style to erect into a model. Hadad was published in 1825, during my second year in college, and to me it was the opening of a new heaven of imagination. The leading characters possessed me for months, and the bright, clear, harmonious language was, for a long time, constantly in my ears. The author was pointed out to me, soon after, and for once, I saw a poet whose mind was well imaged in his person. In no part of the world have I seen a man of more distinguished mien, or of a more inborn dignity and elegance of address. His person was very finely proportioned, his carriage chivalric and high-bred, and his countenance purely and brightly intellectual. Add to this a sweet voice, a stamp of high courtesy on everything he uttered, and singular simplicity and taste in dress, and you have the portrait of one who, in other days, would have been the mirror of chivalry, and the flower of nobles and troubadours. Hillhouse was no less distinguished in oratory.

. . . Hillhouse had fallen upon days of thrift, and many years of his life which he should have passed either in his study, or in the councils of the nation, were enslaved to the drudgery of business. His constitution seemed to promise him a vigorous manhood, however, and an old age of undiminished fire, and when he left his mercantile pursuits, and retired to the beautiful and poetic home of "Sachem's Wood," his friends looked upon it as the commencement of a ripe and long enduring career of literature. In harmony with such a life were all his surroundings—scenery, society, domestic refinement, and companionship—and never looked promise fairer for the realization of a dream of glory. That he had laid out something of such a field in the future, I chance to know, for, though my acquaintance with him was slight, he confided to me in a casual conversation, the plan of a series of dramas, different from all he had attempted, upon which he designed to work with the first mood and leisure he could command. And with his scholarship, knowledge of life, taste, and genius, what might not have been expected from its fulfilment? But his hand is cold, and his lips still, and his light, just rising to its meridian, is lost now to the world. Love and honor to the memory of such a man.

Henry Wadsworth Longfellow, 1807–.

(Manual, pp. 503, 505.)

From "Hyperion."

206. The Interrupted Legend.

One by one the objects of our affection depart from us. But our affections remain, and like vines stretch forth their broken, wounded tendrils for support. The bleeding heart needs a balm to heal it; and there is none but the love of its kind,—none but the affection of a human heart. Thus the wounded, broken affections of Flemming began to lift themselves from the dust and cling around this new object. Days and weeks passed; and, like the Student Crisostomo, he ceased to love, because he began to adore. And with this adoration mingled the prayer, that, in that hour when the world is still, and the voices that praise are mute, and reflection cometh like twilight, and the maiden, in her day dreams, counted the number of her friends, some voice in the sacred silence of her thoughts might whisper his name.

They were sitting together one morning, on the green, flowery meadow, under the ruins of Burg Unspunnen. She was sketching the ruins. The birds were singing, one and all, as if there were no aching hearts, no sin nor sorrow, in the world. So motionless was the bright air, that the shadow of the trees lay engraven on the grass. The distant snow-peaks sparkled in the sun, and nothing frowned, save the square tower of the old ruin above them.

"What a pity it is," said the lady, as she stopped to rest her weary fingers, "what a pity it is, that there is no old tradition connected with this ruin!"

"I will make you one, if you wish," said Flemming.

"Can you make old traditions?"

"O, yes! I made three, the other day, about the Rhine, and one very old one about the Black Forest. A lady with dishevelled hair; a robber with a horrible slouched hat; and a night storm among the roaring pines."

"Delightful! Do make one for me."

"With the greatest pleasure. Where will you have the scene? Here, or in the Black Forest."

"In the Black Forest, by all means! Begin."

"I will unite this ruin and the forest together. But first promise not to interrupt me. If you snap the golden threads of thought, they will float away on the air like the film of the gossamer, and I shall never be able to recover them."

"I promise."

"Listen, then, to the Tradition of 'THE FOUNTAIN OF OBLIVION.'"

"Begin."

Flemming was reclining on the flowery turf, at the lady's feet, looking up with dreamy eyes into her sweet face, and then into the leaves of the linden-trees overhead.

"Gentle Lady! Dost thou remember the linden trees of Bülach,—those tall and stately trees, with velvet down upon their shining leaves, and rustic benches underneath their overhanging eaves? A leafy dwelling, fit to be the home of elf or fairy, where first I told my love to thee, thou cold and stately Hermione! A little peasant girl stood near, and listened all the while, with eyes of wonder and delight, and an unconscious smile, to hear the stranger still speak on in accents deep yet mild,—none else was with us in that hour, save God and that little child!"

"Why, it is in rhyme!"

"No, no! the rhyme is only in your imagination. You promised not to interrupt me, and you have already snapped asunder the gossamer threads of as sweet a dream as was ever spun from a poet's brain."

"It certainly did rhyme!"

Henry Reed, 1808-1854. (Manual, p. 501.)

From "Lectures on English History."

207. Legendary Period of British History.

It would be a weary, and probably vain inquiry to consider minutely the claims which such historical materials have on our belief; and so little is there attractive in the legends of British history, that I need not attempt to dwell upon any of the alleged facts. But I wish before passing from this part of my subject, briefly to examine the curious tenacity with which the belief in this legendary literature was once held and to show that it was not relinquished until a more critical standard of historic belief was adopted, and scientific investi gation took the place of uninquiring and passive credulity. It has been said that no man, before the sixteenth century, presumed to doubt that the Britons were descended from Brutus the Trojan; and it is equally certain that no modern writer could presume confidently to assert it. . . .

. . . It is most difficult for us, in these later days of higher standards of historic credibility, to form anything like an adequate conception, of the entire and unquestioning confidence which was felt for the story of British origin, and the race of ancient British kings. Of this feeling there is a curious proof in a transaction in the reign of Edward I., when the sovereignty of Scotland was claimed by the English monarch. The Scots sought the interposition and protection of the pope, alleging that the Scottish realm belonged of right to the see of Rome. Boniface VIII., a pontiff not backward in asserting the claims of the papacy, did interpose to check the English conquest, and was answered by an elaborate and respectful epistle from Edward, in which the English claim is most carefully and confidently derived from the conquest of the whole country by the Trojans in the times of Eli and Samuel—assuredly a very respectable antiquity of some two thousand four hundred years. No Philadelphia estate could be more methodically traced back to the proprietary title of William Penn, than was this claim to Scotland up to Brutus, the exile from Troy. . . . Now, all this is set forth with the most imperturbable seriousness, and with an air of complete assurance of the truth. It appears, too, to have fully answered the purpose intended; and the Scots, finding that the papal antiquity was but a poor defence against such claims, and as if determined not to be outdone by the Southron, replied in a document asserting their independence by virtue of descent from Scota, one of the daughters of Pharaoh. The pope seems to have been silenced in a conflict of ancestral authority, in which the succession of St. Peter seemed quite a modern affair, when overshadowed by such Trojan and Egyptian antiquity.

Caroline M. Kirkland, 1808–1864. (Manual, p. 484.)

From "Forest Life."

208. The Felling of a Great Tree.

One darling tree,—a giant oak which looked as if half a dozen Calibans might have been pegged in its knotty entrails —this one tree, the grandfather of the forest, we thought we had saved. It stood a little apart,—it shadowed no man's land,—it shut the broiling sun from nobody's windows, so we hoped it might be allowed to die a natural death. But one unlucky day, a family fresh from "the 'hio" removed into a house which stood at no great distance from this relic of primeval grandeur. These people were but little indebted to fortune, and the size of their potato-patch did not exactly correspond with the number of rosy-cheeks within doors. So the loan of a piece of ground was a small thing to ask or to grant. Upon this piece of lent land stood our favorite oak. The potatoes were scarcely peeping green above the soil, when we observed that the great boughs which we looked at admiringly a dozen times a day, as they towered far above the puny race around them, remained distinct in their outline, instead of exhibiting the heavy masses of foliage which had usually clothed them before the summer heat began. Upon nearer inspection it was found that our neighbor had commenced his plantation by the operation of girdling the tree, for which favor he expected our thanks, observing pithily that "nothing wouldn't never grow under sich a great mountain as that!" It is well that "Goth" and "Vandal" are not actionable.

Yet the felling of a great tree has something of the sublime in it. When the axe first falls on the trunk of a stately oak, laden with the green wealth of a century, or a pine whose aspiring peak might look down on a moderate church steeple, the contrast between the puny instrument and the gigantic result to be accomplished approaches the ridiculous. But as "the eagle towering in his pride of place was, by a mousing owl, hawked at and killed," so the leaf-crowned monarch of the wood has no small reason to quiver at the sight of a long-armed Yankee approaching his deep-rooted trunk with an awkward axe. One blow seems to accomplish nothing: not even a chip falls. But with another stroke comes a broad slice of the bark, leaving an ominous, gaping wound. Another pair of blows extends the gash, and when twenty such have fallen, behold a girdled tree. This would suffice to kill, and a melancholy death it is; but to fell is quite another thing. . . . Two deep incisions are made, yet the towering crown sits firm as ever. And now the destroyer pauses,—fetches breath,—wipes his beaded brow, takes a wary view of the bearings of the tree,—and then with a slow and watchful care recommences his work. The strokes fall doubtingly, and many a cautious glance is cast upward, for the whole immense mass now trembles, as if instinct with life, and conscious of approaching ruin. Another blow! it waves,—a groaning sound is heard— . . . yet another stroke is necessary. It is given with desperate force, and the tall peak leaves its place with an easy sailing motion accelerated every instant, till it crashes prone on the earth, sending far and wide its scattered branches, and letting in the sunlight upon the cool, damp, mossy earth, for the first time perhaps in half a century.

From "Western Clearings."

209. The Bee Tree.

One of the greatest temptations to our friend Silas, and to most of his class, is a bee hunt. Neither deer, nor 'coons, nor prairie hens, nor even bears, prove half as powerful enemies to anything like regular business, as do these little thrifty vagrants of the forest. The slightest hint of a bee tree will entice Silas Ashburn and his sons from the most profitable job of the season, even though the defection is sure to result in entire loss of the offered advantage; and if the hunt prove successful, the luscious spoil is generally too tempting to allow of any care for the future, so long as the "sweet'nin" can be persuaded to last. "It costs nothing," will poor Mrs. Ashburn observe; "let 'em enjoy it. It isn't often we have such good luck."

Margaret Fuller Ossoli, 1810–1850. (Manual, p. 502.)

From "At Home and Abroad."

210. Character of Carlyle.

Accustomed to the infinite wit and exhuberant richness of his writings, his talk is still an amazement and a splendor scarcely to be faced with steady eyes. He does not converse,—only harangues. It is the usual misfortune of such marked men (happily not one invariable or inevitable) that they cannot allow other minds room to breathe and show themselves in their atmosphere, and thus miss the refreshment and instruction which the greatest never cease to need from the experience of the humblest. Carlyle allows no one a chance, but bears down all opposition, not only by his wit and onset of words, resistless in their sharpness as so many bayonets, but by actual physical superiority, raising his voice and rushing on his opponent with a torrent of sound. This is not the least from unwillingness to allow freedom to others; on the contrary, no man would more enjoy a manly resistance to his thought; but it is the impulse of a mind accustomed to follow out its own impulse as the hawk its prey, and which knows not how to stop in the chase. Carlyle, indeed, is arrogant and overbearing, but in his arrogance there is no littleness or self-love: it is the heroic arrogance of some old Scandinavian conqueror,—it is his nature, and the untamable impulse that has given him power to crush the dragons. You do not love him, perhaps, nor revere, and perhaps, also, he would only laugh at you if you did; but you like him heartily, and like to see him the powerful smith, the Siegfried, melting all the old iron in his furnace till it glows to a sunset red, and burns you if you senselessly go too near. He seemed to me quite isolated, lonely as the desert; yet never was man more fitted to prize a man, could he find one to match his mood. He finds such, but only in the past. He sings rather than talks. He pours upon you a kind of satirical, heroical, critical poem, with regular cadences, and generally catching up near the beginning some singular epithet, which serves as a *refrain* when his song is full, or with which as with a knitting-needle he catches up the stitches, if he has chanced now and then to let fall a row. For the higher kinds of poetry he has no sense, and his talk on that subject is delightfully and gorgeously absurd; he sometimes stops a minute to laugh at it himself, then begins anew with fresh vigor; for all the spirits he is driving before him seem to him as Fata Morgana; ugly masks in fact, if he can but make them turn about, but he laughs that they seem to others such dainty Ariels. He puts out his chin sometimes till it looks like the beak of a bird, and his eyes flash bright instinctive meanings like Jove's bird; yet he is not calm and grand enough for the eagle: he is more like the falcon, and yet not of gentle blood enough for that either. He is not exactly like anything but himself, and therefore you cannot see him without the most hearty refreshment and good-will, for he is original, rich, and strong enough to afford a thousand faults; one expects some wild land in a rich kingdom. His talk, like his books, is full of pictures, his critical strokes masterly; allow for his point of view, and his survey is admirable. He is a large subject; I cannot speak more nor wiselier of him now, nor needs it; his works are true, to blame and praise him, the Siegfried of England, great and powerful, if not quite invulnerable, and of a might rather to destroy evil than legislate for good. At all events, he seems to be what Destiny intended, and represents fully a certain side; so we make no remonstrance as to his being and proceeding for himself, though we sometimes must for us.

Oliver Wendell Holmes, 1809–. (Manual, p. 520.)

From "The Autocrat of the Breakfast Table."

211. Consequences of Exposing an old Error.

Did you never, in walking in the fields, come across a large flat stone which had lain, nobody knows how long, just where you found it, with the grass forming a little hedge, as it were, all round it, close to its edges,—and have you not, in obedience to a kind of feeling that told you it had been lying there long enough, insinuated your stick, or your foot, or your fingers, under its edge, and turned it over as a housewife turns a cake, when she says to herself, "It's done brown enough by this time?" What an odd revelation, and what an unforeseen and unpleasant surprise to a small community, the very existence of which you had not suspected, until the sudden dismay and scattering among its members produced by your turning the old stone over! Blades of grass flattened down, colorless, matted together, as if they had been bleached and ironed; hideous crawling creatures, some of them coleopterous or horny-shelled,—turtle-bugs one wants to call them; some of them softer but cunningly spread out and compressed like Lepine watches; (Nature never loses a crack or a crevice, mind you, or a joint in a tavern bedstead, but she always has one of her flat pattern live timekeepers to slide into it;) black, glossy crickets, with their long filaments sticking out like the whips of four-horse stage-coaches; motionless, slug-like creatures, young larvæ, perhaps more horrible in their pulpy stillness than even in the infernal wriggle of maturity. But no sooner is the stone turned and the wholesome light of day let upon this compressed and blinded community of creeping things, than all of them which enjoy the luxury of legs—and some of them have a good many—rush round wildly, butting each other and everything in their way, and end in a general stampede for underground retreats from the region poisoned by sunshine. *Next year* you will find the grass growing tall and green where the stone lay; the ground-bird builds her nest where the beetle had his hole; the dandelion and the buttercup are growing there, and the broad fans of insect-angels open and shut over their golden disks, as the rhythmic waves of blissful consciousness pulsate through their glorified being.

—The young fellow whom they call John saw fit to say, in his very familiar way,—at which I do not choose to take offence, but which I sometimes think it necessary to repress,—that I was coming it rather strong on the butterflies.

No, I replied; there is meaning in each of those images, the butterfly as well as the others. The stone is ancient error. The grass is human nature borne down and bleached of all its color by it. The shapes which are found beneath are the crafty beings that thrive in darkness, and the weaker organisms kept helpless by it. He who turns the stone over is whosoever puts the staff of truth to the old lying incubus, no matter whether he do it with a serious face or a laughing one. The next year stands for the coming time. Then shall the nature which had lain blanched and broken, rise in its full stature and native hues, in the sunshine. Then shall God's minstrels build their nests in the hearts of a new-born humanity. Then shall beauty—Divinity taking outlines and color—light upon the souls of men as the butterfly, image of the beautified spirit rising from the dust, soars from the shell that held a poor grub, which would never have found wings, had not the stone been lifted.

You never need think you can turn over any old falsehood without a terrible squirming and scattering of the horrid little population that dwells under it.

—

212. PLEASURES OF BOATING.

I DARE not publicly name the rare joys, the infinite delights, that intoxicate me on some sweet June morning, when the river and bay are smooth as a sheet of beryl-green silk, and I run along ripping it up with my knife-edged shell of a boat the rent closing after me like those wounds of angels which Milton tells of, but the seam still shining for many a long rood behind me. To lie still, over the Flats, where the waters are shallow, and see the crabs crawling and the sculpins gliding busily and silently beneath the boat,—to rustle in through the long harsh grass that leads up some tranquil creek,—to take shelter from the sunbeams under one of the thousand-footed bridges, and look down its interminable colonnades, crusted with green and oozy growths, studded with minute barnacles, and belted with rings of dark muscles, while overhead, streams and thunders that other river, whose every wave is a human soul flowing to eternity as the river below flows to the ocean,—lying there moored unseen, in loneliness so profound that the columns of Tadmoor in the Desert could not seem more remote from life,—the cool breeze on one's forehead, the stream whispering against the half-sunken pillars,—why should I tell of these things, that I should live to see my beloved haunts invaded and the waves blackened with boats as with a swarm of water-beetles? What a city of idiots we must be, not to have covered this glorious bay with gondolas and wherries, as we have just learned to cover the ice in winter with skaters!

—

From "The Guardian Angel."

213. The Unspoken Declaration.

Myrtle had, perhaps, never so seriously inclined her ear to the honeyed accents of the young pleader. He flattered her with so much tact, that she thought she heard an unconscious echo through his lips of an admiration which he only shared with all around him. But in him he made it seem discriminating, deliberate, not blind, but very real. This it evidently was which had led him to trust her with his ambitions and his plans,—they might be delusions, but he could never keep them from her, and she was the one woman in the world to whom he thought he could safely give his confidence.

The dread moment was close at had. Myrtle was listening

with an instinctive premonition of what was coming,—ten thousand mothers and grandmothers, and great-grandmothers, and so on, had passed through it all in preceding generations, until time reached backwards to the sturdy savage who asked no questions of any kind, but knocked down the primeval great-grandmother of all, and carried her off to his hole in the rock, or into the tree where he had made his nest. Why should not the coming question announce itself by stirring in the pulses, and thrilling in the nerves, of the descendant of all these grandmothers?

She was leaning imperceptibly towards him, drawn by the mere blind elemental force, as the plummet was attracted to the side of Schehallien. Her lips were parted, and she breathed a little faster than so healthy a girl ought to breathe in a state of repose. The steady nerves of William Murray Bradshaw felt unwonted thrills and tremors tingling through them, as he came nearer and nearer the few simple words with which he was to make Myrtle Hazard the mistress of his destiny. His tones were becoming lower and more serious; there were slight breaks once or twice in the conversation; Myrtle had cast down her eyes.

"There is but one word more to add," he murmured softly, as he bent towards her—

A grave voice interrupted him. "Excuse me, Mr. Bradshaw," said Master Byles Gridley, "I wish to present a young gentleman to my friend here. I promised to show him the most charming young person I have the honor to be acquainted with, and I must redeem my pledge. Miss Hazard, I have the pleasure of introducing to your acquaintance my distinguished young friend, Mr. Clement Lindsay.

—

From "Currents and Counter Currents."

214. Mechanism of Vital Action.

But if the student of nature and the student of divinity can once agree that all the forces of the universe, as well as all its power, are immediately dependent upon its Creator,—that He is not only omni*potent* but omni*movent*,—we have no longer any fear of nebular theories, or doctrines of equivocal generation, or of progressive development. . . .

We begin then by examining the general rules which the Creator seems to have prescribed to His own operations. We ask, in the first place, whether He is wont, so far as we know, to employ a great multitude of materials, patterns, and forces, or whether He has seen fit to accomplish many different ends by the employment of a few of these only.

In all our studies of external nature, the tendency of increasing knowledge has uniformly been to show that the rules of creation are simplicity of material, economy of inventive effort, and thrift in the expenditure of force. All the endless forms in which matter presents itself to us, are resolved by chemistry into some three-score supposed simple substances, some of these perhaps being only modifications of the same element. The shapes of beasts and birds, of reptiles and fishes, vary in every conceivable degree; yet a single vertebra is the pattern and representation of the framework of them all, from eels to elephants. The identity reaches still further,—across a mighty gulf of being,—but bridges it over with a line of logic as straight as a sunbeam, and as indestructible as the scymitar-edge that spanned the chasm, in the fable of the Indian Hades. Strange as it may sound, the tail which the serpent trails after him in the dust, and the head of Plato, were struck in the die of the same primitive conception, and differ only in their special adaptation to particular ends. Again, the study of the movements of the universe has led us, from their complex phenomena, to the few simple forces from which they flow. The falling apple and the rolling planet are shown to obey the same tendency. The stick of sealing-wax which draws a feather to it, is animated by the same impulse that convulses the stormy heavens. These generalizations have simplified our view of the grandest material operations, yet we do not feel that creative power and wisdom have been shorn of any single ray, by the demonstrations of Newton, or of Franklin. On the contrary, the larger the collection of seemingly heterogeneous facts we can bring under the rule of a single formula, the nearer we feel that we have reached towards the source of knowledge, and the more perfectly we trace the little arc of the immeasurable circle which comes within the range of our hasty observations, at first like the broken fragments of a many-sided polygon, but at last as a simple curve which encloses all we know, or can know, of nature. To our own intellectual wealth, the gain is like that of the over-burdened traveller, who should exchange hundred-weights of iron for ounces of gold. Evanescent, formless, unstable, impalpable, a fog of uncondensed experiences hovers over our consciousness like an atmosphere of uncombined gases. One spark of genius shoots through it, and its elements rush together and glitter before us in a single translucent drop. It would hardly be extravagant to call Science the art of packing knowledge.

John William Draper,[1] *1810–.*

From the "Human Physiology."

215. Truths in the Ancient Philosophies.

It is not my intention to enter on an examination, or even enumeration, of ancient philosophical opinions, nor to show that many of the doctrines which have been brought forward within the last three centuries existed in embryo in those times. It may, however, be observed that, in the midst of much error, there were those who held just views of the various problems of theology, law, politics, philosophy, and particularly of the fundamental doctrines of natural science, the constitution of the solar system, the geological history of the earth, the nature of chemical forces, the physiological relations of animals and plants.

[1] Distinguished as an author in chemistry and physiology, and as a philosophical historian: a native of England, but long a professor in New York University.

It is supposed by many, whose attention has been casually drawn to the philosophical opinions of antiquity, that the doctrines which we still retain as true came to the knowledge of the old philosophers, not so much by processes of legitimate investigation as by mere guessing or crude speculation, for which there was an equal chance whether they were right or wrong; but a closer examination will show that many of them must have depended on results previously determined or observed by the Africans or Asiatics, and thus they seem to indicate that the human mind has undergone in twenty centuries but little change in its manner of action, and that, commencing with the same data, it always comes to the same conclusions. Nor is this at all dependent on any inherent logic of truth. Very many of the errors of antiquity have re-appeared in our times. If the Greek schools were infected with materialism, pantheism, and atheism, the later progress of philosophy has shown the same characters. To a certain extent, such doctrines will receive an impression from the prevailing creeds, but the arguments which have been appealed to in their favor have always been the same. The distinction between these heresies in ancient and modern times lies chiefly in the grosser characters which they formerly assumed, arising partly from the reflected influence of the existing mythology, and partly from the imperfections of exact knowledge. Even the errors of early antiquity are venerable. We must judge our predecessors by the rules by which we hope posterity will judge us, making a generous allowance for the imperfections of reason, the infirmities of character, and especially for the prejudices of the times. To have devoutly believed in the existence of a human soul, to have looked forward to its continuing after the death of the body, to have expected a future state of rewards and punishments, and to have drawn therefrom, as a philosophical conclusion, the necessity of leading a virtuous life—these, though they may be enveloped in a cloud of errors, are noble results of the intellect of man.

From "Thoughts on the Future Civil Policy of America."

216. PROSPECTIVE INFLUENCES OF THE REPUBLIC.

Now, when we consider the position of the American continent,—its Atlantic front looking upon Europe, its Pacific front looking upon Asia,—when we reflect how much Nature has done for it in the wonderful river system she has bestowed, and how varied are the mineral and agricultural products it yields, it would seem as if we should be constrained by circumstances to carry out spontaneously in practical life the abstract suggestions of policy. . . . . Great undertakings, such as the construction of the Pacific Railroad, pressed into existence by commercial motives and fostered for military reasons, will indirectly accomplish political objects not yielding in importance to those that are obvious and avowed.

A few years more, and the influence of the great republic will resistlessly extend in a direction that will lead to surprising results. . . . The stream of Chinese emigration already setting into California is but the precursor of the flood that is to come. Here are the fields, there are the men. The dominant power on the Pacific Ocean must necessarily exert a controlling influence in the affairs of Asia.

The Roman empire is regarded, perhaps not unjustly, as the most imposing of all human political creations. Italy extended her rule across the eastern and western basins of the Mediterranean Sea, from the confines of Parthia to Spain. A similar central, but far grander, position is occupied by the American continent. The partitions of an interior and narrow sea are replaced by the two great oceans. But, since history ever repeats itself, the maxims that guided the policy of Rome in her advance to sovereignty are not without application here. Her mistakes may be monitions to us.

A great, a homogeneous, and yet an active people, having strength and security in its political institutions, may look forward to a career of glory. It may, without offense, seek to render its life memorable in the annals of the human race.

James Russell Lowell, 1810–. (Manual, pp. 503, 520.)

From "Among my Books."

217. New England two Centuries ago.

I have little sympathy with declaimers about the Pilgrim Fathers, who look upon them all as men of grand conceptions and superhuman foresight. An entire ship's company of Columbuses is what the world never saw. It is not wise to form any theory and fit our facts to it, as a man in a hurry is apt to cram his traveling-bag, with a total disregard of shape or texture. But perhaps it may be found that the facts will only fit comfortably together on a single plan, namely, that the fathers did have a conception (which those will call grand who regard simplicity as a necessary element of grandeur) of founding here a commonwealth on those two eternal bases of Faith and Work; that they had, indeed, no revolutionary ideas of universal liberty; but yet, what answered the purpose quite as well, an abiding faith in the brotherhood of man and the fatherhood of God; and that they did not so much propose to make all things new, as to develop the latent possibilities of English law and English character by clearing away the fences by which the abuse of the one was gradually discommoning the other from the broad fields of natural right. They were not in advance of their age, as it is called, for no one who is so can ever work profitably in it; but they were alive to the highest and most earnest thinking of their time.

---

218. From an "Essay on Dryden."

I do not think he added a single word to the language, unless, as I suspect, he first used *magnetism* in its present sense of moral attraction. What he did in his best writing was, to use the English as if it were a spoken, and not merely an inkhorn language; as if it were his own to do what he pleased with it, as if it need not be ashamed of itself. In this respect, his service to our prose was greater than any other man has ever rendered. He says he formed his style upon Tillotson's (Bossuet, on the other hand, formed *his* upon Corneille's); but I rather think he got it at Will's, for its greatest charm is, that it has the various freedom of talk. In verse, he has a pomp which, excellent in itself, became pompousness in his imitators. But he had nothing of Milton's ear for various rhythm and interwoven harmony. He knew how to give new modulation, sweetness, and force to the pentameter; but in what used to be called pindarics, I am heretic enough to think he generally failed.

—

From "My Study Windows."

219. LOVE OF BIRDS AND SQUIRRELS.

WILSON'S thrush comes every year to remind me of that most poetic of ornithologists. He flits before me through the pine-walk like the very genius of solitude. A pair of pewees have built immemorially on a jutting brick in the arched entrance to the ice-house. Always on the same brick, and never more than a single pair, though two broods of five each are raised there every summer. How do they settle their claim to the homestead? By what right of primogeniture? Once, the children of a man employed about the place oölogized the nest, and the pewees left us for a year or two. I felt towards those boys as the messmates of the Ancient Mariner did towards him after he had shot the albatross. But the pewees came back at last, and one of them is now on his wonted perch, so near my window that I can hear the click of his bill as he snaps a fly on the wing. . . . The pewee is the first bird to pipe up in the morning; and, during the early summer he preludes his matutinal ejaculation of *pewee* with a slender whistle, unheard at any other time. He saddens with the season, and, as summer declines, he changes his note to *eheu, pewee!* as if in lamentation. Had he been an Italian bird, Ovid would have had a plaintive tale to tell about him. He is so familiar as often to pursue a fly through the open window into my library.

There is something inexpressibly dear to me in these old friendships of a lifetime. There is scarce a tree of mine but has had, at some time or other, a happy homestead among its boughs, to which I cannot say,

> "Many light hearts and wings,
> Which now be dead, lodged in thy living bowers."

My walk under the pines would lose half its summer charm were I to miss that shy anchorite, the Wilson's thrush, nor hear in haying time the metallic ring of his song, that justifies his rustic name of *scythe-whet.* I protect my game as jealously as an English squire. If anybody had oölogized a certain cuckoo's nest I know of (I have a pair in my garden every year), it would have left me a sore place in my mind for weeks. I love to bring these aborigines back to the mansuetude they showed to the early voyagers, and before (forgive the involuntary pun), they had grown accustomed to man and knew his savage ways. And they repay your kindness with a sweet familiarity too delicate ever to breed contempt. I have made a Penn-treaty with them, preferring that to the Puritan way with the native, which converted them to a little Hebraism and a great deal of Medford rum. If they will not come near enough to me (as most of them will), I bring them close with an opera-glass,—a much better weapon than a gun. I would not, if I could, convert them from their pretty pagan ways. The only one I sometimes have savage doubts about, is the red squirrel. I *think* he oölogizes; I *know* he eats cherries, (we counted five of them at one time in a single tree, the stones pattering down like the sparse hail that preludes a storm), and that he knaws off the small end of pears to get at the seeds. He steals the corn from under the noses of my poultry. But what would you have? He will come down upon the limb of the tree I am lying under, till he is within a yard of me. He and his mate will scurry up and down the great black-walnut for my diversion, chattering like monkeys. Can I sign his death-warrant who has tolerated me about his grounds so long? Not I. Let them steal, and welcome, I am sure I should, had I the same bringing up and the same temptation. As for the birds, I do not believe there is one of them but does more good than harm; and of how many featherless bipeds can this be said.

—

220. CHAUCER'S LOVE OF NATURE.

HE was the first great poet who really loved outward nature as the source of conscious pleasurable emotion. The Troubadour hailed the return of spring, but with him it was a piece of empty ritualism. Chaucer took a true delight in the new green of the leaves, and the return of singing birds—a delight as simple as that of Robin Hood:—

"In summer when the shaws be sheen,
And leaves be large and long,
It is full merry in fair forest
To hear the small birds' song."

He has never so much as heard of the burthen and the mystery of all this unintelligible world. His flowers and trees and birds have never bothered themselves with Spinoza. He himself sings more like a bird than any other poet, because it never occurred to him, as to Goethe, that he ought to do so. He pours himself out in sincere joy and thankfulness. When we compare Spenser's imitations of him with the original passages, we feel that the delight of the later poet was more in the expression than in the thing itself. Nature, with him, is only to be transfigured by art. We walk among Chaucer's sights and sounds; we listen to Spenser's musical reproduction of them. In the same way the pleasure which Chaucer takes in telling his stories, has, in itself, the effect of consummate skill, and makes us follow all the windings of his fancy with sympathetic interest. His best tales run on like one of our inland rivers, sometimes hastening a little and turning upon themselves in eddies, that dimple without retarding the current, sometimes loitering smoothly, while here and there a quiet thought, a tender feeling, a pleasant image, a golden-hearted verse, opens quietly as a water-lily to float on the surface without breaking it into ripple. . . . Chaucer never shows any signs of effort, and it is a main proof of his excellence that he can be so inadequately sampled by detached passages, by single lines taken away from the connection in which they contribute to the general effect. He has that continuity of thought, that evenly prolonged power, and that delightful equanimity, which characterize the higher orders of mind. There is something in him of the disinterestedness that made the Greeks masters in art. His phrase is never importunate. His simplicity is that of elegance, not of poverty. The quiet unconcern with which he says his best things is peculiar to him among English poets, though Goldsmith, Addison, and Thackeray, have approached it in prose. He prattles inadvertently away, and all the while, like the princess in the story, lets fall a pearl at every other word. It is such a piece of good luck to be natural. It is the good gift which the fairy god-mother brings to her prime favorites in the cradle. If not genius, it is alone what makes genius amiable in the arts. If a man have it not he will never find it; for when it is sought it is gone.

Edgar Allen Poe, 1811–1849. (Manual, p. 510.)

From "The Masque of the Red Death."

221. Chiming of the Clock.

The seventh apartment was closely shrouded in black velvet tapestries that hung all over the ceiling and down the walls, falling in heavy folds upon a carpet of the same material and hue. But in this chamber only, the color of the windows failed to correspond with the decorations. The panes here were scarlet—a deep blood color. Now in no one of the seven apartments was there any lamp or candelabrum, amid the profusion of golden ornaments that lay scattered to and fro, or depended from the roof. There was no light of any kind emanating from lamp or candle within the suite of chambers. But in the corridors that followed the suite, there stood, opposite to each window, a heavy tripod, bearing a brazier of fire, that projected its rays through the tinted glass and so glaringly illumined the room. And thus were produced a multitude of gaudy and fantastic appearances. But in the western or black chamber, the effect of the fire-light that streamed upon the dark hangings through the blood-tinted panes, was ghastly in the extreme, and produced so wild a look upon the countenances of those who entered, that there were few of the company bold enough to set foot within its precincts at all.

It was in this apartment, also, that there stood against the western wall, a gigantic clock of ebony. Its pendulum swung to and fro with a dull, heavy, monotonous clang; and when the minute-hand made the circuit of the face, and the hour was to be stricken, there came from the brazen lungs of the clock a sound which was clear and loud and deep, and exceedingly musical, but of so peculiar a note and emphasis that, at each lapse of an hour, the musicians of the orchestra were constrained to pause, momentarily, in their performance, to hearken to the sound; and thus the waltzers perforce ceased their evolutions; and there was a brief disconcert of the whole gay company; and, while the chimes of the clock yet rang, it was observed that the giddiest grew pale, and the more aged and sedate passed their hands over their brows, as if in confused revery or meditation. But when the echoes had fully ceased, a light laughter at once pervaded the assembly; the musicians looked at each other and smiled, as if at their own nervousness and folly, and made whispering vows, each to the other, that the next chiming of the clock should produce in them no similar emotion; and then, after the lapse of sixty minutes, (which embrace three thousand and six hundred seconds of the Time that flies,) there came yet another chiming of the clock, and then were the same disconcert and tremulousness and meditation as before.

From his "Essays."

222. The Philosophy of Composition.

There is a radical error, I think, in the usual mode of constructing a story. Either history affords a thesis—or one is suggested by an incident of the day—or, at best, the author sets himself to work in the combination of striking events to form merely the basis of his narrative—designing, generally, to fill in with description, dialogue, or autorial comment, whatever crevices of fact, or action, may, from page to page, render themselves apparent.

I prefer commencing with the consideration of an *effect*, keeping originality *always* in view—for he is false to himself who ventures to dispense with so obvious and so easily attainable a source of interest. I say to myself, in the first place, "Of the innumerable effects, or impressions, of which the heart, the intellect, or (more generally) the soul, is susceptible, what one shall I, on the present occasion, select?" Having chosen a novel, first, and secondly a vivid, effect, I consider whether it can be best wrought by incident or tone, whether by ordinary incidents and peculiar tone, or the converse, or by peculiarity both of incident and tone—afterward looking about me (or rather within) for such combinations of event, or tone, as shall best aid me in the construction of the effect.

I have often thought how interesting a magazine paper might be written by any author who would—that is to say, who could—detail, step by step, the process by which any one of his compositions attained its ultimate point of completion. Why such a paper has never been given to the world, I am much at a loss to say—but, perhaps, the autorial vanity has had more to do with the omission than any one other cause. Most writers, poets in especial, prefer having it understood that they compose by a species of fine frenzy, an ecstatic intuition, and would positively shudder at letting the public take a peep behind the scenes, at the elaborate and vacillating crudities of thought—at the true purposes seized only at the last moment—

at the innumerable glimpses of idea that arrived not at the maturity of full view—at the fully matured fancies discarded in despair as unmanageable—at the cautious selections and rejections—at the painful erasures and interpolations—in a word, at the wheels and pinions, the tackle for scene-shifting—the step-ladders and demon-traps—the cock's feathers, the red paint and the black patches, which, in ninety-nine cases out of the hundred, constituted the properties of the literary *histrio.*

I am aware, on the other hand, that the case is by no means common in which an author is at all in condition to retrace the steps by which his conclusions have been attained. In general, suggestions having arisen pell-mell, are pursued and forgotten in a similar manner.

Henry T. Tuckerman,[1] *1813–.*

From "New England Philosophy;" an Essay from "The Optimist."

223. THE HEART SUPERIOR TO THE INTELLECT.

CONSTANT supplies of knowledge to the intellect, and the exclusive cultivation of reason, may, indeed, make a pedant and a logician; but the probability is, these benefits—if such they are—will be gained at the expense of the soul. Sentiment, in its broadest acceptation, is as essential to the true enjoyment and grace of life as mind. Technical information, and that quickness of apprehension which New Englanders call smartness, are not so valuable to a human being as sensibility to the beautiful, and a spontaneous appreciation of the divine influences which fill the realms of vision and of sound, and the world of action and feeling. The tastes, affections, and sentiments are more absolutely the man than his talents or acquirements. And yet it is by, and through, the latter that we are apt to estimate character, of which they are at best but fragmentary evidences. It is remarkable that in the New Testament, allusions to the intellect are so rare, while the "heart" and the "spirit we are of" are ever appealed to. . . . To what end are society, popular education, churches, and all the machinery of culture, if no living truth is elicited which fertilizes, as well as enlightens. Shakespeare undoubtedly owed his marvelous insight into the human soul, to his profound sympathy with man. He might have conned whole libraries on the philosophy of the passions, he might have coldly observed facts for years, and never have conceived of jealousy like Othello's,—the remorse of Macbeth, or love like that of Juliet. . . .

Sometimes, in musing upon genius in its simpler manifestations, it seems as if the great art of human culture consisted chiefly in preserving the glow and freshness of the heart. It is certain that, in proportion as its merely mental strength and attainment take the place of natural sentiment, in proportion as we acquire the habit of receiving all impressions through the reason, the teachings of Nature grow indistinct and cold. . . . It is when we are overcome, and the pride of intellect vanquished before the truth of nature, when instead of coming to a logical decision we are led to bow in profound reverence before the mysteries of life, when we are led back to childhood, or up to God, by some powerful revelation of the sage or minstrel, it is then our natures grow. To this end is all art. Exquisite vocalism, beautiful statuary, and painting, and all true literature, have not for their great object to employ the ingenuity of prying critics, or furnish the world with a set of new ideas, but to move the whole nature by the perfection and truthfulness of their appeal. There is a certain atmosphere exhaled from the inspired page of genius, which gives vitality to the sentiments, and through these, quickens the mental powers. And this is the chief good of books.

H. N. Hudson, 1814–. (Manual, pp. 480, 501.)

From "Preface to the Works of Shakespeare."

224. SHAKESPEARE'S WORKS INSTRUCTIVE.

IT is true, he often lays on us burdens of passion that would not be borne in any other writer. But whether he wrings the heart with pity, or freezes the blood with terror, or fires the soul with indignation, the genial reader still rises from his pages refreshed. The reason of which is, instruction keeps pace with excitement: he strengthens the mind in proportion as he loads it. He has been called the great master of passion: doubtless he is so; yet he makes us think as intensely as he requires us to feel; while opening the deepest fountains of the heart, he at the same time unfolds the highest energies of the head. Nay, with such consummate art does he manage the fiercest tempests of our being, that in a healthy mind the witnessing of them is always attended with an overbalance of pleasure. With the very whirlwinds of passion he so blends the softening and alleviating influences of poetry, that they relish of nothing but sweetness and health. . . . He is not wont to exhibit either utterly worthless or utterly faultless monsters; persons too good, or too bad, to exist; too high to be loved, or too low to be pitied; even his worst characters (unless we should except Goneril and Regan, and even their blood is red like ours) have some slight fragrance of humanity about them, some indefinable touches, which redeem them from utter hatred and execration, and keep them within the pale of human sympathy, or at least of human pity.

Mary Henderson Eastman,[1] about *1815–.*

From "The American Aboriginal Port Folio."

225. LAKE ITASKA, THE SOURCE OF THE MISSISSIPPI.

THERE it lay—the beautiful lake—swaying its folds of crystal water between the hills that guarded it from its birth. There it lay, placid as a sleeping child, the tall pines on the surrounding summits standing like so many motionless and watchful sentinels for its protection.

There was the sequestered birthplace of that mighty mass

[1] This lady—a native of Virginia—has written several interesting books, chiefly relating to Indian tradition.

of waters, that, leaving the wilderness of beauty where they lived undisturbed and unknown, wound their way through many a desolate prairie, and fiercely lashed the time-worn bluffs, whose sides were as walls to the great city, where lived and died the toiling multitude. The lake was as some fair and pure maiden in early youth, so beautiful, so full of repose and truth, that it was impossible to look and not to love. . .

There was but one landing to the lake, our travellers found. It was on a small island, that they called Schoolcraft's Island. On a tall spruce tree they raised the American flag. There was enough in the novelty of the scenery, and of the event, to interest the white men of the party. There was a solemnity mingled with their pleased emotions ; for who had made this grand picture, stretching out in its beauty and majesty before them? What were they, in comparison with the great and good Being upon whose works they were gazing?

—

226. A Plea for the Indians.

The light of the great council-fire—its blaze once illumined the entire country we now call our own—is faintly gleaming out its unsteady and dying rays. Our fathers were guests, and warmed themselves by its hospitable rays ; now we are lords, and rule with an iron hand over those who received kindly, and entertained generously, the wanderer who came from afar to worship his God according to his own will. The very hearth where moulder the ashes of this once never-ceasing fire, is becoming desolate, the decaying embers sometimes starting into a brief brilliancy, and then fading into a gloom more sad, more silent, than ever. Soon will be scattered, as by the winds of heaven, the last ashes that remain. Think of it, O legislator! as thou standest in the Capitol, the great council-hall of thy country ; plead for them, "upon whose pathway death's dark shadow falls."

Mary E. Moragne,[1] *1815–.*

From "The Huguenot Town."

227. RUINS OF THE OLD FRENCH SETTLEMENT.

AN ignorance of the common methods of agriculture practised here, as well as strong prejudices in favor of their former habits of living, prevented them from seizing with avidity on large bodies of land, by individual possession ; but the site of a town being selected, a lot of four acres was apportioned to every citizen. In a short time a hundred houses had risen, in a regularly compact body, in the square of which stood a building superior in size and construction to the rest. . . .

. . . The town was soon busy with the industry of its tradesmen ; silk and flax were manufactured, whilst the cultivators of the soil were taxed with the supply of corn and wine. The hum of cheerful voices arose during the week, mingled with the interdicted songs of praise ; and on the Sabbath the quiet worshippers assembled in their rustic church, listened with fervent response to that faithful pastor, who had been their spiritual leader through perils by sea and land, and who now directed their free, unrestrained devotion to the Lord of the forest.

. . . The woods still wave on in melancholy grandeur, with the added glory of near a hundred years ; but they who once lived and worshipped beneath them—where are they? Shades of my ancestors,—where? No crumbling wreck, no mossy ruin, points the antiquarian research to the place of their sojourn, or to their last resting-places! The traces of a narrow trench, surrounding a square plat of ground, now covered with the interlacing arms of hawthorn and wild honey-suckle, arrest the attention as we are proceeding along a strongly beaten track in the deep woods, and we are assured that this is the site of the "old French town" which has given its name to the portion of country around.

[1] One of the best female writers of South Carolina, who has of late years laid aside her pen.

Richard H. Dana, Jr., 1815–. (Manual, p. 504.)

From "Two years before the Mast."

228. Loss of a Man at Sea.

Death is at all times solemn, but never so much so as at sea. A man dies on shore; his body remains with his friends, and "the mourners go about the streets;" but when a man falls overboard at sea and is lost, there is a suddenness in the event, and a difficulty in realizing it, which give to it an air of awful mystery. A man dies on shore—you follow his body to the grave, and a stone marks the spot. You are often prepared for the event. There is always something which helps you to realize it when it happens, and to recall it when it has passed. A man is shot down by your side in battle, and the mangled body remains an object, and a real evidence; but at sea, the man is near you—at your side—you hear his voice, and in an instant he is gone, and nothing but a vacancy shows his loss. Then too, at sea—to use a homely but expressive phrase—you miss a man so much. A dozen men are shut up together in a little bark, upon the wide, wide sea, and for months and months see no forms and hear no voices but their own, and one is taken suddenly from among them, and they miss him at every turn. It is like losing a limb. There are no new faces or new scenes to fill up the gap. There is always an empty berth in the forecastle, and one man wanting when the small night watch is mustered. There is one less to take the wheel, and one less to lay out with you upon the yard. You miss his form, and the sound of his voice, for habit had made them almost necessary to you, and each of your senses feels the loss.

All these things make such a death peculiarly solemn, and the effect of it remains upon the crew for some time. There is more kindness shown by the officers to the crew, and by the crew to one another. There is more quietness and seriousness. The oath and the loud laugh are gone. The officers are more watchful, and the crew go more carefully aloft. The lost man is seldom mentioned, or is dismissed wtth a sailor's rude eulogy,

"Well, poor George is gone. His cruise is up soon. He knew his work, and did his duty, and was a good shipmate." Then usually follows some allusion to another world, for sailors are almost all believers ; but their notions and opinions are unfixed, and at loose ends. They say,—"God won't be hard upon the poor fellow," and seldom get beyond the common phrase which seems to imply that their sufferings and hard treatment here, will excuse them hereafter. *To work hard, live hard, die hard, and go to hell after all*, would be hard indeed. .

Yet a sailor's life is at best but a mixture of a little good with much evil, and a little pleasure with much pain. The beautiful is linked with the revolting, the sublime with the common-place, and the solemn with the ludicrous.

We had hardly returned on board with our sad report, before an auction was held of the poor man's clothes. The captain had first, however, called all hands aft, and asked them if they were satisfied that everything had been done to save the man, and if they thought there was any use in remaining there longer. The crew all said that it was in vain, for the man did not know how to swim, and was very heavily dressed. So we then filled away and kept her off to her course.

Evert A. Duyckinck, 1816–. (Manual, p. 502.)

Essay from "Arcturus."

229. NEWSPAPERS.

No one, it has been said, ever takes up a newspaper without interest, or lays it down without regret. There is a deeper truth in this observation than at first thought strikes the mind ; it is not the casual disappointment at the loss of fine writing, or the absence of particular topics of news, or the variety of subjects that dispel all deep-settled reflection ; but a newspaper is in some measure a picture of human life, and we can no more read its various paragraphs with pleasure, than we can look back upon the events of any single day with unmingled satisfaction. . . . A man may learn, sitting by his fire-side, more than an angel would desire to know of human life, by reading well a single newspaper. It is an instrument of many tones, running through the whole scale of humanity; from the lightest gayety to the gravest sadness; from the large interests of nations to the humblest affairs of the smallest individual. On its single page we read of Births, Marriages, and Deaths; the daily, almost hourly, register of royalty, how it eat, walked, and laughed; and the single incident the world deems worth recording of the life of poverty—how it died. It is a picture of motley human life; a poet's thought, or an orator's eloquence in one column, and the condemnation of a pickpocket in another. . . .

Doubtless it was a very satisfactory thing for a Roman poet, when the wind was quiet, to get an audience about him, under a portico, and unwind his well-written scroll for an hour or two; but there must have been a vast deal of secret machinery, and influence, and agitation, to keep up his name with the people. The followers of Pythagoras, in another country, we know, said he had a golden leg, and this satisfied the people that his philosophy was divine. Truly were they the dark ages before the invention of newspapers. Besides, what became of literature when the poet's voice in the public bath, or library, where he recited, was drowned by the din of arms? . . .

What would we not give for a newspaper of the days of Homer, with personal recollections of the contractors and commanders in the siege of Troy; a reminiscence of Helen; the unedited fragments of Nestor; or a traditional saying of Ulysses, who may be supposed too wise to have published? What such a passage of literature would be to us, the journal of to-day may be to some long distant age, when it is disentombed from the crumbling corner-stone of some Astor House, Exchange, or Trinity Church, on the deserted shore of an island, once New York. What matters of curiosity would be poured fourth for the attention of the inquisitive; how many learned theories which had sprung up in the interim, put to rest; what anxiety moralists would be under to know the number of churches, the bookseller's advertisements, and the convictions at the Sessions! Some might be supposed to sigh over our lack of improvement, the infant state of the arts, and our ineffectual attempts at electro-magnetism, while others would dwell upon the old times when Broadway was gayer with life, and the world got along better, than it has ever done since.

Horace Binney Wallace,[1] *1817–1852.*

From "Art, Scenery, and Philosophy in Europe."

230. ART AN EMANATION OF RELIGIOUS AFFECTION.

THE spirit, conscious of an emotion of reverence for some unseen subject of its own apprehension, desires to substantiate and fix its deity, and to bring the senses into the same adoring attitude; and this can be done only by setting before them a material representation of the divine. This is illustrated in the universal and inveterate tendency of early nations to idolatry. . . .

How and why was it that the sculpture of the Greeks attained a character so exalted that it shines on through our time, with a beam of glory peculiar and inextinguishable? When we enter the chambers of the Vatican, we are presently struck with the mystic influence that rays from those silent forms that stand ranged along the walls. Like the moral prestige that might encircle the vital presence of divine beings, we behold divinities represented in human shapes idealized into a significance altogether irresistible. What constitutes that idealizing modification we know not; but we feel that it imparts to the figures an interest and impressiveness which natural forms possess not. These sculptured images seem

[1] A young writer of great cultivation and of uncommon promise. His premature death occurred while on a tour in Europe. A native of Philadelphia.

directly to address the imagination. They do not suffer the cold and critical survey of the eye, but awaken an instant and vivid mental consideration.

. . . It has sometimes been suggested that the superiority of the Greeks in delineating the figure, arose from the familiarity with it which they acquired from their frequent opportunities of viewing it nude,—on account of their usages, costumes, climate, &c. This is too superficial an account of that vital faculty of skill and knowledge upon this subject, which was a part of the inherent capacity of the Greek. . . . The outflow and characteristic exercise of Grecian inspiration in sculpture, was in the representation of their mythology, which included heroes, or deified men, as well as gods of the first rank. Later, it extended to winners at the public games, athletes, runners, boxers;—but this class of persons partook, in the national feeling, of a heroic or half-divine superiority. A particular type of form, highly ideal, became appropriate to them, as to the heroes, and to each of the gods. It may be added, that a capacity thus derived from religious impressibility, extended to a great number of natural forms, which were to the Greeks measurably objects of a divine regard. Many animals as connected with the gods, or with sacrifices, were sacred beings to them, and became subjects of their surpassing gift in sculpture. In general, nature,—the visible, the sensible, the actual, was to the Hellenic soul, Religion; as inward and reflective emotions were and are, to the modern European.

Henry David Thoreau, 1817-1862. (Manual, p. 532.)

From "Autumnal Tints."

231. Description of "Poke" or Garget, (*Phytolacca Decandra.*)

Some which stand under our cliffs quite dazzle me with their purple stems now, and early in September. They are as interesting to me as most flowers, and one of the most important fruits of our autumn. Every part is flower, (or fruit,) such is its superfluity of color,—stem, branch, peduncle, pedicel, petiole, and even the at length yellowish purple-veined leaves. Its cylindrical racemes of berries of various hues, from green to dark purple, six or seven inches long, are gracefully drooping on all sides, offering repasts to the birds; and even the sepals from which the birds have picked the berries are a brilliant lake-red, with crimson, flame-like reflections, equal to anything of the kind,—all on fire with ripeness. Hence the *lacca*, from lac, lake. There are at the same time flower-buds, flowers, green berries, dark purple or ripe ones, and these flower-like sepals, all on the same plant.

We love to see any redness in the vegetation of the temperate zone. It is the color of colors. This plant speaks to our blood. It asks a bright sun on it to make it show to best advantage, and it must be seen at this season of the year. On warm hill-sides its stems are ripe by the twenty-third of August. At that date I walked through a beautiful grove of them, six or seven feet high, on the side of one of our cliffs, where they ripen early. Quite to the ground they were a deep brilliant purple with a bloom, contrasting with the still clear green leaves. It appears a rare triumph of Nature to have produced and perfected such a plant, as if this were enough for a summer. What a perfect maturity it arrives at! It is the emblem of a successful life concluded by a death not premature, which is an ornament to Nature. What if we were to mature as perfectly, root and branch, glowing in the midst of our decay, like the Poke! I confess that it excites me to behold them. I cut one for a cane, for I would fain handle and lean on it. I love to press the berries between my fingers, and see their juice staining my hand. To walk amid these upright, branching casks of purple wine, which retain and diffuse a sunset glow, tasting each one with your eye, instead of counting the pipes on a London dock,—what a privilege! For Nature's vintage is not confined to the vine. Our poets have sung of wine, the product of a foreign plant which commonly they never saw, as if our own plants had no juice in them more than the singers. Indeed, this has been called by some the American grape, and though a native of America, its juices are used in some foreign countries to improve the color of the wine; so that the poetaster may be celebrating the virtues of the Poke without knowing it. Here are berries enough to paint afresh the western sky, and play the bacchanal with, if you will. And what flutes its ensanguined stems would make, to be used in such a dance! It is truly a royal plant. I could spend the evening of the year musing amid the Poke-stems. And perchance amid these groves might arise at last a new school of philosophy or poetry.

—

From "Walden, or Life in the Woods."

232. Walden Pond.

The greatest depth was exactly one hundred and two feet, to which may be added the five feet which it has risen since, making one hundred and seven. This is a remarkable depth for so small an area; yet not an inch of it can be spared by the imagination. What if all ponds were shallow? Would it not react on the minds of men? I am thankful that this pond was made deep and pure for a symbol. While men believe in the infinite, some ponds will be thought to be bottomless.

—

From "Life without Principle."

233. Wants of the Age.

I saw, the other day, a vessel which had been wrecked, and many lives lost, and her cargo of rags, juniper-berries, and bitter almonds, was strewn along the shore. It seemed hardly worth the while to tempt the dangers of the sea between Leghorn and New York, for the sake of a cargo of juniper-berries and bitter almonds. America sending to the Old World for her bitters! Is not the sea-brine,—is not shipwreck, bitter enough to make the cup of life go down here? Yet such, to a great extent, is our boasted commerce; and there are those who style themselves statesmen and philosophers who are so blind as to think that progress and civilization depend on precisely this kind of interchange and activity,—the activity of flies about a molasses-hogshead. Very well, observes one, if men were oysters. And very well, answer I, if men were mosquitoes.

Lieutenant Herndon, whom our Government sent to explore the Amazon, and, it is said, to extend the area of Slavery, observed that there was wanting there "an industrious and active population, who know what the comforts of life are, and who have artificial wants to draw out the great resources of the country." But what are the "artificial wants" to be encouraged? Not the love of luxuries, like the tobacco and slaves of, I believe, his native Virginia, nor the ice and granite and other material wealth of our native New England; nor are "the great resources of a country" that fertility or barrenness of soil which produces these. The chief want, in every State that I have been into, was a high and earnest purpose in its inhabitants. This alone draws out "the great resources" of Nature and at last taxes her beyond her resources; for man naturally dies out of her. When we want culture more than potatoes, and illumination more than sugar-plums, then the great resources of a world are taxed and drawn out, and the result, or staple production, is, not slaves, nor operatives, but men,—those rare fruits called heroes, saints, poets, philosophers, and redeemers.

Elizabeth F. Ellett, 1818–. (Manual, pp. 484, 490.)

From "Pioneer Women of the West."

234. ESCAPE OF MARY BLEDSOE FROM THE INDIANS.

IT was not consistent with Spencer's chivalrous character to attempt to save himself by leaving his companion to the mercy of the foe. Bidding her retreat as fast as possible, and encouraging her to keep her seat firmly, he protected her by following more slowly in her rear, with his trusty rifle in his hand. When the Indians in pursuit came too near, he would raise his weapon as if to fire; and as he was known to be an excellent marksman, the savages were not willing to encounter him, but hastened to the shelter of trees, while he continued his retreat. In this manner he kept them at bay for some miles, not firing a single shot—for he knew that his threatening had more effect—until Mrs. Bledsoe reached a station. Her life and his own, were, on this occasion, saved by his prudence and presence of mind; for both would have been lost had he yielded to the temptation to fire. . . .

Bereaved of her husband, sons, and brother-in-law, by the murderous savages, Mrs. Bledsoe was obliged to undertake not only the charge of her husband's estate, but the care of the children, and their education and settlement in life. These duties were discharged with unwavering energy and Christian patience. . . . The record of her worth, and of what she did and suffered, may win little attention from the careless many, who regard not the memory of our "pilgrim mothers;" but the recollection of her gentle virtues has not yet faded from the hearts of her descendants, and those to whom they tell the story of her life will acknowledge her the worthy companion of those noble men to whom belongs the praise of having originated a new colony, and built up a goodly state in the bosom of the forest. Their patriotic labors, their struggles with the surrounding savages, their efforts in the maintenance of the community they had founded,—sealed, as they finally were, with their own blood, and the blood of their sons and relatives,—will never be forgotten while the apprehension of what is noble, generous, and good, survives in the hearts of their countrymen.

James Jackson Jarves, 1818-. (Manual, p. 531.)

From "Art Hints."

235. THE ART IDEA.

THE first duty of art, as we have already intimated, is to make our public buildings and places, as instructive and enjoyable as possible. They should be pleasurable, full of attractive beauty and eloquent teachings. Picturesque groupings of natural objects, architectual surprises, sermons from the sculptor's chisel and the painter's palette, the ravishment of the soul by its superior senses, the refinement of mind and body by the sympathetic power of beauty,—these are a portion of the means which a due estimation of art, as an element of civilization, inspires the ruling will to provide freely for all. If art be kept a rare and tabooed thing, a specialty for the rich and powerful, it excites in the vulgar mind, envy and hate; but proffer it freely to the public, and the public soon learns to delight in and protect it as its rightful inheritance. It also tends to develop a brotherhood of thought and feeling. During the civil strifes of Italy, art flourished and was respected. Indeed, to some extent, it operated as a sort of peace society, and was held sacred when nothing else was. Even rude soldiers, amid the perils and necessities of sieges, turned aside destruction from the walls that sheltered it. The history of art is full of records of its power to soften and elevate the human heart. As soon would man, were it possible, mar one of God's sunsets, as cease to respect what genius has confided to his care, when once his mind has been awakened to its meaning.

The desire for art being awakened, museums to illustrate its technical and historical progress, and galleries to exhibit its master-works, become indispensable. In the light of education, appropriations for such purposes are as much a duty of the government as for any other purpose connected with the true welfare of the people; for its responsibilities extend over the entire social system.

Edwin P. Whipple, 1819-. (Manual, p. 501.)

From "Literature and Life."

236. Wit and Humor in Literature.

Every student of English theological literature knows that much of its best portions gleams with wit. Five of the greatest humorists that ever made the world ring with laughter were priests,—Rabelais, Scarron, Swift, Sterne, and Sydney Smith. The prose works of Milton are radiant with satire of the sharpest kind. Sydney Smith, one of the most benevolent, intelligent and influential Englishmen of the nineteenth century, a man of the most accurate insight and extensive information, embodied the large stores of his practical wisdom in almost every form of the ludicrous. Many of the most important reforms in England are directly traceable to him. He really laughed his countrymen out of some of their most cherished stupidities of legislation.

And now let us be just to Mirth. Let us be thankful that we have in Wit a power before which the pride of wealth and the insolence of office are abased; which can transfix bigotry and tyranny with arrows of lightning; which can strike its object over thousands of miles of space, across thousands of years of time; and which, through its sway over an universal weakness of man, is an everlasting instrument to make the bad tremble and the foolish wince. Let us be grateful for the social and humanizing influences of Mirth. Amid the sorrow, disappointment, agony, and anguish of the world,—over dark thoughts and tempestuous passions, the gloomy exaggerations of self-will, the enfeebling illusions of melancholy,—Wit and Humor, light and lightning, shed their soft radiance, or dart their electric flash. See how life is warmed and illumined by Mirth! See how the beings of the mind, with which it has peopled our imaginations, wrestle with the ills of existence,—feeling their way into the harshest or saddest meditations, with looks that defy calamity; relaxing muscles made rigid with pain; hovering o'er the couch of sickness, with sunshine and laughter in their beneficent faces; softening the austerity of thoughts whose awful shadows dim and darken the brain,—loosening the gripe of Misery as it tugs at the heart-strings! Let us court the society of these gamesome, and genial, and sportive, and sparkling beings, whom Genius has left to us as a priceless bequest; push them not from the daily walks of the world's life; let them scatter some humanities in the sullen marts of business; let them glide in through the open doors of the heart; let their glee lighten up the feast, and gladden the fire-side of home:

"That the night may be filled with music,
And the cares that infest the day
May fold their tents, like the Arabs,
And as silently steal away."

Jane T. L. Worthington,[1] *-1847.* (Manual, p. 524.)

From "Love Sketches."

237. THE SISTERS.

THE sisters were together, together for the last time in the happy home of their childhood. The window before them was thrown open, and the shadows of evening were slowly passing from each familiar outline on which the gazers looked. They were both young and fair; and one, the elder, wore that pale wreath the maiden wears but once. The accustomed smile had forsaken her lip now, and the orange-flowers were scarcely whiter than the cheek they shaded. The sister's hands were clasped in each other, and they sat silently watching the gradual brightening of the crescent moon, and the coming forth, one by one, of the stars. Not a cloud was floating in the quiet sky; the light wind hardly stirred the young leaves, and the air was fraught with the fragrance of early spring flowers. It was the hour when reverie is deepest, and fantasies have the earnestness of truth, when memory is melancholy in its vividness, and we feel, "almost like a reality," the presence of those who may bless our pathway no more. The loved, the lost—

"So many, yet how few!"—

gather around us, not as they are, chastened and troubled by battling with trials and disappointments, but as they used to be, in the glow of unwearied expectation. Old fears flit before us altered into pleasures, and old hopes return bathed in tears.

Alice Cary, 1820–1871. (Manual, p. 484.)

From "Clovernook."

238. The End of the History.

And so with the various seasons of the year. May, with her green lap full of sprouting leaves and bright blossoms, her song-birds making the orchards and meadows vocal, and rippling streams and cultivated gardens; June, with full-blown roses and humming-bees, plenteous meadows and wide cornfields, with embattled lines rising thick and green; August, with reddened orchards and heavy-headed harvests of grain; October, with yellow leaves and swart shadows; December, palaced in snow, and idly whistling through his numb fingers;—all have their various charm; and in the rose-bowers of summer, and as we spread our hands before the torches of winter, we say joyfully, "Thou hast made all things beautiful in their time." We sit around the fireside, and the angel feared and dreaded by us all comes in, and one is taken from our midst. Hands that have caressed us, locks that have fallen over us like a bath of beauty, are hidden beneath shroud-folds. We see the steep edges of the grave, and hear the heavy rumble of the clods; and, in the burst of passionate grief, it seems that we can never still the crying of our hearts. But the days rise and set, dimly at first, and seasons come and go, and, by little and little, the weight rises from the heart, and the shadows drift from before the eyes, till we feel again the spirit of gladness, and see again the old beautv of the world.

Donald G. Mitchell, 1822–. (Manual, pp. 504, 531.)

From "Wayside Hints."

239. A TALK ABOUT PORCHES.

A COUNTRY house without a porch is like a man without an eyebrow; it gives expression, and gives expression where you most want it. The least office of a porch is that of affording protection against the rain-beat and the sun-beat. It is an interpreter of character; it humanizes bald walls and windows; it emphasizes architectural tone; it gives hint of hospitality; it is a hand stretched out (figuratively and lumberingly, often) from the world within to the world without.

At a church door even, a porch seems to me to be a blessed thing, and a most worthy and patent demonstration of the overflowing Christian charity, and of the wish to give shelter. Of all the images of wayside country churches which keep in my mind, those hang most persistently and agreeably, which show their jutting, defensive rooflets to keep the brunt of the storm from the church-goer while he yet fingers at the latch of entrance.

I doubt if there be not something beguiling in a porch over the door of a country shop—something that relieves the odium of bargaining, and imbues even the small grocer with a flavor of cheap hospitalities. The verandas (which is but a long translation of porch) that stretch along the great river front of the Bellevue Hospital, diffuse somehow a gladsome cheer over that prodigious caravansery of the sick; and I never see the poor creatures in their bandaged heads and their flannel gowns, enjoying their convalescence in the sunshine of those exterior corridors, but I reckon the old corridors for as much as the young doctors, in bringing them from convalescence into strength, and a new fight with the bedevilments of the world.

What shall we say, too, of inn porches? Does anybody doubt their fitness? Is there any question of the fact—with any person of reasonably imaginative mood—that Falstaff and

Nym and Bardolph, and the rest, once lolled upon the benches of the porch that overhung the door of the Boar's Head Tavern, Eastcheap? Any question about a porch, and a generous one, at the Tabard, Southwark—presided over by that wonderful host who so quickened the story-telling humors of the Canterbury pilgrims of Master Chaucer?

Then again, in our time, if one were to peel away the verandas and the exterior corridors from our vast watering-place hostelries, what an arid baldness of wall and of character would be left! All sentiment, all glowing memories, all the music of girlish footfalls, all echoes of laughter and banter and rollicking mirth, and tenderly uttered vows would be gone.

King David when he gave out to his son Solomon the designs for the building of the Temple, included among the very first of them, (1 Chron. XXVIII. 11) the "pattern of a porch." It is not, however, of porches of shittim-wood and of gold, that I mean to talk just now—nor even of those elaborate architectural features which will belong of necessity to the entrance-way of every complete study of a country house. I plead only for some little mantling hood about every exterior door-way, however humble.

There are hundreds of naked, vulgar-looking dwellings, scattered up and down our country highroads, which only need a little deft and adroit adaptation of the hospitable feature which I have made the subject of this paper, to assume an air of modest grace, in place of the present indecorous exposure of a wanton.

Richard Grant White,[1] *1822-.*

From "Memoirs of the Life of William Shakespeare."

240. The Character of Shakespeare's Style.

Writing for the general public, he used such language as would convey his meaning to his auditors,—the common

[1] A native of New York City; distinguished as a student and editor of Shakespeare, and more recently for his critical articles on the English language and grammar.

phraseology of his period. But what a language was that! In its capacity for the varied and exact expression of all moods of mind, all forms of thought, all kinds of emotion, a tongue unequaled by any other known to literature! A language of exhaustless variety; strong without ruggedness, and flexible without effeminacy. A manly tongue; yet bending itself gracefully and lovingly to the tenderest and the daintiest needs of woman, and capable of giving utterance to the most awful and impressive thoughts, in homely words that come from the lips, and go to the heart, of childhood. It would seem as if this language had been preparing itself for centuries to be the fit medium of utterance for the world's greatest poet. Hardly more than a generation had passed since the English tongue had reached its perfect maturity; just time enough to have it well worked into the unconscious usage of the people, when Shakespeare appeared, to lay upon it a burden of thought which would test its extremest capability. He found it fully formed and developed, but not yet uniformed and cramped and disciplined by the lexicographers and rhetoricians,—those martinets of language, who seem to have lost for us in force and flexibility as much as they have gained for us in precision. The phraseology of that day was notably large and simple among ordinary writers and speakers. Among the college-bred writers and their imitators, there was too great a fondness for little conceits; but even with them this was an extraneous blemish, like that sometimes found in the ornament upon a noble building. Shakespeare seized this instrument to whose tones all ears were open, and with the touch of a master he brought out all its harmonies. It lay ready to any hand; but his was the first to use it with absolute control; and among all its successors, great as some are, he has had, even in this single respect, no rival. No unimportant condition of his supreme mastery over expression was his entire freedom from restraint—it may almost be said from consciousness—in the choice of language. He was no precisian, no etymologist, no purist. He was not purposely writing literature. The only criticism that he feared was that of his audience, which represented the English people of all grades above the peasantry. These he wished should not find his writing incomprehensible or dull: no more. If we except the translators of the Bible, Shakespeare wrote the best English that has yet been written.

Thomas Wentworth Higginson, 1823–.

(Manual, p. 531).

From "Atlantic Essays."

241. Elegance of French Style.

In France alone among living nations is literature habitually pursued as an art; and in consequence of this, despite the seeds of decay which imperialism sowed, French prose-writing has no rival in contemporary literature. We cannot fully recognize this fact through translations, because only the most sensational French books appear to be translated. But as French painters and actors now habitually surpass all others even in what are claimed as the English qualities,—simplicity and truth,—so do French prose-writers excel. To be set against the brutality of Carlyle and the shrill screams of Ruskin, there is to be seen across the Channel the extraordinary fact of an actual organization of good writers, the French Academy, whose influence all nations feel. Under their authority we see introduced into literary work an habitual grace and perfection, a clearness and directness, a light and pliable strength, and a fine shading of expression, such as no other tongue can even define. We see the same high standard in their criticism, in their works of research, in the Revue des Deux Mondes, and in short throughout literature. What is there in any other lanaguage, for instance, to be compared with the voluminous writings of Sainte-Beuve, ranging over all history and literature, and carrying into all, that incomparable style, so delicate, so brilliant, so equable, so strong,—touching all themes, not with the blacksmith's hand of iron, but with the surgeon's hand of steel.

In the average type of French novels, one feels the superiority to the English in quiet power, in the absence of the sensational and exaggerated, and in keeping close to the level of real human life. They rely for success upon perfection of style, and the most subtle analysis of human character; and therefore they are often painful,—just as Thackeray is painful,—because they look at artificial society, and paint what they see. Thus they dwell often on unhappy marriages, because such things grow naturally from the false social system in France. On the other hand, in France there is very little house-breaking, and bigamy is almost impossible, so that we hear delightfully little about them; whereas, if you subtract these from the current English novels, what is there left?

Charles Godfrey Leland,[1] *1824–.*

From "Meister Karl's Sketch-book."

242. Aspect of Nuremberg.

There is a picturesque disorder—a lyrical confusion about the entire place, which is perfectly irresistible. Turrets shoot up in all sorts of ways, on all sorts of occasions, upon all sorts of houses; and little boxes, with delicate Gothic windows, cling to their sides and to one another, like barnacles to a ship; while the houses themselves are turned round and about in so many positions that you wonder that a few are not upside down or lying on their sides by way of completing the original arrangement of no arrangement at all. It always seemed to me as if the buildings in Nuremberg had, like the furniture in Irving's tale, been indulging over night in a very irregular

[1] A native of Philadelphia, who has resided much abroad, and pursued a varied literary career; he possesses a familiarity with the German language and character, which he has turned to good account in the comic ballads by Hans Breitman.

dance, and suddenly stopped in the most complicated part of a confusion worse confounded. Galleries, quaint staircases, and towers with projecting upper stories, as well as eccentric chimneys, demented door-ways, insane weather-vanes, and highly original steeples, form the most common-place materials in building; and it has more than once occurred to me that the architects of this city, even at the present day, must have imbibed their principles; not from the lecture-room, but from the most remarkable inspirations of some romantic scene-painter. During the last two centuries men appear to have striven, with a most uncommendable zeal, all over Christendom, to root out and extirpate every trace of the Gothic. In Nuremberg alone they have religiously preserved what little they originally had in domestic architecture, and added to it. . . .

Nuremberg, like Avignon, is one of the very few cities which have retained in an almost perfect state, the feudal walls and turrets with which they were invested by the middle ages. At regular intervals along these walls occur little towers, for their defence, reminding one of beads strung on a rosary; the great watch-tower at the gate, with its projecting machicolation, forming the pendent cross,—the whole serving to guard the town within from the dangers of war, even as the rosary protects the city of Mansoul from the attacks of Sin and Death—though, sooth to say, since the invention of gunpowder and the Reformation, both the one and the other appear to have lost much of their former efficacy. Directly through the center of the town runs a small stream called the Pegnitz, "dividing the town into two nearly equal halves, named after the two great churches situated within them; the northern being termed St. Sebald's, and the southern, St. Lawrence side."

In the northern part of the division of St. Sebaldus rises a high hill, formed, at the summit, of vast rocks, on which is situated the ancient Reicheveste, or Imperial Castle, whose origin is fairly lost in the dark old days of Heathenesse. From it the traveller can obtain an admirable view of the romantic town below. In regarding it, I was irresistibly reminded of the remarkable resemblance existing between most of its buildings and the children's toys manufactured by the ingenious artisans of Nuremberg and its vicinity.

George William Curtis, 1824–. (Manual, p. 504.)

From "Nile Notes of a Howadji."

243. UNDER THE PALMS.

THENCEFORWARD, in the land of Egypt, palms are perpetual. They are the only foliage of the Nile; for we will not harm the modesty of a few mimosas and sycamores, by foolish claims. They are the shade of the mud villages, marking their site in the landscape, so that the groups of palms are the number of villages. They fringe the shore and the horizon. The sun sets golden behind them, and birds sit swinging upon their boughs and float gloriously among their trunks; on the ground beneath are flowers; the sugar-cane is not harmed by the ghostly shade, nor the tobacco, and the yellow flowers of the cotton-plant star its dusk at evening. The children play under them; the old men crone and smoke; the surly bison and the conceited camels repose. The old Bible pictures are ceaselessly painted, but with softer, clearer colors, than in the venerable book.

. . . But the eye never wearies of palms, more than the ear of singing-birds. Solitary they stand upon the sand, or upon the level, fertile land in groups, with a grace and dignity that no tree surpasses. Very soon the eye beholds in their forms the original type of the columns which it will afterwards admire in the temples. Almost the first palm is architecturally suggestive, even in those western gardens—but to artists living among them and seeing only them! men's hands are not delicate in the early ages, and the fountain fairness of the palms is not very flowingly fashioned in the capitals; but in the flowery perfection of the Parthenon the palm triumphs. The forms of those columns came from Egypt, and that which was the suspicion of the earlier workers, was the success of more delicate designing. So is the palm inwound with our art, and poetry, and religion, and of all trees would the Howadji be a palm, wide-waving peace and plenty, and feeling his kin to the Parthenon and Raphæl's pictures.

But nature is absolute taste, and has no pure ornament, so that the palm is no less useful than beautiful. The family is infinite, and ill understood. The cocoa-nut, date, and sago, are all palms. Ropes and sponges are wrought of their tough interior fibre. The various fruits are nutritious; the wood, the roots, and the leaves, are all consumed. It is one of nature's great gifts to her spoiled sun-darlings. Whoso is born of the sun is made free of the world. Like the poet Thompson, he may put his hands in his pockets and eat apples at leisure.

John L. McConnel, 1826–. (Manual, p. 510.)

From "Western Characters."

244. The Early Western Politician.

He was tall, gaunt, angular, swarthy, active, and athletic. His hair was invariably black as the wing of the raven. Even in that small portion which the cap of raccoon-skin left exposed to the action of sun and rain, the gray was but thinly scattered, imparting to the monotonous darkness only a more iron character. . . . A stoop in the shoulders indicated that, in times past, he had been in the habit of carrying a heavy rifle, and of closely examining the ground over which he walked; but what the chest thus lost in depth it gained in breadth. His lungs had ample space in which to play. There was nothing pulmonary even in the drooping shoulders. . . .

From shoulders thus bowed hung long, muscular arms, sometimes, perhaps, dangling a little ungracefully, but always under the command of their owner, and ready for any effort, however violent. These were terminated by broad, bony hands, which looked like grapnels; their grasp, indeed, bore no faint resemblance to the hold of those symmetrical instruments. Large feet, whose toes were usually turned in, like those of the Indian, were wielded by limbs whose vigor and activity were in keeping with the figure they supported. Imagine, with these peculiarities, a free, bold, rather swaggering gait, a swarthy complexion, and comformable features and tones of voice, and, excepting his costume, you have before your fancy a complete picture of the early western politician.

Sarah J. Lippincott,[1] about *1833–.* (Manual, p. 484.)

From "Records of Five Years."

245. DEATH IN TOWN AND COUNTRY.

UP the long ascent it moved,—that shadow of our mortal sorrow and perishable earthly estate, that shadow of the dead man's hearse, along the way his feet had often trod, past the spring over whose brink he may have often bent with thirsting lip, past lovely green glades, mossy banks, and fairy forests of waving ferns, on which his eye had often dwelt with a vague and soft delight; and so passed out of our view. But its memory went not out of our hearts that day.

In this pure, healthful region, where nature seems so unworn, so youthful and vigorous, where dwell simplicity, humble comfort, and quiet happiness, death has startled us as something strange and unnatural. . . .

How different is it in the city! . . . There, on many a corner, one is confronted with the black, significant sign of the undertaker's "dreadful trade," or comes upon some marble-yard, filled with a ghastly assemblage of anticipatory gravestones and monuments; graceful broken columns, which are to typify the lovely incompleteness of some young life now full of beauty and promise; melancholy, drooping figures, types of grief forever inconsolable, destined, perhaps, to

[1] Originally and very favorably known by the assumed name of "Grace Greenwood."

stand proxy for mourning young widows now happy wives; sculptured lambs, patiently waiting to take their places above the graves of little children whom yet smiling mothers nightly lay to sleep in soft cribs, without the thought of a deeper dark and silence of a night not far away, or of the dreary beds soon to be prepared for their darlings "i' the earth."

Francis Bret Harte,[1] *1837-.*

From "The Luck of Roaring Camp," &c.

246. Birth of a Child in a Miner's Camp.

. . . The camp lay in a triangular valley, between two hills and a river. The only outlet was a steep trail over the summit of a hill that faced the cabin, now illuminated by the rising moon. The suffering woman might have seen it from the rude bunk whereon she lay,—seen it winding like a silver thread until it was lost in the stars above.

A fire of withered pine-boughs added sociability to the gathering. By degrees the natural levity of Roaring Camp returned. Bets were freely offered and taken regarding the result. Three to five that "Sal would get through with it," even, that the child would survive; side bets as to the sex and complexion of the coming stranger. . . .

In the midst of an excited discussion an exclamation came from those nearest the door, and the camp stopped to listen. Above the swaying and moaning of the pines, the swift rush of the river, and the crackling of the fire, rose a sharp, querulous cry. The pines stopped moaning, the river ceased to rush, and the fire to crackle. It seemed as if Nature had stopped to listen too.

The camp rose to its feet as one man! It was proposed to explode a barrel of gunpowder; but, in consideration of the situation of the mother, better counsels prevailed, and only a

[1] Prominent among the more recent American writers; a native of New York, but long resident in California: noted for his vivid portraiture of the early life, and remarkable scenery of that State, in a style uncommonly suggestive.

few revolvers were discharged; for, whether owing to the rude surgery of the camp, or some other reason, Cherokee Sal was sinking fast. Within an hour she had climed, as it were, the rugged road that led to the stars, and so passed out of Roaring Camp, its sin and shame, forever. . . .

I do not think that the announcement disturbed them much, except in speculation as to the fate of the child. "Can he live now?" was asked of Stumpy. The answer was doubtful. The only other being of Cherokee Sal's sex and maternal condition in the settlement, was an ass. There was some conjecture as to fitness, but the experiment was tried. It was less problematical than the ancient treatment of Romulus and Remus, and apparently as successful.

Strange to say, the child thrived. Perhaps the invigorating climate of the mountain camp was compensatien for maternal deficiencies. Nature took the foundling to her broader breast. In that rare atmosphere of the Sierra foot-hills—that air pungent with balsamic odor, that ethereal cordial at once bracing and exhilarating—he may have found food and nourishment, or a subtle chemistry that transmuted asses' milk to lime and phosphorus. Stumpy inclined to the belief that it was the latter and good nursing. "Me and that ass," he would say, "has been father and mother to him! Don't you," he would add, apostrophizing the helpless bundle before him, "never go back on us."

William Dean Howells, 1837–. (Manual, p. 531.)

From "Venetian Life."

247. SNOW IN VENICE.

. . . THE lofty crest of the bell-tower was hidden in the folds of falling snow, and I could no longer see the golden angel upon its summit. But looked at across the Piazza, the beautiful outline of St. Mark's Church was perfectly penciled in the air, and the shifting threads of the snow-fall were woven into a spell of novel enchantment around a structure that always seemed to me too exquisite in its fantastic loveliness to be anything but the creation of magic. The tender snow had compassionated the beautiful edifice for all the wrongs of time, and so hid the stains and ugliness of decay that it looked as if just from the hands of the builder—or, better said, just from the brain of the architect. There was marvellous freshness in the colors of the mosaics in the great arches of the façade; and all that glorious harmony into which the temple rises, of marble scrolls and leafy exuberance airily supporting the statues of the saints, was a hundred times etherialized by the purity and whiteness of the drifting flakes. The snow lay lightly on the golden globes that tremble like peacock-crests above the vast domes, and plumed them with softest white; it robed the saints in ermine; and it danced over all its work as if exulting in its beauty. . . .

Through the wavering snow-fall, the Saint Theodore upon one of the granite pillars of the Piazzetta did not show so grim as his wont is, and the winged lion on the other might have been a winged lamb, so mild and gentle he looked by the tender light of the storm. The towers of the island churches loomed faint and far away in the dimness; the sailors in the rigging of the ships that lay in the Basin, wrought like phantoms among the shrouds; the gondolas stole in and out of the opaque distance, more noiselessly and dreamily than ever; and a silence almost palpable, lay upon the mutest city in the world.

Mary Abigail Dodge,[1] *1838–.*

From "Wool Gathering."

248. Scenery of the Upper Mississippi.

Up the broad, cold, steel-blue river we wind steadily to its Northern home. No flutter of its orange groves, no fragrance of its Southern roses, no echo of its summer lands, can pene-

[1] Born in Massachusetts, author of numerous magazine articles of merit and earnestness, afterwards republished as books; known to her readers as Gail Hamilton.

trate these distances. Only prophecies of the sturdy North are here,—the glitter of the Polar sea, the majesty of Arctic solitudes. The imagination is touched. The eye looks out upon a hemisphere. Vast spaces, lost ages, the unsealed mysteries of cold and darkness and eternal silence, sweep around the central thought, and people the wilderness with their solemn symbolism. Prettiness of gentle slope, wealth and splendor of hue, are not wanting, but they shine with veiled light. Mountains come down to meet the Great River. The mists of the night lift slowly away, and we are brought suddenly into the presence-chamber. One by one they stand out in all their rugged might, only softened here and there by fleecy clouds still clinging to their sides, and shining pink in the ruddy dawn. Bold bluffs that have come hundreds of miles from their inland home guard the river. They rise on both sides, fronting us, bare and black, layer of solid rock piled on solid rock, defiant fortifications of some giant race, crowned here and there with frowning tower; here and there overborne and overgrown with wild-wood beauty, vine and moss and manifold leafage, gorgeous now with the glory of the vanishing summer. It is as if the everlasting hills had parted to give the Great River entrance to the hidden places of the world. And then the bold bluffs break into sharp cones, lonely mountains rising head and shoulders above their brethren, and keeping watch over the whole country; groups of mountains standing sentinels on the shores, almost leaning over the river, and hushing us to breathless silence as we sail through their awful shadow. And then the earth smiles again, the beetling cliffs recede into distances, and we glide through a pleasant valley. Green levels stretch away to the foot of the far cliffs, level with the river's blue, and as smooth,—sheltered and fertile, and fit for future homes. Nay, already the pioneer has found them, and many a hut and cottage and huddle of houses show whence art and science and all the amenities of human life, shall one day radiate. And even as we greet them we have left them, and the heights clasp us again, the hills overshadow us, the solitude closes around us.

LATER MISCELLANEOUS WRITERS.

George Washington[1], *1732–1799.*

From a Letter to Sir John Sinclair.

249. Natural Advantages of Virginia.

The United States, as you well know, are very extensive, more than fifteen hundred miles between the northeastern and southwestern extremities; all parts of which, from the seaboard to the Appalachian Mountains, which divide the eastern from the western waters, are entirely settled; though not as compactly as they are susceptible of; and settlements are progressing rapidly beyond them.

Within so great a space, you are not to be told, that there is a great variety of climates, and you will readily suppose, too, that there are all sorts of land, differently improved, and of various prices, according to the quality of the soil, its contiguity to, or remoteness from, navigation, the nature of the improvements, and other local circumstances. . . .

. Notwithstanding these abstracts, and although I may incur the charge of partiality in hazarding such an opinion at this time, I do not hesitate to pronounce, that the lands on the waters of the Potomac will in a few years be in greater demand and in higher estimation, than in any other part of the United States. But, as I ought not to advance this doctrine without assigning reasons for it, I will request you to examine a general map of the United States; and the following facts will strike you at first view; that they lie in the most temperate latitude of the United States, that the main river runs in a *direct* course to the expanded parts of the western country, and approximates nearer to the principal branches of the Ohio, than any other eastern water, and of course must become a

[1] Washington's correspondence was voluminous, and on the subjects relating to climate, agriculture, and internal improvements, he wrote with interest and ability. The letter to Sinclair is characteristic.

great, if not (under all circumstances), the best highway into that region; that the upper seaport of the Potomac is considerably nearer to a large portion of Pennsylvania, than that portion is to Philadelphia, besides accommodating the settlers thereof with inland navigation for more than two hundred miles; that the amazing extent of tide navigation, afforded by the bay and rivers of the Chesapeake, has scarcely a parallel.

When to these it is added, that a site at the junction of the inland and tide navigations of that river is chosen for the permanent seat of the general government, and is in rapid preparation for its reception; that the inland navigation is nearly completed, to the extent above mentioned; that its lateral branches are capable of great improvement at a small expense, through the most fertile parts of Virginia in a southerly direction, and crossing Maryland and extending into Pennsylvania in a northerly one, through which, independently of what may come from the western country, an immensity of produce will be water-borne, thereby making the Federal City the great emporium of the United States; I say, when these things are taken into consideration, I am under no apprehension of having the opinion I have given, relative to the value of land on the Potomac, controverted by impartial men.

Matthew F. Maury,[1] *1806–1873.*

From "The Physical Geography of the Sea."

250. The Mariner's Guide across the Deep.

So to shape the course on voyages as to make the most of the winds and currents at sea, is the perfection of the navigator's art. How the winds blow, and the currents flow, along this route or that, is no longer matter of opinion or subject of speculation, but it is a matter of certainty determined by actual observation. . . . The winds and the weather daily en-

[1] Formerly an officer of the navy, eminent for his scientific researches and writings on maritime subjects; a native of Virginia.

countered by hundreds who have sailed on the same voyage before him, and "the distance made good" by each one from day to day, have been tabulated in a work called Sailing Directions, and they are so arranged that he may daily see how much he is ahead of time, or how far he is behind time; nay, his path has been literally blazed through the winds for him on the sea; mile-posts have been set up on the waves, and finger-boards planted, and time-tables furnished for the trackless waste, by which the ship-master, on his first voyage to any port, may know as well as the most experienced trader whether he be in the right road or no.

. . . The route that affords the bravest winds, the fairest sweep, and the fastest running to be found among ships, is the route to and from Australia. But the route which most tries a ship's prowess is the outward-bound voyage to California. The voyage to Australia and back, carries the clipper ship along a route which, for more than three hundred degrees of longitude, runs with the "brave west winds" of the southern hemisphere. With these winds alone, and with their bounding seas which follow fast, the modern clipper, without auxiliary power, has accomplished a greater distance in a day than any sea-steamer has ever been known to reach. With these fine winds and heaving seas, those ships have performed their voyages of circumnavigation in sixty days.

—

251. The Gulf Stream.

As a rule, the hottest water of the Gulf Stream is at, or near, the surface; and as the deep-sea thermometer is sent down, it shows that these waters, though still far warmer than the waters on either side at corresponding depths, gradually become less and less warm until the bottom of the current is reached. There is reason to believe that the warm waters of the Gulf Stream are nowhere permitted, in the oceanic economy, to touch the bottom of the sea. There is everywhere a cushion of cool water, between them and the solid parts of the earth's crust. This arrangement is suggestive, and strikingly beautiful. One of the benign offices of the Gulf Stream is to convey heat from the Gulf of Mexico, where otherwise it would become excessive, and to dispense it in regions beyond the Atlantic, for the amelioration of the climates of the British Islands and of all Western Europe. Now cold water is one of the best non-conductors of heat, and if the warm water of the Gulf Stream was sent across the Atlantic in contact with the solid crust of the earth,—comparatively a good conductor of heat,—instead of being sent across, as it is, in contact with a cold non-conducting cushion of cool water to fend it from the bottom, much of its heat would be lost in the first part of the way, and the soft climates of both France and England would be, as that of Labrador, severe in the extreme, ice-bound, and bitterly cold.

Ormsby M. Mitchell,[1] *1810-1862.*

252. The Great Unfinished Problems of the Universe.

I do not pretend to indorse the theory of Mädler with reference to his central sun. If I did indorse it, it would amount simply to nothing at all, for he needs no indorsement of mine. But it is one of the great unfinished problems of the universe, which remains yet to be solved. Future generations yet are to take it up. Materials for its solution are to accumulate from generation to generation, and possibly from century to century. Nay, I know not but thousands of years will roll away before the slow movements of these far distant orbs shall so accumulate as to give us the data whereby the resolution may be absolutely accomplished. But shall we fail to work because the end is far off? Had the old astronomer that once stood upon the watch-tower in Babylon, and there marked the coming of the dreaded eclipse, said, "I care not for this; this is

1 An astronomer, and a favorite lecturer on the science; a native of Kentucky.

the business of posterity; let posterity take care of itself; I will make no record"—and had, in succeeding ages, the sentinel in the watch-tower of the skies said, "I will retire from my post; I have no concern with these matters, which can do me no good; it is nothing that I can do for the age in which I live,"—where should we have been to-night? Shall we not do, for those who are to follow us, what has been done for us by our predecessors? Let us not shrink from the responsibility which comes down upon the age in which we live. The great and mighty problem of the universe has been given to the whole human family for its solution. Not by any clime, not by any age, not by any nation, not by any individual man or mind, however great or grand, has this wondrous solution been accomplished; but it is the problem of humanity, and it will last as long as humanity shall inhabit the globe on which we live and move.

—

No, here is the temple of our Divinity. Around us and above us rise sun and system, cluster and universe. And I doubt not that in every region of this vast empire of God, hymns of praise and anthems of glory are rising and reverberating from sun to sun, and from system to system, heard by Omnipotence alone, across immensity, and through eternity.

WRITERS ON NATURAL HISTORY, SCENERY, &c.

William Bartram, 1739-1813. (Manual, p. 490.)

From the "Travels through the Carolinas," &c.

253. Scenes on the Upper Oconee.

At this rural retirement were assembled a charming circle of mountain vegetable beauties. . . . Some of these roving beauties stroll over the mossy, shelving, humid rocks, or from off the expansive wavy boughs of trees, bending over the floods, salute their delusive shade, playing on the surface; some plunge their perfumed heads and bathe their flexile limbs in the silver stream; whilst others by the mountain breezes are tossed about, their blooming tuffts bespangled with pearly and crystalline dew-drops collected from the falling mists, glistening in the rainbow arch. Having collected some valuable specimens at this friendly retreat, I continued my lonesome pilgrimage. My road for a considerable time led me winding and turning about the steep rocky hills; the descent of some of which was very rough and troublesome, by means of fragments of rocks, slippery clay and talc: but after this I entered a spacious forest, the land having gradually acquired a more level surface: a pretty grassy vale appears on my right, through which my wandering path led me, close by the banks of a delightful creek, which sometimes falling over steps of rocks, glides gently with serpentine meanders through the meadows.

After crossing this delightful brook and mead, the land rises again with sublime magnificence, and I am led over hills and vales, groves and high forests, vocal with the melody of the feathered songsters; the snow-white cascades glittering on the sides of the distant hills.

It was now afternoon; I approached a charming vale, amidst sublimely high forests, awful shades! Darkness gathers around; far distant thunder rolls over the trembling hills: the black clouds with august majesty and power, move slowly forwards, shading regions of towering hills, and threatening all the destruction of a thunder-storm: all around is now still as death, not a whisper is heard, but a total inactivity and silence seem to pervade the earth; the birds afraid to utter a chirrup, in low tremulous voices take leave of each other, seeking covert and safety: every insect is silenced, and nothing heard but the roaring of the approaching hurricane. The mighty cloud now expands its sable wings, extending from north to south, and is driven irresistibly on by the tumultuous winds, spreading its livid wings around the gloomy concave, armed with terrors of thunder and fiery shafts of lightning. Now the lofty forests bend low beneath its fury; their limbs and wavy boughs are tossed about and catch hold of each other; the mountains tremble and seem to reel about, and the ancient hills to be shaken to their foundations: the furious storm sweeps along, smoking through the vale and over the resounding hills: the face of the earth is obscured by the deluge descending from the firmament, and I am deafened by the din of the thunder. The tempestuous scene damps my spirits, and my horse sinks under me at the tremendous peals, as I hasten on for the plain.

From his "Travels in the Carolinas, Florida," &c.

254. The Wood Pelican of Florida.

This solitary bird does not associate in flocks, but is generally seen alone, commonly near the banks of great rivers, in vast marshes or meadows, especially such as are caused by inundations, and also in the vast deserted rice plantations: he stands alone on the topmost limb of tall dead cypress trees, his neck contracted or drawn in upon his shoulders, and beak resting like a long scythe upon his breast: in this pensive posture and solitary situation, it looks extremely grave, sorrowful, and melancholy, as if in the deepest thought.

Alexander Wilson, 1766–1813. (Manual, p. 504.)

From the "American Ornithology."

255. Nest of the Red-headed Woodpecker.

Notwithstanding the care which this bird, in common with the rest of its genus, takes to place its young beyond the reach of enemies, within the hollows of trees, yet there is one deadly foe, against whose depredations neither the height of the tree nor the depth of the cavity is the least security. This is the black snake, who frequently glides up the trunk of the tree, and, like a skulking savage, enters the woodpecker's peaceful apartment, devours the eggs or helpless young, in spite of the cries and flutterings of the parents, and, if the place be large enough, coils himself up in the spot they occupied, where he will sometimes remain for several days. The eager school-boy, after hazarding his neck to reach the woodpecker's hole, at the triumphant moment when he thinks the nestlings his own, and strips his arm, launching it down into the cavity, and grasping what he conceives to be the callow young, starts with horror at the sight of a hideous snake, and almost drops from his giddy pinnacle, retreating down the tree with terror and precipitation. Several adventures of this kind have come to my knowledge; and one of them was attended with serious consequences, where both snake and boy fell to the ground, and a broken thigh, and long confinement, cured the adventurer completely of his ambition for robbing woodpeckers' nests.

—

256. THE WHITE-HEADED, OR BALD, EAGLE.

ELEVATED on the high dead limb of some gigantic tree that commands a wide view of the neighboring shore and ocean, he seems calmly to contemplate the motions of the various feathered tribes that pursue their busy avocations below,—the snow-white Gulls slowly winnowing the air; the busy *Tringæ* coursing along the sands; trains of Ducks streaming over the surface; silent and watchful Cranes, intent and wading; clamorous crows; and all the winged multitudes that subsist by the bounty of this vast liquid magazine of nature. High over all these hovers one, whose action instantly arrests his whole attention. By his wide curvature of wing, and sudden suspension in air, he knows him to be the Fish Hawk, settling over some devoted victim of the deep. His eye kindles at the sight, and balancing himself with half-opened wings, on the branch, he watches the result. Down, rapid as an arrow from heaven, descends the distant object of his attention, the roar of its wings reaching the ear as it disappears in the deep, making the surges foam around. At this moment, the eager looks of the Eagle are all ardor; and levelling his neck for flight, he sees the Fish Hawk once more emerge, struggling with his prey, and mounting in the air with screams of exultation. These are the signal for our hero, who launching into the air, instantly gives chase, and soon gains on the Fish Hawk; each exerts his utmost to mount above the other, displaying in these rencontres the most elegant and sublime aerial evolutions. The unincumbered Eagle rapidly advances, and is just on the point of reaching his opponent, when, with a sudden scream, probably of despair and honest execration, the latter drops his fish ; the Eagle poising himself for a moment, as if to take a more certain aim, descends like a whirlwind, snatches it in his grasp ere it reaches the water, and bears his ill-gotten booty silently away to the woods.

Stephen Elliott,[1] *1771-1830.*

From "Views of Nature."

257. Completeness and Variety of Nature.

What is there that will not be included in the history of nature? The earth on which we tread, the air we breathe, the waters around the earth, the material forms that inhabit its surface, the mind of man, with all its magical illusions and all its inherent energy, the planets that move around our system, the firmament of heaven—the smallest of the invisible atoms which float around our globe, and the most majestic of the orbs that roll through the immeasurable fields of space—all are parts of one system, productions of one power, creations of one intellect, the offspring of Him, by whom all that is inert and inorganic in creation was formed, and from whom all that have life derive their being.

Of this immense system,—all that we can examine,—this

[1] Distinguished as a writer and scholar, and especially for his work on the Botany of South Carolina and Georgia; a native of South Carolina.

little globe that we innerit, is full of animation, and crowded with forms, organized, glowing with life, and generally sentient. No space is unoccupied; the exposed surface of the rock is incrusted with living substances; plants occupy the bark, and decaying limbs, of other plants; animals live on the surface, and in the bodies, of other animals; inhabitants are fashioned and adapted to equatorial heats, and polar ice;—air, earth, and ocean teem with life;—and if to other worlds the same proportion of life and of enjoyment has been distributed which has been allotted to ours, if creative benevolence has equally filled every other planet of every other system, nay, even the suns themselves, with beings, organized, animated, and intelligent, how countless must be the generations of the living! What voices which we cannot hear, what languages that we cannot understand, what multitudes that we cannot see, may, as they roll along the stream of time, be employed hourly, daily, and forever, in choral songs of praise, hymning their great Creator!

And when, in this almost prodigal waste of life, we perceive that every being, from the puny insect which flutters in the evening ray; from the lichen which we can scarcely distinguish on the mouldering rock; from the fungus that springs up and re-animates the mass of dead and decomposing substances; that every living form possesses a structure as perfect in its sphere, an organization sometimes as complex, always as truly and completely adapted to its purposes and modes of existence as that of the most perfect animal; when we discover them all to be governed by laws as definite, as immutable, as those which regulate the planetary movements, great must be our admiration of the wisdom which has arrayed, and the power which has perfected this stupendous fabric.

Nor does creation here cease. There are beyond the limits of our system, beyond the visible forms of matter, other principles, other powers, higher orders of beings, an immaterial world which we cannot yet know; other modes of existence which we cannot comprehend; yet however inscrutable to us, this spiritual world must be guided by its own unerring laws, and the harmonious order which reigns in all we can see and understand, ascending through theseries of immortal and invisible existence, must govern even the powers and dominions, the seraphim and cherubim, that surround the throne of God himself.

John James Audubon, 1776-1851. (Manual, p. 504.)

From the "Ornithological Biography."

258. The Passenger Pigeon.

I cannot describe to you the extreme beauty of their aerial evolutions, when a hawk chanced to press upon the rear of a flock. At once, like a torrent, and with a noise like thunder, they rushed into a compact mass, pressing upon each other towards the centre. In these almost solid masses, they darted forward in undulating and angular lines, descended and swept close over the earth ·ith inconceivable velocity, mounted perpendicularly so as to resemble a vast column, and when high, were seen wheeling and twisting within their continued lines, which then resembled the coils of a gigantic serpent.

It is extremely interesting to see flock after flock performing exactly the same evolutions which had been traced as it were, in the air, by a preceding flock. Thus should a hawk have charged on a group at a certain spot, the angles, curves, and undulations that have been described by the birds, in their efforts to escape from the dreaded talons of the plunderer, are undeviatingly followed by the next group that comes up. Should the by-stander happen to witness one of these affrays, and, struck with the rapidity and elegance of the motions exhibited, feel desirous of seeing them repeated, his wishes will be gratified, if he only remain in the place until the next group comes up.

As soon as the pigeons discover a sufficiency of food to entice them to alight, they fly around in circles, reviewing the country below. During their evolutions, on such occasions, the dense mass which they form, exhibits a beautiful appearance, as it changes its direction, now displaying a glistening sheet of azure, when the backs of the birds come simultaneously into view, and anon, suddenly presenting a mass of rich purple. They then pass lower, over the woods, and for a moment are lost among the foliage, but again emerge, and are seen gliding aloft. They now alight, but the next moment, as if suddenly alarmed, they take to wing, producing by the flapping of their wings a noise like the roar of distant thunder, and sweep through the forests to see if danger is near. Hunger, however, soon brings them to the ground. When alighted, they are seen industriously throwing up the withered leaves in quest of the falling mast. The rear ranks are continually rising, passing over the main body, and alighting in front, in such rapid succession, that the whole flock seems still on wing. The quantity of ground thus swept is astonishing, and so completely has it been cleared, that the gleaner who might follow in their rear, would find his labor completely lost.

---

259. EMIGRANTS REMOVING WESTWARD.

I THINK I see them at this moment harnessing their horses and attaching them to their wagons, which are already filled with bedding, provisions, and the younger children; while on the outside are fastened spinning-wheels and looms, and a bucket filled with tar and tallow swings between the hind wheels. Several axes are secured to the bolster, and the feeding-trough of the horses contains pots, kettles, and pans. The servant, now become a driver, rides the near saddled horse; the wife is mounted on another; the worthy husband shoulders his gun; and his sons, clad in plain, substantial homespun, drive the cattle ahead, and lead the procession, followed by the hounds and other dogs.

260. INTEREST OF EXPLORATION IN THE REMOTE WEST.

How delightful, I have often exclaimed, must have been the feelings of those enthusiastic naturalists, my friends Nuttall and Townsend, while traversing the ridges of the Rocky Mountains! How grand and impressive the scenery presented to their admiring gaze, when from an elevated station they saw the mountain torrent hurling its foamy waters over the black crags of the rugged ravine, while on wide-spread wings the Great Vulture sailed overhead watching the departure of the travellers, that he might feast on the Salmon which in striving to ascend the cataract had been thrown on the stony beach! Now the weary travellers are resting on the bank of a brawling brook, along which they are delighted to see the lively Dipper frisking wren-like from stone to stone. On the stunted bushes above them some curious Jays are chattering, and as my friends are looking upon the gay and restless birds, they are involuntarily led to extend their gaze to the green slope beneath the more distant crags, where they spy a mountain sheep, watching the movements of the travellers as well as those of yon wolves stealing silently toward the fleet-footed animal. Again the pilgrims are in motion; they wind their pathless way round rocks and fissures; they have reached the greatest height of the sterile platform; and as they gaze on the valleys whose waters hasten to join the Pacific Ocean, and bid adieu, perhaps for the last time, to the dear friends they have left in the distant east, how intense must be their feelings, as thoughts of the past and the future blend themselves in their anxious minds! But now I see them, brother-like, with lighter steps, descending toward the head waters of the famed Oregon. They have reached the great stream, and seating themselves in a canoe, shoot adown the current, gazing on the beautiful shrubs and flowers that ornament the banks, and the majestic trees that cover the sides of the valley, all new to them, and presenting a wide field of discovery. The melodies of unknown songsters enliven their spirits, and glimpses of gaudily plumed birds excite their desire to search those beautiful thickets; but time is urgent, and onward they must speed. A deer crosses the stream, they pursue and capture it; and it being now evening, they land and soon form a camp, carefully concealed from the prying eyes of the lurking savage. The night is past, the dawn smiles upon the refreshed travellers, who launch their frail bark; and, as they slowly float on the stream, both listen attentively to the notes of the Red-and-White-winged Troopial, and wonder how similar they are to those of the "Red-winged Starling;" they think of the affinities of species, and especially of those of the lively birds composing this beautiful group.

Daniel Drake,[1] *1785-1852.*

From a "Picture of Cincinnati, &c."

261. Objects of the Western Mound-Builders.

No objects in the State of Ohio seem to have more forcibly arrested the attention of travellers, nor employed a greater number of pens, than its antiquities. It is to be regretted, however, that so hastily and superficially have they been examined by strangers, and so generally neglected by ourselves, that the materials for a full description have not yet been collected. . . .

The forests over these remains exhibit no appearances of more recent growth than in other parts. Trees, several hundred years old, are in many places seen growing out of the ruins of others, which appear to have been of equal size. . .

Those at Cincinnati, for example, exhibit so few of the characters of a defensive work, that General Wayne, upon attentively surveying them in 1794, was of opinion that they were not designed for that purpose. It was from the examination of valley-works only, that Bishop Madison was led to

[1] A native of New Jersey, who was taken when very young, to the West, where he became distinguished as a medical professor and practitioner. His recollections and sketches are very valuable.

deny that the remains of the western country were ever intended for defence, and to conclude that they were enclosures for permanent residence. It would be precipitate to assert that the relics found in the valleys were for this purpose, and those of the uplands for defence. But while it is certain that the latter were military posts, it seems highly probable that the former were for ordinary abode in times of peace. They were towns and the seats of chiefs, whose perishable parts have crumbled into earth, and disappeared with the generations which formed them. Many of them might have been calculated for defence, as well as for habitations; but the latter must have been the chief purpose for which they were erected. On the contrary, the hill-constructions, which are generally in the strongest military positions of the country, were designed solely for defence, in open and vigorous war.

John Bachman,[1] *1790–1873.*

From "The Quadrupeds of North America."

262. The Opossum.

We can imagine to ourselves the surprise with which the opossum was regarded by Europeans, when they first saw it. Scarcely anything was known of the marsupial animals, as New Holland had not as yet opened its unrivalled stores of singularities to astonish the world. Here was a strange animal, with the head and ears of the pig, sometimes hanging on the limb of a tree, and occasionally swinging like the monkey by the tail. Around that prehensile appendage a dozen sharp-nosed, sleek-headed young had entwined their own tails, and were sitting on the mother's back. The astonished traveller approaches this extraordinary compound of an animal, and touches it cautiously with a stick. Instantly it seems to be struck with some mortal disease: its eyes close, it falls to the

[1] A clergyman of the Lutheran church, for many years a citizen of Charleston, South Carolina, but originally from New York; eminent for his attainments and writings in natural history and science.

ground, ceases to move, and appears to be dead. He turns it on its back, and perceives on its stomach a strange, apparently artificial opening. He puts his fingers into the extraordinary pocket, and lo, another brood of a dozen or more young, scarcely larger than a pea, are hanging in clusters on the teats. In pulling the creature about, in great amazement, he suddenly receives a gripe on the hand; the twinkling of the half-closed eye, and the breathing of the creature, evince that it is not dead; and he adds a new term to the vocabulary of his language, that of "playing 'possum."

. . . . When the young are four weeks old, they begin from time to time to relax their hold on the teats, and may now be seen with their heads occasionally out of the pouch. A week later, and they venture to steal occasionally from their snug retreat in the pouch, and are often seen on the mother's back, securing themselves by entwining their tails around hers. In this situation she moves from place to place in search of food, carrying her whole family along with her, to which she is much attached, and in whose defence she exhibits a considerable degree of courage, growling at any intruder, and ready to use her teeth with great severity on man or dog. In travelling, it is amusing to see this large family moving about. Some of the young, nearly the size of rats, have their tails entwined around the legs of the mother, and some around her neck,—thus they are dragged along. They have a mild and innocent look, and are sleek, and in fine condition, and this is the only age in which the word pretty can be applied to the Opossum. At this period, the mother in giving sustenance to so large a family, becomes thin, and is reduced to one-half of her previous weight. The whole family of young remain with her about two months, and continue in the vicinity till autumn. In the meantime, a second, and often a third brood, is produced, and thus two or more broods of different ages may be seen, sometimes with the mother, and at other times not far off.

. . . Hunting the Opossum is a very favorite amusement among domestics and field laborers on our Southern plantations, of lads broke loose from school in the holidays, and even of gentlemen, who are sometimes more fond of this sport than of the less profitable and more dangerous and fatiguing one of hunting the gray fox by moonlight. Although we have never participated in an Opossum hunt, yet we have observed that it afforded much amusement to the sable group that in the majority of instances make up the hunting party, and we have on two or three occasions been the silent and gratified observers of the preparations that were going on, the anticipations indulged in, and the excitement apparent around us.

J. A. Lapham.[1]

From "Wisconsin, its Geography," &c.

263. THE SMALLER LAKES.

BESIDES these immense lakes, Wisconsin abounds in those of smaller size, scattered profusely over her whole surface. They are from one to twenty or thirty miles in extent. Many of them are the most beautiful that can be imagined—the water deep, and of crystal purity and clearness, surrounded by sloping hills and promontories, covered with scattered groves and clumps of trees. Some are of a more picturesque kind, being more rugged in their appearance, with steep, rocky bluffs, crowned with cedar, hemlock, spruce, and other evergreen trees of a similar character. Perhaps a small rocky island will vary the scene, covered with a conical mass of vegetation, the low shrubs and bushes being arranged around the margin, and the tall trees in the centre. These lakes usually abound in fish of various kinds, affording food for the pioneer settler; and among the pebbles on their shores may occasionally be found fine specimens of agate, carnelian, and other precious stones. In the bays, where the water is shallow, and but little affected

[1] The age of this meritorious and industrious writer we have not been able to learn. The second edition of his book on Wisconsin appeared in 1846.

by the winds, the wild rice grows in abundance, affording subsistence for the Indian, and attracting innumerable water-birds to these lakes.

---

264. ANCIENT EARTHWORKS.

THERE is a class of ancient earthworks in Wisconsin, not before found in any other country. . . . Some have a resemblance to the buffalo, the eagle, or crane, or to the turtle or lizard. One, representing the human form, near the Blue Mounds, is, according to R. C. Taylor, Esq., one hundred and twenty feet in length: it lies in an east and west direction, the head towards the west, with the arms and legs extended. The body or trunk is thirty feet in breadth, the head twenty-five, and its elevation above the general surface of the prairie is about six feet. Its conformation is so distinct, that there can be no possibility of mistake in assigning it to the human figure.

Charles Wilkins Webber, 1819–1856.

(Manual, p. 505.)

From "Wild Scenes and Song-birds."

265. THE MOCKING-BIRD.

THE next spring a new melody filled the air. A melody such as I had never heard before burst in clear and overwhelming raptures from the meadows where I had first seen the graceful stranger with the white-barred wings, last year. . . . I saw it now leaping up from its favorite perch on a tree-top much in the manner I had observed before, but now it was in a different mood and seemed to mount thus spirit-like upon the wilder ecstasies, and floating fall upon the subsiding cadence, of that passionate song it poured into the listening ear of love, for I could see his mate, with fainter bars across her wings, where she sat upon a thornbush near, and listened.

When this magnificent creature commenced to sing, the very air was burdened with a thousand different notes; but his voice rose clear and melodiously loud above them all. As I listened, one song after another ceased suddenly, until, in a few minutes, and before I could realize that it was so, I found myself hearkening to that solitary voice. This is a positive fact. I looked around me in astonishment. What! Are they awed? But his song only now grew more exulting, and, as if feeling his triumph, he bounded yet higher, with each new gush, and in swift and quivering raptures dived, skimmed, and floated round—round—then rose to fall again more boldly on the billowy storm of sound.

. . . This curious phenomenon I have witnessed many times since. Even in the morning choir, when every little throat seems strained in emulation, if the mocking-bird breathes forth in one of its mad, bewildered, and bewildering extravaganzas, the other birds pause almost invariably, and remain silent until his song is done. This, I assure you, is no figment of the imagination, or illusion of an excited fancy; it is just as substantial a fact as any other one in natural history. Whether the other birds stop from envy, as has been said, or from awe, cannot be so well ascertained, but I believe it is from the sentiment of awe, for as I certainly have felt it myself in listening to the mocking-bird, I do not know why these inferior creatures should not also.

Charles Lanman, 1819–. (Manual, p. 505.)

From "Haw-ho-noo."

266. Maple-Sugar-Making among the Indians.

It is in the month of April, and the hunting season is at an end. Albeit, the ground is covered with snow, the noonday sun has become quite powerful; and the annual offering has been made to the Great Spirit, by the medicine-men, of the first product of one of the earliest trees in the district. This being the preparatory signal for extensive business, the women of the encampment proceed to make a large number of wooden troughs (to receive the liquid treasure), and after these are finished, the various trees in the neighborhood are tapped, and the juice begins to run. In the mean time the men of the party have built the necessary fires, and suspended over them their earthen, brass, or iron kettles. The sap is now flowing in copious streams, and from one end of the camp to the other is at once presented an animated and romantic scene, which continues day and night, until the end of the sugar season. The principal employment to which the men devote themselves, is that of lounging about the encampment, shooting at marks, and playing the moccasin game; while the main part of the labor is performed by the women, who not only attend to the kettles, but employ all their leisure time in making the beautiful birchen mocucks, for the preservation and transportation of the sugar when made; the sap being brought from the troughs to the kettles, by the boys and girls. Less attention than usual is paid by the Indians at such times to their meals; and unless game is very easily obtained, they are quite content to depend upon the sugar alone.

It was now about the middle of June, and some fifty birchen canoes have just been launched upon the waters of Green Bay. They are occupied by our Ottawa sugar-makers, who have started upon a pilgrimage to Mackinaw. The distance is near two hundred miles, and as the canoes are heavily laden not only with mocucks of sugar, but with furs collected by the hunters during the past winter, and the Indians are travelling at their leisure, the party will probably reach their desired haven in the course of ten days. Well content with their accumulated treasures, both the women and the men are in a particularly happy mood, and many a wild song is heard to echo over the placid lake. As the evening approaches, day after day they seek out some convenient landing place, and, pitching the wigwams on the beach, spend a goodly portion of the night carousing and telling stories around their camp fires, resuming their voyage after a morning sleep, long after the sun has risen above the blue waters of the east. Another sunset hour, and the cavalcade of canoes is quietly gliding into the crescent bay of Mackinaw, and, reaching a beautiful beach at the foot of a lofty bluff, the Indians again draw up their canoes,—again erect their wigwams. And, as the Indian traders have assembled on the spot, the more improvident of the party immediately proceed to exhibit their sugar and furs, which are usually disposed of for flour and pork, blankets and knives, guns, ammunition, and a great variety of trinkets, long before the hour of midnight.

Ephraim C. Squier, 1821-. (Manual, p. 504.)

From "Aboriginal Monuments of the West."

267. Indian Pottery.

The site of every Indian town throughout the west is marked by the fragments of pottery scattered around it; and the cemeteries of the various tribes abound with rude vessels of clay, piously deposited with the dead. Previous to the discovery, the art of the potter was much more important, and its practice more general than it afterwards became, upon the introduction of metallic vessels. The mode of preparing and moulding the materials is minutely described by the early observers, and seems to have been common to all the tribes, and not to have varied materially from that day to this. The work devolved almost exclusively upon the women, who kneaded the clay and formed the vessels. Experience seems to have suggested the means of so tempering the material as to resist the action of fire; accordingly we find pounded shells, quartz, and sometimes simple coarse sand from the streams mixed with the clay. None of the pottery of the present races, found in the Ohio valley, is destitute of this feature; and it is not uncommon, in certain localities, where from the abundance of fragments, and from other circumstances, it is supposed the manuufacture was specially carried on, to find quantities of the decayed shells of the fresh water molluscs, intermixed with the earth, probably brought to the spot to be used in the process. Amongst the Indians along the Gulf, a greater degree of skill was displayed than with those on the upper waters of the Mississippi, and on the lakes. Their vessels were generally larger and more symmetrical, and of a superior finish. They moulded them over gourds and models, and baked them in ovens. In the construction of those of large size, it was customary to model them in baskets of willow or splints, which, at the proper period, were burned off, leaving the vessel perfect in form, and retaining the somewhat ornamental markings of their moulds. Some of those found on the Ohio seem to have been modelled in bags or nettings of coarse thread or twisted bark. These practices are still retained by some of the remote western tribes.

Benjamin Silliman, 1779–1864. (Manual, p. 505.)

From "A Tour to Canada."

268. The Falls of Montmorenci.

. . . The Montmorenci, after a gentle previous declivity, which greatly increases its velocity, takes its stupendous leap of two hundred and forty feet, into a chasm among the rocks, where it boils and foams in a natural rocky basin, from which, after its force is in some measure exhausted in its own whirlpools and eddies, it flows away in a gentle stream towards the St. Lawrence. The fall is nearly perpendicular, and appears not to deviate more than three or four degrees from it. This deviation is caused by the ledges of rock below, and is just sufficient to break the water completely into foam and spray. .

The effect on the beholder is most delightful. The river, at some distance, seems suspended in a sheet of billowy foam, and contrasted as it is, with the black frowning abyss into which it falls, it is an object of the highest interest. As we approached nearer to its foot, the impressions of grandeur and sublimity were, in the most perfect manner imaginable, blended with those of extreme beauty.

This river is of so considerable a magnitude, that, precipitated as it is from this amazing height, the thundering noise, and mighty rush of waters, and the never-ceasing wind and rain produced by the fall, powerfully arrest the attention: the spectator stands in profound awe, mingled with delight, especially when he contrasts the magnitude of the fall, with that of a villa, on the edge of the dark precipices of frowning rock which form the western bank, and with the casual spectators looking down from the same elevation.

The sheet of foam which breaks over the ridge, is more and more divided as it is dashed against the successive layers of rocks, which it almost completely veils from view; the spray becomes very delicate and abundant, from top to bottom, hanging over, and revolving around the torrent, till it becomes lighter and more evanescent than the whitest fleecy clouds of summer, than the finest attenuated web, than the lightest gossamer, constituting the most airy and sumptuous drapery that can be imagined. Yet, like the drapery of some of the Grecian statues, which, while it veils, exhibits more forcibly the form beneath, this does not hide, but exalts the effect produced by this noble cataract.

The rainbow we saw in great perfection; bow within bow, and (what I never saw elsewhere so perfectly), as I advanced into the spray, the bow became complete, myself being a part of its circumference, and its transcendent glories moving with every change of position.

This beautiful and splendid sight was to be enjoyed only by advancing quite into the shower of spray; as if, in the language of ancient poetry, and fable, the genii of the place, pleased with the beholder's near approach to the seat of their empire, decked the devotee with the appropriate robes of the cataract, the vestal veil of fleecy spray, and the heavenly splendors of the bow.

John L. Stephens, 1805–1852. (Manual, p. 504.)

From the "Travels in Central America."

269. DISCOVERY OF A RUINED CITY IN THE WOODS.

THE sight of this unexpected monument put at rest, at once and forever, in our minds, all uncertainty in regard to the character of American antiquities, and gave us the assurance that the objects we were in search of were interesting, not only as the remains of an unknown people, but as works of art, proving, like newly-discovered historical records, that the people who once occupied the continent of America were not savages. With an interest perhaps stronger than we had ever felt in wandering among the ruins of Egypt, we followed our guide, who, sometimes missing his way, with a constant and vigorous use of his machete, conducted us through the thick forest, among half-buried fragments, to fourteen monuments of the same character and appearance, some with more elegant designs, and some in workmanship equal to the finest monuments of the Egyptians; one displaced from its pedestal by enormous roots; another locked in the close embrace of branches of trees, and almost lifted out of the earth; another hurled to the ground, and bound down by huge vines and creepers; and one standing, with its altar before it, in a grove of trees which grew around it, seemingly to shade and shroud it as a sacred thing; in the solemn stillness of the woods it seemed a divinity mourning over a fallen people. The only sounds that disturbed the quiet of this buried city, were the noise of monkeys moving among the tops of the trees, and the cracking of dry branches broken by their weight. They moved over our heads in long and swift processions, forty or fifty at a time; some, with little ones wound in their long arms, walking out to the end of boughs, and holding on with their hind feet, or a curl of the tail, sprang to a branch of the next tree, and with a noise like a current of wind, passed on into the depths of the forest. It was the first time we had seen these mockeries of humanity, and with the strange monuments around us, they seemed like wandering spirits of the departed race, guarding the ruins of their former habitations.

. . . We sat down on the very edge of the wall, and strove in vain to penetrate the mystery by which we were surrounded. Who were the people that built this city? In the ruined cities of Egypt,—even in the long lost Petra, the stranger knows the story of the people whose vestiges are around him. America, say historians, was peopled by savages; but savages never reared these structures, savages never carved these stones.

John Charles Fremont, 1813–. (Manual, p. 505.)

From "Report of an Exploring Expedition."

270. Ascent of a Peak of the Rocky Mountains.

We continued climbing, and in a short time reached the crest. I sprang upon the summit, and another step would have precipitated me into an immense snow field five hundred feet below. To the edge of this field was a sheer icy precipice; and then, with a gradual fall, the field sloped off for about a mile, until it struck the foot of another lower ridge. I stood on a narrow crest, about three feet in width, with an inclination of about 20° N., 51° E. As soon as I had gratified the first feelings of curiosity, I descended, and each man ascended in his turn; for I would only allow one at a time to mount the unstable and precarious slab, which it seemed a breath would hurl into the abyss below. We mounted the barometer in the snow of the summit, and fixing a ramrod in a crevice, unfurled the national flag to wave in the breeze, where never flag waved before. During our morning's ascent, we had met no sign of animal life, except the small sparrow-like bird already mentioned. A stillness the most profound, and a terrible solitude forced themselves constantly on the mind, as the great features of the place. Here, on the summit, where the stillness was absolute, unbroken by any sound, and the solitude complete, we thought ourselves beyond the region of animated life; but while we were sitting on the rock, a solitary bee (*bromus*, the humble bee) came winging his flight from the eastern valley, and lit on the knee of one of the men.

---

271. THE COLUMBIA RIVER, OREGON.

THE Columbia is the only river which traverses the whole breadth of the country, breaking through all the ranges, and entering the sea. Drawing its waters from a section of ten degrees of latitude in the Rocky Mountains, which are collected into one stream by three main forks (Lewis', Clark's, and the North Fork) near the center of the Oregon valley, this great river thence proceeds by a single channel to the sea, while its three forks lead each to a pass in the mountains which opens the way into the interior of the continent. This fact in relation to the rivers of this region, gives an immense value to the Columbia. Its mouth is the only inlet and outlet, to and from the sea ; its three forks lead to the passes in the mountains; it is therefore the only line of communication between the Pacific and the interior of North America; and all operations of war or commerce, of national or social intercourse, must be conducted upon it. This gives it a value beyond estimation, and would involve irreparable injury if lost. In this unity and concentration of its waters, the Pacific side of our continent differs entirely from the Atlantic side, where the waters of the Alleghany mountains are dispersed into many rivers, having their different entrances into the sea, and opening many lines of communication with the interior.

Elisha Kent Kane,[1] *1822-1857.*

From "Arctic Explorations."

272. THE DISCOVERY OF AN OPEN SEA.

As Morton, leaving Hans and his dogs, passed between Sir

[1] A traveller, explorer, and writer of high merit; a native of Philadelphia, and a Surgeon in the Navy. His early death was much deplored.

John Franklin Island and the narrow beach-line, the coast became more wall-like, and dark masses of porphyritic rock abutted into the sea. With growing difficulty, he managed to climb from rock to rock, in hopes of doubling the promontory and sighting the coasts beyond, but the water kept encroaching more and more on his track.

It must have been an imposing sight, as he stood at this termination of his journey, looking out upon the great waste of waters before him. Not a "speck of ice," to use his own words, could be seen. There, from a height of four hundred and eighty feet, which commanded a horizon of almost forty miles, his ears were gladdened with the novel music of dashing waves; and a surf, breaking in among the rocks at his feet, stayed his farther progress.

Beyond this cape all is surmise. The high ridges to the north-west dwindled off into low blue knobs, which blended finally with the air. Morton called the cape, which baffled his labors, after his commander; but I have given it the more enduring name of Cape Constitution.

. . . I am reluctant to close my notice of this discovery of an open sea without adding that the details of Mr. Morton's narrative harmonized with the observations of all our party. I do not propose to discuss here the causes or conditions of this phenomenon. How far it may extend—whether it exist simply as a feature of the immediate region, or as part of a great and unexplored area communicating with the Polar basin, and what may be the argument in favor of one or the other hypothesis, or the explanation which reconciles it with established laws—may be questions for men skilled in scientific deductions Mine has been the more humble duty of recording what we saw. Coming as it did, a mysterious fluidity in the midst of vast plains of solid ice, it was well calculated to arouse emotions of the highest order; and I do not believe there was a man among us who did not long for the means of embarking upon its bright and lonely waters.

Bayard Taylor, 1825-. (Manual, pp. 505, 523, 531.)

From "Eldorado."

273. Monterey, California.

No one can be in Monterey a single night, without being startled and awed by the deep, solemn crashes of the surf, as it breaks along the shore. There is no continuous roar of the plunging waves, as we hear on the Atlantic seaboard; the slow, regular swells—quiet pulsations of the great Pacific's heart—roll inward in unbroken lines, and fall with single grand crashes, with intervals of dead silence between. They may be heard through the day, if one listens, like a solemn undertone to all the shallow noises of the town; but at midnight, when all else is still, those successive shocks fall upon the ear with a sensation of inexpressible solemnity. All the air, from the pine forests to the sea, is filled with a light tremor, and the intermitting beats of sound are strong enough to jar a delicate ear. Their constant repetition at last produces a feeling something like terror. A spirit worn and weakened by some scathing sorrow could scarcely bear the reverberation.

---

274. Approach to San Francisco, California.

Sunset came on as we approached the strait opening from Pablo Bay into the Bay of San Francisco. The cloudless sky became gradually suffused with a soft rose-tint, which covered its whole surface, painting alike the glassy sheet of the bay, and glowing most vividly on the mountains to the eastward. The color deepened every moment, and the peaks of the Coast Range burned with a rich vermilion light, like that of a live coal. This faded gradually into as glowing a purple, and at last into a blue as intense as that of the sea at noon-day. The first effect of the light was most wonderful; the mountains stretched around the horizon like a belt of varying fire and amethyst, between the two roseate deeps of air and water; the shores were transmuted into solid, the air into fluid gems. Could the pencil faithfully represent this magnificent transfiguration of Nature, it would appear utterly unreal and impossible to eyes which never beheld the reality. . . . It lingered, and lingered, changing almost imperceptibly and with so beautiful a decay, that one lost himself in the enjoyment of each successive charm, without regret for those which were over. The dark blue of the mountains deepened into their night-garb of dusky shadow without any interfusion of dead, ashy color, and the heaven overhead was spangled with all its stars long before the brilliant arch of orange in the west had sunk below the horizon. I have seen the dazzling sunsets of the Mediterranean flush the beauty of its shores, and the mellow skies which Claude used to contemplate from the Pincian Hill; but lovely as they are in my memory, they seem cold and pale when I think of the splendor of such a scene, on the Bay of San Francisco.

The Little Land of Appenzell.

275. Swiss Scenery,—A Battlefield; Picturesque Dwellings.

On the right lay the land of Appenzell,—not a table-land, but a region of mountain, ridge, and summit, of valley and deep, dark gorge, green as emerald, up to the line of snow, and so thickly studded with dwellings, grouped or isolated, that there seemed to be one scattered village as far as the eye could reach. To the south, over forests of fir, the Sentis lifted his huge towers of rock, crowned with white, wintry pyramids.

Here, where we are, said the postillion, "was the first battle; but there was another, two years afterwards, over there, the other side of Trogen, where the road goes down to the Rhine. Stoss is the place, and there's a chapel built on the very spot. Duke Frederick of Austria came to help the Abbott Runo, and the Appenzellers were only one to ten against them. It was a great fight, they say, and the women helped,—not with pikes and guns, but in this way: they put on white shirts, and came out of the woods, above where the fighting was going on. Now when the Austrians and the Abbot's people saw them, they thought there were spirits helping the Appenzellers, (the women were all white you see, and too far off to show plainly,) and so they gave up the fight, after losing nine hundred knights and troopers. After that, it was ordered that the women should go first to the sacrament, so that no man might forget the help they gave in that battle. And the people go every year to the chapel, on the same day when it took place."

If one could only transport a few of these houses to the United States! Our country architecture is not only hideous, but frequently unpractical, being at worst, shanties, and at best, city residences set in the fields. An Appenzell farmer lives in a house from forty to sixty feet square, and rarely less than four stories in height. The two upper stories, however, are narrowed by the high, steep roof, so that the true front of the house is one of the gables. The roof projects at least four feet on all sides, giving shelter to balconies of carved wood, which cross the front under each row of windows. The outer walls are covered with upright, overlapping shingles, not more than two or three inches broad, and rounded at the ends, suggesting the scale armor of ancient times. This covering secures the greatest warmth; and when the shingles have acquired from age that rich burnt-sienna tint which no paint could exactly imitate, the effect is exceedingly beautiful. The lowest story is generally of stone, plastered and whitewashed. The stories are low, (seven to eight feet) but the windows are placed side by side, and each room is thoroughly lighted. Such a house is very warm, very durable, and, without any apparent expenditure of ornament, is externally so picturesque that no ornament could improve it. . . .

The view of a broad Alpine landscape dotted all over with such beautiful homes, from the little shelf of green hanging on the sides of a rocky gorge, and the strips of sunny pasture between the ascending forests, to the very summits of the lower heights and the saddles between them, was something quite new in my experience.

NOVELISTS AND WRITERS OF FICTION.

Charles Brockden Brown, 1771–1810.

(Manual, pp. 478, 505.)

From "Ormond."

276. The Yellow Fever in Philadelphia.

As she approached the house to which she was going, her reluctance to proceed increased. Frequently she paused to recollect the motives that had prescribed this task, and to re-enforce her purposes. At length she arrived at the house. Now, for the first time, her attention was excited by the silence and desolation that surrounded her. This evidence of fear and of danger struck upon her heart. All appeared to have fled from the presence of this unseen and terrible foe. The temerity of adventuring thus into the jaws of the pest, now appeared to her in glaring colors.

. . . She cast her eye towards the house opposite to where she now stood. Her heart drooped on perceiving proofs that the dwelling was still inhabited. The door was open, and the windows in the second and third story were raised. Near the entrance, in the street, stood a cart. The horse attached to it, in his form, and furniture, and attitude, was an emblem of torpor and decay. His gaunt sides, motionless limbs, his gummy and dead eyes, and his head hanging to the ground, were in unison with the craziness of the vehicle to which he belonged, and the paltry and bedusted harness which covered him. No attendant nor any human face was visible. The stillness, though at an hour customarily busy, was uninterrupted, except by the sound of wheels moving at an almost indistinguishable distance.

She paused for a moment to contemplate this unwonted spectacle. Her trepidations were mingled with emotions not unakin to sublimity; but the consciousness of danger speedily prevailed, and she hastened to acquit herself of her engagement. She approached the door for this purpose, but before she could draw the bell, her motions were arrested by sounds from within. The staircase was opposite the door. Two persons were now discovered descending the stair. They lifted between them a heavy mass, which was presently discerned to be a coffin. Shocked by this discovery, and trembling, she withdrew from the entrance.

Washington Allston, 1779–1843. (Manual, pp. 504, 510.)

From "Monaldi."

277. Impersonation of the Power of Evil.

The light (which descended from above) was so powerful, that for nearly a minute I could distinguish nothing, and I rested on a form attached to the wainscoting. I then put up my hand to shade my eyes, when—the fearful vision is even now before me—I seemed to be standing before an abyss in space, boundless and black. In the midst of this permeable pitch stood a colossal mass of gold, in shape like an altar, and girdled about by a huge serpent, gorgeous and terrible; his body flecked with diamonds, and his head, an enormous carbuncle, floating like a meteor on the air above. Such was the Throne. But no words can describe the gigantic Being that sat thereon—the grace, the majesty, its transcendent form—and yet I shuddered as I looked, for its superhuman countenance seemed, as it were, to radiate falsehood; every feature was in contradiction—the eye, the mouth, even to the nostril—whilst the expression of the whole was of that unnatural softness which can only be conceived of malignant blandishment. It was the appalling beauty of the King of Hell. The frightful discord vibrated through my whole frame, and I turned for relief to the figure below. . . . But I had turned from the first, only to witness in the second object, its withering fascination. I beheld the mortal conflict between the conscience and the will—the visible struggle of a soul in the toils of sin.

—

From his "Letters."

278. On a Picture by Carracci.

The subject was the body of the virgin borne for interment by four apostles. The figures are colossal; the tone dark, and of tremendous color. It seemed, as I looked at it, as if the ground shook at their tread, and the air was darkened by their grief.

—

279. Originality of Mind.

An original mind is rarely understood until it has been *reflected* from some half dozen congenial with it; so averse are men to admitting the true in an unusual form; whilst any novelty, however fantastic, however false, is greedily swallowed.

James K. Paulding, 1779-1860. (Manual, p. 510.)

From "Letters from the South."

280. Character of the Dutch and German Settlers.

In almost every part of the United States where I have chanced to be, except among the Dutch, the Germans, and the Quakers, people seem to build everything extempore and pro tempore, as if they looked forward to a speedy removal or did not expect to want it long. Nowhere else, it seems to me, do people work more for the present, less for the future, or live so commonly up to the extent of their means. If we build houses, they are generally of wood, and hardly calculated to outlast the builder. If we plant trees, they are generally Lombardy poplars, that spring up of a sudden, give no more shade than a broom stuck on end, and grow old with their planters.

Still, however, I believe all this has a salutary and quickening influence on the character of the people, because it offers another spur to activity, stimulating it not only by the hope of gain, but the necessity of exertion to remedy passing inconveniences. Thus the young heir, instead of stepping into the possession of a house completely finished, and replete with every convenience—an estate requiring no labor or exertion to repair its dilapidations, finds it absolutely necessary to bestir himself to complete what his ancestor had only begun, and thus is relieved from the tedium and temptations of idleness.

But you can always tell when you get among the Dutch and the Quakers, for there you perceive that something has been done for posterity. Their houses are of stone, and built for duration, not for show. If a German builds a house, its walls are twice as thick as others—if he puts down a gate-post, it is sure to be nearly as thick as it is long. Every thing about him, animate and inanimate, partakes of this character of solidity. His wife even is a jolly, portly dame, his children chubby rogues, with legs shaped like little old-fashioned mahogany bannisters—his barns as big as fortresses—his horses like mammoths—his cattle enormous—and his breeches surprisingly redundant in linseywoolsey. It matters not to him, whether the form of sideboards or bureaus changes, or whether other people wear tight breeches or cossack pantaloons in the shape of meal-bags. Let fashion change as it may, his low, round-crowned, broad-brimmed hat, keeps its ground, his galligaskins support the same liberal dimensions, and his old oaken chest and clothes-press of curled maple, with the Anno Domini of their construction upon them, together with the dresser glistening with pewter-plates, still stand their ground, while the baseless fabrics of fashion fade away, without leaving a wreck behind. Ceaseless and unwearied industry is his delight, and enterprise and speculation his abhorrence. Riches do not corrupt, nor poverty depress him; for his mind is a sort of Pacific ocean, such as the first navigators described it—unmoved by tempests, and only intolerable from its dead and tedious calms.

Thus he moves on, and when he dies his son moves on in the same pace, till generations have passed away, without one of the name becoming distinguished by his exploits or his crimes. These are useful citizens, for they bless a country with useful works, and add to its riches. But still, though industry, prudence, and economy are useful habits, they are selfish after all, and can hardly aspire to the dignity of virtues, except as they are preservatives against active vices.

—

From "Westward Ho."

281. Abortive Towns.

Zeno Paddock and his wife Mrs. Judith, departed from the village, never to return. Such was the reputation of the proprietor of the Western Sun, that a distinguished speculator, who was going to found a great city at the junction of Big Dry, and Little Dry, Rivers, made him the most advantageous offers to come and establish himself there, and puff the embryo bantling into existence as fast as possible. He offered him a whole square next to that where the college, the court-house, the church, the library, the athenæum, and all the public buildings were situated. . . . Truth obliges us to say, that on his arrival at the city of New Pekin, as it was called, he found it covered with a forest of trees, each of which would take a man half a day to walk round; and that on discovering the square in which all the public buildings were situated, he found, to his no small astonishment, on the very spot where the court-house stood on the map, a flock of wild turkeys gobbling like so many lawyers, and two or three white-headed owls sitting on the high trees listening with most commendable gravity. . . . Zeno set himself down, began to print his paper in a great hollow sycamore, and to live on anticipation, as many great speculators had done before him.

James Fenimore Cooper, 1789–1851. (Manual, pp. 478, 495, 506.)

From "The Pioneers."

282. THE SHOOTING MATCH.

IN the mean while, as Billy Kirby was preparing himself for another shot, Natty left the goal, with an extremely dissatisfied manner, muttering to himself, and speaking aloud—

"There hasn't been such a thing as a good flint sold at the foot of the lake, since the time when the Indian traders used to come into the country;—and if a body should go into the flats along the streams in the hills, to hunt for such a thing, it's ten to one but they will be all covered up with the plough. Heigho! its seems to me, that just as the game grows scarce, and a body wants the best of ammunition, to get a livelihood, everything that's bad falls on him, like a judgment. But I'll change the stone, for Billy Kirby has'nt the eye for such a mark, I know."

The wood-chopper seemed now entirely sensible that his reputation in a great measure depended on his care; nor did he neglect any means to ensure his success. He drew up his rifle, and renewed his aim, again and again, still appearing reluctant to fire. No sound was heard from even Brom, during these portentous movements, until Kirby discharged his piece, with the same want of success as before. Then, indeed, the shouts of the negro rung through the bushes, and sounded among the trees of the neighboring forest, like the outcries of a tribe of Indians. He laughed, rolling his head, first on one side, then on the other, until nature seemed exhausted with mirth. He danced, until his legs were wearied with motion, in the snow; and in short, he exhibited all that violence of joy that characterizes the mirth of a thoughtless negro.

The wood-chopper had exerted his art, and felt a proportionate degree of disappointment at his failure. He first examined the bird with the utmost attention, and more than once suggested that he had touched its feathers, but the voice of the multitude was against him, for it felt disposed to listen to the often-repeated cries of the black, to "gib a nigger fair play."

Finding it impossible to make out a title to the bird, Kirby turned fiercely to the black, and said—

"Shut your oven, you crow! Where is the man that can hit a turkey's head at a hundred yards? I was a fool for trying. You need'nt make an uproar like a falling pine-tree about it. Show me the man who can do it."

"Look this a-way, Billy Kirby," said Leather-Stocking, "and let them clear the mark, and I'll show you a man who's made better shots afore now, and that when he's been hard pressed by the savages and wild beasts."

* * * * * * *

Although Natty Bumppo* had certainly made hundreds of more momentous shots, at his enemies or his game, yet he never exerted himself more to excel. He raised his piece three several times; once to get his range; once to calculate his distance; and once because the bird, alarmed by the death-like stillness that prevailed, turned its head quickly to examine its foes. But the fourth time he fired. The smoke, the report, and the momentary shock, prevented most of the spectators from instantly knowing the result; but Elizabeth, when she saw her champion drop the end of his rifle in the snow, and open his mouth in one of its silent laughs, and then proceed very coolly to recharge his piece, knew that he had been successful. The boys rushed to the mark, and lifted the turkey on high, lifeless, and with nothing but the remnant of a head.

"Bring in the critter," said Leather-Stocking, "and put it at the feet of the lady. I was her deputy in the matter, and the bird is her property." . . . Elizabeth handed the black a piece of silver as a remuneration for his loss, which had some effect in again unbending his muscles, and then expressed to her companion her readiness to return homeward.

*Another name of Leather-Stocking.

From "The Pilot."

283. LONG TOM COFFIN.

THE seaman who was addressed by this dire appellation arose slowly from the place where he was stationed as cockswain of the boat, and seemed to ascend high in air by the gradual evolution of numberless folds in his body. When erect, he stood nearly six feet and as many inches in his shoes, though, when elevated in his most perpendicular attitude, there was a forward inclination about his head and shoulders, that appeared to be the consequence of habitual confinement in limited lodgings. . . . One of his hands grasped, with a sort of instinct, the staff of a bright harpoon, the lower end of which he placed firmly on the rock, as, in obedience to the order of his commander, he left the place, where, considering his vast dimensions, he had been established in an incredibly small space.

. . . The hardy old seaman, thus addressed, turned his grave visage on his commander, and replied with a becoming gravity,—

"Give me a plenty of sea-room, and good canvas, where there is no occasion for pilots at all, sir. For my part, I was born on board a chebacco-man, and never could see the use of more land than now and then a small island, to raise a few vegetables, and to dry your fish—I'm sure the sight of it always makes me feel uncomfortable, unless we have the wind dead off shore."

. . . "I am more than half of your mind, that an island now and then is all the terra firma that a seaman needs."

"It's reason and philosophy, sir," returned the sedate cockswain; "and what land there is, should always be a soft mud, or a sandy ooze, in order that an anchor might hold, and to make soundings sartin. I have lost many a deep-sea, besides hand-leads by the dozens, on rocky bottoms; but give me the roadstead where a lead comes up light, and an anchor heavy. There's a boat pulling athwart our fore-foot, Captain Barnstable; shall I run her aboard, or give her a berth, sir."

From "The Prairie."

284. Death of the Aged Trapper, in the Pawnee Village.

The trapper had remained nearly motionless for an hour. His eyes alone had occasionally opened and shut. When opened, his gaze seemed fastened on the clouds which hung around the western horizon, reflecting the bright colors, and giving form and loveliness to the glorious tints of an American sunset. The hour, the calm beauty of the season, the occasion, all conspired to fill the spectators with solemn awe. Suddenly, while musing on the remarkable position in which he was placed, Middleton felt the hand which he held grasp his own with incredible power, and the old man, supported on either side by his friends, rose upright to his feet. For a moment he looked about him, as if to invite all in presence to listen (the lingering remnant of human frailty), and then, with a fine military elevation of the head, and with a voice that might be heard in every part of that numerous assembly, he pronounced the word "Here!"

A movement so entirely unexpected, and the air of grandeur and humility which were so remarkably united in the mien of the trapper, together with the clear and uncommon force of his utterance, produced a short period of confusion in the faculties of all present. When Middleton and Hard-Heart, each of whom had involuntarily extended a hand to support the form of the old man, turned to him again, they found that the subject of their interest was removed forever beyond the necessity of their care.

From "The Red Rover."

285. Escape from the Wreck.

. . . The boat was soon cleared of what, under their circumstances, was literally lumber; leaving, however, far more than enough to meet all their wants, and not a few of their comforts, in the event that the elements should accord the permission to use them.

Then, and not till then, did Wilder relax in his exertions. He had arranged his sails ready to be hoisted in an instant; he had carefully examined that no straggling rope connected the boat to the wreck, to draw them under with the foundering mass; and he had assured himself that food, water, compass, and the imperfect instruments that were there then in use to ascertain the position of a ship, were all perfectly disposed of in their several places, and ready to his hand. When all was in this state of preparation he disposed of himself in the stern of the boat, and endeavored by the composure of his manner, to inspire his less resolute companions with a portion of his own firmness.

The bright sunshine was sleeping in a thousand places on every side of the silent and deserted wreck. The sea had subsided to such a state of utter rest that it was only at long intervals that the huge and helpless mass, on which the ark of the expectants lay, was lifted from its dull quietude, to roll heavily, for a moment in the washing waters, and then to settle lower into the greedy and absorbing element. Still the disappearance of the hull was slow, and even tedious, to those who looked forward with such impatience to its total immersion, as to the crisis of their own fortunes. . . .

* * * * * * *

Then came the moon, with its mild and deceptive light, to throw the delusion of its glow on the varying but ever frightful scene.

"See," said Wilder, as the luminary lifted its pale and melancholy orb out of the bed of the ocean; "we shall have light for our hazardous launch!"

"Is it at hand?" demanded Mrs. Wyllis, with all the resolution of manner she could assume in so trying a situation.

"It is—the ship has already brought her scuppers to the water. Sometimes a vessel will float until saturated with the brine. If ours sink at all, it will be soon."

"If at all! Is there then hope that she can float?"

"None!" said Wilder, pausing to listen to the hollow and threatening sounds which issued from the depths of the vessel, as the water broke through her divisions, in passing from side to side, and which sounded like the groaning of some heavy monster in the last agony of nature. "None; she is already losing her level!"

His companions saw the change; but not for the empire of the world, could either of them have uttered a syllable. Another low, threatening, rumbling sound was heard, and then the pent air beneath blew up the forward part of the deck, with an explosion like that of a gun.

"Now grasp the ropes I have given you!" cried Wilder, breathless with his eagerness to speak.

His words were smothered by the rushing and gurgling of waters. The vessel made a plunge like a dying whale; and raising its stern high into the air, glided into the depths of the sea, like the leviathan seeking his secret places. The motionless boat was lifted with the ship, until it stood in an attitude fearfully approaching to the perpendicular. As the wreck descended, the bows of the launch met the element, burying themselves nearly to filling; but buoyant and light, it rose again, and, struck powerfully on the stern by the settling mass, the little ark shot ahead, as though it had been driven by the hand of man. Still, as the water rushed into the vortex, every thing within its influence yielded to the suction; and at the next instant, the launch was seen darting down the declivity, as if eager to follow the vast machine, of which it had so long formed a dependant, through the same gaping whirlpool, to the bottom. Then it rose, rocking to the surface, and for a moment, was tossed and whirled like a bubble circling in the eddies of a pool. After which, the ocean moaned, and slept again; the moon-beams playing across its treacherous bosom, sweetly and calm, as the rays are seen to quiver on a lake that is embedded in sheltering mountains.

From "The History of the United States Navy."

286. NAVAL RESULTS OF THE WAR OF 1812.

THUS terminated the war of 1812, so far as it was connected with the American marine. The navy came out of this struggle with a vast increase of reputation. The brilliant style in which the ships had been carried into action, the steadiness and rapidity with which they had been handled, and the fatal accuracy of their fire, on nearly every occasion, produced a new era in naval warfare. Most of the frigate actions had been as soon decided as circumstances would at all allow, and in no instance was it found necessary to keep up the fire of a sloop-of-war an hour, when singly engaged. Most of the combats of the latter, indeed, were decided in about half that time. The execution done in these short conflicts was often equal to that made by the largest vessels of Europe in general actions, and, in some of them, the slain and wounded comprised a very large proportion of the crews.

It is not easy to say in which nation this unlooked-for result created the most surprise, America or England. In the first it produced a confidence in itself that had been greatly wanted, but which, in the end, perhaps, degenerated to a feeling of self-esteem and security that were not without danger, or entirely without exaggeration. . . . The ablest and bravest captains of the English fleet were ready to admit that a new power was about to appear on the ocean, and that it was not improbable the battle for the mastery of the seas would have to be fought over again.

. . . That the tone and discipline of the service were high, is true; but it must be ascribed to moral, and not to physical, causes, to that aptitude in the American character for the sea which has been so constantly manifested, from the day the first pinnace sailed along the coast, on the trading voyages of the seventeenth century, down to the present moment.

Many false modes of accounting for the novel character that had been given to naval battles were resorted to, and among other reasons, it was affirmed that the American vessels of war sailed with crews of picked seamen. That a nation which practiced impressment should imagine that another in which enlistments were voluntary, could possess an advantage of this nature, infers a strong disposition to listen to any means but the right one to account for an unpleasant truth. It is not known that a single vessel left the country, the case of the Constitution on her two last cruises excepted, with a crew that could be deemed extraordinary in this respect. No American man-of-war ever sailed with a complement composed of nothing but able seamen; and some of the hardest fought battles that occurred during this war, were fought by ships' companies that were materially worse than common. The people that manned the vessels on Lake Champlain, in particular, were of a quality much inferior to those usually found in ships of war. Neither were the officers, in general, old or very experienced. The navy itself dated but fourteen years back, when the war commenced; and some of the commanders began their professional careers several years after the first appointments had been made. Perhaps one half of the lieutenants in the service at the peace of 1815, had first gone on board ship within six years from the declaration of the war, and very many of them within three or four. So far from the midshipmen having been masters and mates of merchantmen, as was reported at the time, they were generally youths that first went from the ease and comforts of the paternal home, when they appeared on the quarter-deck of a man-of-war.

Catharine M. Sedgwick, 1789–1867.

(Manual, p. 484.)

From "Hope Leslie."

287. The Minister condemning Vain Apparel.

Mr. Cotton, the regular pastor, rose to remind his brethren of the decree "that private members should be very sparing in their questions and observations after public sermons," and to say that he should postpone any further discussion of the precious points before them, as it was now near nine o'clock, after which it was not suitable for any Christian family to be unnecessarily abroad.

Hope now, and many others, instinctively rose, in anticipation of the dismissing benediction; but Mr. Cotton waved his hand for them to sit down till he could communicate to the congregation the decision to which the ruling elders and himself had come on the subject of the last Sabbath sermon. "He would not repeat what he had before said upon that lust of costly apparel which was fast gaining ground, and had already, as was well known, crept into godly families. He was pleased that there were among them gracious women, ready to turn at a rebuke, as was manifested in many veils being left at home that were floating over the congregation like so many butterflies' wings in the morning. Economy," he justly observed, "was, as well as simplicity, a Christian grace; and, therefore, the rulers had determined that those persons who had run into the excess of immoderate veils and sleeves, embroidered caps, and gold and silver lace, should be permitted to wear them out, but new ones should be forfeited."

This sumptuary regulation announced, the meeting was dismissed.

Madame Winthrop whispered to Everell that she was going, with his father, to look in upon a sick neighbor, and would thank him to see her niece home. Everell stole a glance at Hope, and dutifully offered his arm to Miss Downing.

Hope, intent only on one object, was hurrying out of the pew, intending, in the jostling of the crowd, to escape alone; but she was arrested by Madame Winthrop's saying, "Miss Leslie, Sir Philip offers you his arm;" and at the same moment, her aunt stooped forward to beg her to wait a moment, till she could send a message to Deacon Knowles' wife, that she might wear her new gown with the Turkish sleeves, the next day. . . . "It is but doing as a body would be done by, to let Mistress Knowles know she may come out in her new gown to-morrow."

From "The Linwoods."

288. Kosciusko's Garden at West Point.

The harmonies of Nature's orchestra were the only and the fitting sounds in this seclusion; the early wooing of the birds; the water from the fountains of the heights, that, filtering through the rocks, dropped from ledge to ledge with the regularity of a water-clock; the ripple of the waves, as they broke upon the rocky points of the shore, or softly kissed its pebbly margin; and the voice of the tiny stream, that, gliding down a dark, deep, and almost hidden channel in the rocks, disappeared and welled up again in the center of the turfy slope, stole over it, and trickled down the lower ledge of granite to the river. Tradition has named this little, green shelf on the rocks, "Kosciusko's Garden;" but, as no traces have been discovered of any other than Nature's plantings, it was probably merely his favorite retreat, and, as such, is a monument of his taste and love of nature.

John Neal, 1793–. (Manual, p. 510.)

From "Randolph."

289. The Nature of True Poetry.

Poetry is the naked expression of power and eloquence; but, for many hundred years, poetry has been confounded with false music, measure, and cadence, the soul with the body, the thought with the language, the manner of speaking with the mode of thinking. . . . What I call poetry, has nothing to do with art or learning. It is a natural music, the music of woods and waters, not that of the orchestra. . . . Poetry is a religion, as well as a music. Nay, it is eloquence. It is whatever affects, touches, or disturbs the animal or moral sense of man. I care not how poetry may be expressed, nor in what language; it is still poetry; as the melody of the waters, wherever they may run, in the desert or the wilderness, among the rocks or the grass, will always be melody. . . .

It is not the composition of a master, the language of art, painfully and entirely exact, but is the wild, capricious melody of *nature,* pathetic or brilliant, like the roundelay of innumerable birds whistling all about you, in the wind and water, sky and air, or the coquetting of a river breeze over the fine strings of an Æolian harp, concealed among green leaves and apple blossoms.

John Pendleton Kennedy, 1795–1870.

(Manual, pp. 490, 510.)

From "Swallow Barn."

290. THE MANSION AND THE BARN.

SWALLOW BARN is an aristocratical old edifice, which sits, like a brooding hen, on the southern bank of the James River. It looks down upon a shady pocket, or nook, formed by an indentation of the shore, from a gentle acclivity, thinly sprinkled with oaks, whose magnificent branches afford habitation to sundry friendly colonies of squirrels and woodpeckers.

This time-honored mansion was the residence of the family of Hazards. . . .

The main building is more than a century old. It is built with thick brick walls, but one story in height, and surmounted by a double-faced or hipped roof, which gives the idea of a ship, bottom upwards. Later buildings have been added to this, as the wants or ambition of the family have expanded. These are all constructed of wood, and seem to have been built in defiance of all laws of congruity, just as convenience required. . . .

. . . Beyond the bridge, at some distance, stands a prominent object in the perspective of this picture,—the most venerable appendage to the establishment,—a huge barn, with an immense roof hanging almost to the ground, and thatched a foot thick with sun-burnt straw, which reaches below the eaves in ragged flakes. It has a singularly drowsy and decrepit aspect.

291. A Disappointed Politician.

"Things are getting worse and worse," replied the other. "I can see how it's going. Here, the first thing General Jackson did, when he came in, he wanted to have the president elected for six years; and, by and by, they will want him for ten; and now they want to cut up our orchards and meadows, whether or no. That's just the way Bonaparte went on. What's the use of states, if they are all to be cut up with canals, and railroads, and tariffs? No, no, gentlemen; you may depend Old Virginny's not going to let Congress carry on in her day."

"How can they help it?" asked Sandy.

"We haven't *fout* and bled," rejoined the other, taking out of his pocket a large piece of tobacco, and cutting off a quid, as he spoke in a somewhat subdued tone,—"we haven't *fout* and bled for our liberties to have our posterity and their land circumcised after this rate, to suit the figaries of Congress. So let them try it when they will."

"Mr. Ned Hazard, what do you call state rights?" demanded Sandy.

"It's a sort of a law," said the other speaker, taking the answer to himself, "against cotton and wool."

From his "Life of William Wirt."

292. Wirt's Style of Oratory.

He became, in the maturity of his career, one of the most philosophic and accomplished lawyers of his time. In earlier life, he was remarked for a florid imagination, and a power of vivid declamation,—faculties which are but too apt to seduce their possessor to waste his strength in that flimsier eloquence, which more captivates the crowd without the bar, than the Judge upon the bench, and whose fatal facility often ensnares ambitious youth capable of better things, by its cheap applause and temptation to that indolence which may be indulged without loss of popularity. The public seem to have ascribed to Mr. Wirt some such reputation as this, when he first attracted notice. He came upon the broader theater of his fame under this disadvantage. He was aware of it himself, and labored with matchless perseverance to disabuse the tribunals, with which he was familiar, of this disparaging opinion. How he succeeded, his compeers at the bar have often testified. None amongst them ever brought to the judgment-seat a more complete preparation for trial:—none ever more thoroughly argued a case through minute analysis and nice discrimination of principles. In logical precision of mind, clearness of statement, full investigation of complicated points, and close comparison of precedents, he had no superior at the bar of the Supreme Court. He often relieved the tedium of argument with playful sallies of wit and humor. He had a prompt and effective talent for this exercise, to which his extensive and various reading administered abundant resource; and he indulged it not less to the gratification of his auditory than to the aid of his cause. . . . In such tactics, Mr. Wirt was well versed. In sarcasm and invective he was often exceedingly strong, and denounced with a power that made transgressors tremble; but the bent of his nature being kindly and tolerant of error, he took more pleasure in exciting the laugh, than in conjuring the spirit of censure or rebuke.

His manner in speaking was singularly attractive. His manly form, his intellectual countenance and musical voice, set off by a rare gracefulness of gesture, won, in advance, the favor of his auditory. He was calm, deliberate, and distinct in his enunciation, not often rising into any high exhibition of passion, and never sinking into tameness. His key was that of earnest and animated argument, frequently alternated with that of a playful and sprightly humor. His language was neat, well chosen, and uttered without impediment or slovenly repetition. The tones of his voice played, with a natural skill, through the various cadences most appropriate to express the flitting emotions of his mind, and the changes of his thought.

To these external properties of his elocution, we may ascribe the pleasure which persons of all conditions found in listening to him. Women often crowded the court-rooms to hear him, and as often astonished him, not only by the patience, but the visible enjoyment with which they were wont to sit out his argument to the end,—even when the topic was too dry to interest them, or too abstruse for them to understand his discourse. . . . His oratory was not of that strong, bold, and impetuous nature which is often the chief characteristic of the highest eloquence, and which is said to sway the Senate with absolute dominion, and to imprison or set free the storm of human passion, in the multitude, according to the speaker's will. It was smooth, polished, scholar-like, sparkling with pleasant fancies, and beguiling the listener by its varied graces, out of all note or consciousness of time.

William Ware, 1797–1852. (Manual, p. 510.)

From "Aurelian, or Rome in the Third Century."

293. The Christian Martyr.

When now he had stood there not many minutes, one of the doors of the vivaria was suddenly thrown back, and bounding forth with a roar that seemed to shake the walls of the theatre, a lion of huge dimensions leaped upon the arena. Majesty and power were inscribed upon his lordly limbs; and, as he stood there where he had first sprung, and looked round upon the multitude, how did his gentle eye and noble carriage, with which no one for a moment could associate meanness, or cruelty, or revenge, cast shame upon the human monsters assembled to behold a solitary, unarmed man torn limb from limb! When he had in this way looked upon that cloud of faces, he then turned, and moved round the arena through its whole circumference, still looking upwards upon those who filled the seats, not till he had come again to the point from which he started so much as noticing him who stood his victim in the midst. Then, as if apparently for the first time becoming conscious of his presence, he caught the form of Probus, and, moving slowly towards him, looked steadfastly upon him, receiving in return the settled gaze of the Christain. Standing there still a while, each looking upon the other, he then walked round him, then approached nearer, making suddenly, and for a moment, those motions which indicated the roused appetite; but, as it were, in the spirit of self-rebuke, he immediately retreated a few paces, and lay down in the sand, stretching out his head towards Probus, and closing his eyes, as if for sleep.

Lydia Maria Child, 1802-. (Manual, p. 484.)

From "Autumnal Leaves."

294. ILL TEMPER CONTAGIOUS.

IT is curious to observe how a man's spiritual state reflects itself in the people and animals around him; nay, in the very garments, trees, and stones.

Reuben Black was an infestation in the neighborhood where he resided. The very sight of him produced effects similar to the Hindoo magical tune called Raug, which is said to bring on clouds, storms, and earthquakes. His wife seemed lean, sharp, and uncomfortable. The heads of his boys had a bristling aspect, as if each individual hair stood on end with perpetual fear. The cows poked out their horns horizontally, as soon as he opened the barn-yard gate. The dog dropped his tail between his legs, and eyed him askance, to see what humor he was in. The cat looked wild and scraggy, and had been known to rush straight up the chimney when he moved towards her. Fanny Kemble's expressive description of the Pennsylvania stage-horses was exactly suited to Reuben's poor old nag. "His hide resembled an old hair-trunk." Continual whipping and kicking had made him such a stoic, that no amount of blows could quicken his pace, and no chirruping could change the dejected drooping of his head. All his natural language said, as plainly as a horse *could* say it, that he was a most unhappy beast. Even the trees on Reuben's premises had a gnarled and knotted appearance. The bark wept little sickly tears of gum, and the branches grew awry, as if they felt the continual discord, and made sorry faces at each other behind their owner's back. His fields were red with sorrel, or run over with mullein. Every thing seemed as hard and arid as his own visage. Every day, he cursed the town and the neighborhood, because they poisoned his dogs, and stoned his hens, and shot his cats. Continual law-suits involved him in so much expense, that he had neither time nor money to spend on the improvement of his farm.

Against Joe Smith, a poor laborer in the neighborhood, he had brought three suits in succession. Joe said he had returned a spade he borrowed, and Reuben swore he had not. He sued Joe, and recovered damages, for which he ordered the sheriff to seize his pig. Joe, in his wrath, called him an old swindler, and a curse to the neighborhood. These remarks were soon repeated to Reuben. He brought an action for slander, and recovered twenty-five cents. Provoked at the laugh this occasioned, he watched for Joe to pass by, and set his big dog upon him, screaming furiously, "Call me an old swindler again, will you." An evil spirit is more contagious than the plague. Joe went home and scolded his wife, and boxed little Joe's ears, and kicked the cat; and not one of them knew what it was all for. A fortnight after, Reuben's big dog was found dead by poison. Whereupon he brought another action against Joe Smith, and not being able to prove him guilty of the charge of dog-murder, he took his revenge by poisoning a pet lamb belonging to Mrs. Smith. Thus the bad game went on, with mutual worriment and loss. Joe's temper grew more and more vindictive, and the love of talking over his troubles at the grog-shop increased on him. Poor Mrs. Smith cried, and said it was all owing to Reuben Black; for a better hearted man never lived than her Joe, when she first married him.

Robert M. Bird, 1803–1854. (Manual, p. 510.)

From "Nick of the Woods: a Tale of Kentucky."

295. THE QUAKER HUNTSMAN.

"I HAVE a thing to say to thee, which it concerns thee and the fair maid, thee cousin, to know. There was a will, friend, a true and lawful last will and testament of thee deceased uncle, in which theeself and thee cousin was made the sole heirs of the same. Truly, friend, I did take it from the breast of the villain that plotted thee ruin; but, truly, it was taken from me again, I know not how."

"I have it safe," said Roland, displaying it, for a moment, with great satisfaction, to Nathan's eyes. "It makes me master of wealth, which you, Nathan, shall be the first to share. You must leave this wild life of the border, go with me to Virginia—"

"I, friend!" exclaimed Nathan, with a melancholy shake of the head; "thee would not have me back in the Settlements, to scandalize them that is of my faith? No, friend; my lot is cast in the woods, and thee must not ask me again to leave them. And, friend, thee must not think I have served thee for the lucre of money or gain; for truly these things are now to me as nothing. The meat that feeds me, the skins that cover, the leaves that make my bed, are all in the forest around me, to be mine when I want them; and what more can I desire? Yet, friend, if thee thinks theeself obliged by whatever I have done for thee, I would ask of thee one favor that thee can grant."

"A hundred!" said the Virginian, warmly.

"Nay, friend," muttered Nathan, with both a warning and beseeching look, "all that I ask is, that thee shall say nothing of me that should scandalize and disparage the faith to which I was born."

"I understand you," said Roland, "and will remember your wish. . . . Come with us, Nathan; come with us."

But Nathan, ashamed of the weakness which he could not

resist, had turned away to conceal his emotion, and, stalking silently off, with the ever-faithful Peter at his heels, was soon hidden from their eyes.

Nathaniel Hawthorne, about *1805–1864.*

(Manual, pp. 505, 508.)

From the "Twice-Told Tales."

296. Portrait of Edward Randolph.

Within the antique frame which so recently had enclosed a sable waste of canvas, now appeared a visible picture—still dark, indeed, in its hues and shadings, but thrown forward in strong relief. . . . The whole portrait started so distinctly out of the background, that it had the effect of a person looking down from the wall at the astonished and awe-stricken spectators. The expression of the face, if any words can convey an idea of it, was that of a wretch detected in some hideous guilt, and exposed to the bitter hatred, and laughter, and withering scorn of a vast, surrounding multitude. There was the struggle of defiance, beaten down and overwhelmed by the crushing weight of ignominy. The torture of the soul had come forth upon the countenance. It seemed as if the picture, while hidden behind the cloud of immemorial years, had been all the time acquiring an intenser depth and darkness of expression, till now it gloomed forth again, and threw its evil omen over the present hour. Such, if the wild legend may be credited, was the portrait of Edward Randolph, as he appeared when a people's curse had wrought its influence upon his nature.

---

297. Description of an Old Sailor.

Many such a day did I sit snugly in Mr. Bartlett's store, attentive to the yarns of Uncle Parker—uncle to the whole village by right of seniority, but of southern blood, with no kindred in New England. His figure is before me now, enthroned upon a mackerel barrel—a lean, old man, of great height, but bent with years, and twisted into an uncouth shape by seven broken limbs; furrowed, also, and weather-worn, as if every gale, for the better part of a century, had caught him somewhere on the sea. He looked like a harbinger of tempest, a shipmate of the Flying Dutchman. . . . One of Uncle Parker's eyes had been blown out with gunpowder, and the other did but glimmer in its socket. Turning it upward as he spoke, it was his delight to tell of cruises against the French, and battles with his own ship-mates, when he and an antagonist used to be seated astride of a sailor's chest, each fastened down by a spike-nail through his trousers, and there to fight it out.

—

From the "Blithedale Romance."

298. A Picture of Girlhood.

Priscilla had now grown to be a very pretty girl, and still kept budding and blossoming, and daily putting on some new charm, which you no sooner became sensible of than you thought it worth all she had previously possessed. So unformed, vague, and without substance, as she had come to us, it seemed as if we could see Nature shaping out a woman before our very eyes, and yet had only a more reverential sense of the mystery of a woman's soul and frame. Yesterday, her cheek was pale,—to-day it had a bloom. Priscilla's smile, like a baby's first one, was a wondrous novelty. Her imperfections and short-comings affected me with a kind of playful pathos, which was as absolutely bewitching a sensation as ever I experienced. After she had been a month or two at Blithedale, her animal spirits waxed high, and kept her pretty constantly in a state of bubble and ferment, impelling her to far more bodily activity than she had yet strength to endure. She was very fond of playing with the other girls out of doors. There is hardly another sight in the world so pretty as that of a company of young girls, almost women grown, at play, and so giving themselves up to their airy impulse that their tiptoes barely touch the ground.

Girls are incomparably wilder and more effervescent than boys, more untamable, and regardless of rule and limit, with an ever-shifting variety, breaking continually into new modes of fun, yet with a harmonious propriety through all. Their steps, their voices, appear free as the wind, but keep consonance with a strain of music inaudible to us. Young men and boys, on the other hand, play according to recognized law, old, traditionary games, permitting no caprioles of fancy, but with scope enough for the outbreak of savage instincts. . .

Especially it is delightful to see a vigorous young girl run a race, with her head thrown back, her limbs moving moref riskily than they need, and an air between that of a bird and a young colt. But Priscilla's peculiar charm, in a foot-race, was the weakness and irregularity with which she ran. . . .

When she had come to be quite at home among us, I used to fancy that Priscilla played more pranks, and perpetrated more mischief, than any other girl in the community. For example, I once heard Silas Foster, in a very gruff voice, threatening to rivet three horse-shoes round Priscilla's neck, and chain her to a post, because she, with some other young people, had clambered upon a load of hay, and caused it to slide off the cart. How she made her peace I never knew; but very soon afterwards I saw old Silas, with his brawny hands round Priscilla's waist, swinging her to and fro, and finally depositing her on one of the oxen, to take her first lessons in riding. She met with terrible mishaps in her efforts to milk a cow; she let the poultry into the garden; she generally spoilt whatever part of the dinner she took in charge; she broke crockery; she dropped our biggest pitcher into the well; and—except with her needle and those little wooden instruments for purse-making—was as unserviceable a member of society as any young lady in the land. There was no other sort of efficiency about her. Yet everybody was kind to Priscilla; everybody loved her and laughed at her to her face, and did not laugh behind her back; everybody would have given her half of his last crust, or the bigger share of his plum-cake. These were pretty certain indications that we were all conscious of a pleasant weakness in the girl, and considered her not quite able to look after her own interests, or fight her battle with the world.

From "The Marble Faun."

299. SCULPTURE: ART AND ARTISTS.

A SCULPTOR, indeed, to meet the demands which our preconceptions make upon him, should be even more indispensably a poet than those who deal in measured verse and rhyme. His material, or instrument, which serves him in the stead of shifting and transitory language, is a pure, white, undecaying substance. It insures immortality to whatever is wrought in it, and therefore makes it a religious obligation to commit no idea to its mighty guardianship, save such as may repay the marble for its faithful care, its incorruptible fidelity, by warming it with an etherial life. Under this aspect, marble assumes a sacred character; and no man should dare to touch it unless he feels within himself a certain consecration and a priesthood, the only evidence of which, for the public eye, will be the high treatment of heroic subjects, or the delicate evolution of spiritual, through material beauty. . . .

No ideas such as the foregoing—no misgivings suggested by them—probably troubled the self complacency of most of these clever sculptors. Marble, in their view, had no such sanctity as we impute to it. . . .

Yet we love the artists, in every kind; even these, whose merits we are not quite able to appreciate. Sculptors, painters, crayon sketchers, or whatever branch of æsthetics they adopted, were certainly pleasanter people, as we saw them that evening, than the average whom we meet in ordinary society. They were not wholly confined within the sordid compass of practical life; they had a pursuit which, if followed faithfully out, would lead them to the beautiful, and always had a tendency thitherward, even if they lingered to gather up golden drops by the wayside. Their actual business (though they talked about it very much as other men talk of cotton, politics, flour barrels, and sugar) necessarily illuminated their conversation with something akin to the ideal. . . .

As interesting as any of these relics was a large portfolio of old drawings, some of which, in the opinion of their possessor, bore evidence on their faces of the touch of master-hands. . . . According to the judgment of several connoisseurs, Raphael's own hand had communicated its magnetism to one of these sketches; and if genuine, it was evidently his first conception of a favorite Madonna, now hanging in the private apartment of the Grand Duke, at Florence. . . . There were at least half a dozen others, to which the owner assigned as high an origin. It was delightful to believe in their authenticity, at all events; for these things make the spectator more vividly sensible of a great painter's power, than the final glow and perfected art of the most consummate picture that may have been elaborated from them. There is an effluence of divinity in the first sketch; and there, if any where, you find the pure light of inspiration, which the subsequent toil of the artist serves to bring out in stronger lustre, indeed, but likewise adulterates it with what belongs to an inferior mood. The aroma and fragrance of new thought were perceptible in these designs, after three centuries of wear and tear. The charm lay partly in their very imperfection; for this is suggestive, and sets the imagination at work; whereas, the finished picture, if a good one, leaves the spectator nothing to do, and if bad, confuses, stupefies. disenchants, and disheartens him.

From the "English Note Books."

300. Ruins of Furness Abbey.

The most interesting part is that which was formerly the church, and which, though now roofless, is still surrounded by walls, and retains the remnants of the pillars that formerly supported the intermingling curves of the arches. The floor is all overgrown with grass strewn with fragments and capitals of pillars. It was a great and stately edifice, the length of the nave and choir having been nearly three hundred feet, and that of the transept more than half as much. The pillars along the nave were alternately, a round solid one, and a clustered one. Now, what remains of some of them is even with the ground; others present a stump just high enough to form a seat; and others are perhaps a man's height from the ground; and all are mossy, and with grass and weeds rooted into their chinks, and here and there a tuft of flowers giving its tender little beauty to their decay. The material of the edifice is a soft red stone, and it is now extensively overgrown with a lichen of a very light gray hue, which at a little distance makes the walls look as if they had long ago been whitewashed and now had partially returned to their original color. The arches of the nave and transept were noble and immense; there were four of them together, supporting a tower which has long since disappeared,—arches loftier than I ever conceived to have been made by man. Very possibly, in some cathedral that I have seen, or am yet to see, there may be arches as stately as these, but I doubt whether they can ever show to such advantage in a perfect edifice as they do in this ruin,—most of them broken, only one, as far as I recollect, still completing its sweep. In this state they suggest a greater majesty and beauty than any finished human work can show; the crumbling traces of the half-obliterated design producing somewhat of the effect of the first idea of any thing admirable, when it dawns upon the mind of an artist or a poet,—an idea which, do what he may, he is sure to fall short of in his attempt to embody it. . . .

Conceive all these shattered walls, with here and there an arched door, or the great arched vacancy of a window; these broken stones and monuments scattered about; these rows of pillars up and down the nave, these arches, through which a giant might have stepped, and not needed to bow his head, unless in reverence to the sanctity of the place,—conceive it all, with such verdure and embroidery of flowers as the gentle, kindly moisture of the English climate procreates on all old things, making them more beautiful than new, conceive it with the grass for sole pavement of the long and spacious aisle, and the sky above for the only roof. The sky, to be sure, is more majestic than the tallest of those arches; and yet these latter, perhaps, make the stronger impression of sublimity, because they translate the sweep of the sky to our finite comprehension. It was a most beautiful, warm, sunny day, and the ruins had all the pictorial advantage of bright light, and deep shadows. I must not forget that birds flew in and out among the recesses, and chirped and warbled, and made themselves at home there. Doubtless, the birds of the present generation are the posterity of those who first settled in the ruins, after the Reformation; and perhaps the old monks of a still earlier day may have watched them building about the abbey, before it was a ruin at all.

—

From the "American Note Books."

301. Scenery of the Merrimac.

I never could have conceived that there was so beautiful a river-scene in Concord as this of the North Branch. The stream flows through the midmost privacy and deepest heart of a wood, which, as if but half satisfied with its presence, calm, gentle and unobtrusive as it is, seems to crowd upon it, and barely to allow it passage, for the trees are rooted on the very verge of the water, and dip their pendent branches into it. On one side there is a high bank forming the side of a hill, the Indian name of which I have forgotten, though Mr. Thoreau told it to me; and here in some instances the trees stand leaning over the river, stretching out their arms as if about to plunge in headlong. On the other side, the bank is almost on a level with the water, and there the quiet congregation of trees stood with feet in the flood, and fringed with foliage down to its very surface. Vines here and there twine themselves about bushes or aspens or alder-trees, and hang their clusters, though scanty and infrequent this season, so that I can reach them from my boat. I scarcely remember a scene of more complete and lovely seclusion than the passage of the river through this wood. Even an Indian canoe in olden times, could not have floated onward in deeper solitude than my boat. I have never elsewhere had such an opportunity to observe how much more beautiful reflection is than what we call reality. The sky and the clustering foliage on either hand, and the effect of sunlight as it found its way through the shade, giving lightsome hues in contrast with the quiet depth of the prevailing tints, all these seemed unsurpassably beautiful when beheld in upper air. But on gazing downward, there they were, the same even to the minutest particular, yet arrayed in ideal beauty which satisfied the spirit incomparably more than the actual scene. I am half convinced that the reflection is indeed the reality, the real thing which Nature imperfectly images to our grosser sense. At any rate the disembodied shadow is nearest to the soul.

From the "French and Italian Note Books."

302. A DUNGEON OF ANCIENT ROME.

WE were now in the deepest and ugliest part of the old Mamertine Prison, one of the few remains of the kingly period of Rome, and which served the Romans as a state prison for hundreds of years before the Christian era. A multitude of criminals or innocent persons, no doubt, have languished here in misery, and perished in darkness. Here Jugurtha starved; here Catiline's adherents were strangled; and methinks, there can not be in the world another such an evil den, so haunted with black memories and indistinct surmises of guilt and suffering. In old Rome, I suppose, the citizens never spoke of this dungeon above their breath. It looks just as bad as it is; round, only seven paces across, yet so obscure that our tapers could not illuminate it from side to side,—the stones of which it is constructed being as black as midnight. The custode showed us a stone post at the side of the cell, with the hole in the top of it, into which, he said, St. Peter's chain had been fastened; and he uncovered a spring of water, in the middle of the stone floor, which he told us had miraculously gushed up to enable the Saint to baptize his jailor. The miracle was perhaps the more easily wrought, inasmuch as Jugurtha had found the floor of the dungeon oozy with wet. However, it is best to be as simple and childlike as we can in these matters; and whether St. Peter stamped his visage into the stone, and wrought this other miracle or no, and whether or no he ever was in the prison at all, still the belief of a thousand years and more, gives a sort of reality and substance to such traditions. The custode dipped an iron ladle into the miraculous water, and we each of us drank a sip; and, what is very remarkable, to me it seemed hard water and almost brackish, while many persons think it the sweetest in Rome. I suspect that St. Peter still dabbles in this water, and tempers its qualities according to the faith of those who drink it.

William Gilmore Simms, 1806–1870.

(Manual, pp. 490, 510.)

From "Eutaw, a Sequel to The Foragers."

303. The Battle of Eutaw.

Up to this moment nothing had seemed more certain than the victory of the Americans. The consternation in the British camp was complete. Everything was given up for lost by a considerable portion of the army. The commissaries destroyed their stores, the loyalists and American deserters, dreading the rope, seizing every horse which they could command, fled incontinently for Charleston, whither they carried such an alarm that the stores along the road were destroyed, and the trees felled across it for the obstruction of the victorious Americans, who were supposed to be pressing down upon the city with all their might.

Equally deceived were the conquerors. Flushed with success, the infantry scattered themselves about the British camp, which, as all the tents had been left standing, presented a thousand objects to tempt the appetites of a half-starved and half-naked soldiery. Insubordination followed disorder. . . .

No more could be done. The laurels won in the first act of this exciting drama, were all withered in the second. Both parties claimed a victory. It belonged to neither. The British were beaten from the field at the point of the bayonet, sought shelter in a fortress, and repulsed their assailants from that fortress. It is to the shame and discredit of the Americans that they were repulsed. The victory was in their hands.

From the "Life of Francis Marion."

304. CHARACTER AND SERVICES OF GENERAL MARION.

No commander had ever been more solicitous of the safety and comfort of his men. It was this which had rendered him so sure of their fidelity, which had enabled him to extract from them such admirable service. This simple entreaty stayed their quarrels; . . . No duel took place among his officers during the whole of his command.

The province which was assigned to his control by Governor Rutledge, was the constant theatre of war. He was required to cover an immense extent of country. With a force constantly unequal and constantly fluctuating, he contrived to supply its deficiencies by the resources of his own vigilance and skill. His personal bravery was frequently shown, and the fact that he himself conducted an enterprise, was enough to convince his men that they were certain to be led to victory. . . . He had no lives to waste, and the game he played was that which enabled him to secure the greatest results, with the smallest amount of hazard. Yet, when the occasion seemed to require it, he could advance and strike with an audacity, which in the ordinary relations of the leader with the soldier, might well be thought inexcusable rashness. . . . The reader will perceive a singular discrepancy between the actual events detailed in the life of every popular hero, and the peculiar fame which he holds in the minds of his countrymen. Thus, while Marion is every where regarded as the peculiar representative in the southern States, of the genius of partizan warfare, we are surprised, when we would trace, in the pages of the annalist, the sources of this fame, to find the details so meagre and so unsatisfactory. Tradition mumbles over his broken memories, which we vainly strive to pluck from his lips, and bind together in coherent and satisfactory records. The spirited surprise, the happy ambush, the daring onslaught, the fortunate escape,—these, as they involve no monstrous slaughter,—no murderous strife of masses,—no rending of walled towns and sack of cities, the ordinary historian disdains. The military reputation of Marion consists in the frequent performance of deeds, unexpectedly, with inferior means, by which the enemy was annoyed and dispirited, and the hearts and courage of his countrymen warmed into corresponding exertions with his own. To him we owe that the fires of patriotism were never extinguished, even in the most disastrous hours, in the low country of South Carolina. He made our swamps and forests sacred, as well because of the refuge which they gave to the fugitive patriot, as for the frequent sacrifices which they enabled him to make, on the altars of liberty and a befitting vengeance. . . . It is enough that his fame has entered largely into that of his country, forming a valuable portion of its national stock of character. His memory is in the very hearts of our people.

Harriet Beecher Stowe, 1812-. (Manual, p. 484.)

From "Uncle Tom's Cabin."

305. MEMORIALS OF A DEAD CHILD.

AT the door, however, he stopped a moment, and then coming back, he said, with some hesitation,—

"Mary, I don't know how you'd feel about it, but there's that drawer full of things—of—of—poor little Henry's." So saying, he turned quickly on his heel, and shut the door after him.

His wife opened the little bedroom door adjoining her room, and taking the candle, set it down on the top of a bureau there; then from a small recess she took a key, and put it thoughtfully in the lock of a drawer, and made a sudden pause, while two boys, who, boy-like, had followed close on her heels, stood looking, with silent, significant glances, at their mother. And O, mother that reads this, has there never been in your house a drawer, or a closet, the opening of which has been to you like the opening again of a little grave? Ah! happy mother that you are, if it has not been so.

Mrs. Bird slowly opened the drawer. There were little coats, of many a form and pattern, piles of aprons, and rows of small stockings; and even a pair of little shoes, worn and rubbed at the toes, were peeping from the folds of a paper. There was a toy horse and wagon, a top, a ball,—memorials gathered with many a tear and many a heart-break! She sat down by the drawer, and leaning her head on her hands over it, wept till the tears fell through her fingers into the drawer; then, suddenly raising her head, she began, with nervous haste, selecting the plainest and most substantial articles, and gathering them into a bundle.

"Mamma," said one of the boys, gently touching her arm, "are you going to give away *those* things?"

"My dear boys," she said, softly and earnestly, "if our dear loving little Henry looks down from heaven, he would be glad to have us do this. I could not find it in my heart to give them away to any common person — to anybody that was happy; but I give them to a mother more heart-broken and sorrowful than I am; and I hope God will send his blessing with them!"

From "Old-Town Folks."

306. The Old Meeting House.

Going to meeting, in that state of society into which I was born, was as necessary and inevitable a consequence of waking up on Sunday morning, as eating one's breakfast. Nobody thought of staying away,—and, for that matter, nobody wanted to stay away. Our weekly life was simple, monotonous, and laborious; and the chance of seeing the whole neighborhood together in their best clothes on Sunday, was a thing which, in the dearth of all other sources of amusement, appealed to the idlest and most unspiritual of loafers. They who did not care for the sermon or the prayers, wanted to see Major Broad's scarlet coat and laced ruffles, and his wife's brocade dress, and the new bonnet which Lady Lothrop had just had sent up from Boston. Whoever had not seen these would be out of society for a week to come, and not be able to converse understandingly on the topics of the day.

The meeting on Sunday united in those days, as nearly as possible, the whole population of a town,—men, women, and children. There was then in a village but one fold and one shepherd, and long habit had made the tendency to this one central point so much a necessity to every one, that to stay away from "meetin," for any reason whatever, was always a secret source of uneasiness. I remember in my early days, sometimes when I had been left at home by reason of some of the transient ailments of childhood, how ghostly and supernatural the stillness of the whole house and village outside the meeting-house used to appear to me, how loudly the clock ticked and the flies buzzed down the window-pane, and how I listened in the breathless stillness to the distant psalm-singing, the solemn tones of the long prayer, and then to the monotone of the sermon, and then again to the closing echoes of the last hymn, and thought sadly, what if some day I should be left out, when all my relations and friends had gone to meeting in the New Jerusalem, and hear afar the music from the crystal walls.

The arrangement of our house of worship in Oldtown was somewhat peculiar, owing to the fact of its having originally been built as a missionary church for the Indians. The central portion of the house, usually appropriated to the best pews, was in ours devoted to them; and here were arranged benches of the simplest and most primitive form; on which were collected every Sunday, the thin and wasted remnants of what once was a numerous and powerful tribe. There were four or five respectable Indian families, who owned comfortable farms in the neighborhood, and came to meeting in their farm-wagons, like any of their white neighbors.

. . . Besides our Indian population, we had also a few negroes, and a side gallery was appropriated to them. . . . One of them was that of Aunt Nancy Prime, famous for making election-cake and ginger-pop, and who was sent for at all the great houses on occasions of high festivity, as learned in all mysteries relating to the confection of cakes and pies. A tight, trig, bustling body she, black and polished as ebony, smooth-spoken and respectful, and quite a favorite with everybody. Nancy had treated herself to an expensive luxury in the shape of a husband,—an idle, worthless mulatto man, who was owned as a slave in Boston. Nancy bought him, by intense labors in spinning flax, but found him an undesirable acquisition, and was often heard to declare, in the bitterness of her soul, when her husband returned from his drinking bouts, that she should never buy another nigger, she knew. Prominent there was the stately form of old Boston Foodah, an African Prince, who had been stolen from the coast of Guinea in early youth, and sold in Boston at some period of antiquity whereto the memory of man runneth not.

Maria J. McIntosh, 1815–. (Manual, p. 484.)

From "Two Pictures."

307. Debate between Webster and Hayne.

. . . Webster, Clay, Calhoun—the triumvirate to which, it is to be feared, we shall long have to look back as to our last, were still living; and as Augusta Moray gazed on the dark, melancholy eyes of the first, shadowed by that wonderful brow, or looked into the face of the second, where if prescient thought sometimes rose as a flitting cloud, it was chased away before the glow of the warm heart and the quick kindling fancy, or turned to the sharp angular lines and firmly compressed lips that marked the iron strength of the third, she felt that she stood in the midst of her dream fulfilment. The session was one of peculiar interest. Great questions agitated the public mind, and were treated greatly. Two great parties, springing from the very foundations of our civil polity, strove for supremacy in our legislative halls The one, looking into the depths of our colonial history, took its stand on the unquestionable truth, that each state of the Union was sovereign over herself, from which was drawn the corollary, that she was as free to leave as she had been to enter the Union. The other contended that the present constitution of these United States defined the boundary of the powers of each state, as well as of the great whole into which they had been voluntarily fused; that to look behind that, was such a resort to first principles or natural rights, as is involved in revolution, and must be decided as revolution ever is, by the relative strength of the ruling and the revolting forces.

On neither side was there any trickery, any bullying, any flimsy display of rhetorical power. All was grand as the subject for which they contended, solemn as the doom to which they seemed approaching. In the chief magistrate of that time all saw the unflinching executor of the nation's will—a man whose words were the sure prefigurements of his deeds. Their verdict must be carefully weighed, for it would be surely executed In stern silence each sat to hear, to deliberate, to judge. The sharp logic and fiery vehemence of Hayne called up no angry flash, roused no personal vindictiveness; and the deep tones of Webster found as ready an entrance to southern as to northern hearts, while in those powerful words which seemed the fit weapons of a nation's champion, his mighty mind swept away all that opposed it, save that principle which lay imbedded in the very deepest stratum of the life of his opponents, and which could not be torn away from them till feeling and life were extinct.

It was in the capital, and in the presence of these great men, that Augusta liked best to find herself. We are afraid she did not always listen when men of more ordinary power occupied the floor,—the gallery was an excellent dreaming place at such times.

Catharine Anne Warfield,[1] *1817–.*

From "The Romance of Beauseincourt."

308. VIEW OF THE SKY BY NIGHT.

I HAD derived great and constant pleasure from the undisturbed possession of this place of promenade during my whole sojourn. . . . Often, when my mind had been distracted with anxious cares, I had literally walked down its excitement and anguish in my fierce and rapid movements to and fro, over its smooth painted floor, the daily care of Sylphy, who might be heard in the hot season busily employed in refreshing it with mop and broom and water during the first hours of the morning, the pleasant, dewy freshness of which operation might be felt gratefully in the atmosphere of our heated chamber.

The long gallery was very solitary, of course, at an hour like this, and it was with a feeling of calm relief that I paced its lonely length, stopping at intervals to look out upon the night; one of cloudy sultriness, occasionally relieved by gusts of

[1] One of our most accomplished female writers: a native of Mississippi, but long resident in Kentucky.

warm, damp wind, that bore the distant odors of swamp and forest on its wings, and promised speedy rain. Here and there in the dappled heavens were liquid purple spaces, like the open sea described by Arctic voyagers, around which hung masses of silvery clouds, projecting like ice cliffs; and into these patches of sky the large yellow moon would now and then sail majestically, suddenly emerging, like a ship from a fog, from the fleecy screen that veiled her light, to cross these spaces, and plunge into mist and shadow again.

There was something in the whole effect calculated to absorb the mind of an absent dreamer, intent on the future, and for the first time for many weeks putting aside all foreign considerations, in favor of self too long merged in others and neglected.

Herman Melville, 1819–. (Manual, p. 505.)

From "Moby Dick."

309. Sperm Whale Fishing.

It was a sight full of quick wonder and awe! The vast swells of the omnipotent sea; the surging, hollow roar they made as they rolled along the eight gunwales, like gigantic bowls in a boundless bowling-green; the brief suspended agony of the boat, as it would tip for an instant on the knife-like edge of the sharper waves, that almost seemed threatening to cut it in two; the sudden profound dip into the watery glens and hollows; the keen spurrings and goadings to gain the top of the opposite hill; the headlong, sled-like slide down its other side; all these, with the cries of the headsmen and harpooners, and the shuddering gasps of the oarsmen, with the wondrous sight of the ivory Pequod bearing down upon her boats, with outstretched sails, like a wild hen after her screaming brood; all this was thrilling. Not the raw recruit, marching from the bosom of his wife into the fever heat of his first battle; not the dead man's ghost, encountering the first unknown phantom in the other world; neither of these can feel stranger and stronger emotions than that man does, who for the first time finds himself pulling into the charmed, churned circle of the hunted sperm whale.

Soon we were running through a suffusing wide veil of mist; neither ship nor boat to be seen.

"Give way, men," whispered Starbuck, drawing still further aft the sheet of his sail; "there is time to kill a fish yet before the squall comes. There's white water again! close to! Spring!" Though not one of the oarsmen was then facing the life and death peril so close to them ahead, yet with their eyes on the intense countenance of the mate in the stern of the boat, they knew that the imminent instant had come; they heard, too, an enormous wallowing sound as of fifty elephants stirring in their litter. Meanwhile the boat was still booming through the mist, the waves curling and hissing around us like the erected crests of enraged serpents.

"That's his hump. *There, there,* give it to him!" whispered Starbuck.

A short rushing sound leaped out of the boat; it was the darted iron of Queequeg. Then all in one welded commotion, came an invisible push from astern, while forward the boat seemed striking on a ledge; the sail collapsed and exploded; a gush of scalding vapor shot up near by; something rolled and tumbled like an earthquake beneath us. The whole crew were half suffocated as they were tossed helter-skelter into the white curdling cream of the squall. Squall, whale, and harpoon had all blended together; and the whale, merely grazed by the iron, escaped.

Though completely swamped, the boat was nearly unharmed. Swimming round it we picked up the floating oars, and lashing them across the gunwale, tumbled back to our places. There we sat up to our knees in the sea, the water covering every rib and plank, so that to our downward gazing eyes, the suspended craft seemed a coral boat grown up to us from the bottom of the ocean.

Josiah Gilbert Holland, 1819–.

From The Bay Path.

310. The Wedding-Present.

John Woodcock was the first to break the silence. Rising from his seat, and making his way out of the crowd around him, he crossed the room to where his daughter was standing absorbed in, and half bewildered by the scene, and whispering a few words in her ear, took her by the hand, and led her before the married pair. Mary extended her hand to him instantly and cordially, and exclaimed, "I knew that you would come to me and congratulate me."

"That wan't my arrant any way," said Woodcock bluntly, "and I should'nt begin with you if it was."

"Why John! I am astonished!" exclaimed the bride; "I thought you was one of the best friends I had in the world."

But Mary was somewhat affected with Woodcock's seriousness, and, with no reply to Holyoke, beyond a smile, she asked Woodcock's reasons for the statement he had made.

"I didn't come up here to talk about this, and p'raps it aint the right time to do it, but there's no use backin' down when you begin. I've got a consait that men and women aint built out of the same kind of timber. Look at my hand—a great pile o' bones covered with brown luther, with the hair on,—and then look at yourn. White oak ain't bass, is it? Every man's hand aint so black as mine, and every woman's aint so white as yourn, but there's always difference enough to show, and there's just as much odds in their doin's and dispositions as there is in their hands. I know what women be. I've wintered and summered with 'em, and take 'em by and large, they're better'n men. Now and then a feller gets hitched to a hedgehog, but most of 'em get a woman that's too good for 'em. They're gentle and kind, and runnin' over with good feelin's, and will stick to a fellow a mighty sight longer'n he'll stick to himself. My woman's dead and gone, but if there wan't any women in the world, and I owned it, I'd sell out for three shillin's, and throw in stars enough to make it an object for somebody to take it off my hands.

"Some time ago," resumed Woodcock, "I heerd the little ones and some of the old ones tellin' what they was goin' to give Mary Pynchon when she got married; and it set me to thinkin' what I could give her, for I knew if anybody ought to give her anything, it was me. But I hadn't any money, and I couldn't send to the Bay for anything, and I shouldn't 'a known what to get if I could. I might have shot a buck, but I couldn't 'a brought it to the weddin', and it didn't seem exactly ship-shape to give her anything she could eat up and forget. So I thought I'd give her a keepsake my wife left me when she died. It's all I've got of any vally to me, and it's somethin' that'll grow better every day it is kep', if you'll take care of it. I don't know what'll come of me, and I want to leave it in good hands."

The bride began to grow curious, and despite their late repulse the group began to collect again.

"It's a queer thing for a present, perhaps, (and Woodcock's lip began to quiver and his eye to moisten,) but I hope it'll do you some service. 'Taint anything't you can wear in your hair, or throw over your shoulders. It's—it's—"

"It's what?" inquired Mary, with an encouraging smile.

Woodcock took hold of the hand of his child, and placing it in that of the questioner, burst out with, "God knows that's the handle to it," and retreated to the window, where he spent several minutes looking out into the night, and endeavoring to repress the spasms of a choking throat. Neither Mary Holyoke nor her husband could disguise their emotions, as they saw before them the living testimonial of Woodcock's gratitude and trust. Mary stooped and kissed the gift-child, who clung to her as if, contrary to her father's statement, she was an article of wearing apparel.

John Esten Cooke,[1] *1830-.*

From "Estcourt, or the Memoirs of a Virginia Gentleman."

311. The Portrait.

"I see you are prepared now," said the painter; "the thought I endeavored to suggest has entered your mind, for I read the expression in your face like an open book. Well, see if I have deceived you—look!"

And as he spoke, the painter removed a green curtain from the frame of a picture, so arranged that the full light of the middle window fell upon it.

Estcourt almost cried out with astonishment. Here, before him, as though ready to start from the canvas, was the woman who had been his fate—who had died long years before; there in the full blaze of light, he saw her who had thrown the shadow upon his existence, which still clouded it, fresh, softly smiling, alive almost on the speaking and eloquent canvas. The blue eyes beamed with a tender and subdued sweetness, the delicate forehead, with its soft brown curls, rose airily above the perfectly arched brows, the innocent lips were half parted, and the portrait seemed almost ready to move from its frame, and descend, a living woman, into the apartment.

—

312. Aspects of Summer.

The glory of the summer deepened and grew more intense, the foliage assumed a darker tint of emerald, the sky glowed with a more dazzling blue, and the songs of the busy harvesters came sad and slow, like the long, melancholy swell of pensive sighs across the hills and fields, dying away finally into the "harvest home," which told that the golden grain would wave no more in the wind until another year. The "harvest moon" looked down on bare fields now, and June was dead.

[1] Conspicuous among the younger writers of Virginia, of which State he is a native; author of many novels.

At last came August, the month of great white clouds and imperial sunsets, the crowning hours of the rich summer, soon to fade away into the yellow autumn, the month of reveries and dreams on the banks of shadowy streams, or beneath the old majestic trees of silent forests.

Sarah A. Dorsey,[1] about *1835-*.

From "Lucia Dare."

313. SCENERY AND SOCIETY AT NATCHEZ, MISSISSIPPI.

THE village of Natchez, under the hill, was clustered close to the water's edge; the bluffs rose precipitously, garnished with pine trees, and locusts, and tufted grasses; the vista here terminated in Brown's beautiful gardens, gay with flower-beds and closely-clipped hedges. Far away over the river stretched the broad emerald plain of Louisiana, level with the stream, extending for many, many miles, its champaign checkered with groups of white plantation-houses, spotted with groves of trees, rich in autumnal beauty, glowing with crimson, gold, and green, softened by veils of long, gray moss. This plain was dotted with lovely lakes, whose waters shone in the slanting rays of the declining sun. . . . The sun went down quickly, as he does at sea, a round, red fire-ball, while light, splendid clouds of purple, pink, lilac, and gray, on the blue, blue heavens, refracted the ascending, slender, quivering rays of the disappearing orb, the type of Deity in all natural religions, the Totem of the Natchez Indians. Beloved city—bright "city of the Sun"! How often have I paced with restless child's feet, the road that Lucian was now traveling over, and listened, as he did, but more lingeringly, to the sounds of gentle human life, stirring within thy peaceful homes! How often have I thanked God for my beautiful childhood's home—for my precious Southern Land—for its sunshine, its verdure, its forests, its flowers, its perfume; but oh! above all, for the

[1] Prominent among the living authors of Louisiana.

loving, refined, intelligent, gentle race of people it was my great, my priceless privilege, to be born amongst—a people worthy to live with, yes, *worthy to die for!* The stern besom of war has wept over you, beloved Natchez—your fairest homes have been desolated, your lovely gardens are now only remembrances—your family circles are broken up—your bravest sons are sleeping in the dust of death, or weeping tears of bitterness in exile—your daughters, bowed down with penury and grief, are mourning beside their darkened firesides—your joyous households transferred to other and kindlier lands. The forms of my kindred faded into phantoms of the past—strangers sit now in the place that once was mine; but yet, thou art lovely, still beloved in thy ruin, in thy desolation—city of my heart—city of my love—city of my childish joy! Oh! city of my dead!

Anne Moncure Crane.[1]

From "Opportunity;" a Novel.

314. Impression of a Sea Scene.

The tide had been out, but it was now rising; and they stood silently watching the long, low waves dissolve in foam, whose white edges each time crept nearer and nearer their feet. No one was conscious of the duration of the silence. The sea's monotony of motion and sound seemed to fill the void, and lull them to quietude. But beautiful as was the scene that lay before her, Harvey gradually forgot it. . . .

The two women had been nearly facing each other; and in a moment or two Harvey put his hand upon Rose's shoulder, and with the other, motioned her to look out upon the sea at her side. As she obeyed, her faint, inarticulate expression of surprise and pleasure made both men follow her example. It was only a coasting vessel, which had come rather close to the shore, and was sailing swiftly by, before the freshening breeze;

[1] A young authoress of Maryland; has written two novels of unusual promise.

but its broad, white sails, with the moonlight upon them, and its gliding, soundless motion, gave it an unearthly effect, as of a phantom of light floating between the dark sea and sky, or a great white-winged spirit sweeping past. When it had vanished into the distance and darkness, Rose turned, and looked up at Harvey with mute but half-parted lips, with eyes dilating with light, only this for a moment, but Miss Berney knew she had accomplished her wish.

The others also did not speak. But Grahame made an involuntary angry movement of his foot upon the sand.

Mary Clemmer Ames,[1] about *1837–.*

From "A Woman's Right."

315. A Railway Depot in the Country.

. . . Yet this depot was the centre of attraction for miles around. It was the grand hall of re-union for all the people of the scattered town, not second in importance even to the meeting-house. Here, twice a day, stopped the great Western and Eastern trains, the two fiery arteries through which flowed all the tumultuous life of the vast outer world that had ever come to this secluded hamlet. Its primitive inhabitants in their isolated farm-houses, under the hills and on the stony mountain-moors, could never have realized the existence of another world than the green, grand world of nature around them and above them, and would have been as oblivious of the great god "News" as the denizens of Greenland, if it had not been for the daily visits of this Cyclops with the burning eye. Now twice a day, the shriek of his diabolical whistle pierced the umbrageous woods and hilly gorges for miles away, and its cry to many a solitary household was the epoch of the day. Hearing it, John mounted his nag and scampered away to the station for the Boston journals of yes-

[1] An active writer, chiefly known as a newspaper correspondent from Washington; a native of Vermont, has published a novel of much descriptive vigor.

terday. Seth harnessed Peggy, and drove off in the buggy in all possible haste, to see if the mail had brought a letter from Amzi who was in New York, or from Nimrod who had gone to work in "Bosting," or if the train had brought Sally and her children from the city, who were expected home on a visit. Here, under pretext of waiting for the cars, congregated the drones and supernumeraries of the different neighborhoods, lounging on the steps, hacking the benches with their jack-knives for hours together, while they discussed politics, and talked over their own and their neighbors' affairs.

A walk to the station on a summer evening, was more to the boys and girls of this rural region, than a Broadway promenade to a metropolitan belle. Their day's task done, here they met in pairs, comparing finery and indulging in flirtations, with an impunity which would not have been tolerated by their elders at the Sunday recess in the meeting-house. Then, besides, it was such an exciting sight to see the cars come in, to see the long rows of strange faces, and to catch glimpses of the new fashions at their open windows. Besides, at rare intervals, a real city lady would actually alight at the rustic station of Hilltop, followed by an avalanche of trunks, "larger than hen-houses," the girls would afterwards affirm to their astonished mothers, when it was discovered that the city-lady, in her languishing necessity for country-air, had really condescended to come in search of a remote country-cousin. Besides the fine lady, sometimes small companies of dashing young gentlemen, with fishing-rods and retinues of long-eared dogs, or a long-haired artist with a portfolio under his arm, all lured by the mountains and woods and streams, to seek pleasure in far different ways, would alight at the station, and ask of some staring rustic where they could find the hotel.

CHAPTER IV.

POETS.

Francis Hopkinson,[1] *1737–1791.*

From "The Battle of the Kegs."[2]

315.

GALLANTS, attend, and hear a friend
Trill forth harmonious ditty;
Strange things I'll tell, which late befell
In Philadelphia city.

'Twas early day, as poets say,
Just when the sun was rising,
A soldier stood on a log of wood,
And saw a thing surprising.

As in amaze he stood to gaze,—
The truth can't be denied, sir,—
He spied a score of kegs, or more,
Come floating down the tide, sir.

A sailor, too, in jerkin blue,
This strange appearance viewing,
First rubbed his eyes, in great surprise,
Then said some mischief's brewing.

. . . . .

Some fire cried, which some denied,
But said the earth had quakéd;
And girls and boys, with hideous noise,
Ran through the streets half naked.

. . . . . .

[1] A prominent author of the revolutionary era.

[2] In the revolutionary war, while the British held Philadelphia, some floating torpedoes were one day sent down the river to destroy their vessels, and this novel mode of attack caused the alarm described by the poet.

The royal band now ready stand,
All ranged in dread array, sir,
With stomach stout, to see it out,
And make a bloody day, sir.

The cannons roar from shore to shore;
The small arms make a rattle;
Since wars began, I'm sure no man
E'er saw so strange a battle.

. . . . . .

A hundred men, with each a pen,
Or more,—upon my word, sir,
It is most true,—would be too few
Their valor to record, sir.

John Trumbull, 1750-1831. (Manual, pp. 490, 512.)

From "McFingal."

316.

Though this, not all his time was lost on,
He fortified the town of Boston,
Built breastworks that might lend assistance
To keep the patriots at a distance;
For, howsoe'er the rogues might scoff,
He liked them best the farthest off;
Works of important use to aid
His courage when he felt afraid.

. . . . . .

For Providence, disposed to tease us,
Can use what instruments it pleases;
To pay a tax, at Peter's wish,
His chief cashier was once a fish.

. . . . . .

An English bishop's cur of late
Disclosed rebellions 'gainst the State;

So frogs croaked Pharaoh to repentance,
And lice delayed the fatal sentence:
And Heaven can ruin you at pleasure,
By Gage, as soon as by a Cæsar.
Yet did our hero in these days
Pick up some laurel-wreaths of praise;
And as the statuary of Seville
Made his cracked saint an excellent devil,
So, though our war small triumph brings,
We gained great fame in other things.
Did not our troops show great discerning,
And skill, your various arts in learning?
Outwent they not each native noodle
By far, in playing Yankee-doodle?
Which, as 'twas your New England tune,
'Twas marvellous they took so soon.
And ere the year was fully through,
Did they not learn to foot it too,
And such a dance as ne'er was known
For twenty miles on end lead down?
Did they not lay their heads together,
And gain your art to tar and feather,
When Colonel Nesbitt, thro' the town,
In triumph bore the country-clown?
Oh! what a glorious work to sing
The veteran troops of Britain's king,
Adventuring for th'heroic laurel
With bag of feathers and tar-barrel!
To paint the cart where culprits ride,
And Nesbitt marching at its side.
Great executioner and proud,
Like hangman high on Holborn road;
And o'er the slow-drawn rumbling car,
The waving ensigns of the war!

Philip Freneau, 1752-1832. (Manual, pp. 486, 511.)

From "An Indian Burying-ground."

317.

In spite of all the learned have said,
  I still my old opinion keep;
The posture that we give the dead,
  Points out the soul's eternal sleep.

Not so the ancients of these lands;—
  The Indian, when from life released,
  Again is seated with his friends,
  And shares again the joyous feast.

His imaged birds, and painted bowl,
  And venison, for a journey dressed,
Bespeak the nature of the soul,—
  Activity, that wants no rest.

His bow, for action ready bent,
  And arrows, with a head of bone,
Can only mean that life is spent,
  And not the finer essence gone.

. . . . .

Here still a lofty rock remains,
  On which the curious eye may trace,
Now wasted half by wearing rains,
  The fancies of a ruder race.

. . . .

By midnight moons, o'er moistening dews,
  In vestments for the chase arrayed,
The hunter still the deer pursues,
  The hunter and the deer—a shade.

David Humphreys, 1753-1818. (Manual, p. 512.)

From "The Happiness of America."

318. Recollections of the War.

I too, perhaps, should Heaven prolong my date,
The oft-repeated tale shall oft relate;
Shall tell the feelings in the first alarms,
Of some bold enterprise the unequalled charms;
Shall tell from whom I learnt the martial art,
With what high chiefs I played my early part—
With Parsons first—

. . . .

Death-daring Putnam—then immortal Greene—
Then how great Washington my youth approved,
In rank preferred, and as a parent loved.
With him what hours on warlike plains I spent,
Beneath the shadow of th' imperial tent;
With him how oft I went the nightly round
Through moving hosts, or slept on tented ground;
From him how oft—(nor far below the first,
In high behests and confidential trust)—
From him how oft I bore the dread commands,
Which destined for the fight the eager bands;
With him how oft I passed the eventful day,
Rode by his side, as down the long array
His awful voice the columns taught to form,
To point the thunders and direct the storm.
But, thanks to Heaven! those days of blood are o'er;
The trumpet's clangor, the loud cannon's roar.

. . . .

No more this hand, since happier days succeed,
Waves the bright blade, or reins the fiery steed.
No more for martial fame this bosom burns;
Now white-robed Peace to bless a world returns;
Now fostering Freedom all her bliss bestows,
Unnumbered blessings for unnumbered woes.

Samuel J. Smith,[1] *1771-1835.*

319. Peace, be still.

When, on his mission from his home in heaven,
In the frail bark the Saviour deigned to sleep,
The tempest rose—with headlong fury driven,
The wave-tossed vessel whirled along the deep:
Wild shrieked the storm amid the parting shrouds,
And the vexed billows dashed the darkening clouds.

Ah! then how futile human skill and power,—
"Save us! we perish in the o'erwhelming wave!"
They cried, and found in that tremendous hour,
"An eye to pity, and an arm to save."
He spoke, and lo! obedient to His will,
The raging waters, and the winds were still.

And thou, poor trembler on life's stormy sea,
Where dark the waves of sin and sorrow roll,
To Him for refuge from the tempest flee,—
To Him, confiding, trust the sinking soul;
For O, He came to calm the tempest-tossed,
To seek the wandering, and to save the lost.

For thee, and such as thee, impelled by love,
He left the mansions of the blessed on high;
Mid sin, and pain, and grief, and fear, to move,
With lingering anguish, and with shame to die.
The debt to Justice, boundless Mercy paid,
For hopeless guilt, complete atonement made.

O, in return for such surpassing grace,
Poor, blind, and naked, what canst thou impart?
Canst thou no offering on his altar place?
Yes, lowly mourner; give him all thy heart:
That simple offering he will not disown,—
That living incense may approach his throne.

[1] A gentleman of fortune and literary culture; a life-long resident in the country, in his native State, New Jersey.

William Clifton, 1772–1799. (Manual, p. 512.)

From lines "To Fancy,"

320. Pleasures of Imagination.

Is my lonely pittance past?
Fleeting good too light to last?
Lifts my friend the latch no more?
Fancy, thou canst all restore;
Thou canst, with thy airy shell,
To a palace raise my cell.

. . . . .

With thee to guide my steps, I'll creep
In some old haunted nook to sleep,
Lulled by the dreary night-bird's scream,
That flits along the wizard stream,
And there, till morning 'gins appear,
The tales of troubled spirits hear.

Sweet's the dawn's ambiguous light,
Quiet pause 'tween day and night,
When afar the mellow horn
Chides the tardy gaited morn,
And asleep is yet the gale
On sea-beat mount, and rivered vale.
But the morn, though sweet and fair;
Sweeter is when thou art there;
Hymning stars successive fade,
Fairies hurtle through the shade,
Lovelorn flowers I weeping see,
If the scene is touched by thee.

. . . . .

Thus through life with thee I'll glide,
Happy still what'er betide,
And while plodding sots complain
Of ceaseless toil and slender gain,
Every passing hour shall be
Worth a golden age to me.

Robert Treat Paine, 1773–1811. (Manual, p. 512.)

From "The Ruling Passion."

321. The Miser.

Next comes the miser; palsied, jealous, lean,
He looks the very skeleton of Spleen!
'Mid forests drear, he haunts, in spectred gloom,
Some desert abbey or some druid's tomb;
Where hearsed in earth, his occult riches lay,
Fleeced from the world, and buried from the day.
With crutch in hand, he points his mineral rod,
Limps to the spot, and turns the well-known sod.
While there, involved in night, he counts his store
By the soft tinklings of the golden ore,
He shakes with terror lest the moon should spy,
And the breeze whisper, where his treasures lie.

This wretch, who, dying, would not take one pill,
If, living, he must pay a doctor's bill,
Still clings to life, of every joy bereft;
His God is gold, and his religion theft!
And, as of yore, when modern vice was strange,
Could leathern money current pass on 'change,
His reptile soul, whose reasoning powers are pent
Within the logic bounds of cent. per cent.,
Would sooner coin his ears than stocks should fall,
And cheat the pillory, than not cheat at all!

John Blair Linn,[1] *1777–1804.*

From "The Powers of Genius."

322. Wretchedness of Savage Life.

The human fabric early from its birth,
Feels some fond influence from its parent earth;

[1] A Presbyterian clergyman, who died prematurely; an associate and connection of Charles Brockden Brown. Has left several poems of merit. A native of Pennsylvania.

In different regions different forms we trace,
Here dwells a feeble, there an iron race;
Here genius lives, and wakeful fancies play,
Here noiseless stupor sleeps its life away.

. . . .

Chill through his trackless pines the hunter passed,
His yell arose upon the howling blast;
Before him fled, with all the speed of fear,
His wealth—and victim, yonder helpless deer.
Saw you the savage man, how fell and wild,
With what grim pleasure, as he passed, he smiled?
Unhappy man! a wretched wigwam's shed
Is his poor shelter, some dry skins his bed;
Sometimes alone upon the woodless height
He strikes his fire, and spends his watchful night;
His dog with howling bays the moon's red beam,
And starts the wild deer in his nightly dream.
Poor savage man! for him no yellow grain
Waves its bright billows o'er the fruitful plain;
For him no harvest yields its full supply,
When winter hurls his tempest through the sky.
No joys he knows but those which spring from strife,
Unknown to him the charms of social life.
Rage, malice, envy, all his thoughts control,
And every dreadful passion burns his soul.
Should culture meliorate his darksome home,
And cheer those wilds where he is wont to roam;

. . . .

Should fields of tillage yield their rich increase,
And through his wastes walk forth the arts of peace,
His sullen soul would feel a genial glow,
Joy would break in upon the night of woe;
Knowledge would spread her mild, reviving ray,
And on his wigwam rise the dawn of day.

Francis S. Key, 1779–1843. (Manual, p. 523.)

323. The Star-Spangled Banner.

O say, can you see, by the dawn's early light,
  What so proudly we hailed, at the twilight's last gleaming?
Whose broad stripes and bright stars, through the perilous fight,
  O'er the ramparts we watched, were so gallantly streaming;
And the rocket's red glare, the bombs bursting in air,
Gave proof through the night that our flag was still there:
O say, does that Star-Spangled Banner yet wave
O'er the land of the free and the home of the brave?

On that shore, dimly seen through the mist of the deep,
  Where the foe's haughty host in dread silence reposes,
What is that which the breeze, o'er the towering steep,
  As it fitfully blows, now conceals, now discloses?
Now it catches the gleam of the morning's first beam,
In full glory reflected now shines in the stream:
'Tis the Star-Spangled Banner; O, long may it wave
O'er the land of the free and the home of the brave!

And where are the foes who so vauntingly swore
  That the havoc of war, and the battle's confusion,
A home and a country should leave us no more?
  Their blood has washed out their foul footsteps' pollution.
No refuge could save the hireling and slave
From the terror of flight, or the gloom of the grave;
And the Star-Spangled Banner in triumph doth wave
O'er the land of the free and the home of the brave!

O thus be it ever, when freemen shall stand
  Between their loved homes and the war's desolation;
Blest with victory and peace, may the heav'n-rescued land
  Praise the Power that hath made and preserved us a nation!
Then conquer we must, when our cause it is just,
And this be our motto, "In God is our trust;"
And the Star-Spangled Banner in triumph shall wave
O'er the land of the free and the home of the brave!

Washington Allston, 1779–1843. (Manual, pp. 504, 510.)

From the "Sylphs of the Seasons."

324.

METHOUGHT, within a desert cave,
Cold, dark, and solemn as the grave,
I suddenly awoke.
It seemed of sable night the cell
Where, save when from the ceiling fell
An oozing drop, her silent spell
No sound had ever broke.

There motionless I stood alone,
Like some strange monument of stone
Upon a barren wild;
Or like (so solid and profound
The darkness seemed that walled me round)
A man that's buried under ground,
Where pyramids are piled.

. . . . . .

Then spake the Sylph of Spring serene,
"'Tis I thy joyous heart, I ween,
With sympathy shall move:
For I with living melody
Of birds in choral symphony,
First waked thy soul to poesy,
To piety and love.

"When thou, at call of vernal breeze,
And beckoning bough of budding trees,
Hast left thy sullen fire;
And stretched thee in some mossy dell,
And heard the browsing wether's bell,
Blithe echoes rousing from their cell
To swell the tinkling choir:

. . . . . .

"Or lured by some fresh-scented gale
That wooed the mooréd fisher's sail
    To tempt the mighty main,
Hast watched the dim, receding shore,
Now faintly seen the ocean o'er,
Like hanging cloud, and now no more
    To bound the sapphire plain.

"Then, wrapped in night, the scudding bark,
(That seemed, self-poised amid the dark,
    Through upper air to leap,)
Beheld, from thy most fearful height,
The rapid dolphin's azure light
Cleave, like a living meteor bright,
    The darkness of the deep."

John Pierpont, 1785–1866. (Manual, p. 513.)

325. A Temperance Song.

In Eden's green retreats,
  A water-brook—that played
Between soft, mossy seats,
  Beneath a plane tree's shade,
    Whose rustling leaves
      Danced o'er its brink—
      Was Adam's drink,
    And also Eve's.

. . . . .

And, when the man of God
  From Egypt led his flock,
They thirsted, and his rod
  Smote the Arabian rock,
    And forth a rill
      Of water gushed,
      And on they rushed,
    And drank their fill.

Had Moses built a still,
And dealt out to that host
To every man his gill,
And pledged him in a toast,
Would cooler brains,
Or stronger hands,
Have braved the sands
Of those hot plains?

If Eden's strength and bloom,
Cold water thus hath given,
If e'en beyond the tomb,
It is the drink of heaven,
Are not good wells
And crystal springs
The very things
For our Hotels?

---

326. THE PILGRIM FATHERS.

THE Pilgrim Fathers,—where are they?
The waves that brought them o'er
Still roll in the bay, and throw their spray,
As they break along the shore:
Still roll in the bay, as they roll'd that day
When the Mayflower moor'd below,
When the sea around was black with storms,
And white the shore with snow.

The mists, that wrapp'd the Pilgrim's sleep,
Still brood upon the tide;
And his rocks yet keep their watch by the deep,
To stay its waves of pride.
But the snow-white sail, that he gave to the gale
When the heavens look'd dark, is gone;—
As an angel's wing, through an opening cloud,
Is seen, and then withdrawn.

The Pilgrim exile,—sainted name!
 The hill, whose icy brow
Rejoiced when he came, in the morning's flame,
 In the morning's flame burns now.
And the moon's cold light, as it lay that night
 On the hill-side and the sea,
Still lies where he laid his houseless head;—
 But the Pilgrim,—where is he?

The Pilgrim Fathers are at rest.
 When summer's throned on high,
And the world's warm breast is in verdure dress'd
 Go, stand on the hill where they lie.
The earliest ray of the golden day
 On that hallow'd spot is cast;
And the evening sun, as he leaves the world,
 Looks kindly on that spot last.

The Pilgrim *spirit* has not fled;
 It walks in the noon's broad light;
And it watches the bed of the glorious dead,
 With their holy stars, by night.
It watches the bed of the brave who have bled,
 And shall guard this ice-bound shore,
Till the waves of the bay, where the Mayflower lay,
 Shall foam and freeze no more.

James G. Percival, 1786–1856. (Manual, p. 515.)

327. The Coral Grove.

Deep in the wave is a coral grove,
Where the purple mullet and gold-fish rove;
Where the sea-flower spreads its leaves of blue,
That never are wet with the falling dew,
But in bright and changeful beauty shine,
Far down in the green and glassy brine.

The floor is of sand, like the mountain drift,
And the pearl-shells spangle the flinty snow;
From coral rocks, the sea-plants lift
Their boughs, where the tides and billows flow;
The water is calm and still below,
For the winds and waves are absent there,
And the sands are bright as the stars that glow
In the motionless fields of upper air.
There, with its waving blade of green,
The sea-flag streams through the silent water,
And the crimson leaf of the dulse is seen
To blush like a banner bathed in slaughter.
There, with a light and easy motion,
The fan-coral sweeps through the clear, deep sea,
And the yellow and scarlet tufts of ocean
Are bending like corn on the upland lea,
And life, in rare and beautiful forms,
Is sporting amid those bowers of stone.

Richard H. Dana, 1787–. (Manual, pp. 501, 504, 514.)

From "The Buccaneer."

328.

A sweet, low voice, in starry nights,
  Chants to his ear a 'plaining song;
Its tones come winding up the heights,
  Telling of woe and wrong;
And he must listen, till the stars grow dim,
The song that gentle voice doth sing to him.

O, it is sad that aught so mild
  Should bind the soul with bands of fear;
That strains to soothe a little child
  The man should dread to hear!

But sin hath broke the world's sweet peace, unstrung
The harmonious chords to which the angels sung.

. . . . . .

But he no more shall haunt the beach,
Nor sit upon the tall cliff's crown,
Nor go the round of all that reach,
Nor feebly sit him down,
Watching the swaying weeds; another day,
And he'll have gone far hence that dreadful way.

To-night the charmèd number's told.
"Twice have I come for thee," it said.
"Once more, and none shall thee behold.
Come, live one, to the dead!"
So hears his soul, and fears the coming night,
Yet sick and weary of the soft, calm light.

Again he sits within that room;
All day he leans at that still board;
None to bring comfort to his gloom,
Or speak a friendly word.
Weakened with fear, lone, haunted by remorse,
Poor, shattered wretch, there waits he that pale horse.

Richard Henry Wilde, 1789–. (Manual, pp. 521, 501.)

329. My Life is Like the Summer Rose.

My life is like the summer rose
That opens to the morning sky,
But, ere the shades of evening close,
Is scattered on the ground to die;
Yet on that rose's humble bed
The softest dews of night are shed,
As if she wept such waste to see;
But none shall drop a tear for me.

My life is like the autumn leaf
  That trembles in the moon's pale ray;
Its hold is frail, its state is brief,
  Restless, and soon to pass away;
But when that leaf shall fall and fade,
The parent tree will mourn its shade,
The winds bewail the leafless tree;
But none shall breathe a sigh for me.

My life is like the print which feet
  Have left on Tampa's desert strand;
Soon as the rising tide shall beat,
  Their track will vanish from the sand;
Yet, as if grieving to efface
All vestige of the human race,
On that lone shore loud moans the sea;
But none shall thus lament for me.

James A. Hillhouse, 1789–1844. (Manual, p. 487.)

From "Hadad."

330.

Hadad. CONFIDE in me.
I can transport thee, O, to a paradise
To which this Canaan is a darksome span.
Beings shall welcome, serve thee, lovely as angels;
The elemental powers shall stoop, the sea
Disclose her wonders, and receive thy feet
Into her sapphire chambers; orbèd clouds
Shall chariot thee from zone to zone, while earth,
A dwindled islet, floats beneath thee. Every
Season and clime shall blend for thee the garland.
The Abyss of time shall cast its secrets, ere
The flood marred primal nature, ere this orb
Stood in her station. Thou shalt know the stars,
The houses of eternity, their names,
Their courses, destiny—all marvels high.
Tam. Talk not so madly.

From "The Judgment."

331.

As, when from some proud capital that crowns
Imperial Ganges, the reviving breeze
Sweeps the dank mist, or hoary river fog
Impervious mantled o'er her highest towers,
Bright on the eye rush Bramah's temples, capp'd
With spiry tops, gay-trellised minarets,
Pagods of gold, and mosques with burnish'd domes,
Gilded, and glistening in the morning sun,
So from the hill the cloudy curtains roll'd,
And, in the lingering lustre of the eve,
Again the Saviour and his seraphs shone.
Emitted sudden in his rising, flash'd
Intenser light, as toward the right hand host
Mild turning, with a look ineffable,
The invitation he proclaim'd in accents
Which on their ravish'd ears pour'd thrilling, like
The silver sound of many trumpets, heard
Afar in sweetest jubilee: then, swift
Stretching his dreadful sceptre to the left,
That shot forth horrid lightnings, in a voice
Clothed but in half its terrors, yet to them
Seem'd like the crush of heaven, pronounced the doom.
The sentence utter'd as with life instinct,
The throne uprose majestically slow;
Each angel spread his wings; in one dread swell
Of triumph mingling as they mounted, trumpets
And harps, and golden lyres, and timbrels sweet,
And many a strange and deep-toned instrument
Of heavenly minstrelsy unknown on earth,
And angels' voices, and the loud acclaim
Of all the ransom'd like a thunder shout,
Far through the skies melodious echoes roll'd
And faint hosannas distant climes return'd.

John M. Harney,[1] *1789–1855.*

From "Crystallina: a Fairy Tale."

332.

On the stormy heath a ring they form;
 They place therein the fearful maid,
And round her dance in the howling storm.
 The winds beat hard on her lovely head;
 But she clasped her hands, and nothing said.

O, 'twas, I ween, a ghastly sight
 To see their uncouth revelry.
The lightning was the taper bright,
 The thunder was the melody,
 To which they danced with horrid glee.

The fierce-eyed owl did on them scowl,
 The bat played round on leathern wing,
The coal-black wolf did at them howl,
 The coal-black raven did croak and sing,
 And o'er them flap his dusky wing.

An earthquake heaved beneath their feet,
 Pale meteors revelled in the sky,
The clouds sailed by like a routed fleet,
 The night-winds shrieked as they passed by,
 The dark-red moon was eclipsed on high.

Charles Sprague, 1791–. (Manual, p. 514.)

From "Curiosity."

333. The Newspaper.

Turn to the Press—its teeming sheets survey,
Big with the wonders of each passing day;
Births, deaths, and weddings, forgeries, fires, and wrecks,
Harangues and hailstorms, brawls and broken necks;

[1] One of the earliest poets of the West, but a native of Delaware.

Where half-fledged bards, on feeble pinions, seek
An immortality of near a week;
Where cruel eulogists the dead restore,
In maudlin praise, to martyr them once more;
Where ruffian slanderers wreak their coward spite,
And need no venomed dagger while they write.

. . . .

Yet, sweet or bitter, hence what fountains burst,
While still the more we drink the more we thirst.
Trade hardly deems the busy day begun
Till his keen eye along the page has run;
The blooming daughter throws her needle by,
And reads her schoolmate's marriage with a sigh;
While the grave mother puts her glasses on,
And gives a tear to some old crony gone.
The preacher, too, his Sunday theme lays down
To know what last new folly fills the town.
Lively or sad, life's meanest, mightiest things,
The fate of fighting cocks, or fighting kings—
Nought comes amiss; we take the nauseous stuff,
Verjuice or oil, a libel or a puff.

Lydia H. Sigourney, 1791–1865. (Manual, pp. 484, 523.)

334. The Widow at her Daughter's Bridal.

Deal gently, thou whose hand hath won
  The young bird from its nest away,
Where, careless, 'neath a vernal sun,
  She gayly carolled day by day;
The haunt is lone, the heart must grieve,
  From where her timid wing doth soar
They pensive lisp at hush of eve,
  Yet hear her gushing song no more.

Deal gently with her; thou art dear,
  Beyond what vestal lips have told,
And, like a lamb from fountains clear,
  She turns, confiding, to thy fold.
She round thy sweet, domestic bower
  The wreath of changeless love shall twine,
Watch for thy step at vesper hour,
  And blend her holiest prayer with thine.

Deal gently, thou, when, far away,
  'Mid stranger scenes her foot shall rove,
Nor let thy tender care decay;
  The soul of woman lives in love.
And shouldst thou, wondering, mark a tear,
  Unconscious, from her eyelids break,
Be pitiful, and soothe the fear
  That man's strong heart may ne'er partake.

A mother yields her gem to thee,
  On thy true breast to sparkle rare;
She places 'neath thy household tree
  The idol of her fondest care;
And, by thy trust to be forgiven
  When judgment wakes in terror wild,
By all thy treasured hopes of heaven,
  Deal gently with the widow's child.

William O. Butler,[1] *1793–.*

From "The Boatman's Horn."

335.

O BOATMAN, wind that horn again;
  For never did the listening air
  Upon its lambent bosom bear
So wild, so soft, so sweet a strain.

[1] A native of Kentucky; a favorite Western poet; at one time prominent as a politician.

What though thy notes are sad and few,
  By every simple boatman blown?
Yet is each pulse to nature true,
  And melody in every tone.
How oft, in boyhood's joyous day,
  Unmindful of the lapsing hours,
I've loitered on my homeward way,
  By wild Ohio's bank of flowers,
While some lone boatman from the deck
  Poured his soft numbers to that tide,
As if to charm from storm and wreck
  The boat where all his fortunes ride!
Delighted Nature drank the sound,
  Enchanted Echo bore it round
In whispers soft and softer still,
From hill to plain, and plain to hill.

---

336. The Battle-field of Raisin.

The battle 's o'er; the din is past;
Night's mantle on the field is cast;
The Indian yell is heard no more;
The silence broods o'er Erie's shore.
At this lone hour I go to tread
The field where valor vainly bled;
To raise the wounded warrior's crest,
Or warm with tears his icy breast;
To treasure up his last command,
And bear it to his native land.
It may one pulse of joy impart
To a fond mother's bleeding heart,
Or, for a moment, it may dry
The tear-drop in the widow's eye.
Vain hopes, away! The widow ne'er
Her warrior's dying wish shall hear.

The passing zephyr bears no sigh;
No wounded warrior meets the eye;
Death is his sleep by Erie's wave;
Of Raisin's snow we heap his grave.
How many hopes lie buried here—
 The mother's joy, the father's pride,
The country's boast, the foeman's fear,
 In 'wildered havoc, side by side!
Lend me, thou silent queen of night,
Lend me a while thy waning light,
That I may see each well-loved form
That sank beneath the morning storm.

***William Cullen Bryant*, *1794–*.** (Manual, pp. 487, 524.)

From his "Poems."

337. LINES TO A WATER FOWL.

 WHITHER, midst falling dew,
While glow the heavens with the last steps of day,
Far through their rosy depths dost thou pursue
 Thy solitary way?

 Vainly the fowler's eye
Might mark thy distant flight to do thee wrong,
As, darkly seen against the crimson sky,
 Thy figure floats along.

 Seek'st thou the plashy brink
Of weedy lake, or marge of river wide,
Or where the rocking billows rise and sink
 On the chafed ocean side ?

 There is a Power whose care
Teaches thy way along that pathless coast,—
The desert and illimitable air,—
 Lone wandering, but not lost.

All day thy wings have fanned,
At that far height, the cold, thin atmosphere,
Yet stoop not, weary, to the welcome land,
Though the dark night is near.

And soon that toil shall end,
Soon shalt thou find a summer home and rest,
And scream among thy fellows; reeds shall bend
Soon, o'er thy sheltered nest.

Thou'rt gone; the abyss of heaven
Hath swallowed up thy form; yet on my heart
Deeply hath sunk the lesson thou hast given,
And shall not soon depart.

He who, from zone to zone,
Guides through the boundless sky thy certain flight,
In the long way that I must tread alone,
Will lead my steps aright.

From "The Antiquity of Freedom."

338. Freedom Irrepressible.

O Freedom, thou art not, as poets dream,
A fair, young girl, with light and delicate limbs,
And wavy tresses gushing from the cap
With which the Roman master crowned his slave
When he took off the gyves. A bearded man,
Armed to the teeth, art thou; one mailéd hand
Grasps the broad shield, and one the sword; thy brow,
Glorious in beauty though it be, is scarred
With tokens of old wars; thy massive limbs
Are strong with struggling. Power at thee has launched
His bolts, and with his lightnings smitten thee.
They could not quench the life thou hast from heaven.
Merciless power has dug thy dungeon deep,
And his swart armorers, by a thousand fires,

Have forged thy chain; yet, while he deems thee bound,
The links are shivered, and the prison walls
Fall outward; terribly thou springest forth,
As springs the flame above a burning pile,
And shoutest to the nations, who return
Thy shoutings, while the pale oppressor flies.

—

From "Thanatopsis."

339. Communion with Nature, Soothing.

To him who in the love of Nature holds
Communion with her visible forms, she speaks
A various language; for his gayer hours
She has a voice of gladness, and a smile,
An eloquence of beauty, and she glides
Into his darker musings, with a mild
And healing sympathy, that steals away
Their sharpness, ere he is aware. When thoughts
Of the last bitter hour come like a blight
Over thy spirit, and sad images
Of the stern agony, and shroud, and pall,
And breathless darkness, and the narrow house,
Make thee to shudder, and grow sick at heart;—
Go forth, under the open sky, and list
To Nature's teachings, while from all around—
Earth and her waters, and the depths of air,—
Comes a still voice. Yet a few days, and thee
The all-beholding sun shall see no more
In all his course; nor yet in the cold ground,
Where thy pale form was laid, with many tears,
Nor in the embrace of ocean, shall exist
Thy image. Earth, that nourished thee, shall claim
Thy growth, to be resolved to earth again,
And lost each human trace, surrendering up
Thine individual being, shalt thou go
To mix for ever with the elements,

To be a brother to the insensible rock,
And to the sluggish clod which the rude swain
Turns with his share, and treads upon. The oak
Shall send his roots abroad, and pierce thy mould.

. . . .

As the long train
Of ages glide away, the sons of men,
The youth in life's green spring, and he who goes
In the full strength of years, matron, and maid,
And the sweet babe, and the gray-headed man,—
Shall one by one be gathered to thy side,
By those, who in their turn shall follow them.
So live, that when thy summons comes to join
The innumerable caravan, that moves
To that mysterious realm where each shall take
His chamber in the silent halls of death,
Thou go not like the quarry-slave at night,
Scourged to his dungeon, but, sustained and soothed
By an unfaltering trust, approach thy grave,
Like one who wraps the drapery of his couch
About him, and lies down to pleasant dreams.

—

340. The Living Lost.

Matron! the children of whose love,
Each to his grave, in youth had passed,
And now the mould is heaped above
The dearest and the last!
Bride! who dost wear the widow's veil
Before the wedding flowers are pale!
Ye deem the human heart endures
No deeper, bitterer grief than yours.

Yet there are pangs of keener wo,
Of which the sufferers never speak,

Nor to the world's cold pity show
  The tears that scald the cheek,
Wrung from their eyelids by the shame
And guilt of those they shrink to name,
Whom once they loved with cheerful will,
And love, though fallen and branded, still.

Weep, ye who sorrow for the dead;
  Thus breaking hearts their pain relieve;
And reverenced are the tears ye shed,
  And honored ye who grieve.
The praise of those who sleep in earth,
The pleasant memory of their worth,
The hope to meet when life is past,
Shall heal the tortured mind at last.

But ye, who for the living lost
  That agony in secret bear,
Who shall with soothing words accost
  The strength of your despair?
Grief for your sake is scorn for them
Whom ye lament, and all condemn;
And o'er the world of spirits lies
A gloom from which ye turn your eyes.

---

341. THE SONG OF THE SOWER.

BRETHREN, the sower's task is done.
The seed is in its Winter bed.
Now let the dark-brown mould be spread,
  To hide it from the sun,
And leave it to the kindly care
Of the still earth and brooding air.
As when the mother, from her breast,
Lays the hushed babe apart to rest,
And shades its eyes, and waits to see

How sweet its waking smile will be.
The tempest now may smite, the sleet
All night on the drowned furrow beat,
And winds that from the cloudy hold
Of winter, breathe the bitter cold,
Stiffen to stone the yellow-mould,
Yet safe shall lie the wheat;
Till, out of heaven's unmeasured blue,
Shall walk again the genial year,
To wake with warmth, and nurse with dew,
The germs we lay to slumber here.
O blessed harvest yet to be!
Abide thou with the love that keeps,
In its warm bosom tenderly,
The life which wakes, and that which sleeps.
The love that leads the willing spheres
Along the unending track of years,
And watches o'er the sparrow's nest,
Shall brood above thy winter rest,
And raise thee from the dust, to hold
Light whisperings with the winds of May;
And fill thy spikes with living gold,
From Summer's yellow ray.
Then, as thy garners give thee forth,
On what glad errands shalt thou go,
Wherever, o'er the waiting earth,
Roads wind, and rivers flow!
The ancient East shall welcome thee
To mighty marts beyond the sea;
And they who dwell where palm-groves sound
To summer winds the whole year round,
Shall watch, in gladness, from the shore,
The sails that bring thy glistening store.

342. The Planting of the Apple-tree.

Come, let us plant the apple-tree!
Cleave the tough greensward with the spade;
Wide let its hollow bed be made;
There gently lay the roots, and there
Sift the dark mould with kindly care,
  And press it o'er them tenderly,
As, round the sleeping infant's feet,
We softly fold the cradle-sheet:
  So plant we the apple-tree.

What plant we in the apple-tree?
Buds, which the breath of summer days
Shall lengthen into leafy sprays;
Boughs, where the thrush with crimson breast
Shall haunt and sing and hide her nest.
  We plant upon the sunny lea
A shadow for the noontide hour,
A shelter from the summer shower,
  When we plant the apple-tree.

What plant we in the apple-tree?
Sweets for a hundred flowery springs,
To load the May-wind's restless wings,
When, from the orchard-row, he pours
Its fragrance through our open doors;
  A world of blossoms for the bee;
Flowers for the sick girl's silent room;
For the glad infant, sprigs of bloom,
  We plant with the apple-tree.

What plant we in the apple-tree?
Fruits that shall swell in sunny June,
And redden in the August noon,
And drop as gentle airs come by
That fan the blue September sky;

While children, wild with noisy glee,
Shall scent their fragrance as they pass,
And search for them the tufted grass
At the foot of the apple-tree.

And when above this apple-tree
The winter stars are quivering bright,
And winds go howling through the night,
Girls, whose young eyes o'erflow with mirth,
Shall peel its fruit by cottage-hearth,
And guests in prouder homes shall see,
Heaped with the orange and the grape,
As fair as they in tint and shape,
The fruit of the apple-tree.

The fruitage of this apple-tree,
Winds, and our flag of stripe and star,
Shall bear to coasts that lie afar,
Where men shall wonder at the view,
And ask in what fair groves they grew;
And they who roam beyond the sea,
Shall look, and think of childhood's day,
And long hours passed in summer play
In the shade of the apple-tree.

Each year shall give this apple-tree
A broader flush of roseate bloom,
A deeper maze of verdurous gloom,
And loosen, when the frost-clouds lower,
The crisp brown leaves in thicker shower;
The years shall come and pass, but we
Shall hear no longer, where we lie,
The summer's songs, the autumn's sigh,
In the boughs of the apple-tree.

And time shall waste this apple tree.
Oh, when its aged branches throw
Thin shadows on the sward below,

Shall fraud and force and iron-will
Oppress the weak and helpless still?
What shall the tasks of mercy be,
Amid the toils, the strifes, the tears
Of those who live when length of years
Is wasting this apple-tree?

"Who planted this old apple-tree?"
The children of that distant day
Thus to some aged man shall say;
And gazing on its mossy stem,
The gray-haired man shall answer them:
"A poet of the land was he,
Born in the rude, but good old times;
'Tis said he made some quaint old rhymes
On planting the apple-tree."

Maria Brooks, 1795–1845. (Manual, p. 523.)

343. MARRIAGE.

THE bard has sung, God never formed a soul
Without its own peculiar mate, to meet
Its wandering half, when ripe to crown the whole
Bright plan of bliss, most heavenly, most complete!

But thousand evil things there are that hate
To look on happiness: these hurt, impede,
And, leagued with time, space, circumstance, and fate,
Keep kindred heart from heart, to pine, and pant, and bleed.

And as the dove to far Palmyra flying,
From where her native founts of Antioch beam,
Weary, exhausted, longing, panting, sighing,
Lights sadly at the desert's bitter stream;

So, many a soul, o'er life's drear desert faring,
Love's pure, congenial spring unfound, unquaffed,
Suffers, recoils, then thirsty and despairing
Of what it would, descends, and sips the nearest draught.

Joseph Rodman Drake, 1795–1820. (Manual, p. 517.)

From "The Culprit Fay."

344. The Fay's Departure.

. . . .

The moon looks down on old Crow-nest,
She mellows the shades, on his shaggy breast,
And seems his huge grey form to throw
In a silver cone on the wave below;
His sides are broken by spots of shade,
By the walnut bough and the cedar made,
And through their clustering branches dark
Glimmers and dies the fire-fly's spark—
Like starry twinkles that momently break,
Through the rifts of the gathering tempest's rack.

The stars are on the moving stream,
  And fling, as its ripples gently flow,
A burnished length of wavy beam
  In an eel-like, spiral line below;
The winds are whist, and the owl is still,
  The bat in the shelvy rock is hid.
And naught is heard on the lonely hill
But the cricket's chirp, and the answer shrill
  Of the gauze-winged katy-did;
And the plaint of the wailing whip-poor-will,
  Who mourns unseen, and ceaseless sings,
Ever a note of wail and woe,
  Till morning spreads her rosy wings,
And earth and sky in her glances grow.

The moth-fly, as he shot in air,
Crept under the leaf, and hid her there;
The katy-did forgot its lay,
The prowling gnat fled fast away,
The fell mosquito checked his drone

And folded his wings till the Fay was gone,
And the wily beetle dropped his head,
And fell on the ground as if he were dead;
They crouched them close in the darksome shade,
  They quaked all o'er with awe and fear,
For they had felt the blue-bent blade,
  And writhed at the prick of the elfin spear;
Many a time on a summer's night,
When the sky was clear, and the moon was bright,
They had been roused from the haunted ground,
By the yelp and bay of the fairy hound;
They had heard the tiny bugle-horn,
They had heard the twang of the maize-silk string,
When the vine-twig bows were tightly drawn,
And the nettle shaft through air was borne,
Feathered with down of the hum-bird's wing.
And now they deemed the courier-ouphe,
  Some hunter sprite of the elfin ground;
And they watched till they saw him mount the roof
  That canopies the world around;
Then glad they left their covert lair,
And freaked about in the midnight air.

Fitz-Greene Halleck, 1795–1869. (Manual, p. 515.)

345. Marco Bozzaris.

At midnight, in his guarded tent,
  The Turk was dreaming of the hour
When Greece, her knee in suppliance bent,
  Should tremble at his power:
In dreams, through camp and court he bore
The trophies of a conqueror;
  In dreams his song of triumph heard;
Then wore his monarch's signet ring:
Then pressed that monarch's throne—a king;

As wild his thoughts, and gay of wing,
  As Eden's garden bird.

At midnight, in the forest shades,
  Bozzaris ranged his Suliote band,
True as the steel of their tried blades,
  Heroes in heart and hand.
There had the Persian thousands stood,
There had the glad earth drunk their blood
  On old Platœa's day;
And now there breathed that haunted air
The sons of sires that conquer'd there,
With arm to strike and soul to dare,
  As quick, as far as they.

An hour pass'd on—the Turk awoke;
  That bright dream was his last;
He woke to hear his sentries shriek,
"To arms! they come! the Greek! the Greek!"
He woke—to die, midst flame, and smoke,
And shout, and groan, and sabre-stroke,
  And death-shots, falling thick and fast
As lightnings from the mountain-cloud;
And heard, with voice as trumpet loud,
  Bozzaris cheer his band:
"Strike—till the last arm'd foe expires;
Strike—for your altars and your fires;
Strike—for the green graves of your sires:
  God, and your native land!"

They fought—like brave men, long and well;
  They piled that ground with Moslem slain;
They conquer'd—but Bozzaris fell,
  Bleeding at every vein.
His few surviving comrades saw—
His smile when rang their proud hurrah,
  And the red field was won:

Then saw in death his eyelids close
Calmly, as to a night's repose
  Like flowers at set of sun.

Come to the bridal chamber, Death!
  Come to the mother's, when she feels,
For the first time, her first-born's breath;
  Come when the blessed seals
That close the pestilence, are broke,
And crowded cities wail its stroke;
Come in consumption's ghastly form,
The earthquake shock, the ocean storm;
Come when the heart beats high and warm,
  With banquet-song, and dance, and wine;
And thou art terrible; the tear,
The groan, the knell, the pall, the bier,
And all we know, or dream, or fear,
  Of agony, are thine.

But to the hero, when his sword
  Has won the battle for the free,
Thy voice sounds like a prophet's word;
And in its hollow tones are heard
  The thanks of millions yet to be.
Come, when his task of fame is wrought—
Come, with her laurel-leaf blood-bought—
  Come, in her crowning hour—and then
Thy sunken eye's unearthly light
To him is welcome as the sight
  Of sky and stars to prison'd men:
Thy grasp is welcome as the hand
Of brother in a foreign land;
Thy summons welcome as the cry
That told the Indian isles were nigh,
  To the world-seeking Genoese;
When the land-wind from woods of palm,
And orange-groves, and fields of balm,
  Blew o'er the Haytian seas.

Bozzaris! with the storied brave
  Greece nurtured in her glory's time,
Rest thee—there is no prouder grave,
  E'en in her own proud clime.
She wore no funeral weeds for thee,
  Nor bade the dark hearse wave its plume,
Like torn branch from death's leafless tree,
In sorrow's pomp and pageantry,
  The heartless luxury of the tomb:
But she remembers thee as one
Long loved and for a season gone,
For thee her poet's lyre is wreathed,
Her marble wrought, her music breathed:
For thee she rings the birth-day bells;
Of thee her babes' first lisping tells,
For thine, her evening prayer is said
At palace couch, and cottage bed;
Her soldier, closing with the foe,
Gives for thy sake a deadlier blow;
His plighted maiden, when she fears
For him, the joy of her young years,
Thinks of thy fate, and checks her tears.
  And she, the mother of thy boys,
Though in her eye and faded cheek
Is read the grief she will not speak,
  The memory of her buried joys,
And even she who gave thee birth,
Will by their pilgrim-circled hearth,
  Talk of thy doom without a sigh:
For thou art Freedom's now, and Fame's,
One of the few, the immortal names,
  That were not born to die.

From "Fanny."

346. THE BROKEN MERCHANT.

FANNY! 'twas with her name my song began;
 'Tis proper and polite her name should end it;
If in my story of her woes, or plan
 Or moral can be traced, 'twas not intended;
And if I've wronged her, I can only tell her
I'm sorry for it—so is my bookseller.

. . . . . .

Her father sent to Albany a prayer
 For office, told how fortune had abused him,
And modestly requested to be mayor—
 The council very civilly refused him;
Because, however much they might desire it,
The "public good," it seems, did not require it.

Some evenings since, he took a lonely stroll
 Along Broadway, scene of past joys and evils;
He felt that withering bitterness of soul,
 Quaintly denominated the "blue devils;"
And thought of Bonaparte and Belisarius,
Pompey, and Colonel Burr, and Caius Marius.

And envying the loud playfulness and mirth
 Of those who passed him, gay in youth and hope,
He took at Jupiter a shilling's worth
 Of gazing, through the showman's telescope;
Sounds as of far-off bells came on his ears,
He fancied 'twas the music of the spheres.

He was mistaken, it was no such thing,
 'Twas Yankee Doodle, played by Scudder's band;
He muttered, as he lingered listening,
 Something of freedom and our happy land;
Then sketched, as to his home he hurried fast,
This sentimental song—his saddest and his last.

John G. C. Brainard, 1796–1828. (Manual, p. 523.)

From Lines "To the Connecticut River."

347. The Past and the Present.

From that lone lake, the sweetest of the chain,
That links the mountain to the mighty main,
Fresh from the rock and swelling by the tree,
Rushing to meet, and dare, and breast the sea—
Fair, noble, glorious river! in thy wave
The sunniest slopes and sweetest pastures lave;
The mountain torrent, with its wintry roar,
Springs from its home and leaps upon thy shore:
The promontories love thee—and for this
Turn their rough cheeks, and stay thee for thy kiss.

. . . .

Dark as the forest leaves that strew the ground,
The Indian hunter here his shelter found;
Here cut his bow and shaped his arrows true,
Here built his wigwam and his bark canoe,
Speared the quick salmon leaping up the fall,
And slew the deer without the rifle-ball.

. . . .

What Art can execute, or Taste devise,
Decks thy fair course and gladdens in thine eyes—
As broader sweep the bendings of thy stream,
To meet the southern sun's more constant beam.
Here cities rise, and sea-washed commerce hails
Thy shores and winds with all her flapping sails,
From Tropic isles, or from the torrid main—
Where grows the grape, or sprouts the sugar-cane—
Or from the haunts where the striped haddock play,
By each cold northern bank and frozen bay.
Here, safe returned from every stormy sea,
Waves the striped flag, the mantle of the free—
That star-lit flag, by all the breezes curled
Of yon vast deep whose waters grasp the world.

Robert C. Sands, 1799–1832. (Manual, p. 504.)

From "Weehawken."

348. Historical Reminiscences.

Eve o'er our path is stealing fast;
Yon quivering splendors are the last
The sun will fling, to tremble o'er
The waves that kiss the opposing shore;
His latest glories fringe the height
Behind us, with their golden light.

. . . . . .

Yet should the stranger ask what lore
Of by-gone days, this winding shore,
Yon cliffs, and fir-clad steeps, could tell
If vocal made by Fancy's spell,
The varying legend might rehearse
Fit themes for high romantic verse.

O'er yon rough heights and moss-clad sod
Oft hath the stalwart warrior trod;
Or peered with hunter's gaze, to mark
The progress of the glancing bark.
Spoils, strangely won on distant waves,
Have lurked in yon obstructed caves.

When the great strife for Freedom rose,
Here scouted oft her friends and foes,
Alternate, through the changeful war,
And beacon-fires flashed bright and far;
And here, when Freedom's strife was won,
Fell, in sad feud, her favored son;—

Her son,—the second of the band,
The Romans of the rescued land.
Where round yon capes the banks descend,
Long shall the pilgrim's footsteps bend;
There, mirthful hearts shall pause to sigh
There, tears shall dim the patriot's eye.

There last he stood. Before his sight
Flowed the fair river, free and bright;
The rising Mart, and isles and bay,
Before him in their glory lay,—
Scenes of his love and of his fame,—
The instant ere the death-shot came.

George W. Doane, 1799–1859. (Manual, p. 523.)

From "Evening."

349.

Softly now the light of day
Fades upon my sight away;
Free from care, from labor free,
Lord, I would commune with thee.

Thou, whose all-pervading eye
  Nought escapes, without, within,
Pardon each infirmity,
  Open fault, and secret sin.

Soon for me the light of day
Shall forever pass away;
Then, from sin and sorrow free,
Take me, Lord, to dwell with thee!

Thou who sinless, yet hast known
  All of man's infirmity;
Then, from thy eternal throne,
  Jesus, look with pitying eye.

George P. Morris, 1801–1864. (Manual, p. 523.)

350. Highlands of the Hudson.

Where Hudson's wave o'er silvery sands
  Winds through the hills afar,

Old Crow-nest like a monarch stands,
  Crowned with a single star.
And there amid the billowy swells
  Of rock-ribbed, cloud-capped earth,
My fair and gentle Ida dwells,
  A nymph of mountain birth.

The snow-flake that the cliff receives—
  The diamonds of the showers—
Spring's tender blossoms, buds, and leaves—
  The sisterhood of flowers—
Morn's early beam, eve's balmy breeze—
  Her purity define;—
But Ida 's dearer far than these
  To this fond breast of mine.

George D. Prentice, 1802-1869. (Manual, p. 487.)

From "The Mammoth Cave."

351. Contrast of Nature Without.

All day, as day is reckoned on the earth,
I've wandered in these dim and awful aisles,
Shut from the blue and breezy dome of heaven.
. . . And now
I'll sit me down upon yon broken rock,
To muse upon the strange and solemn things
Of this mysterious realm.
All day my steps
Have been amid the beautiful, the wild,
The gloomy, the terrific; crystal founts
Almost invisible in their serene
And pure transparency, high pillared domes
With stars and flowers, all fretted like the halls
Of Oriental monarchs—rivers dark,
And drear, and voiceless, as Oblivion's stream,
That flows through Death's dim vale of silence,—gulfs

All fathomless, down which the loosened rock
Plunges, until its far-off echoes come
Fainter and fainter, like the dying roll
Of thunders in the distance.
. . . Beautiful
Are all the thousand snow-white gems that lie
In these mysterious chambers, gleaming out
Amid the melancholy gloom, and wild
These rocky hills and cliffs, and gulfs, but far
More beautiful and wild, the things that greet
The wanderer in our world of light,—the stars
Floating on high, like islands of the blest,—
The autumn sunsets glowing like the gate
Of far-off Paradise; the gorgeous clouds
On which the glories of the earth and sky
Meet, and commingle; earth's unnumbered flowers,
All turning up their gentle eyes to heaven;
The birds, with bright wings glancing in the sun,
Filling the air with rainbow miniatures;
The green old forests surging in the gale;
The everlasting mountains, on whose peaks
The setting sun burns like an altar-flame.

Charles Constantine Pise, 1802–1866.

(Manual, p. 532.)

From "The Pleasures of Religion."

352. The Rainbow.

Mark, o'er yon wild, as melts the storm away,
The rainbow tints their various hues display;
Beauteous, though faint, though deeply shaded, bright,
They span the clearing heavens, and charm the sight.
Yes, as I gaze, methinks I view—the while,
Hope's radiant form, and Mercy's genial smile.
Who doth not see, in that sweet bow of heaven,

Circling around the twilight hills of even,
Religion's light, which o'er the wilds of life
Shoots its pure rays through misery and strife;
Soothes the lone bosom, as it pines in woe,
And turns to heaven this barren world below?
O, what were man, did not her hallowed ray
Disperse the clouds that thicken on his way!
A weary pilgrim, left in cheerless gloom,
To grope his midnight journey to the tomb;
His life a tempest, death, a wreck forlorn,
In sorrow dying, as in sorrow born.

From "The Tourist."

353. VIEW AT GIBRALTAR.

AND from this height, how beauteous to survey
The neighboring shores, the bright cerulean bay:
Myriads of sails are swelling on the deep,
And oars, in myriads, through the waters sweep.
Behold, in peace, all nations here unite,
Their various pennons streaming to the sight:
The red cross glows, the Danish crown appears,
The half-moon rises, and the lion rears,
But mark, bold-towering o'er the conscious wave,
The starry banners of my country brave,
Stream like a meteor to the wooing breeze,
And float all-radiant o'er the sunny seas!
Hail, native flag! for ever mayst thou blow—
Hope to the friend, and terror to the foe!
Again I hail thee, Calpe! on thy steep
I wandered high, and gazed upon the deep!
Nature's best fortress, which no warlike foe,
No martial scheme, can ever overthrow.
Art, too, had added strength, and given a grace
That smooths the rugged aspect of thy face.

What wondrous halls along the mountain made!
What trains of cannon in those halls arrayed!
They frown imperious from their lofty state,
Prepared around to deal the scourge of fate.

Elijah P. Lovejoy,[1] *1802–1816.*

From "Lines to my Mother."

354.

There is a fire that burns on earth,
  A pure and holy flame;
It came to men from heavenly birth,
  And still it is the same
As when it burned the chords along
That bore the first-born seraph's song;
  Sweet as the hymn of gratitude
That swelled to Heaven when "all was good."
No passion in the choirs above
Is purer than a mother's love.

. . . . . .

My mother! I am far away
  From home, and love, and thee;
And stranger hands may heap the clay
  That soon may cover me;
Yet we shall meet—perhaps not here,
But in yon shining, azure sphere;
And if there's aught assures me more,
  Ere yet my spirit fly,
That Heaven has mercy still in store
  For such a wretch as I,
'Tis that a heart so good as thine
Must bleed, must burst, along with mine.

[1] Born in Maine, but lived at the West; was editor of a religious newspaper, which early assailed slavery as wrong; lost his life in defending his press against a mob at Alton, Illinois, July, 1836.

And life is short, at best, and time
  Must soon prepare the tomb;
And there is sure a happier clime
  Beyond this world of gloom.
And should it be my happy lot,
  After a life of care and pain,
  In sadness spent, or spent in vain,
To go where sighs and sin are not,
  'Twill make the half my heaven to be,
  My mother, evermore with thee.

Edward Coate Pinkney, 1802–1828. (Manual, p. 521.)

355. A HEALTH.

I FILL this cup to one made up of loveliness alone;
A woman, of her gentle sex the seeming paragon,
To whom the better elements and kindly stars have given
A form so fair, that, like the air, 'tis less of earth than heaven.

Her every tone is music's own, like those of morning birds;
And something more than melody dwells ever in her words.
The coinage of her heart are they, and from her lips each flows,
As one may see the burdened bee forth issue from the rose.

Affections are as thoughts to her, the measures of her hours;
Her feelings have the fragrance and the freshness of young flowers;
And lovely passions, changing oft, so fill her, she appears
The image of themselves by turns, the idol of past years.

Of her bright face, one glance will trace a picture on the brain,
And of her voice, in echoing hearts a sound must long remain;
But memory such as mine of her, so very much endears
When death is nigh, my latest sigh will not be life's, but hers.

I fill this cup to one made up of loveliness alone,
A woman, of her gentle sex, the seeming paragon.
Her health! and would on earth there stood some more of
such a frame,
That life might be all poetry, and weariness a name.

Ralph Waldo Emerson, 1803–. (Manual, pp. 478, 503, 531.)

356. HYMN SUNG AT THE COMPLETION OF THE CONCORD MONUMENT.

BY the rude bridge that arched the flood,
Their flag to April's breeze unfurled,
Here once the embattled farmers stood,
And fired the shot heard round the world.

The foe long since in silence slept;
Alike the conqueror silent sleeps;
And Time the ruined bridge has swept
Down the dark stream which seaward creeps.

On this green bank, by this soft stream,
We set to-day a votive stone,
That memory may their deed redeem,
When, like our sires, our sons are gone.

Spirit, that made those heroes dare
To die, or leave their children free,
Bid Time and Nature gently spare
The shaft we raise to them and thee.

From "May Day."

357. DISAPPEARANCE OF WINTER.

NOT for a regiment's parade,
Nor evil laws or rulers made,

Blue Walden rolls its cannonade,
But for a lofty sign
Which the Zodiac threw,
That the bondage-days are told,
And waters free as winds shall flow.
Lo! how all the tribes combine
To rout the flying foe.
See, every patriot oak-leaf throws
His elfin length upon the snows,
Not idle, since the leaf all day
Draws to the spot the solar ray,
Ere sunset quarrying inches down,
And half-way to the mosses brown;
While the grass beneath the rime
Has hints of the propitious time,
And upward pries and perforates
Through the cold slab a thousand gates,
Till the green lances peering through
Bend happy in the welkin blue.

. . . . .

The ground-pines wash their rusty green,
The maple-tops their crimson tint,
On the soft path each track is seen,
The girl's foot leaves its neater print.
The pebble loosened from the frost
Asks of the urchin to be tost.
In flint and marble beats a heart,
The kind Earth takes her children's part,
The green lane is the school-boy's friend,
Low leaves his quarrel apprehend,
The fresh ground loves his top and ball,
The air rings jocund to his call,
The brimming brook invites a leap,
He dives the hollow, climbs the steep.
The youth reads omens where he goes,
And speaks all languages, the rose.

The wood-fly mocks with tiny noise
The far halloo of human voice;
The perfumed berry on the spray
Smacks of faint memories far away.
A subtle chain of countless rings
The next unto the farthest brings,
And, striving to be man, the worm
Mounts through all the spires of form.

—

From "Voluntaries II."

358. Inspiration of Duty.

In an age of joys and toys,
Wanting wisdom, void of right,
Who shall nerve heroic boys
To hazard all in Freedom's fight,—
Break shortly off their jolly games,
Forsake their comrades gay,
And quit proud homes and youthful dames,
For famine, toil, and fray?
Yet on the nimble air benign
Speed nimbler messages,
That waft the breath of grace divine
To hearts in sloth and ease.
So nigh is grandeur to our dust,
So near is God to man,
When duty whispers low, *Thou must*,
The youth replies, *I can*.

. . . .

Stainless soldier on the walls,
Knowing this,—and knows no more,—
Whoever fights, whoever falls
Justice conquers evermore,
Justice after as before.—

Thomas C. Upham,[1] *1799–1873.*

359. ON A SON LOST AT SEA.

BOY of my earlier days and hopes! Once more,
Dear child of memory, of love, of tears!
I see thee, as I saw in days of yore,
As in thy young, and in thy lovely, years.

The same in youthful look, the same in form;
The same the gentle voice I used to hear;
Though many a year hath passed, and many a storm
Hath dashed its foam around thy cruel bier.

Deep in the stormy ocean's hidden cave
Buried, and lost to human care and sight,
What power hath interposed to rend thy grave?
What arm hath brought thee thus to life and light?

I weep,—the tears my aged cheek that stain,
The throbs that once more swell my aching breast,
Embodying one of anxious thought and pain,
That wept and watched around that place of rest.

O leave me not, my child! Or, if it be,
That, coming thus, thou canst not longer stay,
Yet shall this kindly visit's mystery
Give rise to hopes that never can decay.

Dear cherished image from thy stormy bed!
Child of my early woe, and early joy!
'Tis thus at last the sea shall yield her dead,
And give again my loved, my buried boy.

[1] A philosophical and religious writer of much merit and earnestness; author of a volume of poems; for a long time professor of moral and mental philosophy in Bowdoin College. A native of New Hampshire.

Jacob Leonard Martin,[1] *1805–1848.*

360. The Church of Santa Croce, Florence.

Tomb of the mighty dead,[2] illustrious shrine,
Where genius, in the majesty of death,
Reposes solemn, sepulchred beneath,
Temple o'er every other fane divine!
Dark Santa Crocé, in whose dust recline
Their mouldering relics whose immortal wreath
Blooms on, unfaded by Time's withering breath,
In these proud ashes what a prize is thine!
Sure it is holy ground I tread upon;
Nor do I breathe unconsecrated air,
As, rapt, I gaze on each undying name.
These monuments are fragments of the throne
Once reared by genius on this spot so fair,
When Florence was the seat of arts and early fame.

Geo. W. Bethune, 1805–1862. (Manual, p. 487.)

Invocation.

361. Mythology gives place to Christianity.

Hushed is their song; from long-frequented grove,
  Pale Memory, are thy bright-eyed daughters gone;
No more in strains of melody and love,
  Gush forth thy sacred waters, Helicon;
Prostrate on Egypt's plain, Aurora's son,
  God of the sunbeam and the living lyre,
No more shall hail thee with mellifluous tone;
  Nor shall thy Pythia, raving from thy fire,
Speak of the future sooth to those who would inquire.

No more at Delos, or at Delphi now,
  Or e'en at mighty Ammon's Lybian shrine,
The white-robed priests before the altar bow,

[1] A native of North Carolina; best known in political life, but meritorious in literature.

[2] In this church repose Galileo, Michael Angelo, Alfieri, and other illustrious Italians.

To slay the victim and to pour the wine,
While gifts of kingdoms round each pillar twine;
Scarce can the classic pilgrim, sweeping free
From fallen architrave the desert vine,
Trace the dim names of their divinity—
Gods of the ruined temples, where, oh where! are ye?

The Naiad bathing in her crystal spring,
The guardian Nymph of every leafy tree,
The rushing Æolus on viewless wing,
The flower-crowned Queen of every cultured lea,
And he who walked, with monarch-tread, the sea,
The awful Thunderer, threatening them aloud,
GOD! were their vain imaginings of Thee,
Who saw Thee only through the illusive cloud
That sin had flung around their spirits, like a shroud.

As fly the shadows of uncertain night,
On misty vapors of the early day,
When bursts o'er earth the sun's resplendent light—
Fantastic visions! they have passed away,
Chased by the purer Gospel's orient ray.
My soul's bright waters flow from out thy throne,
And on my ardent breast thy sunbeam's play;
Fountain of thought! True Source of light! I own
In joyful strains of praise, thy sovereign power alone.

O breathe upon my soul thy Spirit's fire,
That I may glow like seraphim on high,
Or rapt Isaiah kindling o'er his lyre;
And sent by Thee, let holy Hope be nigh,
To fill with prescient joy my ravished eye,
And gentle Love; to tune each jarring string
Accordant with the heavenly harmony;
Then upward borne, on Faith's aspiring wing,
The praises of my God to listening earth, I sing.

Charles Fenno Hoffman, 1806–. (Manual, pp. 487, 505, 519.)

From "The Vigil of Faith."

362. The Red Man's Heaven.

White man! I say not that they lie
Who preach a faith so dark and drear,
That wedded hearts in yon cold sky
Meet not as they were mated here.
But scorning not thy faith, thou must
Stranger, in mine have equal trust,—
The Red man's faith, by Him implanted,
Who souls to both our bodies granted.
Thou know'st in life we mingle not;
Death cannot change our different lot!
He who hath placed the White man's heaven
Where hymns in vapory clouds are chanted,
To harps by angel fingers play'd,
Not less on his Red children smiles,
To whom a land of souls is given,
Where in the ruddy West array'd,
Brighten our blessed hunting isles.

. . . . . .

Those blissful Islands of the West!
I've seen, myself, at sunset time,
The golden lake in which they rest;
Seen, too, the barks that bear The Blest,
Floating toward that fadeless clime:
First dark, just as they leave our shore,
Their sides then brightening more and more,
Till in a flood of crimson light
They melted from my straining sight.
And she who climb'd the storm-swept steep,
She who the foaming wave would dare,
So oft love's vigil here to keep,—

Stranger, albeit thou think'st I dote,
I know, I know she watches there!
Watches upon that radiant strand,
Watches to see her lover's boat
Approach The Spirit-Land.

He ceased, and spoke no more that night,
Though oft, when chillier blew the blast,
I saw him moving in the light
The fire, that he was feeding, cast;
While I, still wakeful, ponder'd o'er
His wondrous story more and more.
I thought, not wholly waste the mind
Where Faith so deep a root could find,
Faith which both love and life could save,
And keep the first, in age still fond,
Thus blossoming this side the grave
In steadfast trust of fruit beyond.
And when in after years I stood
By INCA-PAH-CHO's haunted water,
Where long ago that hunter woo'd
In early youth its island daughter,
And traced the voiceless solitude
Once witness of his loved one's slaughter—
At that same season of the leaf
In which I heard him tell his grief,—
I thought some day I'd weave in rhyme,
That tale of mellow autumn time.

William Gilmore Simms, 1806–1870. (Manual, pp. 523, 490, 510.)

From "The Cassique of Accabee."

363. NATURE INSPIRES SENTIMENT.

IT was a night of calm. O'er Ashley's waters
Crept the sweet billows to their own soft tune,

While she, most bright of Keawah's fair daughters,
  Whose voice might spell the footsteps of the moon,
      As slow we swept along,
      Poured forth her own sweet song—
  A lay of rapture not forgotten soon.

Hushed was our breathing, stayed the lifted oar,
  Our spirits rapt, our souls no longer free,
While the boat, drifting softly to the shore,
  Brought us within the shades of Accabee.
      "Ah!" sudden cried the maid,
      In the dim light afraid,
  "'Tis here the ghost still walks of the old Yemassee."

And sure the spot was haunted by a power
  To fix the pulses in each youthful heart;
Never was moon more gracious in a bower,
  Making delicious fancy-work for art,
      Weaving so meekly bright
      Her pictures of delight,
  That, though afraid to stay, we sorrowed to depart.

"If these old groves are haunted"—sudden then,
  Said she, our sweet companion,—"it must be
By one who loved, and was beloved again,
  And joy'd all forms of loveliness to see:—
      Here, in these groves they went,
      Where love and worship, blent,
  Still framed the proper God for each idolatry.

"It could not be that love should here be stern,
  Or beauty fail to sway with sov'reign might;
These from so blessèd scenes should something learn,
  And swell with tenderness, and shape delight:
      These groves have had their power,
      And bliss, in by-gone hour,
  Hath charm'd with sight and song the passage of the night."

"It were a bliss to think so;" made reply
  Our Hubert—"yet the tale is something old,
That checks us with denial;—and our sky,
  And these brown woods that, in its glittering fold,
      Look like a fairy clime,
      Still unsubdued by time,
  Have evermore the tale of wrong'd devotion told."

"Give us thy legend, Hubert;" cried the maid;—
  And, with down-dropping oars, our yielding prow
Shot to a still lagoon, whose ample shade
  Droop'd from the gray moss of an old oak's brow:
      The groves, meanwhile, lay bright,
      Like the broad stream, in light,
  Soft, sweet as ever yet the lunar loom display'd.

—

Nathaniel Parker Willis, 1807–1867.

(Manual, pp. 504, 519.)

From the "Sacred Poems."

364. Hagar in the Wilderness.

. . . . . .

The morning pass'd, and Asia's sun rose up
In the clear heaven, and every beam was heat.
The cattle of the hills were in the shade,
And the bright plumage of the Orient lay
On beating bosoms in her spicy trees.
It was an hour of rest; but Hagar found
No shelter in the wilderness, and on
She kept her weary way, until the boy
Hung down his head, and open'd his parch'd lips
For water; but she could not give it him.
She laid him down beneath the sultry sky,—
For it was better than the close, hot breath
Of the thick pines,—and tried to comfort him,-
But he was sore athirst, and his blue eyes

Were dim and bloodshot, and he could not know
Why God denied him water in the wild.

She sat a little longer, and he grew
Ghastly and faint, as if he would have died.
It was too much for her, she lifted him,
And bore him further on, and laid his head
Beneath the shadow of a desert shrub;
And, shrouding up her face, she went away,
And sat to watch where he could see her not,
Till he should die; and watching him, she mourned:

"God stay thee in thine agony, my boy!
I cannot see thee die; I cannot brook
Upon thy brow to look,
And see death settle on my cradle-joy.
How have I drunk the light of thy blue eye!
And could I see thee die?

"I did not dream of this when thou wert straying,
Like an unbound gazelle, among the flowers;
Or wearing rosy hours,
By the rich gush of water-sources playing,
Then sinking weary to thy smiling sleep,
So beautiful and deep.

"O, no! and when I watch'd by thee the while,
And saw thy bright lip curling in thy dream,
And thought of the dark stream
In my own land of Egypt, the far Nile,
How pray'd I that my father's land might be
An heritage for thee!

"And now the grave for its cold breast hath won thee,
And thy white, delicate limbs the earth will press;
And, O, my last caress
Must feel thee cold, for a chill hand is on thee.

How can I leave my boy, so pillow'd there
    Upon his clustering hair!"

  She stood beside the well her God had given
To gush in that deep wilderness, and bathed
The forehead of her child until he laugh'd
In his reviving happiness, and lisp'd
His infant thought of gladness at the sight
Of the cool plashing of his mother's hand.

---

365. UNSEEN SPIRITS.

THE shadows lay along Broadway,—
  'Twas near the twilight tide,—
And slowly there, a lady fair
  Was walking in her pride.
Alone walked she, yet viewlessly
  Walked spirits at her side.

Peace charmed the street beneath her feet,
  And honor charmed the air,
And all astir looked kind on her,
  And called her good as fair;
For all God ever gave to her,
  She kept with chary care.

She kept with care her beauties rare,
  From lovers warm and true;
For her heart was cold to all but gold,
  And the rich came not to woo.
Ah, honored well, are charms to sell,
  When priests the selling do!

Now, walking there, was one more fair—
  A slight girl, lily pale,
And she had unseen company
  To make the spirit quail;

'Twixt want and scorn, she walked forlorn,
  And nothing could avail.

No mercy now can clear her brow
  For this world's peace to pray;
For, as love's wild prayer dissolved in air,
  Her woman's heart gave way,
And the sin forgiven by Christ in heaven
  By man is cursed alway.

Henry Wadsworth Longfellow, 1807–.

(Manual, pp. 503, 505, 519, 531.)

366. Lines to Resignation.

There is no flock, however watched and tended
  But one dead lamb is there!
There is no fireside, howso'er defended,
  But has one vacant chair!

The air is full of farewells to the dying,
  And mournings for the dead;
The heart of Rachel, for her children crying,
  Will not be comforted!

Let us be patient! these severe afflictions
  Not from the ground arise,
But oftentimes celestial benedictions
  Assume this dark disguise.

We see but dimly through the mists and vapors;
  Amid these earthly damps,
What seem to us but sad, funereal tapers
  May be heaven's distant lamps.

There is no Death! What seems so is transition.
  This life of mortal breath
Is but a suburb of the life elysian,
  Whose portal we call Death.

She is not dead,—the child of our affection,—
  But gone unto that school
Where she no longer needs our poor protection,
  And Christ himself doth rule.

In that great cloister's stillness and seclusion,
  By guardian angels led,
Safe from temptation, safe from sin's pollution,
  She lives, whom we call dead.

Day after day we think what she is doing
  In those bright realms of air;
Year after year, her tender steps pursuing,
  Behold her grown more fair.

Thus do we walk with her, and keep unbroken
  The bond which nature gives,
Thinking that our remembrance, though unspoken,
  May reach her where she lives.

Not as a child shall we again behold her;
  For when with raptures wild
In our embraces we again enfold her,
  She will not be a child;

But a fair maiden, in her Father's mansion,
  Clothed with celestial grace;
And beautiful with all the soul's expansion
  Shall we behold her face.

And though at times impetuous with emotion
  And anguish long suppressed,
The swelling heart heaves, moaning like the ocean,
  That cannot be at rest,—

We will be patient, and assuage the feeling
  We may not wholly stay;
By silence sanctifying, not concealing,
  The grief that must have way.

From "The Seaside and The Fireside."

367. THE WEDDING; THE LAUNCH; THE SHIP.

THE prayer is said,
The service read,
The joyous bridegroom bows his head;
And in tears the good old Master
Shakes the brown hand of his son,
Kisses his daughter's glowing cheek
In silence, for he cannot speak,
And ever faster
Down his own the tears begin to run.
The worthy pastor—
The Shepherd of that wandering flock,
That has the ocean for its wold,
That has the vessel for its fold,
Leaping ever from rock to rock—
Spake, with accents mild and clear,
Words of warning, words of cheer,
But tedious to the bridegroom's ear.

. . . . .

Then the Master,
With a gesture of command,
Waved his hand;
And at the word,
Loud and sudden there was heard,
All around them and below,
The sound of hammers, blow on blow,
Knocking away the shores and spurs.
And see! she stirs!
She starts,—she moves,—she seems to feel
The thrill of life along her keel,
And, spurning with her foot the ground,
With one exulting, joyous bound,
She leaps into the ocean's arms!

And lo! from the assembled crowd
There rose a shout, prolonged and loud,
That to the ocean seemed to say,—
"Take her, O bridegroom, old and gray,
Take her to thy protecting arms,
With all her youth and all her charms!"
How beautiful she is! How fair
She lies within those arms, that press
Her form with many a soft caress
Of tenderness and watchful care!
Sail forth into the sea, O ship!
Through wind and wave, right onward steer!
The moistened eye, the trembling lip,
Are not the signs of doubt or fear.

Sail forth into the sea of life,
O gentle, loving, trusting wife,
And safe from all adversity
Upon the bosom of that sea
Thy comings and thy goings be!
For gentleness and love and trust
Prevail o'er angry wave and gust;
And in the wreck of noble lives
Something immortal still survives!

Thou, too, sail on, O Ship of State!
Sail on, O Union strong and great!
Humanity with all its fears,
With all the hopes of future years,
Is hanging breathless on thy fate!
We know what master laid thy keel,
What workman wrought thy ribs of steel,
Who made each mast, and sail, and rope,
What anvils rang, what hammers beat,
In what a forge and what a heat
Were shaped the anchors of thy hope!
Fear not each sudden sound and shock,

'Tis of the wave and not the rock;
'Tis but the flapping of the sail,
And not a rent made by the gale!
In spite of rock and tempest-roar,
In spite of false lights on the shore,
Sail on, nor fear to breast the sea!
Our hearts, our hopes, are all with thee,
Our hearts, our hopes, our prayers, our tears,
Our faith triumphant o'er our fears,
Are all with thee,—are all with thee.

—

From "Evangeline."

368. Song of the Mocking-bird, at Sunset.

Softly the evening came. The sun, from the western horizon,
Like a magician, extended his golden wand o'er the landscape;
Twinkling vapors arose; and sky and water and forest
Seemed all on fire at the touch, and melted and mingled together.
Hanging between two skies, a cloud with edges of silver,
Floated the boat, with its dripping oars, on the motionless water.
Filled was Evangeline's heart with inexpressible sweetness.
Touched by the magic spell, the sacred fountains of feeling
Glowed with the light of love, as the skies and waters around her.
Then from a neighboring thicket the mocking-bird, wildest of singers,
Swinging aloft on a willow spray that hung o'er the water,
Shook from his little throat such floods of delirious music,
That the whole air and the woods and the waves seemed silent to listen.
Plaintive at first were the tones and sad; then soaring to madness,
Seemed they to follow or guide the revel of frenzied Bacchantes.

Single notes were then heard, in sorrowful, low lamentation;
Till, having gathered them all, he flung them abroad in derision,
As when, after a storm, a gust of wind through the tree-tops
Shakes down the rattling rain in a crystal shower on the branches.
With such a prelude as this, and hearts that throbbed with emotion,
Slowly they entered the Têche, where it flows through the green Opelousas,
And through the amber air, above the crest of the woodland,
Saw the column of smoke that arose from a neighboring dwelling;—
Sounds of a horn they heard, and the distant lowing of cattle.

—

From "The Song of Hiawatha."

369. HIAWATHA'S DEPARTURE.

ON the shore stood Hiawatha,
Turned and waved his hand at parting;
On the clear and luminous water
Launched his birch canoe for sailing,
From the pebbles of the margin
Shoved it forth into the water;
Whispered to it, "Westward! westward!"
And with speed it darted forward.

And the evening sun descending
Set the clouds on fire with redness,
Burned the broad sky, like a prairie,
Left upon the level water
One long track and trail of splendor,
Down whose streams, as down a river,
Westward, westward Hiawatha
Sailed into the fiery sunset,
Sailed into the purple vapors,
Sailed into the dusk of evening.

And the people from the margin
Watched him floating, rising, sinking,
Till the birch canoe seemed lifted
High into that sea of splendor,
Till it sank into the vapors
Like the new moon slowly, slowly
Sinking in the purple distance.
And they said, "Farewell for ever!"
Said, "Farewell, O Hiawatha!"
And the forests, dark and lonely,
Moved through all their depth of darkness,
Sighed, "Farewell, O Hiawatha!"
And the waves upon the margin
Rising, rippling on the pebbles,
Sobbed, "Farewell, O Hiawatha!"
And the heron, the Shu-shuh-gah,
From her haunts among the fen-lands,
Screamed, "Farewell, O Hiawatha!"
Thus departed Hiawatha,
Hiawatha the beloved,
In the glory of the sunset,
In the purple mists of evening,
To the regions of the home-wind,
Of the Northwest wind Keewaydin,
To the islands of the Blessed,
To the kingdom of Ponemah,
To the land of the Hereafter!

William D. Gallagher, 1808–. (Manual, p. 523.)

370. The Laborer.

Stand up—erect! Thou hast the form,
And likeness of thy God!—who more?
A soul as dauntless mid the storm
Of daily life, a heart as warm
And pure, as breast e'er bore.

What then?—Thou art as true a Man
  As moves the human mass among;
As much a part of the Great plan
That with creation's dawn began,
  As any of the throng.

Who is thine enemy? the high
  In station, or in wealth the chief?
The great, who coldly pass thee by,
With proud step and averted eye?
  Nay! nurse not such belief.

. . . . .

No:—uncurbed passions—low desires—
  Absence of noble self-respect—
Death, in the breast's consuming fires,
To that high Nature which aspires
  For ever, till thus checked:

. . . . .

True, wealth thou hast not: 'tis but dust!
  Nor place; uncertain as the wind!
But that thou hast, which, with thy crust
And water, may despise the lust
  Of both—a noble mind.

With this and passions under ban,
  True faith, and holy trust in God,
Thou art the peer of any man.
Look up, then—that thy little span
  Of life, may be well trod!

John G. Whittier, 1808–. (Manual, pp. 490, 522.)

371. What the Voice Said.

Maddened by Earth's wrong and evil,
  "Lord," I cried in sudden ire,
"From thy right hand, clothed with thunder,
  Shake the bolted fire!

"Love is lost, and Faith is dying;
  With the brute, the man is sold;
And the dropping blood of labor
  Hardens into gold.

. . . . . .

"Thou, the patient Heaven upbraiding,"
  Spake a solemn Voice within;
"Weary of our Lord's forbearance,
  Art thou free from sin?

. . . . . .

"Earnest words must needs be spoken
  When the warm heart bleeds or burns
With its scorn of wrong, or pity
  For the wronged, by turns.

"But, by all thy nature's weakness,
  Hidden faults and follies known,
Be thou, in rebuking evil,
  Conscious of thine own.

"Not the less shall stern-eyed Duty
  To thy lips her trumpet set,
But with harsher blasts shall mingle
  Wailings of regret."

Cease not, Voice of holy speaking,
  Teacher sent of God, be near,
Whispering through the day's cool silence,
  Let my spirit hear!

So, when thoughts of evil doers
  Waken scorn, or hatred move,
Shall a mournful fellow-feeling
  Temper all with love.

From "The Tent on the Beach."

372. THE ATLANTIC TELEGRAPH.

O LONELY bay of Trinity,
  O dreary shores, give ear!
Lean down unto the white-lipped sea
  The voice of God to hear!

From world to world his couriers fly,
  Thought-winged, and shod with fire;
The angel of his stormy sky
  Rides down the sunken wire.

What saith the herald of the Lord?
  "The world's long strife is done;
Close wedded by that mystic cord,
  Its continents are one.

And one in heart, as one in blood,
  Shall all her peoples be;
The hands of human brotherhood
  Are clasped beneath the sea.

"Through Orient seas, o'er Afric's plain
  And Asian mountains borne,
The vigor of the Northern brain
  Shall nerve the world outworn.

"From clime to clime, from shore to shore,
  Shall thrill the magic thread;
The new Prometheus steals once more
  The fire that wakes the dead."

Throb on, strong pulse of thunder! beat
  From answering beach to beach;
Fuse nations in thy kindly heat,
  And melt the chains of each!

Wild terror of the sky above,
  Glide tamed and dumb below!
Bear gently, Ocean's carrier-dove,
  Thy errands to and fro.

Weave on, swift shuttle of the Lord,
  Beneath the deep so far,
The bridal robe of earth's accord,
  The funeral shroud of war!

For lo! the fall of Ocean's wall,
  Space mocked, and time outrun;
And round the world the thought of all
  Is as the thought of one!

The poles unite, the zones agree,
  The tongues of striving cease;
As on the sea of Galilee,
  The Christ is whispering, Peace!

From Snow-Bound.

373. Description of a Snow Storm.

  The sun that brief December day
  Rose cheerless over hills of gray,
  And, darkly circled, gave at noon
  A sadder light than waning moon,
Slow tracing down the thickening sky
Its mute and ominous prophecy,
A portent seeming less than threat,
It sank from sight before it set.
A chill no coat, however stout,
Of homespun stuff could quite shut out,
A hard, dull bitterness of cold,
  That checked, mid-vein, the circling race
  Of life-blood in the sharpened face,

The coming of the snow-storm told.
The wind blew east: we heard the roar
Of Ocean on his wintry shore,
And felt the strong pulse throbbing there
Beat with low rhythm our inland air.

. . . . .

Unwarmed by any sunset light
The gray day darkened into night,
A night made hoary with the swarm
And whirl-dance of the blinding storm,
A zigzag wavering to and fro
Crossed and recrossed the wingéd snow:
And ere the early bed-time came
The white drift piled the window-frame,
And, through the glass, the clothes-line posts
Looked in like tall and sheeted ghosts.

So all night long the storm rolled on:
The morning broke without a sun;
In tiny spherule traced with lines
Of Nature's geometric signs,
In starry flake and pellicle,
All day the hoary meteor fell;
And, when the second morning shone,
We looked upon a world unknown,
On nothing we could call our own.
Around the glistening wonder bent
The blue walls of the firmament,
No cloud above, no earth below,—
A universe of sky and snow!

From "The Pennsylvania Pilgrim."

374. The Quaker's Creed.

. . . . . .

Gathered from many sects, the Quaker brought
His old beliefs, adjusting to the thought
That moved his soul, the creed his fathers taught.

One faith alone, so broad that all mankind
Within themselves its secret witness find,
The soul's communion with the Eternal Mind,

The Spirit's law, the Inward Rule and Guide,
Scholar and peasant, lord and serf, allied,
The polished Penn, and Cromwell's Ironside.

As still in Hemskerck's Quaker meeting, face
By face, in Flemish detail, we may trace
How loose-mouthed boor, and fine ancestral grace,

Sat in close contrast,—the clipt-headed churl,
Broad market-dame, and simple serving-girl,
By skirt of silk and periwig in curl!

For soul touched soul; the spiritual treasure-trove
Made all men equal, none could rise above,
Nor sink below, that level of God's love.

So, with his rustic neighbors sitting down,
The homespun frock beside the scholar's gown,
Pastorius, to the manners of the town

Added the freedom of the woods, and sought
The bookless wisdom by experience taught,
And learned to love his new-found home, while not

Forgetful of the old; the seasons went
Their rounds, and somewhat to his spirit lent
Of their own calm and measureless content.

Glad even to tears, he heard the robin sing
His song of welcome to the Western spring,
And bluebird borrowing from the sky his wing.

And when the miracle of autumn came,
And all the woods with many-colored flame
Of splendor, making summer's greenness tame,

Burned unconsumed, a voice without a sound
Spake to him from each kindled bush around
And made the strange, new landscape holy ground.

Albert Pike, 1809-. (Manual, p. 523.)

From "Lines on the Rocky Mountains."

375. THE EVERLASTING HILLS.

THE deep, transparent sky is full
Of many thousand glittering lights—
Unnumbered stars that calmly rule
The dark dominions of the night.
The mild, bright moon has upward risen,
Out of the gray and boundless plain,
And all around the white snows glisten,
Where frost, and ice, and silence, reign,—
While ages roll away, and they unchanged remain.

These mountains, piercing the blue sky
With their eternal cones of ice,—
The torrents dashing from on high,
O'er rock, and crag, and precipice,—
Change not, but still remain as ever,
Unwasting, deathless, and sublime,
And will remain while lightnings quiver,
Or stars the hoary summits climb,
Or rolls the thunder-chariot of eternal Time.

Anne C. Lynch Botta.

From her "Poems."

376. THE DUMB CREATION.

DEAL kindly with those speechless ones,
That throng our gladsome earth;
Say not the bounteous gift of life
Alone is nothing worth.

What though with mournful memories
  They sigh not for the past?
What though their ever joyous now
  No future overcast.

No aspirations fill their breast
  With longings undefined;
They live, they love, and they are blest
  For what they seek they find.

They see no mystery in the stars,
  No wonder in the plain,
And Life's enigma wakes in them,
  No questions dark and vain.

To them earth is a final home,
  A bright and blest abode;
Their lives unconsciously flow on
  In harmony with God.

To this fair world our human hearts
  Their hopes and longings bring,
And o'er its beauty and its bloom,
  Their own dark shadows fling.

Between the future and the past
  In wild unrest we stand,
And ever as our feet advance,
  Retreats the promised land.

And though Love, Fame, and Wealth, and Power
  Bind in their gilded bond,
We pine to grasp the unattained—
  The *something* still beyond.

And, beating on their prison bars,
  Our spirits ask more room,
And with unanswered questionings,
  They pierce beyond the tomb.

Then say thou not, oh, doubtful heart!
  There is no life to come:
That in some tearless, cloudless land,
  Thou shalt not find thy home.

Oliver Wendell Holmes, 1809–. (Manual, pp. 478, 520.)

From his Poems.

377. THE LAST LEAF.

I SAW him once before,
As he passed by the door,
    And again
The pavement stones resound,
As he totters o'er the ground
    With his cane.

. . . . .

My grandmamma has said,—
Poor old lady, she is dead
    Long ago,—
That he had a Roman nose,
And his cheek was like a rose
    In the snow.

But now his nose is thin,
And it rests upon his chin
    Like a staff,
And a crook is in his back,
And a melancholy crack
    In his laugh.

I know it is a sin
For me to sit and grin
    At him here;
But the old three-cornered hat,
And the breeches, and all that,
    Are so queer!

And if I should live to be
The last leaf upon the tree
In the spring,—
Let them smile, as I do now,
At the old forsaken bough
Where I cling.

From "The Professor at the Breakfast Table."

378. A Mother's Secret.

. . . . . .

They reach the holy place, fulfill the days
To solemn feasting given, and grateful praise.
At last they turn, and far Moriah's height
Melts into southern sky and fades from sight.
All day the dusky caravan has flowed
In devious trails along the winding road,—
(For many a step their homeward path attends,
And all the sons of Abraham are as friends.)
Evening has come,—the hour of rest and joy;—
Hush! hush! that whisper,—"Where is Mary's boy?"
O weary hour! O aching days that passed,
Filled with strange fears, each wilder than the last:
The soldier's lance,—the fierce centurion's sword,—
The crushing wheels that whirl some Roman lord,—
The midnight crypt that sucks the captive's breath,—
The blistering sun on Hinnom's vale of death!
Thrice on his cheek had rained the morning light,
Thrice on his lips the mildewed kiss of night,
Crouched by some porphyry column's shining plinth,
Or stretched beneath the odorous terebinth.
At last, in desperate mood, they sought once more
The Temple's porches, searched in vain before;
They found him seated with the ancient men,—
The grim old rufflers of the tongue and pen,—
Their bald heads glistening as they clustered near,
Their gray beards slanting as they turned to hear,

Lost in half-envious wonder and surprise
That lips so fresh should utter words so wise.
And Mary said,—as one who, tried too long,
Tells all her grief and half her sense of wrong,—
"What is this thoughtless thing which thou hast done?
Lo, we have sought thee sorrowing, O my son!"
Few words he spake, and scarce of filial tone,—
Strange words, their sense a mystery yet unknown;
Then turned with them and left the holy hill,
To all their mild commands obedient still.
The tale was told to Nazareth's sober men,
And Nazareth's matrons told it oft again;
The maids retold it at the fountain's side;
The youthful shepherds doubted or denied;
It passed around among the listening friends,
With all that fancy adds and fiction lends,
Till newer marvels dimmed the young renown
Of Joseph's son, who talked the Rabbies down.
But Mary, faithful to its lightest word,
Kept in her heart the sayings she had heard,
Till the dread morning rent the Temple's veil,
And shuddering Earth confirmed the wondrous tale.

Youth fades; love droops; the leaves of friendship fall;
A mother's secret hope outlives them all.

Willis Gaylord Clark, 1810–1841. (Manual, pp. 503, 523.)

From his "Literary Remains."

379. AN INVITATION TO EARLY PIETY.

COME, while the morning of thy life is glowing—
Ere the dim phantoms thou art chasing die;
Ere the gay spell which earth is round thee throwing,
Fade like the sunset of a summer sky;

Life hath but shadows, save a promise given,
  Which lights the future with a fadeless ray;
O, touch the sceptre—win a hope in heaven—
  Come—turn thy spirit from the world away.

Then will the crosses of this brief existence,
  Seem airy nothings to thine ardent soul;
And shining brightly in the forward distance,
  Will of thy patient race appear the goal;
Home of the weary! where in peace reposing,
  The spirit lingers in unclouded bliss,
Though o'er its dust the curtained grave is closing—
  Who would not *early* choose a lot like this?

James Russell Lowell, 1819-. (Manual, p. 520.)

From his "Miscellaneous Poems," &c.

380. A Song.

Violet! sweet violet!
Thine eyes are full of tears;
    Are they wet
    Even yet,
With the thought of other years?
Or with gladness are they full,
For the night so beautiful,
And longing for those far-off spheres?

Loved-one of my youth thou wast,
Of my merry youth,
    And I see,
    Tearfully,
All the fair and sunny past,
All its openness and truth,
Ever fresh and green in thee
As the moss is in the sea.

Thy little heart, that hath with love
Grown colored like the sky above,
On which thou lookest ever,—
Can it know
All the woe
Of hope for what returneth never,
All the sorrow and the longing
To these hearts of ours belonging?

Out on it! no foolish pining
For the sky
Dims thine eye,
Or for the stars so calmly shining;
Like thee let this soul of mine
Take hue from that wherefor I long,
Self-stayed and high, serene and strong,
Not satisfied with hoping—but divine.

Violet! dear violet!
Thy blue eyes are only wet
With joy and love of him who sent thee,
And for the fulfilling sense
Of that glad obedience
Which made thee all that Nature meant thee!

From "The Present Crisis."

381. IMPORTANCE OF A NOBLE DEED.

WHEN a deed is done for Freedom, through the broad earth's aching breast
Runs a thrill of joy prophetic, trembling on from east to west,
And the slave, where'er he cowers, feels the soul within him climb
To the awful verge of manhood, as the energy sublime
Of a century, bursts full-blossomed on the thorny stem of Time.

. . . .

Once, to every man and nation, comes the moment to decide,
In the strife of Truth with Falsehood, for the good or evil side;
Some great cause, God's new Messiah, offering each the bloom
or blight,
Parts the goats upon the left hand, and the sheep upon the right,
And the choice goes by for ever, 'twixt that darkness and that
light.

. . . .

We see dimly in the Present what is small and what is great,
Slow of faith how weak an arm may turn the iron helm of fate,
But the soul is still oracular; amid the market's din,
List the ominous stern whisper from the Delphic cave within,—
"They enslave their children's children, who make compromise
with sin."

From The Atlantic Monthly.

382. The Spaniards' Graves at the Isles of Shoals.

O sailors, did sweet eyes look after you,
The day you sailed away from sunny Spain?
Bright eyes that followed fading ship and crew,
Melting in tender rain?

Did no one dream of that drear night to be,
Wild with the wind, fierce with the stinging snow,
When, on yon granite point that frets the sea,
The ship met her death-blow?

Fifty long years ago these sailors died:
(None know how many sleep beneath the waves:)
Fourteen gray head-stones, rising side by side,
Point out their nameless graves,—

Lonely, unknown, deserted, but for me,
And the wild birds that flit with mournful cry,
And sadder winds, and voices of the sea
That moans perpetually.

Wives, mothers, maidens, wistfully, in vain
  Questioned the distance for the yearning sail,
That, leaning landward, should have stretched again
    White arms wide on the gale,

To bring back their beloved. Year by year,
  Weary they watched, till youth and beauty passed,
And lustrous eyes grew dim, and age drew near,
    And hope was dead at last.

Still summer broods o'er that delicious land,
  Rich, fragrant, warm with skies of golden glow:
Live any yet of that forsaken band
    Who loved so long ago?

O Spanish women, over the far seas,
  Could I but show you where your dead repose!
Could I send tidings on this northern breeze,
    That strong and steady blows!

Dear dark-eyed sisters, you remember yet
  These you have lost, but you can never know
One stands at their bleak graves whose eyes are wet
    With thinking of your woe!

Edgar Allen Poe. (Manual, p. 510.)

From his Works.

383. "THE RAVEN."

ONCE upon a midnight dreary, while I pondered, weak and weary,
Over many a quaint and curious volume of forgotten lore,—
While I nodded, nearly napping, suddenly there came a tapping,
As of some one gently rapping, rapping at my chamber door;
"'Tis some visitor," I muttered, "tapping at my chamber door,—
    Only this, and nothing more."

Ah! distinctly I remember, it was in the bleak December,
And each separate dying ember wrought its ghost upon the
floor.
Eagerly I wished the morrow;—vainly I had sought to borrow,
From my books, surcease of sorrow,—sorrow for the lost
Lenore,—
For the rare and radiant maiden whom the angels name
Lenore,—
Nameless here for evermore.

And the silken, sad, uncertain rustling of each purple curtain
Thrilled me—filled me with fantastic terrors never felt before;
So that now, to still the beating of my heart, I stood repeating,
"'Tis some visitor entreating entrance at my chamber door—
Some late visitor entreating entrance at my chamber door;
This it is, and nothing more."

Presently my soul grew stronger: hesitating then no longer,
"Sir," said I, "or madam, truly your forgiveness I implore;
But the fact is, I was napping, and so gently you came rapping,
And so faintly you came tapping, tapping at my chamber door,
That I scarce was sure I heard you." Here I opened wide the
door;
Darkness there,—and nothing more.

Deep into that darkness peering, long I stood there wondering,
fearing,
Doubting, dreaming dreams no mortal ever dared to dream
before;
But the silence was unbroken, and the stillness gave no token,
And the only word there spoken was the whisper'd word,
"Lenore!"
This I whisper'd, and an echo murmur'd back the word,
"Lenore!"
Merely this, and nothing more.

Back into the chamber turning, all my soul within me burning,
Soon again I heard a tapping, something louder than before.

"Surely," said I,—"surely that is something at my window-
lattice;
Let me see, then, what thereat is, and this mystery explore,—
Let my heart be still a moment, and this mystery explore;—
'Tis the wind, and nothing more."

Open here I flung the shutter, when, with many a flirt and
flutter,
In there stepped a stately Raven of the saintly days of yore.
Not the least obeisance made he; not a minute stopped or staid
he;
But with mien of lord or lady, perched above my chamber
door,—
Perched upon a bust of Pallas, just above my chamber door,—
Perched, and sat, and nothing more.

Then, this ebony bird beguiling my sad fancy into smiling,
By the grave and stern decorum of the countenance it wore,
"Though thy crest be shorn and shaven, thou," I said, "art
sure no craven,
Ghastly, grim, and ancient Raven wandering from the nightly
shore—
Tell me what thy lordly name is on the night's Plutonian shore!"
Quoth the Raven, "Nevermore."

Much I marvell'd this ungainly fowl to hear discourse so plainly,
Though its answer little meaning, little relevancy bore;
For we cannot help agreeing that no living human being
Ever yet was bless'd with seeing bird above his chamber door,—
Bird or beast upon the sculptured bust above his chamber door,—
With such name as "Nevermore."

But the Raven, sitting lonely on that placid bust, spoke only
That one word, as if his soul in that one word he did outpour.
Nothing further then he utter'd; not a feather then he
flutter'd—
Till I scarcely more than mutter'd, "Other friends have flown
before—

On the morrow *he* will leave me, as my Hopes have flown before,"
Then the bird said, "Nevermore."

Startled at the stillness broken by reply so aptly spoken,
"Doubtless," said I, "what it utters is its only stock and store,
Caught from some unhappy master whom unmerciful disaster
Follow'd fast and follow'd faster, till his songs one burden bore—
Till the dirges of his Hope that melancholy burden bore
Of 'Never—never—more!'"

But the Raven still beguiling all my sad soul into smiling,
Straight I wheel'd a cushioned seat in front of bird, and bust, and door;
Then upon the velvet sinking, I betook myself to linking
Fancy unto fancy, thinking what this ominous bird of yore—
What this grim, ungainly, ghastly, gaunt, and ominous bird of yore
Meant in croaking "Nevermore."

This I sat engaged in guessing, but no syllable expressing
To the fowl, whose fiery eyes now burned into my bosom's core;
This and more I sat divining, with my head at ease reclining
On the cushion's velvet lining that the lamp-light gloated o'er,
But whose velvet violet lining which the lamp-light gloated o'er
She shall press, ah, never more!

Then methought, the air grew denser, perfumed from an unseen censer
Swung by seraphim whose footfalls tinkled on the tufted floor.
"Wretch," I cried, "thy God hath lent thee—by these angels he hath sent thee
Respite—respite and nepenthe from thy memories of Lenore!
Quaff, O quaff, this kind nepenthe, and forget this lost Lenore!"
Quoth the Raven, "Never more."

"Prophet," said I, "thing of evil! prophet still, if bird or devil!—
Whether tempter sent, or whether tempest toss'd thee here ashore,
Desolate, though all undaunted, on this desert land enchanted—
On this home by Horror haunted—tell me truly, I implore—
Is there—is there balm in Gilead?—tell me—tell me, I implore!"
Quoth the Raven, "Never more."

"Prophet!" said I, "thing of evil!—prophet still, if bird or devil!
By that heaven that bends above us—by that God we both adore—
Tell this soul, with sorrow laden, if within the distant Aidenn,
It shall clasp a sainted maiden whom the angels name Lenore—
Clasp a rare and radiant maiden whom the angels name Lenore!"
Quoth the Raven, "Never more."

"Be that word our sign of parting, bird or fiend!" I shrieked, upstarting—
"Get thee back into the tempest and the Night's Plutonian shore!
Leave no black plume as a token of that lie thy soul hath spoken!
Leave my loneliness unbroken!—quit the bust above my door!
Take thy beak from out my heart, and take thy form from off my door!
Quoth the Raven, "Never more."

And the Raven, never flitting, still is sitting, still is sitting,
On the pallid bust of Pallas just above my chamber door;
And his eyes have all the seeming of a demon's that is dreaming,
And the lamp-light o'er him streaming throws his shadow on the floor;
And my soul from out that shadow, that lies floating on the floor,
Shall be lifted—never more.

Alfred B. Street, 1811–. (Manual, pp. 522, 531.)

From his "Poems."

384. An Autumn Landscape.

Overhead
There is a blending of cloud, haze, and sky;
A silvery sheet, with spaces of soft hue;
A trembling veil of gauze is stretched athwart
The shadowy hill-sides and dark forest-flanks;
A soothing quiet broods upon the air,
And the faint sunshine winks with drowsiness.
Far sounds melt mellow on the ear: the bark,
The bleat, the tinkle, whistle, blast of horn,
The rattle of the wagon-wheel, the low,
The fowler's shot, the twitter of the bird,
And even the hue of converse from the road.

. . . . .

The sunshine flashed on streams,
Sparkled on leaves, and laughed on fields and woods.
All, all was life and motion, as all now
Is sleep and quiet. Nature in her change
Varies each day, as in the world of man
She moulds the differing features. Yea, each leaf
Is variant from its fellow. Yet her works
Are blended in a glorious harmony,
For thus God made his earth. Perchance His breath
Was music when He spake it into life,
Adding thereby another instrument
To the innumerable choral orbs
Sending the tribute of their grateful praise
In ceaseless anthems towards His sacred throne.

—

From "Drawings and Tintings."

385. The Falls of the Mongaup.

Struggling along the mountain path,
We hear, amid the gloom,

Like a roused giant's voice of wrath,
  A deep-toned, sullen boom:
Emerging on the platform high,
Burst sudden to the startled eye
Rocks, woods, and waters, wild and rude—
A scene of savage solitude.

Swift as an arrow from the bow;
  Headlong the torrent leaps,
Then tumbling round, in dazzling snow
  And dizzy whirls it sweeps;
Then, shooting through the narrow aisle
Of this sublime cathedral pile,
Amidst its vastness, dark and grim,
It peals its everlasting hymn.

Pyramid on pyramid of rock
  Towers upward, wild and riven,
As piled by Titan hand, to mock
  The distant smiling heaven.
And where its blue streak is displayed,
Branches their emerald net-work braid
So high, the eagle in his flight
Seems but a dot upon the sight.

Here column'd hemlocks point in air
  Their cone-like fringes green;
Their trunks hang knotted, black and bare,
  Like spectres o'er the scene;
Here lofty crag and deep abyss,
And awe-inspiring precipice;
There grottoes bright in wave-worn gloss,
And carpeted with velvet moss.

No wandering ray e'er kissed with light
  This rock-walled sable pool,
Spangled with foam-gems thick and white,
  And slumbering deep and cool;

But where yon cataract roars down,
Set by the sun, a rainbow crown
Is dancing o'er the dashing strife—
Hope glittering o'er the storm of life.

Beyond, the smooth and mirror'd sheet
  So gently steals along,
The very ripples, murmuring sweet,
  Scarce drown the wild bee's song;
The violet from the grassy side
Dips its blue chalice in the tide;
And, gliding o'er the leafy brink,
The deer, unfrightened, stoops to drink.

Myriads of man's time-measured race
  Have vanished from the earth,
Nor left a memory of their trace,
  Since first this scene had birth;
These waters, thundering now along,
Joined in Creation's matin-song;
And only by their dial-trees
Have known the lapse of centuries!

Laura M. H. Thurston, 1812–1842. (Manual, p. 524.)

386. Lines on Crossing the Alleghanies.

I hail thee, Valley of the West,
  For what thou yet shalt be!
I hail thee for the hopes that rest
  Upon thy destiny!
Here from this mountain height, I see
Thy bright waves floating rapidly,
  Thine emerald fields outspread;
And feel that in the book of fame,
Proudly shall thy recorded name
  In later days be read.

Oh! brightly, brightly glow thy skies
  In Summer's sunny hours!
The green earth seems a paradise
  Arrayed in summer flowers!
But oh! there is a land afar,
Whose skies to me all brighter are,
  Along the Atlantic shore!
For eyes beneath their radiant shrine
In kindlier glances answered mine:
  Can these their light restore?

Upon the lofty bound I stand,
  That parts the East and West;
Before me lies a fairy land;
  Behind—*a home of rest!*
Here, Hope her wild enchantment flings,
Portrays all bright and lovely things,
  My footsteps to allure—
But *there*, in memory's light I see
All that was once most dear to me—
  My young heart's cynosure!

Francis S. Osgood, 1812–1850. (Manual, p. 523.)

387. "THE PARTING."

I LOOKED not, I sighed not, I dared not betray
The wild storm of feeling that strove to have way,
For I knew that each sign of the sorrow *I* felt
Her soul to fresh pity and passion would melt,
And calm was my voice, and averted my eyes,
As I parted from all that in being I prize.

I pined but one moment that form to enfold,
Yet the hand that touched hers, like the marble was cold,—
I heard her voice falter a timid farewell,

Nor trembled, though soft on my spirit it fell,
And she knew not, she dreamed not, the anguish of soul
Which only my pity for her could control.

It is over—the loveliest dream of delight
That ever illumined a wanderer's night!
Yet one gleam of comfort will brighten my way,
Though mournful and desolate ever I stray:
It is this—that to her, to my idol, I spared
The pang that her love could have softened and shared!

Harriet Beecher Stowe. (Manual, p. 484.)

From the "Religious Poems."

389. The Peace of Faith.

When winds are raging o'er the upper ocean,
  And billows wild contend with angry roar,
'Tis said, far down, beneath the wild commotion,
  That peaceful stillness reigneth evermore.

Far, far beneath, the noise of tempests dieth,
  And silver waves chime ever peacefully,
And no rude storm, how fierce soe'er it flieth,
  Disturbs the Sabbath of that deeper sea.

So to the heart that knows Thy love, O Purest!
  There is a temple, sacred evermore,
And all the babble of life's angry voices
  Dies in hushed stillness at its peaceful door.

Far, far away, the roar of passion dieth,
  And loving thoughts rise calm and peacefully,
And no rude storm, how fierce soe'er it flieth,
  Disturbs that soul that dwells, O Lord, in Thee.

O Rest of rests! O Peace, serene, eternal!
  Thou ever livest, and Thou changest never;
And in the secret of Thy presence dwelleth
  Fullness of joy, for ever and for ever.

390. "ONLY A YEAR."

ONE year ago,—a ringing voice,
    A clear blue eye,
And clustering curls of sunny hair,
    Too fair to die.

Only a year,—no voice, no smile,
    No glance of eye,
No clustering curls of golden hair,
    Fair but to die!

One year ago,—what loves, what schemes
    Far into life!
What joyous hopes, what high resolves,
    What generous strife!

The silent picture on the wall,
    The burial stone,
Of all that beauty, life, and joy
    Remain alone!

One year,—one year,—one little year,
    And so much gone!
And yet the even flow of life
    Moves calmly on.

The grave grows green, the flowers bloom fair,
    Above that head;
No sorrowing tint of leaf or spray
    Says he is dead.

No pause or hush of merry birds
    That sing above,
Tells us how coldly sleeps below
    The form we love.

Where hast thou been this year, beloved?
    What hast thou seen?

What visions fair, what glorious life,
Where thou hast been?

The veil! the veil! so thin, so strong!
'Twixt us and thee;
The mystic veil! when shall it fall,
That we may see?

Not dead, not sleeping, not even gone,
But present still,
And waiting for the coming hour
Of God's sweet will.

Lord of the living and the dead,
Our Saviour dear!
We lay in silence at thy feet
This sad, sad year!

Henry T. Tuckerman.

From his "Poems."

391. The Statue of Washington.

The quarry whence thy form majestic sprung,
Has peopled earth with grace,
Heroes and gods that elder bards have sung,
A bright and peerless race,
But from its sleeping veins ne'er rose before,
A shape of loftier name
Than his, who Glory's wreath with meekness wore,
The noblest son of fame
Sheathed is the sword that Passion never stained;
His gaze around is cast,
As if the joys of Freedom, newly gained,
Before his vision passed;
As if a nation's shout of love and pride
With music filled the air,

And his calm soul was lifted on the tide
  Of deep and grateful prayer;
As if the crystal mirror of his life
  To fancy sweetly came,
With scenes of patient toil and noble strife,
  Undimmed by doubt or shame;
As if the lofty purpose of his soul
  Expression would betray—
The high resolve Ambition to control,
  And thrust her crown away!
O, it was well in marble, firm and white,
  To carve our hero's form,
Whose angel guidance was our strength in fight,
  Our star amid the storm;
Whose matchless truth has made his name divine,
  And human freedom sure,
His country great, his tomb earth's dearest shrine,
  While man and time endure!
And it is well to place his image there,
  Beneath the dome he blest;
Let meaner spirits who its councils share,
  Revere that silent guest!
Let us go up with high and sacred love,
  To look on his pure brow,
And as, with solemn grace, he points above,
  Renew the patriot's vow!

John G. Saxe, 1816–. (Manual, p. 523, 531.)

From "Early Rising."

392. THE BLESSING OF SLEEP.

"GOD bless the man who first invented sleep!"
  So Sancho Panza said, and so say I:
And bless him, also, that he didn't keep
  His great discovery to himself; nor try

To make it—as the lucky fellow might—
A close monopoly by patent-right!

. . . . .

'Tis beautiful to leave the world a while
  For the soft visions of the gentle night;
And free, at last, from mortal care or guile,
  To live as only in the angels' sight,
In Sleep's sweet realm so cosily shut in,
Where, at the worst, we only dream of sin!

So let us sleep, and give the Maker praise.
  I like the lad, who, when his father thought
To clip his morning nap by hackneyed praise
  Of vagrant worm by early songster caught,
Cried, "Served him right!—it's not at all surprising;
The worm was punished, sir, for early rising!"

—

393. "Ye Tailyor-man; a contemplative ballad."

Right jollie is ye tailyor-man
  As annie man may be;
And all ye daye, upon ye benche
  He worketh merrilie.

And oft, ye while in pleasante wise
  He coileth up his lymbes,
He singeth songs ye like whereof
  Are not in Watts his hymns.

And yet he toileth all ye while
  His merrie catches rolle;
As true unto ye needle as
  Ye needle to ye pole.

What cares ye valiant tailyor-man
  For all ye cowarde fears?

Against ye scissors of ye Fates,
He points his mightie shears.

He heedeth not ye anciente jests
That witless sinners use;
What feareth ye bolde tailyor-man
Ye hissinge of a goose?

He pulleth at ye busie threade,
To feede his lovinge wife
And eke his childe; for unto them
It is the threade of life.

He cutteth well ye rich man's coate,
And with unseemlie pride,
He sees ye little waistcoate in
Ye cabbage bye his side.

Meanwhile ye tailyor-man his wife,
To labor nothing loth,
Sits bye with readie hande to baste
Ye urchin, and ye cloth.

Full happie is ye tailyor-man
Yet is he often tried,
Lest he, from fullness of ye dimes,
Wax wanton in his pride.

Full happie is ye tailyor-man,
And yet he hath a foe,
A cunning enemie that none
So well as tailyors knowe.

It is ye slipperie customer
Who goes his wicked wayes,
And wears ye tailyor-man his coate,
But never, never payes!

From "The Money King."

394. Ancient and Modern Ghosts Contrasted.

In olden times,—if classic poets say
The simple truth, as poets do to-day,—
When Charon's boat conveyed a spirit o'er
The Lethean water to the Hadean shore,
The fare was just a penny,—not too great,
The moderate, regular, Stygian statute rate.
Now, for a shilling, he will cross the stream,
(His paddles whirling to the force of steam!)
And bring, obedient to some wizard power,
Back to the Earth more spirits in an hour,
Than Brooklyn's famous ferry could convey,
Or thine, Hoboken, in the longest day!
Time was when men bereaved of vital breath,
Were calm and silent in the realms of Death;
When mortals dead and decently inurned
Were heard no more; no traveler returned,
Who once had crossed the dark Plutonian strand,
To whisper secrets of the spirit-land,—
Save when perchance some sad, unquiet soul—
Among the tombs might wander on parole,—
A well-bred ghost, at night's bewitching noon,
Returned to catch some glimpses of the moon,
Wrapt in a mantle of unearthly white,
(The only rapping of an ancient sprite!)
Stalked round in silence till the break of day,
Then from the Earth passed unperceived away.

Now all is changed: the musty maxim fails,
And dead men *do* repeat the queerest tales!
Alas, that here, as in the books, we see
The travelers clash, the doctors disagree!
Alas, that all, the further they explore,
For all their search are but confused the more!

Ye great departed!—men of mighty mark,—
Bacon and Newton, Adams, Adam Clarke,

Edwards and Whitefield, Franklin, Robert Hall,
Calhoun, Clay, Channing, Daniel Webster,—all
Ye great quit-tenants of this earthly ball,—
If in your new abodes ye cannot rest,
But must return, O, grant us this request:
Come with a noble and celestial air,
To prove your title to the names ye bear!
Give some clear token of your heavenly birth;
Write as good English as ye wrote on earth!
Show not to all, in ranting prose and verse,
The spirit's progress is from bad to worse;
And, what were once superfluous to advise,
Don't tell, I beg you, such egregious lies!—
Or if perchance your agents are to blame,
Don't let them trifle with your honest fame;
Let chairs and tables rest, and "rap" instead,
Ay, "knock" your slippery "Mediums" on the head!

—

395. "Boys."

"The proper study of mankind is man,"—
The most perplexing one, no doubt, is woman,
The subtlest study that the mind can scan,
Of all deep problems, heavenly or human!

But of all studies in the round of learning,
From nature's marvels down to human toys,
To minds well fitted for acute discerning,
The very queerest one is that of boys!

If to ask questions that would puzzle Plato,
And all the schoolmen of the Middle Age,—
If to make precepts worthy of old Cato,
Be deemed philosophy, your boy 's a sage!

If the possession of a teeming fancy,
(Although, forsooth, the younker doesn't know it,)

Which he can use in rarest necromancy,
Be thought poetical, your boy 's a poet!

If a strong will and most courageous bearing,
If to be cruel as the Roman Nero;
If all that 's chivalrous, and all that 's daring,
Can make a hero, then the boy 's a hero!

But changing soon with his increasing stature,
The boy is lost in manhood's riper age,
And with him goes his former triple nature,—
No longer Poet, Hero, now, nor Sage!

—

396. Sonnet to a Clam.

Inglorious friend! most confident I am
Thy life is one of very little ease;
Albeit men mock thee with their similes,
And prate of being "happy as a clam!"
What though thy shell protects thy fragile head
From the sharp bailiffs of the briny sea?
Thy valves are, sure, no safety-valves to thee,
While rakes are free to desecrate thy bed,
And bear thee off,—as foemen take their spoil,—
Far from thy friends and family to roam;
Forced, like a Hessian, from thy native home,
To meet destruction in a foreign broil!
Though thou art tender, yet thy humble bard
Declares, O clam! thy case is shocking hard!

Lucy Hooper, 1816–1841. (Manual, p. 524.)

397. "The Death-Summons."

A voice is on mine ear—a solemn voice:
I come, I come, it calls me to my rest;

Faint not, my yearning heart; rejoice, rejoice;
  Soon shalt thou reach the gardens of the blest:
On the bright waters there, the living streams,
  Soon shalt thou launch in peace thy weary bark,
Waked by rude waves no more from gentle dreams,
  Sadly to feel that earth to thee is dark—
Not bright as once; O, vain, vain memories, cease,
I cast your burden down—I strive for peace.

I heed the warning voice: oh, spurn me not,
  My early friend; let the bruised heart go free:
Mine were high fancies, but a wayward lot
  Hath made my youthful dreams in sadness flee;
Then chide not, I would linger yet awhile,
  Thinking o'er wasted hours, a weary train,
Cheered by the moon's soft light, the sun's glad smile,
  Watching the blue sky o'er my path of pain,
Waiting my summons: whose shall be the eye
To glance unkindly—I have come to die!

Sweet words—to die! O, pleasant, pleasant sounds,
  What bright revealings to my heart they bring;
What melody, unheard in earth's dull rounds,
  And floating from the land of glorious Spring
The eternal home! my weary thoughts revive,
  Fresh flowers my mind puts forth, and buds of love,
Gentle and kindly thoughts for all that live,
  Fanned by soft breezes from the world above:
And pausing not, I hasten to my rest—
Again, O, gentle summons, thou art blest!

Catharine Ann Warfield.

398. "THE RETURN TO ASHLAND."[1]

UNFOLD the silent gates,
The Lord of Ashland waits
Patient without, to enter his domain;
Tell not who sits within,
With sad and stricken mien,
That he, her soul's beloved, hath come again.

Long hath she watched for him,
Till hope itself grew dim,
And sorrow ceased to wake the frequent tear;
But let these griefs depart,
Like shadows from her heart—
Tell her, the long expected host is here.

He comes—but not alone,
For darkly pressing on,
The people pass beneath his bending trees,
Not as they came of yore,
When torch and banner bore
Their part amid exulting harmonies.

But still, and sad, they sweep
Amid the foliage deep,
Even to the threshold of that mansion gray,
Whither from life's unrest,
As an eagle seeks his nest,
It ever was his wont to flee away.

And he once more hath come
To that accustomed home,
To taste a calm, life never offered yet;
To know a rest so deep,
That they who watch and weep,
In this vain world may well its peace regret.

[1] The home of Henry Clay.

Arthur Cleveland Coxe, 1818–. (Manual, p. 523.)

399. THE HEART'S SONG.

IN the silent midnight watches,
  List thy bosom door;
How it knocketh, knocketh, knocketh,
  Knocketh evermore!
Say not 'tis thy pulse 's beating;
  'Tis thy heart of sin;
'Tis thy Saviour knocks, and crieth,
  "Rise, and let me in."

Death comes down with reckless footstep
  To the hall and hut:
Think you Death will tarry knocking
  Where the door is shut?
Jesus waiteth, waiteth, waiteth;
  But thy door is fast.
Grieved, away thy Saviour goeth;
  Death breaks in at last.

Then 'tis thine to stand entreating
  Christ to let thee in,
At the gate of heaven beating,
  Wailing for thy sin.
Nay, alas! thou foolish virgin,
  Hast thou then forgot?
Jesus waited long to know thee,—
  Now he knows thee not.

William Ross Wallace, 1819–. (Manual, p. 523.)

400. THE NORTH EDDA.

NOBLE was the old North Edda,
  Filling many a noble grave,
That for "man the one thing needful
  In his world is to be brave."

This, the Norland's blue-eyed mother
  Nightly chanted to her child,
While the Sea-King, grim and stately,
  Looked upon his boy and smiled.

. . . .

Let us learn that old North Edda
  Chanted grandly on the grave,
Still for man the one thing needful
  In his world is to be brave.

Valkyrs yet are forth and choosing
  Who must be among the slain;
Let us, like that grim old Sea-King,
  Smile at Death upon the plain,—

Smile at tyrants leagued with falsehood,
  Knowing Truth, eternal, stands
With the book God wrote for Freedom
  Always open in her hands,—

Smile at fear when in our duty,
  Smile at Slander's Jotun-breath,
Smile upon our shrouds when summoned
  Down the darkling deep of death.

Valor only grows a manhood;
  Only this upon our sod,
Keeps us in the golden shadow
  Falling from the throne of God.

Walter Whitman, 1819–.[1]

From Leaves of Grass.

401. The Brooklyn Ferry at Twilight.

I too, many and many a time cross'd the river, the sun
  half an hour high;

[1] Was born in New York in 1819, and has been printer, teacher, and later, an official at Washington. His poetry, though irregular in form, and often coarse in sentiment, is decidedly original and vigorous.

I watched the Twelfth-month sea-gulls—I saw them high in
the air, floating with motionless wings, oscillating their
bodies,
I saw how the glistening yellow lit up parts of their bodies,
and left the rest in strong shadow,
I saw the slow-wheeling circles, and the gradual edging toward
the south.

I too saw the reflection of the summer sky in the water,
Had my eyes dazzled by the shimmering track of beams,
Look'd at the fine centrifugal spokes of light round the shape
of my head in the sun-lit water,
Look'd on the haze on the hills southward and south-westward,
Look'd on the vapor as it flew in fleeces tinged with violet,
Look'd towards the lower bay to notice the arriving ships,
Saw their approach, saw aboard those that were near me,
Saw the white sails of schooners and sloops, saw the ships at
anchor,
The sailors at work in the rigging, or out astride the spars,
The round masts, the swimming motion of the hulls, the slen-
der serpentine pennants,
The large and small steamers in motion, the pilots in their
pilot-houses,
The white wake left by the passage, the quick tremulous whirl
of the wheels,
The flags of all nations, the falling of them at sun-set,
The scallop-edged waves in the twilight, the ladled cups, the
frolicsome crests and glistening,
The stretch afar growing dimmer and dimmer, the gray walls
of the granite store-houses by the docks,
On the river the shadowy group, the big steam-tug closely
flank'd on each side by the barges—the hay-boat, the
belated lighter,
On the neighboring shore, the fires from the foundry chimneys burning high and glaringly into the night.

Casting their flicker of black, contrasted with wild red and yellow light, over the tops of houses, and down into the clefts of streets.

These and all else, were to me the same as they are to you;
I project myself a moment to tell you—also I return.

Amelia B. Welby, 1819-1852. (Manual, p. 523.)

402. "The Bereaved."

It is a still and lovely spot
  Where they have laid thee down to rest;
The white rose and forget-me-not
  Bloom sweetly on thy breast,
And birds and streams with liquid lull
Have made the stillness beautiful.

And softly through the forest bars
  Light, lovely shapes, on glossy plumes,
Float ever in, like wingéd stars,
  Amid the purpling glooms.
Their sweet songs, borne from tree to tree,
Thrill the light leaves with melody.

Alas! too deep a weight of thought
  Had filled thy heart in youth's sweet hour;
It seemed with love and bliss o'erfraught;
  As fleeting passion-flower
Unfolding 'neath a southern sky,
To blossom soon, and soon to die.

Alas! the very path I trace,
  In happier hours thy footsteps made;
This spot was once thy resting place,
  Within the silent shade.
Thy white hand trained the fragrant bough
That drops its blossoms o'er me now.

. . . .

31

Yet in those calm and blooming bowers
  I seem to feel thy presence still,
Thy breath seems floating o'er the flowers,
  Thy whisper on the hill;
The clear, faint starlight, and the sea,
Are whispering to my heart of thee.

No more thy smiles my heart rejoice,
  Yet still I start to meet thy eye,
And call upon the low, sweet voice,
  That gives me no reply—
And list within my silent door
For the light feet that come no more.

Rebecca S. Nichols, about ***1820–.*** (Manual, pp. 503, 524.)

From "Musings."

403.

How like a conquerer the king of day
  Folds back the curtains of his orient couch,
Bestrides the fleecy clouds, and speeds his way
  Through skies made brighter by his burning touch;
For, as a warrior from the tented field
  Victorious, hastes his wearied limbs to rest,
So doth the sun his brazen sceptre yield,
  And sink, fair Night, upon thy gentle breast.

. . . . . .

Fair Vesper, when thy golden tresses gleam
  Amid the banners of the sunset sky,
Thy spirit floats on every radiant beam
  That gilds with beauty thy sweet home on high:
Then hath my soul its hour of deepest bliss,
  And gentle thoughts like angels round me throng,
Breathing of worlds (O, how unlike to this!)
  Where dwell eternal melody and song.

Alice Carey.

"The Old House."

404. ATTRACTIONS OF OUR EARLY HOME.

MY little birds, with backs as brown
  As sand, and throats as white as frost,
I've searched the summer up and down,
  And think the other birds have lost
The tunes, you sang so sweet, so low,
About the old house, long ago.

My little flowers, that with your bloom
  So hid the grass you grew upon,
A child's foot scarce had any room
  Between you,—are you dead and gone?
I've searched through fields and gardens rare,
Nor found your likeness any where.

My little hearts, that beat so high
  With love to God, and trust in men,
Oh come to me, and say if I
  But dream, or was I dreaming then,
What time we sat within the glow
Of the old house-hearth, long ago?

My little hearts, so fond, so true,
  I searched the world all far and wide,
And never found the like of you:
  God grant we meet the other side
The darkness 'twixt us, now that stands,
In that new house not made with hands!

Sidney Dyer,[1] about *1820–*.

405. THE POWER OF SONG.

HOWEVER humble be the bard who sings,
  If he can touch one chord of love that slumbers,
His name, above the proudest line of kings,
  Shall live immortal in his truthful numbers.

The name of him who sung of "Home, sweet home,"[2]
  Is now enshrined with every holy feeling;
And though he sleeps beneath no sainted dome,
  Each heart a pilgrim at his shrine is kneeling.

The simple lays that wake no tear when sung,
  Like chords of feeling from the music taken,
Are, in the bosom of the singer, strung,
  Which every throbbing heart-pulse will awaken.

Austin T. Earle,[3] *1821–*.

From "Warm Hearts had We."

406.

THE autumn winds were damp and cold,
  And dark the clouds that swept along,
As from the fields, the grains of gold
  We gathered, with the husker's song.
Our hardy forms, though thinly clad,
  Scarce felt the winds that swept us by,
For she a child, and I a lad,
  Warm hearts had we, my Kate and I.

We heaped the ears of yellow corn,
  More worth than bars of gold to view:

[1] A Baptist clergyman, who has lived for many years at Indianapolis, Indiana; the author of numerous songs.
[2] John Howard Payne.
[3] Was born in Tennessee; a well-known Western writer of both verse and prose.

The crispy covering from it torn,
  The noblest grain that ever grew;
Nor heeded we, though thinly clad,
  The chilly winds that swept us by;
For she a child, and I a lad,
  Warm hearts had we, my Kate and I.

Thomas Buchanan Read, *1822-1872.* (Manual, p. 523.)

From "Sylvia, or the Last Shepherd."

407. The Mournful Mowers.

. . . . . .

Thus sang the shepherd crowned at noon
  And every breast was heaved with sighs;—
Attracted by the tree and tune,
  The winged singers left the skies.

Close to the minstrel sat the maid;
  His song had drawn her fondly near:
Her large and dewy eyes betrayed
  The secret to her bosom dear.

The factory people through the fields,
  Pale men and maids and children pale,
Listened, forgetful of the wheel,
  Till the last summons woke the vale.

And all the mowers rising said,
  "The world has lost its dewy prime;
Alas! the Golden age is dead,
  And we are of the Iron time!

"The wheel and loom have left our homes,—
  Our maidens sit with empty hands,
Or toil beneath yon roaring domes,
  And fill the factory's pallid bands,

"The fields are swept as by a war,
Our harvests are no longer blythe;
Yonder the iron mower's-car,
Comes with his devastating scythe.

"They lay us waste by fire and steel,
Besiege us to our very doors;
Our crops before the driving wheel
Fall captive to the conquerors.

"The pastoral age is dead, is dead!
Of all the happy ages chief;
Let every mower bow his head,
In token of sincerest grief.

"And let our brows be thickly bound
With every saddest flower that blows;
And all our scythes be deeply wound
With every mournful herb that grows."

Thus sang the mowers; and they said,
"The world has lost its dewy prime;
Alas! the Golden age is dead,
And we are of the Iron time!"

Each wreathed his scythe and twined his head;
They took their slow way through the plain:
The minstrel and the maiden led
Across the fields the solemn train.

The air was rife with clamorous sounds,
Of clattering factory—thundering forge,—
Conveyed from the remotest bounds
Of smoky plain and mountain gorge.

Here, with a sudden shriek and roar,
The rattling engine thundered by;
A steamer past the neighboring shore
Convulsed the river and the sky.

The brook that erewhile laughed abroad,
  And o'er one light wheel loved to play,
Now, like a felon, groaning trod
  Its hundred treadmills night and day.

The fields were tilled with steeds of steam,
  Whose fearful neighing shook the vales;
Along the road there rang no team,—
  The barns were loud, but not with flails.

And still the mournful mowers said,
"The world has lost its dewy prime;
Alas! the Golden age is dead,
  And we are of the Iron time!"

—

From "The Closing Scene."

408.

All sights were mellowed, and all sounds subdued,
  The hills seemed farther, and the streams sang low;
As in a dream, the distant woodman hewed
  His winter log, with many a muffled blow.

. . . . . .

The sentinel cock upon the hill-side crew,
  Crew thrice, and all was stiller than before,
Silent, till some replying warder blew
  His alien horn, and then was heard no more.

Where erst the jay, within the elm's tall crest,
  Made garrulous trouble round her unfledged young,
And where the oriole hung her swaying nest,
  By every light wind, like a censer, swung.

. . . . . .

Amid all this, the centre of the scene,
  The white-haired matron, with monotonous tread,
Plied the swift wheel, and, with her joyless mien,
  Sat like a Fate, and watched the flying thread.

. . . . . .

While yet her cheek was bright with summer bloom,
  Her country summoned, and she gave her all;
And twice war bowed to her his sable plume,
  Re-gave the swords to rust upon the wall—

Re-gave the swords, but not the hand that drew,
  And struck for Liberty its dying blow;
Nor him who, to his sire and country true,
  Fell 'mid the ranks of the invading foe.

Long, but not loud, the droning wheel went on,
  Like the low murmur of a hive at noon;
Long, but not loud, the memory of the gone
  Breathed through her lips a sad and tremulous tune.

At last the thread was snapped; her head was bowed;
  Life dropped the distaff through his hands serene;
And loving neighbors smoothed her careful shroud,
  While death and winter closed the autumn scene.

Margaret M. Davidson, 1823–1837. (Manual, p. 523.)

From Lines in Memory of her Sister Lucretia.

409.

O THOU, so early lost, so long deplored!
  Pure spirit of my sister, be thou near;
And, while I touch this hallowed harp of thine,
  Bend from the skies, sweet sister, bend and hear.

For thee I pour this unaffected lay;
  To thee these simple numbers all belong:
For though thine earthly form has passed away,
  Thy memory still inspires my childish song.

Take, then, this feeble tribute; 'tis thine own;
  Thy fingers sweep my trembling heartstrings o'er,

Arouse to harmony each buried tone,
  And bid its wakened music sleep no more.

Long has thy voice been silent, and thy lyre
  Hung o'er thy grave, in death's unbroken rest;
But when its last sweet tones were borne away,
  One answering echo lingered in my breast.

O thou pure spirit! if thou hoverest near,
  Accept these lines, unworthy though they be,
Faint echoes from thy fount of song divine,
  By thee inspired, and dedicate to thee.

John R. Thompson,[1] *1823–1873.*

410. Music in Camp.

Two armies covered hill and plain,
  Where Rappahannock's waters
Ran deeply crimsoned with the stain
  Of battle's recent slaughters.

The summer clouds lay pitched like tents
  In meads of heavenly azure,
And each dread gun of the elements
  Slept in its hid embrazure.

The breeze so softly blew, it made
  No forest leaf to quiver,
And the smoke of the random cannonade
  Rolled slowly from the river.

And now, where circling hills looked down,
  With cannon grimly planted,
O'er listless camp and silent town
  The golden sunset slanted.

[1] Received a liberal education and relinquishing his profession—the law—for literature, was for some years editor of the Southern Literary Messenger. Has written chiefly for the magazines and for the newspapers. A native of Virginia.

When on the fervid air there came
  A strain—now rich and tender;
The music seemed itself aflame
  With day's departing splendor.

. . . .

And yet once more the bugles sang
  Above the stormy riot;
No shout upon the evening rang—
  There reigned a holy quiet.

The sad, slow stream, its noiseless flood
  Poured o'er the glistening pebbles;
All silent now the Yankees stood,
  And silent stood the Rebels.

No unresponsive soul had heard
  That plaintive note's appealing,
So deeply "Home, Sweet Home" had stirred
  The hidden founts of feeling.

Or Blue, or Gray, the soldier sees,
  As by the wand of fairy,
The cottage 'neath the live-oak trees,
  The cabin by the prairie.

Or cold or warm, his native skies
  Bend in their beauty o'er him;
Seen through the tear-mist in his eyes,
  His loved ones stand before him.

As fades the iris after rain
  In April's tearful weather,
The vision vanished, as the strain
  And daylight died together.

But memory, waked by music's art,
  Expressed in simplest numbers,
Subdued the sternest Yankee's heart,
  Made light the Rebel's slumbers.

And fair the form of music shines,
  That bright, celestial creature,
Who still 'mid war's embattled lines,
  Gave this one touch of Nature.

George Henry Boker, 1824–. (Manual, p. 520.)

From the "Ode to a Mountain Oak."

411. The Oak an Emblem.

  Type of unbending Will!
Type of majestic self-sustaining Power!
Elate in sunshine, firm when tempests lower,
May thy calm strength my wavering spirit fill!
    Oh! let me learn from thee,
    Thou proud and steadfast tree,
To bear unmurmuring what stern Time may send;
  Nor 'neath life's ruthless tempests bend:
    But calmly stand like thee,
    Though wrath and storm shake me,
Though vernal hopes in yellow Autumn end,
And, strong in truth, work out my destiny.
    Type of long-suffering Power!
      Type of unbending Will!
    Strong in the tempest's hour,
      Bright when the storm is still;
Rising from every contest with an unbroken heart,
Strengthen'd by every struggle, emblem of might thou art!
Sign of what man can compass, spite of an adverse state,
Still from thy rocky summit, teach us to war with Fate!

---

412. Dirge for a Sailor.

    Slow, slow! toll it low,
    As the sea-waves break and flow;
  With the same dull slumberous motion
  As his ancient mother, Ocean,
    Rocked him on, through storm and calm,
    From the iceberg to the palm:

So his drowsy ears may deem
That the sound which breaks his dream
Is the ever-moaning tide
Washing on his vessel's side.

Slow, slow! as we go,
Swing his coffin to and fro;
As of old the lusty billow
Swayed him on his heaving pillow:
So that he may fancy still,
Climbing up the watery hill,
Plunging in the watery vale,
With her wide-distended sail,
His good ship securely stands
Onward to the golden lands.

Slow, slow! heave-a-ho!—
Lower him to the mould below;
With the well-known sailor ballad,
Lest he grow more cold and pallid
At the thought that Ocean's child,
From his mother's arms beguiled,
Must repose for countless years,
Reft of all her briny tears,
All the rights he owned by birth,
In the dusty lap of earth.

William Allen Butler, 1825-. (Manual, p. 521.)

From "Nothing to Wear."

413.

O LADIES, dear ladies, the next sunny day
Please trundle your hoops just out of Broadway,
From its whirl and its bustle, its fashion and pride,
And the temples of Trade which tower on each side,
To the alleys and lanes, where Misfortune and Guilt
Their children have gathered, their city have built;

Where Hunger and Vice, like twin beasts of prey,
Have hunted their victims to gloom and despair;
Raise the rich, dainty dress, and the fine broidered skirt,
Pick your delicate way through the dampness and dirt,
Grope through the dark dens, climb the rickety stair
To the garret, where wretches, the young and the old,
Half-starved, and half-naked, lie crouched from the cold.
See those skeleton limbs, and those frost-bitten feet,
All bleeding and bruised by the stones of the street;
Hear the sharp cry of childhood, the deep groans that swell
From the poor dying creature who writhes on the floor,
Hear the curses that sound like the echoes of Hell,
As you sicken and shudder and fly from the door;
Then home to your wardrobes, and say, if you dare,
Spoiled children of Fashion—you've nothing to wear!

And O, if perchance there should be a sphere,
Where all is made right which so puzzles us here,

. . . . . .

Where the soul, disenchanted of flesh and of sense,
Unscreened by its trappings, and shows, and pretence,
Must be clothed for the life and the service above,
With purity, truth, faith, meekness, and love;
O daughters of Earth! foolish virgins, beware!
Lest in that upper realm, you have nothing to wear!

Bayard Taylor, 1825-. (Manual, pp. 523, 531.)

From "The Atlantic Monthly."

414. "The Burden of the Day."

I.

Who shall rise and cast away,
First, the Burden of the Day?
Who assert his place, and teach
Lighter labor, nobler speech,

Standing firm, erect, and strong,
Proud as Freedom, free as song?

II.

Lo! we groan beneath the weight
Our own weaknesses create;
Crook the knee and shut the lip,
All for tamer fellowship;
Load our slack, compliant clay
With the Burden of the Day!

III.

Higher paths there are to tread;
Fresher fields around us spread;
Other flames of sun and star
Flash at hand and lure afar;
Larger manhood might we share,
Surer fortune,—did we dare!

IV.

In our mills of common thought
By the pattern all is wrought:
In our school of life, the man
Drills to suit the public plan,
And through labor, love and play,
Shifts the Burden of the Day.

V.

Power of all is right of none!
Right hath each beneath the sun
To the breadth and liberal space
Of the independent race,—
To the chariot and the steed,
To the will, desire, and deed!

VI.

Ah, the gods of wood and stone
Can a single saint dethrone,

But the people who shall aid
'Gainst the puppets they have made?
First they teach and then obey:
'Tis the Burden of the Day.

VII.

Thunder shall we never hear
In this ordered atmosphere?
Never this monotony feel
Shattered by a trumpet's peal?
Never airs that burst and blow
From eternal summits, know?

VIII.

Though no man resent his wrong,
Still is free the poet's song:
Still, a stag, his thought may leap
O'er the herded swine and sheep,
And in pastures far away
Lose the burden of the Day!

John Townsend Trowbridge,[1] *1827–.*

From the Atlantic Monthly

415. "Dorothy in the Garret."

In the low-raftered garret, stooping
  Carefully over the creaking boards,
Old Maid Dorothy goes a-groping
  Among its dusty and cobwebbed hoards;
Seeking some bundle of patches, hid
  Far under the eaves, or bunch of sage,
Or satchel hung on its nail, amid
  The heir-looms of a by-gone age.

[1] After struggling through many early discouragements has attained high repute, both in prose and verse. Has written several novels. New York is his native State.

There is the ancient family chest,
  There the ancestral cards and hatchel;
Dorothy, sighing, sinks down to rest,
  Forgetful of patches, sage, and satchel.
Ghosts of faces peer from the gloom
  Of the chimney, where, with swifts and reel,
And the long-disused, dismantled loom,
  Stands the old-fashioned spinning wheel.

She sees it back in the clean-swept kitchen,
  A part of her girlhood's little world;
Her mother is there by the window, stitching;
  Spindle buzzes, and reel is whirled
With many a click: on her little stool
  She sits, a child by the open door,
Watching, and dabbling her feet in the pool
  Of sunshine spilled on the gilded floor.

Her sisters are spinning all day long;
  To her wakening sense, the first sweet warning
Of daylight come, is the cheerful song
  To the hum of the wheel, in the early morning.
Benjie, the gentle, red-cheeked boy,
  On his way to school, peeps in at the gate;
In neat, white pinafore, pleased and coy,
  She reaches a hand to her bashful mate;

And under the elms, a prattling pair,
  Together they go, through glimmer and gloom:—
It all comes back to her, dreaming there
  In the low-raftered garret room;
The hum of the wheel, and the summer weather,
  The heart's first trouble, and love's beginning,
Are all in her memory linked together;
  And now it is she herself that is spinning.

With the bloom of youth on cheek and lip,
  Turning the spokes with the flashing pin,

Twisting the thread from the spindle-tip,
  Stretching it out and winding it in,
To and fro, with a blithesome tread,
  Singing she goes, and her heart is full,
And many a long-drawn golden thread
  Of fancy, is spun with the shining wool.
. . . .

Henry Timrod,[1] *1829–1867.*

From his "Poems."

416. THE UNKNOWN DEAD.

THE rain is plashing on my sill,
But all the winds of Heaven are still;
And so it falls with that dull sound
Which thrills us in the church-yard ground,
When the first spadeful drops like lead
Upon the coffin of the dead.
Beyond my streaming window-pane,
I cannot see the neighboring vane,
Yet from its old familiar tower
The bell comes, muffled, through the shower
What strange and unsuspected link
Of feeling touched, has made me think—
While with a vacant soul and eye
I watch that gray and stony sky—
Of nameless graves on battle-plains
Washed by a single winter's rains,
Where—some beneath Virginian hills,
And some by green Atlantic rills,
Some by the waters of the West—
A myriad unknown heroes rest?
Ah! not the chiefs, who, dying, see
Their flags in front of victory,

[1] A native of South Carolina. He has a fine poetic sentiment, with much beauty of expression, and is an especial favorite in the South.

Or, at their life-blood's noble cost
Pay for a battle nobly lost,
Claim from their monumental beds
The bitterest tears a nation sheds.
Beneath yon lonely mound—the spot
By all save some fond few, forgot—
Lie the true martyrs of the fight
Which strikes for freedom and for right.
Of them, their patriot zeal and pride,
The lofty faith that with them died,
No grateful page shall farther tell
Than that so many bravely fell;
And we can only dimly guess
What worlds of all this world's distress,
What utter woe, despair, and dearth,
Their fate has brought to many a hearth.
Just such a sky as this should weep
Above them, always, where they sleep;
Yet, haply, at this very hour
Their graves are like a lover's bower;
And Nature's self, with eyes unwet,
Oblivious of the crimson debt
To which she owes her April grace,
Laughs gayly o'er their burial-place.

Susan A. Talley Von Weiss,[1] about ***1830–.***

417. THE SEA-SHELL.

SADLY the murmur, stealing
  Through the dim windings of the mazy shell,
Seemeth some ocean-mystery concealing
    Within its cell.

And ever sadly breathing,
  As with the tone of far-off waves at play,

[1] A native of Virginia; her poetical pieces have been much admired.

That dreamy murmur through the sea-shell wreathing
　　Ne'er dies away.

It is no faint replying
　Of far-off melodies of wind and wave,
No echo of the ocean billow, sighing
　　Through gem-lit cave.

It is no dim retaining
　Of sounds that through the dim sea-caverns swell.
But some lone ocean spirit's sad complaining,
　　Within that cell.

. . . . .

I languish for the ocean—
　I pine to view the billow's heaving crest;
I miss the music of its dream-like motion,
　　That lulled to rest.

How like art thou, sad spirit,
　To many a one, the lone ones of the earth!
Who in the beauty of their souls inherit
　　A purer birth;

. . . .

Yet thou, lone child of ocean,
　May'st never more behold thine ocean-foam,
While they shall rest from each wild, sad emotion,
　　And find their home!

Albert Sutliffe,[1] *1830–.*

418. "May Noon."

The farmer tireth of his half-day toil,
　He pauseth at the plough,
He gazeth o'er the furrow-linéd soil,
　Brown hand above his brow.

[1] A native of Connecticut, but has lived for many years in the West, and latterly in Minnesota.

He hears, like winds lone muffled 'mong the hills,
The lazy river run;
From shade of covert woods, the eager rills
Bound forth into the sun.

The clustered clouds of snowy apple-blooms,
Scarce shivered by a breeze,
With odor faint, like flowers in feverish rooms,
Fall, flake by flake, in peace.

'Tis labor's ebb; a hush of gentle joy,
For man, and beast, and bird;
The quavering songster ceases its employ;
The aspen is not stirred.

But Nature hath no pause; she toileth still;
Above the last-year leaves
Thrusts the lithe germ, and o'er the terraced hill
A fresher carpet weaves.

From many veins she sends her gathered streams
To the huge-billowed main,
Then through the air, impalpable as dreams,
She calls them back again.

She shakes the dew from her ambrosial locks,
She pours adown the steep
The thundering waters; in her palm, she rocks
The flower-throned bee to sleep.

Smile in the tempest, faint and fragile man,
And tremble in the calm!
God plainest shows what great Jehovah can,
In these fair days of balm.

Elijah E. Edwards,[1] *1831–.*

419. "Let Me Rest."

"Let me rest!"
It was the voice of one
Whose life-long journey was but just begun.
With genial radiance shone his morning sun;
The lark sprang up rejoicing from her nest,
To warble praises in her Maker's ear;
The fields were clad in flower-enamelled vest,
And air of balm, and sunshine clear,
Failed not to cheer
That yet unweary pilgrim; but his breast
Was harrowed with a strange, foreboding fear;
Deeming the life to come, at best,
But weariness, he murmured, "Let me rest."

. . . . .

"Let me rest!"
But not at morning's hour,
Nor yet when clouds above my pathway lower;
Let me bear up against affliction's power,
Till life's red sun has sought its quiet west,
Till o'er me spreads the solemn, silent night,
When, having passed the portals of the blessed,
I may repose upon the Infinite,
And learn aright
Why He, the wise, the ever-loving, traced
The path to heaven through a desert waste.
Courage, ye fainting ones! at His behest
Ye pass through labor unto endless rest.

[1] Born in Ohio; of late professor of ancient languages in Minnesota; a contributor in prose and verse to various magazines.

Paul Hamilton Hayne,[1] *1831–.*

420. "OCTOBER."

THE passionate summer's dead! the sky 's aglow
With roseate flushes of matured desire;
The winds at eve are musical and low
As sweeping chords of a lamenting lyre,
Far up among the pillared clouds of fire,
Whose pomp in grand procession upward grows,
With gorgeous blazonry of funereal shows,
To celebrate the summer's past renown.
Ah, me! how regally the heavens look down,
O'ershadowing beautiful autumnal woods,
And harvest-fields with hoarded incense brown,
And deep-toned majesty of golden floods,
That lift their solemn dirges to the sky,
To swell the purple pomp that floateth by.

Rosa V. Johnson Jeffrey[2] about *1832–.*

421. ANGEL WATCHERS.

ANGEL faces watch my pillow, angel voices haunt my sleep,—
And upon the winds of midnight, shining pinions round me sweep;
Floating downward on the starlight, two bright infant-forms I see—
They are mine, my own bright darlings, come from heaven to visit me.

Earthly children smile upon me, but those little ones above,
Were the first to stir the fountains of a mother's deathless love,

[1] A poet and critic of much note; a native of South Carolina.

[2] A native of Mississippi, but of late a resident of Kentucky; the author of several novels, and of many poetical pieces.

And, as now they watch my slumber, while their soft eyes on me shine,
God forgive a mortal yearning still to call his angels mine.

Earthly children fondly call me, but no mortal voice can seem
Sweet as those that whisper "Mother!" 'mid the glories of my dream;
Years will pass, and earthly prattlers cease perchance to lisp my name;
But my angel babies' accents shall be evermore the same.

And the bright band now around me, from their home perchance will rove,
In their strength no more depending on my constant care and love;
But my first-born still shall wander, from the sky in dreams to rest
Their soft cheeks and shining tresses on an earthly mother's breast.

Time may steal away the freshness, or some 'whelming grief destroy
All the hopes that erst had blossomed, in my summer-time of joy;
Earthly children may forsake me, earthly friends perhaps betray,
Every tie that now unites me to this life may pass away;—

But, unchanged, those angel watchers, from their blest immortal home,
Pure and fair, to cheer the sadness of my darkened dreams shall come;
And I cannot feel forsaken, for, though 'reft of earthly love,
Angel children call me "Mother," and my soul will look above.

Sarah J. Lippincott.

From Putnam's Magazine.

422. "ABSOLUTION."

THE long day waned, when spent with pain, I seemed
To drift on slowly toward the restful shore,—
So near, I breathed in balm, and caught faint gleams
Of Lotus-blooms that fringe the waves of death,
And breathless Palms that crown the heights of God.

Then I bethought me how dear hands would close
These wistful eyes in welcome night, and fold
These poor, tired hands in blameless idleness.
In tender mood I pictured forth the spot
Wherein I should be laid to take my rest.

"It shall be in some paradise of graves,
Where Sun and Shade do hold alternate watch;
Where Willows sad trail low their tender green,
And pious Elms build arches worshipful,
O'ertowered by solemn Pines, in whose dark tops
Enchanted storm-winds sigh through summer-nights;
The stalwart exile from fair Lombardy,
And slender Aspens, whose quick, watchful leaves
Give silver challenge to the passing breeze,
And softly flash and clash like fairy shields,
Shall sentinel that quiet camping ground;
The glow and grace of flowers will flood those mounds
An ever-widening sea of billowy bloom;
And not least lovely shall my grave-sod be,
With Myrtles blue, and nestling Violets,
And Star-flowers pale with watching—Pansies, dark,
With mourning thoughts, and Lilies saintly pure;
Deep-hearted Roses, sweet as buried love,
And Woodbine-blossoms dripping honeyed dew
Over a tablet and a sculptured name.

There little song-birds, careless of my sleep,
Shall shake fine raptures from their throats, and thrill
With life's triumphant joy the ear of Death;
And lovely, gauzy creatures of an hour
Preach immortality among the graves.
The chime of silvery waters shall be there—
A pleasant stream that winds among the flowers,
But lingers not, for that it ever hears,
Through leagues of wood and field and towered town,
The great sea calling from his secret deeps."

'Twas here, methought or dreamed, an angel came
And stood beside my couch, and bent on me
A face of solemn questioning, still and stern,
But passing beautiful, and searched my soul
With steady eyes, the while he seemed to say.

What hast thou done here, child, that thy poor dust
Should lie embosomed in such loveliness ?
Why should the gracious trees stand guard o'er thee ?
Hast thou aspired, like them, through all thy life,
And rest and healing with thy shadow cast ?
Have deeds of thine brightened the world like flowers,
And sweetened it with holiest charities ?

. . . . . .

Edmund Clarence Stedman,[1] *1833-.*

From "The Blameless Prince and other Poems."

423. The Mountains.

Two thousand feet in air it stands
Betwixt the bright and shaded lands,
Above the regions it divides
And borders with its furrowed sides.

[1] Was born in Connecticut but has long resided in New York, where he has combined an active business life with literary pursuits—a favorite contributor to the magazines.

The seaward valley laughs with light
Till the round sun o'erhangs this height;
But then, the shadow of the crest
No more the plains that lengthen west
Enshrouds, yet slowly, surely creeps
Eastward, until the coolness steeps
A darkling league of tilth and wold,
And chills the flocks that seek their fold.

Not like those ancient summits lone,
Mont Blanc on his eternal throne,—
The city-gemmed Peruvian peak,—
The sunset portals landsmen seek,
Whose train, to reach the Golden Land,
Crawls slow and pathless through the sand,—
Or that whose ice-lit beacon guides
The mariner on tropic tides,
And flames across the Gulf afar,
A torch by day, by night a star,—
Not thus to cleave the outer skies,
Does my serener mountain rise,
Nor aye forget its gentle birth
Upon the dewey, pastoral earth.

But ever, in the noonday light,
Are scenes whereof I love the sight,—
Broad pictures of the lower world
Beneath my gladdened eyes unfurled.
Irradiate distances reveal
Fair nature wed to human weal;
The rolling valley made a plain;
Its chequered squares of grass and grain;
The silvery rye, the golden wheat,
The flowery elders where they meet,—
Ay, even the springing corn I see,
And garden haunts of bird and bee;

And where, in daisied meadows, shines
The wandering river through its vines,
Move specks at random, which I know
Are herds a-grazing to and fro.

John James Piatt,[1] *1835–*.

From "Landmarks and other Poems."

424. Long Ago.

Though for the soul a lovely Heaven awaits,
Through years of woe,
The Paradise with angels in its gates
Is Long Ago.

The heart's lost Home! Ah, thither winging ever,
In silence, show
Vanishing faces! but they vanish never
In Long Ago!

Ye toil'd through desert sands to reach To-morrow,
With footsteps slow,
Poor Yesterdays! Immortal gleams ye borrow
In Long Ago.

The world is dark: backward our thoughts are yearning,
Our eyes o'erflow:
Sweet Memories, angels to our tears returning,
Leave Long Ago.

We climb: child-roses to our knees are climbing,
From valleys low;
To call us back, dear birds and brooks are rhyming
In Long Ago.

[1] Of Western birth and education. His verse though somewhat crude, has a flow of tenderness and freshness.

Hands clasp'd, tears shed, sad songs are sung!—the fair
Beloved ones, lo!
Shine yonder, through the angel gates of air,
In Long Ago.

Celia Thaxter,[1] *1835-.*

From The Atlantic Monthly.

425. "REGRET."

SOFTLY Death touched her, and she passed away,
Out of this glad, bright world she made more fair;
Sweet as the apple blossoms, when in May,
The orchards flush, of summer grown aware.

All that fresh delicate beauty gone from sight,
That gentle, gracious presence felt no more!
How must the house be emptied of delight!
What shadows on the threshold she passed o'er!

She loved me. Surely I was grateful, yet
I could not give her back all she gave me,—
Ever I think of it with vain regret,
Musing upon a summer by the sea;

Remembering troops of merry girls who pressed
About me, clinging arms and tender eyes,
And love, light scent of roses. With the rest
She came to fill my heart with new surprise.

The day I left them all and sailed away,
While o'er the calm sea, 'neath the soft gray sky
They waved farewell, she followed me to say
Yet once again her wistful, sweet "good by."

At the boat's bow she drooped; her light green dress
Swept o'er the skiff in many a graceful fold,

[1] A native of New Hampshire; long resident on the Isles of Shoals, and remarkable for her vivid pictures of ocean life, in both prose and verse.

Her glowing face, bright with a mute caress,
  Crowned with her lovely hair of shadowy gold:

And tears she dropped into the crystal brine
  For me, unworthy, as we slowly swung
Free of the mooring. Her last look was mine,
  Seeking me still the motley crowd among.

O tender memory of the dead I hold
  So precious through the fret and change of years!
Were I to live till Time itself grew old,
  The sad sea would be sadder for those tears.

Theophilus H. Hill.[1] *1836-.*

From "The Song of the Butterfly."

426.

WHEN the shades of evening fall,
Like the foldings of a pall,—
When the dew is on the flowers,
And the mute, unconscious hours,
Still pursue their noiseless flight
Through the dreamy realms of night,
In the shut or open rose
Ah, how sweetly I repose!

. . . .

And Diana's starry train,
Sweetly scintillant again,
Never sleep while I repose
On the petals of the rose.
Sweeter couch hath who than I?
Quoth the brilliant Butterfly.

[1] Born in North Carolina; in the intervals of his law practice has published a volume of poems.

Life is but a summer day,
Gliding languidly away;
Winter comes, alas! too soon,—
Would it were forever June!
Yet though brief my flight may be,
Fun and frolic still for me!
When the summer leaves and flowers,
Now so beautiful and gay,
In the cold autumnal showers,
Droop and fade, and pine away,
Who would not prefer to die?
What were life to *such as I?*
Quoth the flaunting Butterfly.

Thomas Bailey Aldrich.[1] *1836–.*

From his "Poems."

427. THE CRESCENT AND THE CROSS.

KIND was my friend who, in the Eastern land,
Remembered me with such a gracious hand,
And sent this Moorish Crescent which has been
Worn on the tawny bosom of a queen.

No more it sinks and rises in unrest
To the soft music of her heathen breast;
No barbarous chief shall bow before it more,
No turbaned slave shall envy and adore!

I place beside this relic of the Sun
A cross of Cedar brought from Lebanon,
Once borne, perchance, by some pale monk who trod
The desert to Jerusalem—and his God!

[1] Born in New Hampshire, but long connected with the press in New York. Has produced several volumes of poetry of unusual beauty and finish.

Here do they lie, two symbols of two creeds,
Each meaning something to our human needs,
Both stained with blood, and sacred made by faith,
By tears, and prayers, and martyrdom, and death.

That for the Moslem is, but this for me!
The waning Crescent lacks divinity:
It gives me dreams of battles, and the woes
Of women shut in hushed seraglios.

But when this Cross of simple wood I see,
The Star of Bethlehem shines again for me,
And glorious visions break upon my gloom—
The patient Christ, and Mary at the Tomb!

Francis Bret Harte.

From his "Poems."

428. Dickens in Camp.

Above the pines the moon was slowly drifting,
  The river ran below;
The dim Sierras, far beyond, uplifting
  Their minarets of snow.

The roaring camp-fire, with rude humor, painted
  The ruddy tints of health,
On haggard face, and form that drooped and fainted
  In the fierce race for wealth;

Till one arose, and from his pack's scant treasure
  A hoarded volume drew,
And cards were dropped from hands of listless leisure,
  To hear the tale anew;

And then, while round them shadows gathered faster,
  And as the firelight fell,
He read aloud the book wherein the Master
  Had writ of "Little Nell."

Perhaps 'twas boyish fancy,—for the reader
  Was youngest of them all,—
But, as he read, from clustering pine and cedar,
  A silence seemed to fall.

The fir-trees, gathering closer in the shadows,
  Listened in every spray,
While the whole camp, with "Nell" on English meadows,
  Wandered, and lost their way.

And so in mountain solitudes—o'ertaken
  As by some spell divine—
Their cares dropped from them like the needles shaken
  From out the gusty pine.

Lost is that camp! and wasted all its fire:
  And he who wrought that spell?—
Ah, towering pine and stately Kentish spire,
  Ye have one tale to tell!

Lost is that camp! but let its fragrant story
  Blend with the breath that thrills
With hop-vines' incense all the pensive glory
  That fills the Kentish hills.

And on that grave where English oak and holly
  And laurel wreaths intwine,
Deem it not all a too presumptuous folly,—
  This spray of Western pine!

—

From "East and West Poems."

429. THE TWO SHIPS.

As I stand by the cross on the lone mountain's crest,
  Looking over the ultimate sea,
In the gloom of the mountain a ship lies at rest,
  And one sails away from the lea:

One spreads its white wings on a far-reaching track,
  With pennant and sheet flowing free;
One hides in the shadow with sails laid aback,—
  The ship that is waiting for me!

But lo, in the distance the clouds break away!
  The Gate's glowing portals I see;
And I hear from the outgoing ship in the bay
  The song of the sailors in glee:
So I think of the luminous footprints that bore
  The comfort o'er dark Galilee,
And wait for the signal to go to the shore,
  To the ship that is waiting for me.

Charles Dimitry,[1] *1838–.*

430. "The Sergeant's Story."

    Our army lay,
    At break of day,
A full league from the foe away.
    At set of sun,
    The battle done,
We cheered our triumph, dearly won.

.   .   .   .   .

    All night before,
    We marked the roar
Of hostile guns that on us bore;
    And here and there,
    The sudden blare
Of fitful bugles smote the air.

[1] Of a Louisiana family: is considered one of the most promising of the young writers of the South. The present is a favorable specimen of the poetry of the secession writers.

33

No idle word
The quiet stirred
Among us as the morning neared;
And brows were bent,
As silent went
Unto its post each regiment.

Blank broke the day,
And wan and gray
The drifting clouds went on their way.
So sad the morn,
Our colors torn,
Upon the ramparts drooped forlorn!

At early sun,
The vapors dun
Were lifted by a nearer gun;
At stroke of nine,
Auspicious sign!
The sun shone out along the line.

Then loud and clear,
From cannoneer
And rifleman arose a cheer;
For as the gray
Mists cleared away,
We saw the charging foe's array.

John Hay.[1]

From "Pike County Ballads."

431. THE PRAIRIE.

THE skies are blue above my head,
The prairie green below,

[1] Born in Indiana. Gave up the practice of the law to become Secretary and Aide-de-camp to President Lincoln. Served briefly in the Rebellion war with the rank of Colonel, and was afterward Secretary of Legation at Paris and Madrid, and for some months, Chargé d'Affaires at Vienna. Subsequently applied himself to literature and journalism.

And flickering o'er the tufted grass
  The shifting shadows go,
Vague-sailing, where the feathery clouds
  Fleck white the tranquil skies,
Black javelins darting where aloft
  The whirring pheasant flies.

A glimmering plain in drowsy trance
  The dim horizon bounds,
Where all the air is resonant
  With sleepy summer sounds,—
The life that sings among the flowers,
  The lisping of the breeze,
The hot cicada's sultry cry,
  The murmurous dream of bees.

The butterfly—a flying flower—
  Wheels swift in flashing rings,
And flutters round his quiet kin
  With brave flame-mottled wings.
The wild Pinks burst in crimson fire,
  The Phlox' bright clusters shine,
And Prairie-cups are swinging free
  To spill their airy wine.

. . . .

Far in the East, like low-hung clouds
  The waving woodlands lie;
Far in the West, the glowing plain
  Melts warmly in the sky;
No accent wounds the reverent air,
  No foot-print dints the sod,—
Lone in the light the prairie lies,
  Rapt in a dream of God.

Joaquin Miller.[1]

From "Songs of the Sierras."

432. THE FUTURE OF CALIFORNIA.

DARED I but say a prophecy,
As sang the holy men of old,
Of rock-built cities yet to be
Along those shining shores of gold,
Crowding athirst into the sea,
What wondrous marvels might be told!
Enough to know that empire here
Shall burn her brightest, loftiest star;
Here art and eloquence shall reign,
As o'er the wolf-reared realm of old;
Here learn'd and famous from afar,
To pay their noble court, shall come,
And shall not seek or see in vain,
But look on all, with wonder dumb.

Afar the bright Sierras lie,
A swaying line of snowy white,
A fringe of heaven hung in sight
Against the blue base of the sky.

I look along each gaping gorge,
I hear a thousand sounding strokes,
Like giants rending giant oaks,
Or brawny Vulcan at his forge;
I see pick-axes flash and shine,
And great wheels whirling in a mine.
Here winds a thick and yellow thread,
A moss'd and silver stream instead;
And trout that leap'd its rippled tide
Have turn'd upon their sides and died.

[1] Cincinnatus Heine Miller, commonly known by his assumed name of Joaquin Miller. Born in Indiana, but was taken when very young to Oregon. After a wild career in Oregon and California, he at length studied for the law. His poetry, like his life, is of an eccentric cast.

Lo! when the last pick in the mine
Is rusting red with idleness,
And rot yon cabins in the mould,
And wheels no more croak in distress,
And tall pines reassert command,
Sweet bards along this sunset shore
Their mellow melodies will pour;
Will charm as charmers very wise,
Will strike the harp with master-hand,
Will sound unto the vaulted skies
The valor of these men of old—
The mighty men of 'Forty-nine;
Will sweetly sing and proudly say,
Long, long agone, there was a day
When there were giants in the land.

Joel Chandler Harris,[1] *1846–.*

433. "AGNES."

SHE has a tender, winning way,
And walks the earth with gentle grace,
And roses with the lily play
Amid the beauties of her face.

When'er she tunes her voice to sing,
The song-birds list, with anxious looks,
For it combines the notes of spring
With all the music of the brooks.

Her merry laughter, soft and low,
Is as the chimes of silver bells,—
That like sweet anthems float, and flow
Through woodland groves and bosky dells,

[1] A native of Georgia; is deemed one of the best of the younger poets of the South.

And when the violets see her eyes,
  They flush and glow with love and shame,
They meekly droop with sad surprise,
  As though unworthy of the name.

But still they bloom where'er she throws
  Her dainty glance and smiles so sweet,
And e'en amid stern winter's snows
  The daisies spring beneath her feet.

She wears a crown of Purity,
  Full set with woman's brightest gem,—
A wreath of maiden modesty,
  And Virtue is the diadem.

And when the pansies bloom again,
  And spring and summer intertwine,
Great joys will fall on me like rain,
  For she will be for ever mine!

www.ingramcontent.com/pod-product-compliance
Lightning Source LLC
LaVergne TN
LVHW021301110826
845150LV00003B/452